IRISH LAND LAW

Third Edition

Northern Ireland Edition

IRISH LAND LAW

Third Edition

Northern Ireland Edition

by

J.C.W. Wylie

LL.M. (Harvard), LL.D. (Belfast)
Consultant, A&L Goodbody, Solicitors

Consultant Editor for the Republic of Ireland

The late Hon. Mr Justice Kenny

M.A., LL.B. (N.U.I.), Hon. LL.D. (Dublin)

***Former Judge of the Supreme Court of the
Republic of Ireland***

Bloomsbury Professional

Published by
Bloomsbury Professional
Maxwelton House
41–43 Boltro Road
Haywards Heath
West Sussex
RH16 1BJ

Bloomsbury Professional
The Fitzwilliam Business Centre
26 Upper Pembroke Street
Dublin 2

ISBN 978 1 78043 100 0

British Library Cataloguing-in-Publication Data
A catalogue record for this book is available from the British Library

This edition typeset by Marlex Editorial Services Ltd, Dublin, Ireland
This edition printed in the United Kingdom by Hobbs the Printers Ltd, Totton, Hampshire

Part II

ESTATES AND INTERESTS

Chapter 4

ESTATES

I. INTRODUCTION

A. Estates in Land

[4.001] It has already been explained that in this context the word "estate" relates to the duration for which an interest in land may be held by its owner.[1] An initial ambiguity should be pointed out here; the expressions "interest in land" and "estate in land" have tended to assume rather technical meanings in our law. The word *estate* has come to be used in a narrow sense, to refer to the more important (in terms of size and value) interests in land. The word *interest*, whilst having the wider meaning of all interests that can be created in respect of land (thus including estates), can also be used in a narrower sense to refer to minor interests in land of less importance than estates.[2]

[4.002] The complexity of land law derives in large part from the diversity in the types of estates and lesser interests in land that can be created. This is one of its distinguishing features when a comparison is made with the law of personal property and chattels, though this distinction is not as clear cut as it used to be. Modern commercial practice has done much in recent decades to break down the concept of absolute ownership of chattels. Indeed, commercial law has adopted many of the concepts originally derived from land law in this respect, so that the leasing and mortgaging of valuable chattels like ships and aircraft is quite common.[3] The point to note here, of course, is that this development has taken place in respect of large, valuable chattels, having a reasonably long life expectancy. This characteristic has a connection with the other main distinguishing feature of land, which facilitates its wide fragmentation of ownership. This is that land is virtually indestructible[4] and so there is little risk in creating a wide range of estates and interests in it, some of which may be postponed in enjoyment and possession for decades ahead.

---

[1]   Para **[2.05]** *ante.*

[2]   Eg incorporeal hereditaments, see Ch 6 *post.*

[3]   Though these concepts may not have the same law and rules applied to them in the case of chattels; *cf* eg, the commercial law concepts of hiring, hire purchase, credit-sale and chartering with leasing. On this subject generally, see Lawson and Rudden, *The Law of Property* (2nd ed, 1982); Bell, *Modern Law of Personal Property in England and Ireland* (1989).

[4]   Land, since in this context it includes buildings attached to land, is not strictly indestructible since the buildings can be razed to the ground, even though the ground remains. This point has added significance in the case of blocks of flats, where each flat is separately owned and only the ground floor ones, or those below, are attached to the ground. Considerable conceptual problems occur in England where flats held on freehold tenure are quite common: see George and George, *The Sale of Flats* (5th ed, 1984), and the articles cited in fn 4, para **[1.001]** *ante.* (contd.../)

B. Classification

[4.003] Estates in land fall into two broad categories: *freehold* and *leasehold* estates. It is thus apparent that the epithets "freehold" and "leasehold" are ascribed to two quite distinct concepts, namely, tenure and estates.[5] Generally there is a mutual exclusiveness about these concepts in the sense that one speaks only of land held under freehold tenure for a freehold estate or held under leasehold tenure for a leasehold estate. But in Ireland some confusion occurs because of the practice of creating what appear to be combinations of the concepts. Thus one has concepts like a 'lease' for lives renewable for ever. This creates a freehold estate in the land, but by means of a document creating leasehold tenure between the parties.[6] The same occurs in certain types of fee farm grant, where a freehold estate is granted (a fee simple), but the relationship of landlord and tenant (leasehold tenure) exists between the grantor and grantee. These Irish concepts will be examined in detail below.[7]

[4.004] As one would expect, freehold estates are those which are connected with the feudal system of tenure and much of the law relating to them is clearly grounded on feudal principles. There are three main types: fee simple, fee tail and life estate.[8] The *fee simple* is the largest estate known to our land law, the estate nearest to absolute ownership. It can rarely be quite absolute because of the notion of tenure which decrees that no matter how large the estate, it must be held of someone else, the State or Crown being the ultimate owner.[9] Furthermore, as we shall see, it is quite common for private parties to impose limitations on the holder for the time being of the fee simple estate, so that it becomes even less absolute.[10] In Ireland, as a result of centuries of conveyancing practice, a fee simple absolute was, until recent times, very rare in urban areas of the

---

[4]   (\...contd) Note also the proposals in the Lord Chancellor's Working Group Report (*Commonhold: Freehold Flats and Freehold Ownership of other Interdependent Buildings*, 1987) for a new "commonhold" system similar to the Australian strata title schemes. Despite support from the Lord Chancellor these proposals have yet to be acted upon. The NI Land Law Working Group proposed a similar scheme (see *Final Report* (HMSO, 1990), Pt 3) which has also not yet been acted upon. In Ireland the conceptual problems are fewer because freehold flats are rare; as with most urban land, flats, including those for sale (which are becoming quite common in major urban areas), are held on leasehold tenure, Ch 17 *post*. See Wylie, *Irish Conveyancing Law* (2nd ed, 1996) paras 19.11-22.

[5]   Distinguished at paras **[2.04]-[2.05]** *ante*. When the layman talks about a "freehold property" he is probably combining two concepts; he is referring to property held on freehold tenure for a freehold estate.

[6]   *Cf* a lease for lives combined with a term of years, para **[4.177]** *post*.

[7]   Paras **[4.057]** *et seq, post*. Note that the creation of such "hybrid" estates will be prohibited in NI by the Property (NI) Order 1997: see Articles 28 (fee farm grants), 36 (perpetually renewable leases) and 37 (leases for lives etc). These provisions are discussed later at various points in this chapter.

[8]   Discussed in detail, paras **[4.021]** *et seq*, **[4.112]** *et seq*, and **[4.143]** *et seq, post*.

[9]   In a sense chattels are never owned absolutely either; the State in the Republic of Ireland is ultimate successor to personal property (Succession Act 1965, ss 14 and 73), and the Crown in Northern Ireland succeeds to personal chattels *inter alia* as *bona vacantia* on the death of the owner intestate with no intestate successor (Administration of Estates Act (NI) 1955, ss 16 and 45), paras **[15.27]-[15.28]** *post*.

[10] Paras **[4.046]** *et seq, post*.

country.[11] However, it is a characteristic common to all fees simple that they have the potential to last for ever, with a high probability that they will do so in an age when a last will and testament will avoid the consequences of a death intestate leaving no persons entitled to succeed.[12]

[4.005] The *fee tail*[13] is a lesser estate, where the succession is confined to the descendants of the original holder of the estate. This process of succession cannot be disturbed in Ireland by a will (it could in England[14]), so that there is a much greater probability of an early determination of the estate. The creation of a fee tail estate really belongs to the practices of a bygone age, when land was regarded as the primary and most secure source of wealth. In an age when the paraphernalia of the modern stock market were unknown, most of the wealth of the richer families in the country was tied up with their landed estates and large urban houses, and their lawyer's primary task was to ensure that this land was kept in the family for successive generations. As we shall see, the key tool of the conveyancer in achieving this was the fee tail estate.[15] Nowadays it is rarely created because of two basic reasons. The first is that land is no longer the only main source of wealth, though it remains an investment of considerable value and one of the few which usually increases in value so as to offset, and often outstrip, the fall in the value of money caused by the general inflation which attacks most developed countries' economies. The second is that modern taxation systems impose crippling burdens on many of the older types of family settlement and an estate which decrees a succession to land through various generations incurs heavy capital taxation.[16] Some indication of the problems may be seen from the varied, and often ingenious, attempts in recent decades by owners of large estates and country houses in the British Isles to

---

[11] Paras **[4.057]** *et seq, post.* In the Republic of Ireland they are becoming more common as a result of the prohibition of the creation of future ground rents in respect of dwellings by the Landlord and Tenant (Ground Rents) Act 1978, see para **[1.074]** *ante,* and the acquisition of the fee simple under the Landlord and Tenant (Ground Rents) Act 1967 and Landlord and Tenant (Ground Rents) (No 2) Act 1978, see para **[18.26]** *post* and in due course in NI under the provisions for redemption of ground rents and prohibition of transactions giving rise to such rents in Pt II of the Property (NI) Order 1997, see para **[18.43]** *post.*

[12] Ch 14 *post.*

[13] Also known as an "estate tail," "entail" or "entailed interest" (though this use of the word "interest" as opposed to "estate" can be confusing, see para **[4.001]** *supra*).

[14] Until the creation of such estates was prohibited from 1 January 1997 by the Trusts of Land and Appointment of Trustees Act 1996, Sch 1 para 5: see para **[4.112]** *post.*

[15] Para **[8.005]** *post.*

[16] For the Republic, see now the Capital Acquisitions Tax Act 1976, especially Parts II (gift tax) and III (inheritance tax). This Act imposes a gift tax on gifts taken on or after 28 February 1974 (s 4) and an inheritance tax on an inheritance taken on or after 1 April 1975 (s 10). See O'Callaghan, *Taxation of Estates: The Law in Ireland* (1993) and *Taxation of Trusts: The Law in Ireland* (1993); Bohan, *Capital Acquisitions Tax* (1995). For Northern Ireland, see the UK Finance Act 1975, which imposed a capital transfer tax on gratuitous *inter vivos* transfers made since 26 March 1974 and on the value of deceased persons' estates since 12 March 1975 (s 19). It is now a comprehensive inheritance tax governed by the Inheritance Tax Act 1984 (originally called the Capital Transfer Tax Act 1984, but renamed in 1986), as modified by the Finance Act 1986.

generate revenue from their estates to pay off tax levies. The only alternative is often the selling up of the estate itself.

[4.006] The *life estate* means roughly what the name indicates - an estate to last for someone's life only. The life in question may be that of the grantee, or the grantee may hold for the life of someone else so as to create an estate *pur autre vie*. It should be apparent that without more this estate would be of doubtful commercial value - who is to say how long a life may last? A purchaser is unlikely to risk his money on the basis of an insurance company's actuarial calculations of a person's life expectancy. We shall see that this problem was eventually tackled in a comprehensive manner by legislation.[17] We shall also see that Irish conveyancers provided several variations on this common theme of the life estate, notably the lease for lives renewable for ever[18] and leases for lives combined with terms of years.[19] There is one important distinction between the first two freehold estates and the third, as their names imply. The fee simple and fee tail are what are known as estates of inheritance, ie, on the death of the present holder the estate might descend to his heir[20] (now replaced by persons entitled to succeed so far as the fee simple is concerned[21]). The word 'fee' also indicates that the duration of the estate could be for ever; the words "simple" and "tail" indicate the classes of heir who could inherit.[22] A life estate, however, is not an estate of inheritance, not even where it is held for a life other than that of the grantee and the grantee predeceases that other person. In that case the grantee's heir does not succeed, instead there are special rules as to succession.[23] A life estate cannot *ex hypothesi* last for ever.

[4.007] We turn now to the other main category of estates, namely, *leaseholds*. These are estates which developed much later than freeholds. Indeed, while freeholds were an essential part of the feudal system, leaseholds were never recognised by feudal land law.[24] Prior to the fifteenth century in England they were not even recognised as estates at all nor as creating any interest in land. A lease for a term of years was originally regarded as creating a purely personal contract between the parties and under the doctrine of privity of contract only the original parties to the contract could have any rights or duties under it.[25] It was not until the action of ejectment (a species of the action

---

[17] Ch 8 *post*.

[18] Para **[4.167]** *post*.

[19] Para **[4.177]** *post*. Both will be abolished in NI by the Property (NI) Order 1997, Articles 36 and 37.

[20] Ch 15 *post*.

[21] Succession Act 1965 s 11(1)(RI); Administration of Estates Act (NI) 1955, s 1(3).

[22] Para **[4.024]** *post*.

[23] Para **[4.141]** *post*.

[24] Thus a leaseholder had no seisin and was not liable to pay any feudal services nor subject to any feudal incidents, see para **[2.10]** *ante* and **[4.018]** *post*.

[25] Privity of contract is a technical concept dealing with the persons who may sue on a contract. Originally the only persons who could sue were the parties to it; at a later stage their personal representatives could sue and be sued. The next development was that rights under some contracts could be assigned to another person, who could sue on the contract, but this did not become law until the nineteenth century. See, generally, Clark, *Contract Law in Ireland* (3rd ed, 1992), Ch 17; Wylie, 'Contracts and Third Parties' (1967) 18 NILQ 448.

of trespass[26]) was developed, so as to enable a leaseholder to protect his land and recover it against all comers that a leasehold could be regarded as an estate in land.[27] Yet it was clear that a lease created a form of tenure and equally clear that it was a new type of tenure, not feudal tenure. Thus statutes like *Quia Emptores* did not apply to leases, so that a leasehold tenant was free to make sub-leases and could be restricted from alienation of his estate, according to the terms of his agreement with his landlord.

[4.008] This historical development led to the general principle of our land law that a leasehold estate was always regarded as less than a freehold estate. Indeed, the fundamental distinction was drawn that a leasehold estate was classed as personalty whereas a freehold estate was realty.[28] Freehold estates were classified as realty or real estate because in the early days of the common law an action for their recovery could be brought; the plaintiff got judgment for recovery of the *res*, the thing which was the freehold. But as leaseholds were based on contract there was no known method of getting judgment for their recovery. The action (if any) was for damages and so they were classified as personalty or personal estate. Until recently this was a vitally important distinction because the law of devolution of land on intestacy differed in its application to the deceased's realty and personalty.[29] The distinction remains important because it is quite common for wills to contain general dispositions with respect to the testator's "realty" on the one hand and his "personalty" on the other.[30] But because leaseholds have such a close connection with land and other estates created out of land, they have had a hybrid or composite label ascribed to them. They are frequently called "chattels real"; the word "chattels" indicates the link with personalty and the word "real" the link with realty.

[4.009] Another result of this distinction between freehold and leasehold estates was that a freehold estate could not be created out of a leasehold estate in the early stages of development of our land law system. The basic objection to such a grant at common law was that the holder of a freehold estate had seisin and a leaseholder had no seisin to pass

---

[26] See, generally, Maitland, *Forms of Action* (eds Chaytor and Whittaker, 1936). The real actions, the original feudal forms of action (such as the writ of right and possessory assizes), were abolished by the Real Property Limitation Act 1833, s 36 leaving the action of ejectment as the principal protection for leaseholders *and* freeholders. All forms of action, including ejectment, were abolished by the Common Law Procedure Act 1852, ss 168-221, so that in future an action for recovery of land could be instituted by pleading in ordinary language.

[27] See Holdsworth, *History of English Law*, Vol III, p 4; Megarry and Wade, *The Law of Real Property* (5th ed, 1984), Appendix 1.

[28] Note that under the Local Registration of Title (Ir) Act 1891, Pt IV, freehold titles bought by tenants under the Land Purchase Acts and compulsorily registered under the 1891 Act were to descend on intestacy as personalty, not realty. See now the Registration of Title Act 1964, s 113(2) (RI); Land Registration Act (NI) 1970, s 97 and Sched 14. Also para [3.099] *ante*.

[29] Ch 15, *post*.

[30] Or expressions having the same meaning, such as "real estate" and "personal estate". One interesting point is that since leaseholds were classified as personalty they could be left by will, whereas freehold land could not be devised by will in Ireland until 1634, para [3.020] *ante*.

to the person to whom he intended to convey a freehold estate.[31] New methods of conveyancing were devised to get round this sort of technical objection.[32]

[4.010] There are several types of leasehold estate, which are usually classified into four main categories. It is often said that a major distinguishing feature, in contrast to freehold estates, is the element of certainty of duration attaching to leasehold estates. As we shall see, this is often not a very striking distinction and frequently seems to be a question of degree only.[33] The first category of leasehold estate is one granted for a *certain term*. This sort of estate is common in both Ireland and England, and very long terms of years are particularly common in Ireland.[34] The element of certainty in this case relates to the limit on the estate's duration; there is no certainty at all that such an estate will in fact last for the term agreed, for at least two reasons. One is that something may happen during the course of the lease entitling the lessor to determine it before the term is up.[35] The other is that often a clause is inserted in a lease entitling either party to determine it at any time by serving an appropriate notice to determine on the other party.[36] While there may be a limit on the maximum duration, there is no certainty about the minimum duration.[37]

[4.011] The second category of leasehold estate is a *periodic tenancy*. This is sometimes referred to as a fixed term capable of being rendered certain, but this can cause confusion. The only thing that is fixed is the original minimum period (eg, one week or one month), which will continue for successive periods until such time as either party to the agreement determines the tenancy in the appropriate manner.[38] There is no certainty at all about the maximum duration; if neither party takes any action the successive periods will continue indefinitely, from week to week, month to month or for whatever is the period in question. A maximum limit will be introduced only if and when either party serves a notice to determine the tenancy on a particular date.

[4.012] The next category is a *tenancy at will*. As the name implies this is a tenancy which may also continue indefinitely, but which is determinable by either party at any time. The tenant certainly seems to have tenure, but it is questionable whether he can be

---

[31] Para **[4.019]** *post*.

[32] Ie wills and trusts, see **[5.019]** *post*.

[33] Para **[17.022]** *post*.

[34] Eg, terms of 999 and 10,000 years. See *Re Sergie* [1954] NI 1 (10,000 years) (see *A Casebook on Irish Land Law* (1984), p 70).

[35] Eg, forfeiture for breach of covenant or ejectment for non-payment of rent, Ch 17, *post*.

[36] Ch 17, *post*.

[37] Courts in England have from time to time struck down leases which they construed as coming within this category, but which were not certain enough as regards their duration, the most notorious example being a lease "for the duration of the War". See *Lace v Chantler* [1944] KB 368 (and see the Validation of War-Time Leases Act 1944, 62 LQR 219) and the House of Lords decision in *Prudential Assurance Co Ltd v London Residuary Body* [1992] 2 AC 386, overruling *Re Midland Rly Co's Agreement* [1971] Ch 725 and, on this point, *Ashburn Anstalt v Arnold* [1989] Ch 1. It is doubtful if this point would have the same force in Ireland, see para **[17.022]** *post*.

[38] Para **[17.023]** *post*.

said to hold for an estate. His tenure is so uncertain and insecure that it is difficult to quantify his estate and he seems to have nothing which he could convey to third parties.[39] Another category rather similar to the tenancy at will is a *tenancy at sufferance*. This arises where a tenant "holds over" after his previous tenancy has terminated. Unlike the tenancy at will, the tenant holds without the landlord's assent or dissent. The reason he is not a trespasser is that his original entry was lawful under the terms of his original tenancy agreement; the landlord must re-enter and re-take possession before he can exclude all others as trespassers. So long as the tenant at sufferance is allowed to remain and the landlord does not accept rent from him, his possession excludes any possession by the landlord.[40] Once again it is questionable whether such an interest should be classified as an estate.[41] In passing, it may be mentioned that there is another type of tenancy which involves the concept of "holding over". This is a statutory tenancy, which arises where a tenant is given the right to remain on in possession, subject to the terms and conditions of a previous tenancy agreement,[42] which has since terminated. This sort of tenancy, if it can be called such, is, to some extent, the creation of statute law, such as the rent restriction or similar legislation.[43]

The whole subject of leasehold estates will be dealt with in the later chapter on the law of landlord and tenant.[44]

C. Future Interests

[4.013] An estate in land may be enjoyed either at the present time or in the future. In the language of land law, it may be enjoyed in possession, in reversion or in remainder. If an estate is held in possession it means that the holder has an immediate right to possession and enjoyment of the land to which the estate relates. In the case of a reversion or remainder, on the other hand, this right to possession and enjoyment is postponed to some date in the future and someone else is entitled to it in the meantime. A *reversion* arises where a landowner grants away some estate lesser than his own to be enjoyed in possession by some other person. For example, A, owner of the fee simple estate in Blackacre, grants a life estate to B. B holds the life estate in possession and so

---

[39] See further, the discussion by the Republic's Supreme Court in *Irish Shell & BP Ltd v Costello Ltd* [1984] IR 511 and *Bellew v Bellew* [1982] IR 447; *cf* the English Court of Appeal in *Binions v Evans* [1972] Ch 359.

[40] Note, however, the landlord's option to treat the tenant overholding as a tenant from year to year under s 5 of Deasy's Act 1860, **[17.024]** *post*. On the subject of possession, and its relevance to title to land, see Ch 23, *post*.

[41] Thus such a tenant may be treated as a trespasser in the sense that the modern doctrine of adverse possession operating under the statutes of limitations may apply to him: see para **[23.31]** *post*, and Wylie, *Irish Landlord and Tenant Law*, para 4.039.

[42] Which may be replaced in some respects by statute. Thus legislation like the Rent Acts controlled the amount of rent that could be charged to the statutory tenant.

[43] See paras **[18.35]** and **[18.39]** *post*. This sort of statutory tenancy should not be confused with a 15 year *judicial tenancy* which could be granted to an agricultural tenant under the Land Law (Ir) Act 1881, see para **[1.049]** *ante*.

[44] Ch 17, *post*. See also Wylie, *Irish Landlord and Tenant Law* (looseleaf).

long as that estate lasts A holds his fee simple in reversion. When B dies, his life estate ends and the land reverts in terms of possession and enjoyment to A; the fee simple in reversion becomes once again a fee simple in possession.

[4.014] A *remainder* arises where the grantor creates an estate to be enjoyed in possession in the future by someone other than himself. For example, A, owner of the fee simple in Blackacre, conveys Blackacre to B for life, remainder to C in fee simple. B has a life estate in possession and C has the fee simple in remainder, to be enjoyed in possession when B dies. A has therefore disposed of his entire interest in the property; he has retained no estate or interest in the land, not even a reversion.[45] He would have had a fee simple reversion if instead he had conveyed a fee tail estate only to C.

[4.015] The law relating to future interests is, perhaps, one of the most complex aspects of land law. It has become so because of a clash between two competing policies. One is the principle of allowing landowners freedom to deal with their land, coupled with the desire on the part of testators to decree the future enjoyment of their land long after their deaths. The other is the principle of promotion of land as a commercial asset, to be protected from excessive restrictions on its use and alienation and concentration of control of its ownership in the hands of a few large landowners. Many rules have been devised by the courts and legislatures over the centuries in an attempt to draw a fair balance between these policies. We shall study these further in a later chapter.[46]

D. Interests less than Estates

[4.016] Our land law recognises many interests in land which do not come within the classification of estates in land. It is because there are so many types of this sort of interest in land that the fragmentation of ownership of land can be so complex. Whether or not an interest in land has been created or has arisen is often a difficult question. In recent decades, there has been considerable controversy in the courts, particularly in England, about this matter.[47] The main criterion by which to judge whether a particular interest is an interest in land would seem to be whether that interest will bind successors in title of either or both of the original parties to the contract or conveyance creating the interest in the first place. The point is that land law recognises a wide variety of exceptions to the general principle of the law of contract known as the doctrine of privity of contract.[48] If a mere contractual interest has been created, the original parties to the contract only can be affected by it (by gaining rights or becoming subject to duties enforceable by action in court). If, however, an interest in land is created, it will bind successors in title of the original parties, though how far it will bind successors may

---

[45] The position would be different if a condition precedent were imposed on C's taking possession, so that his remainder was contingent and not vested. This complex subject is discussed in detail in Ch 5, *post*.

[46] Ch 5, *post*.

[47] See Cheshire, 'A New Equitable Interest in Land' (1953) 16 MLR 1; Delany, 'Equitable Interests and "Mere Equities" (1957) 21 Conv 195; Stoljar, 'Licence, Interest and Contract' (1953) 33 CBR 562; Wade, 'Licences and Third Parties' (1952) 68 LQR 337. Also Ch 20 *post*.

[48] See generally Clark, *Contract Law in Ireland* (3rd ed, 1992), Ch 17; Wylie, 'Contracts and Third Parties' (1967) 8 NILQ 448.

vary according to the type of interest in land created. A simple illustration may be given in the case of a lease: L leases his house to T for 99 years; some years later T assigns his lease to A. There are two contracts here; one between L and T and one between T and A; L is not a party to the latter contract and A is not a party to the former. Yet under the law of landlord and tenant, A in effect steps into T's shoes and is treated in law almost as if he were T, so that he obtains most rights T had against L under the contract between L and T, and is subject to most of T's duties towards L under that contract. The converse position obtains if L assigns his reversion to X, so that the relationship between X and A is largely governed by the contract between L and T, the original lease, to which neither of them was a party.[49] As we shall see, many cases have arisen recently where a central issue in the dispute was whether the agreement in question created a lease or a mere licence. But the added complication has also arisen that even a licence may in certain circumstances acquire some of the attributes of an interest in land.[50]

[4.017] Perhaps the best recognised type of interest in land less than an estate is what is commonly called an *incorporeal hereditament*. These interests are called hereditaments because they were classified as realty, as opposed to personalty, for the purposes of the old law of inheritance, ie, devolution on intestacy.[51] They are incorporeal because they do not give any rights to physical objects, such as land itself or buildings (ie, the *corpus*). They are mere rights over land, usually the land of someone else. Common examples are easements (such as a right of way over a neighbour's land), profits *à prendre* (such as a right to shoot or fish on someone else's land) and rentcharges (the right to an annuity charged on land). For the most part they are rights attached to specific pieces of land, though for historical reasons this was not always the case.[52] Other interests in land, apart from incorporeal hereditaments and certain licences, are interests created by conveyancing devices like restrictive covenants[53] or mortgages.[54] In both these cases equity has played an important part in their development.[55]

II. FREEHOLD ESTATES

Before discussing the various categories of freehold estates, there are two fundamental concepts relating to such estates which should be mentioned. One is the concept of *seisin* and the other is the concept of *words of limitation*.

---

[49] See Ch 17, *post*.

[50] Ch 20, *post*.

[51] Ch 15, *post*.

[52] Eg, an advowson, para **[6.018]** *post*. Incorporeal hereditaments are discussed in detail in Ch 6, *post*.

[53] Ch 19, *post*. Note, however, that in NI most freehold covenants, whether positive or restrictive, will become fully enforceable against successors in title, like incorporeal hereditaments, under Article 34 of the Property (NI) Order 1997: see para **[19.048]** *post*.

[54] Ch 12, *post*.

[55] On the role of equity in land law generally, see Ch 3 *ante*.

A. Seisin

[4.018] Seisin was a concept fundamental to the feudal system as it developed in the early centuries. But it is a concept which defies precise definition.[56] The problem is that the concept involves the notion of possession of land, but it is by no means synonymous with possession. Thus a leaseholder has possession of land but he has no seisin; the seisin is in the freeholder from whom he holds his lease, whether directly or indirectly. [57]

[4.019] It eventually became a settled principle under the feudal system that only a freeholder holding under freehold tenure had seisin. So a leaseholder had no seisin, as we have already stated, nor had a copyholder; in a copyholder's case the seisin lay with the lord of the manor. It also became a settled principle that there must always be some person seised at any particular time.[58] Even though a freeholder had parted with possession of the land to someone who could not be seised, the seisin did not lapse and remained in the freeholder. The reasons for these principles were very practical ones. Under the feudal system the services owed could be enforced only against the tenant seised of the land; only those seised were originally recognised by the King's courts. The early actions by which land itself could be recovered, the real actions, could be brought only in respect of disputes over seisin.[59] It was not until several centuries later that the wider concept of possession acquired the same significance and protection in our land law, so that today possession, rather than seisin, is the more important concept.[60]

Seisin had other practical significance. Certain rights on death could be claimed only if the deceased had been seised, eg, rights of dower for a widow and rights of curtesy for a widower.[61] Only the heir of the tenant seised of the land could succeed to the land on that tenant's death. And, as we have seen,[62] in the early days conveyances of freehold land were very technical and formal exercises. The original method was by feoffment with *livery of seisin*, a symbolic ceremony performed by the parties on the land itself.

B. Words of Limitation

[4.020] The concept of words of limitation also derives from the formalistic approach of the feudal system to land transactions. The principle was established that a freehold estate could be created only if the grantor used the words of limitation appropriate for

---

[56] *Long v Myles* (1822) 1 Fox & Sm 1. See Williams, *The Seisin of the Freehold* (1878); Bordwell, 'Seisin and Disseisin' (1921) 34 HLR 592, 717; Maitland 'Mystery of Seisin' (1886) 2 LQR 481, 'Beatitude of Seisin' (1888) 4 LQR 24, 286; Sweet, 'Seisin' (1896) 12 LQR 239; Thorne, 'Livery of Seisin' (1936) 52 LQR 345.

[57] Eg, in the case of a sub-lessee having possession of the land.

[58] Several rules were derived from the feudal approach to the concept of seisin, sometimes known as common law seisin rules. They are discussed in Ch 5, *post*.

[59] Maitland, *Forms of Action at Common Law* (eds Chayton and Whittaker 1936); see also Booth, *Real Actions* (2nd ed, 1811); Lightwood, *Possession of Land* (1894).

[60] Ch 23, *post*.

[61] Para **[4.157]** *post*. See *Long v Myles* (1822) 1 Fox & Sm 1.

[62] Para **[3.023]** *ante*.

that particular estate. The expression "words of limitation" means, therefore, the words delimiting or defining the estate being conveyed. These words are to be distinguished from "words of purchase," which indicate the person to whom the estate is conveyed. Let us take an example to illustrate the distinction: "to A in fee simple". This would be an appropriate formula to use today, as we shall see.[63] Here the words "to A" are the words of purchase and the words "in fee simple" are the words of limitation. This distinction came to be important, particularly with reference to a principle known as the Rule in *Shelley's Case*.[64] The appropriate "magic phrases" to be used in connection with the various freehold estates have varied over the centuries, as a result of statutory interventions. The courts took different approaches according to whether the document was a conveyance made *inter vivos* (ie, between living persons) or a will. These are matters which we shall consider in relation to each particular type of freehold estate, a subject to which we now turn.

III. FEE SIMPLE

A. General

[4.021] It has already been explained that the fee simple estate is the largest estate known to our land law, the estate nearest to absolute ownership of land.[65] It has the potential to last for ever and will end only when an owner for the time being dies intestate, leaving no person entitled to succeed.[66] Indeed, in the Republic of Ireland it is arguable that a fee simple cannot end as the State now succeeds as "ultimate intestate successor" when the owner dies leaving no other person entitled to succeed.[67] Nowadays a fee simple is free from most feudal burdens and, in theory, under general land law the owner is free to use and enjoy the land as he pleases. But this statement must be made subject to many qualifications. First, there is nothing to stop parties to a conveyance imposing restrictions on the use and enjoyment of the land to be held in fee simple. It is true that the law may confine this right of private parties within limits, but as we shall see the exercise of the right means that different categories of fee simple can be created. We shall examine these in a moment, and will then go on to examine the special kinds of conveyances creating a fee simple which are so common in Ireland, fee farm grants.[68] A fee farm grant creates a fee simple with many of the usual characteristics of that estate

---

[63] Para **[4.029]** *post*.

[64] Para **[4.034]** *post*.

[65] Para **[4.004]** *ante*. See also Barton, 'The Rise of the Fee Simple' (1976) 92 LQR 108.

[66] See Ch 15, *post*. An interesting point arises in the case of a squatter barring a fee simple owner; if the principle be accepted that there is no statutory transfer of title or Parliamentary conveyance effected by the statute of limitations, presumably the old fee simple disappears and a new one arises in its place. This subject is discussed in Ch 23, *post*.

[67] Succession Act 1965, s 73.

[68] Para **[4.057]** *post*. It should be noted that the future creation of fee farm grants has been restricted in the Republic by the Landlord and Tenant (Ground Rents) Act 1978. This Act prohibits the future creation of ground rents in respect of dwellings and for these purposes a "lease" includes a fee farm grant, see para **[4.182]** *post*. A similar prohibition on the future creation of fee farm grants is contained in Article 28 of the Property (NI) Order 1997, see *ibid*.

as it developed under English common law, but the real significance of these grants in Ireland is that they create a variety of relationships between the grantors and grantees which could not exist in England. This results in the fee simple estate in these cases acquiring characteristics peculiar to Ireland.

[4.022] The second qualification relates to the land held in fee simple. In this context the Latin maxim *cuius est solum, eius est usque ad coelum et ad inferos*[69] is often cited. Like many maxims in practice it is only an approximation to the truth. At best it can be regarded as a presumption or a rule of thumb for deciding cases of doubt which cannot be disposed of on any other clearer authority. Several cases have arisen involving chattels found under or attached to land belonging to someone else,[70] or becoming affixed to the land so as to become part of it,[71] where the general rule is that the items belong to the landowner.[72] But the fee simple owner will never enjoy such wide-ranging rights as the maxim suggests. He will be subject to rights others have acquired over his land as a result of other land transactions, eg leases and mortgages, or prior sales conferring casements like rights of way. The owner's freedom to do as he pleases on his land is restricted by the general law of tort; he must not cause a public or private nuisance,[73] and may be liable in certain circumstances if dangerous substances escape from his land and injure others,[74] or if others are injured while on his land.[75] The owner's

---

[69] Roughly translated: the owner of the soil is to be taken to own also everything up to the sky and down to the centre of the earth. See the interesting discussion of the maxim, and of its limits, in *Lord Bernstein of Leigh v Skyviews and General Ltd* [1978] QB 479. See also the Republic's Supreme Court decision in *Metropolitan Properties Ltd v O'Brien* [1995] 1 IR 467; *cf Keating & Co Ltd v Jervis Shopping Centre Ltd* unrep, (HC, RI) 1 March 1996; Richardson, 'Private Property Rights in Air Space' (1953) 31 CBR 117.

[70] Eg, *Elwes v Brigg Gas Co* (1886) 33 Ch D 562; *South Staffordshire Water Co v Sharman* [1896] 2 QB 44. See the discussion by the Republic's Supreme Court in *Webb v Ireland* [1988] IR 353, *infra*.

[71] Eg, *Leigh v Taylor* [1902] AC 157 (tapestries fastened by tacks to canvas and pieces of wood nailed to the drawing-room wall of a mansion house); *Holland v Hodgson* (1872) LR 7 CP 328 (mill looms nailed to stone floor of mill); *Elitestone Ltd v Morris* [1997] 2 All ER 513 (bungalow with timber frame walls and suspended floors resting on concrete blocks). The subject of fixtures in relation to life estate owners and tenants is discussed at paras **[4.155]** and **[17.060]** *post*. As regards mortgages, see para **[13.010]** *post*. See also Bingham, 'Some Suggestions Concerning the Law of Fixtures' (1907) 7 Col L Rev 1; Guest and Lever, 'Hire-Purchase, Equipment Leases and Fixtures' (1963) 27 Conv 30); Amos, *Law of Fixtures*.

[72] *Cf* where the item is an unattached chattel in respect of which the landowner has manifested no intention to exercise control over it, nor made any claim to it before it is found by someone else who does claim it: see *Parker v British Airways Board* [1982] QB 1004. A finder may not, however, succeed in a claim as against his employer where the finding occurred in the course of his employment: *McDowell v Ulster Bank* (1899) 33 ILT 225; *cf Crinion v Minister for Justice* [1959] Ir Jur Rep 15. Note that special rules govern "treasure trove": see *infra*.

[73] *Halpin v Tara Mines Ltd* [1976-7] ILRM 28; *Hanrahan v Merck Sharp & Dohme (Ir) Ltd* [1988] ILRM 629; *Belfast City Council v Irish Football Association Ltd* [1988] NI 290.

[74] *Shell-Mex and BP Ltd v Belfast Corporation* [1952] NI 72; *Healy v Bray UDC* [1962-3] Ir Jur Rep 9; see also *Boylan v Dublin Corporation* [1949] IR 60.

[75] *Scully v Boland Ltd* [1962] IR 58; *O'Donoghue v Greene* [1967] IR 40; see also *Cooney v Dockerell & Sons* [1965] Ir Jur Rep 31. And see the Republic's Occupiers' Liability Act 1995; as regards Northern Ireland, the Occupiers' Liability Act (NI) 1957.

rights are subject nowadays to wide-ranging State control and interference, through legislation like the Public Health Acts, Housing Acts and Planning Acts.[76] Furthermore, the ownership of certain things to be found on land lies elsewhere under our law, either at common law or under statute. Indeed, it seems that some things may not be owned at all, eg, wild animals,[77] in respect of which the owner of the land on which they are found has only the exclusive right to catch and appropriate.[78] At common law the Crown was entitled to treasure throve, ie, gold or silver hidden on the land in respect of which the true owner is unknown.[79] In *Webb v Ireland*[80] which involved the famous "Derrynaflan Hoard" of early Christian objects, the Republic's Supreme Court held that this Royal Prerogative right had not survived the 1922 Constitution, but went on to hold that, nevertheless, a right to ownership of all antiquities of national importance (forming part of the national heritage and not confined to articles made of gold and silver[81]) was vested in the State as an inherent attribute of its sovereignty which was recognised and declared by the Constitution.[82] The finder would have no claim to ownership, but might have a claim to reward on the basis of legitimate expectation.[83] In Northern Ireland the common-law rules as to treasure trove have been replaced by the UK statutory scheme introduced by the Treasure Act 1996. Under this "treasure"[84] generally will, when found, vest in the Crown[85] and finders have a duty to notify the coroner for the district in question, who is required to hold an inquest, now usually without a jury.[86] The Crown was also entitled to the foreshore adjoining tidal waters (ie, the land between high and low water marks); this is still the position in Northern Ireland,[87] and in the Republic the

---

[76] See paras **[1.061]**-**[1.062]** and **[1.077]**-**[1.079]** *ante*.

[77] *Blades v Higgs* (1865) 11 HLC 621.

[78] Subject to statutory limitations and prohibitions, see eg, Wild Birds Protection Act 1930 (RI); Wild Birds Protection Acts (NI) 1931 and 1950; Game Preservation Act 1930 (RI); Game Preservation Act (NI) 1928 and Game Law Amendment Act (NI) 1951.

[79] Where treasure is claimed to be found, a coroner is supposed to hold an inquest on the matter, see Coroners Act 1962, s 49 (RI); Coroners Act (NI) 1959, s 33. See Hill, *Treasure Trove in Law and Practice* (1936), especially p 263 *et seq*; Dolly, 'The First Treasure Trove Inquest in Ireland?' (1968) 19 NILQ 182; (1963) 97 ILTSJ 39.

[80] [1988] IR 353.

[81] *Ibid* pp 383 (*per* Finlay CJ) and 390-91 (*per* Walsh J).

[82] See the discussion by Kelly, 'Hidden Treasure and the Constitution' (1988) 10 DULJ 5; Lenihan, 'Royal Prerogatives and the Constitution' (1989) 24 Ir Jur (ns) 1. See also Hogan & Whyte, *Kelly: The Irish Constitution* (3rd ed, 1994), p 1132 *et seq*.

[83] See also the Supreme Court's decision in *Re La Lavia* [1996] 1 ILRM 194. The Court had urged the Oireachtas to introduce a statutory scheme for reward to encourage safekeeping of antiquities and this was done by enactment of the National Monuments (Amendment) Act 1994, s 10.

[84] As defined by s 1, the meaning of which may, however, be altered by statutory instrument (s 2).

[85] Section 4.

[86] Sections 7-9. There is also a statutory provision for rewards, s 11.

[87] Government of Ireland Act 1920, s 4(1); see also the Northern Ireland (Miscellaneous Provisions) Act 1932, s 9.

foreshore is vested in the State.[88] Other matters have been pre-empted by the State through legislation. Thus in the Republic the rights to most minerals, including petroleum[89] have been vested in the State.[90] A similar development has recently taken place in Northern Ireland.[91] Restrictions have been put on the landowner's right to bring actions (for trespass or nuisance) in respect of infringement of the air-space above his land by, eg, aircraft.[92]

B. Creation and Transfer

[4.023] Since the Real Property Act 1845, a fee simple has usually been granted by a deed, ie, a document under seal. A deed is not a requirement because the 1845 Act did not replace the old modes of conveyance, it merely introduced a more convenient alternative.[93] These other modes of conveyance were discussed in more detail in the previous chapter,[94] though it should be noted here that it is extremely unlikely that they would be used today.[95]

C. Words of Limitation

[4.024] It has already been indicated that under the common law appropriate words of limitation had to be used to create a fee simple.[96] The rules were particularly strict in the

---

[88] 1937 Constitution, Article 10; Foreshore Act 1933. See *Howe v Stawell* (1833) Alc & Nap 348; *Hamilton v Att-Gen* (1880) 5 LR Ir 555; *Macnamara v Higgins* (1854) 4 ICLR 326; *Brew v Haren* (1877) 11 ILTR 66; *Stoney v Keane* (1903) 37 ILTR 212; *Mahoney v Neenan* [1966] IR 559. Lee, 'The Right to Take Seaweed from the Seashore' (1967) 18 NILQ 33; also (1955) 89 ILTSJ 131 and 137; Smyth, *The Seashores of Ireland: Public Rights and Restrictions* (1935).

[89] Petroleum and Other Minerals Development Act 1960.

[90] 1922 Constitution, Article 11; 1937 Constitution, Article 10. See also Minerals Development Acts 1940 and 1979; Minerals Exploration and Development Company Act 1941; Minerals Company Acts 1945, 1947 and 1950. See also the Continental Shelf Act 1968. And see *Tara Prospecting Ltd v Minister for Energy* [1993] ILRM 771. See Hogan & Whyte, *Kelly: The Irish Constitution* (3rd ed, 1994), pp 71 *et seq*.

[91] Mineral Development Act (NI) 1969; Petroleum (Production) Act (NI) 1964. The vesting under these Acts was in the then NI Ministry of Commerce.

[92] Air Navigation and Transport Act 1936, s 55 (RI), as amended by s 47 of the Air Navigation and Transport Act 1988; Northern Ireland is governed by the UK Civil Aviation Act 1949, s 40. See *Lord Bernstein of Leigh v Skyviews and General Ltd* [1978] QB 479. Section 40 was held by the European Court of Human Rights not to be a violation of the rights of residents near Heathrow Airport: see *Powell & Raynor v United Kingdom* (1990) 12 EHRR 355.

[93] Section 2, replacing ss 2 and 13 of the Transfer of Property Act 1844. The old modes of conveyance were abolished in England by the Law of Property Act 1925, s 51, under which the deed became the sole method of conveying a fee simple. See paras **[3.025]-[3.030]** *ante*. See also, generally, Wylie, *Irish Conveyancing Law* (1978), Chs 16 and 17.

[94] Paras **[3.023]-[3.024]** *ante*.

[95] Apart from questions of cost and convenience, the old modes do not fit in well with modern conveyancing practice; eg, feoffment with livery of seisin may involve no document capable of registration in the Registry of Deeds, or any title deed or other documentary evidence of title to be supplied to the officials of the Land Registry, see Chs 21 and 22, *post*.

[96] Para **[4.020]** *ante*.

case of freehold estates of inheritance, ie, the fee simple and fee tail, especially where these estates were conveyed *inter vivos*. The early modes of conveyance *inter vivos* were very solemn and ceremonial affairs[97] and this may explain the courts' strict interpretation of them. For centuries wills were not recognised by the Common Law Courts; eventually they were enforced by the Court of Chancery, and then the Statute of Wills (Ireland) 1634 required the Common Law Courts to enforce them.[98] The Court of Chancery was much more liberal in its interpretation of documents, especially wills, seeking as far as possible to give effect to the intention of the parties.[99] When wills came to be recognised at common law this liberal approach to their interpretation survived and so in the following statement of law a distinction still has to be made between conveyances *inter vivos* and wills. The further complication arises that some amendments in the common law position have been made by statute.

1. Conveyances Inter Vivos

(i) At Common Law

At common law a distinction must be made between conveyances to natural persons and conveyances to corporations.

(a) Natural Persons

[4.025] In this case the proper words of limitation for a fee simple were "and his heirs," to be inserted after the name of the grantee. Thus to convey a fee simple to A one would say: "to A and his heirs". The expression "heirs" was like a magic formula.[100] Failure to use it, or an attempt to use some equivalent expression such as "relatives," "issue," "descendants" or even "in fee simple," gave the grantee a life estate only.[101] The same was the position if expressions like "to A for ever" or "to A absolutely" were used.[102] The use, however, of superfluous words would not invalidate a conveyance of a fee simple so long as appropriate words for a fee simple were included.[103] The word "heir" in the singular was not enough,[104] though adding a description to the word "heirs" did not necessarily prevent the conveyance of a fee simple. Thus it seems that "to A and his

---

[97] Para **[3.023]** *ante*.

[98] Para **[3.010]** *ante*.

[99] See, generally, Ch 14, *post*.

[100] See Challis, *Law of Real Property* (3rd ed), Ch XV; Megarry and Wade, *Law of Real Property* (5th ed), pp 49-53. *Kennedy and Lawler v Ryan* [1938] IR 620; see also *Re Fayle and the Irish Feather Co's Contract* [1918] 1 IR 13.

[101] *Jack v Reilly* (1829) 2 Hud & Br 301; *Wood v Davis* (1880) 6 LR Ir 50; *Re Coleman's Estate* [1907] 1 IR 488; *Re Adam's Estate* [1965] IR 57; *Re Houston* [1909] 1 IR 319.

[102] *Lysaght v McGrath* (1881) 11 LR Ir 142; *Cf Twaddle v Murphy* (1881) 8 LR Ir 123 (see *A Casebook on Irish Land Law* (1984) p 113).

[103] In *Twaddle v Murphy* (1881) 8 LR Ir 123, a conveyance to A and B "their heirs and assigns, for the lives of C, D and E, or for 999 years. or for ever, whichever should last longest" was held to pass a fee simple, in this case subject to a perpetual yearly rent (ie a fee farm grant, see para **[4.057]** *post*). See the discussion of this case by Murray J in *Re Courtney* [1981] NI 58.

[104] *Mallory's Case* (1601) 5 Co Rep 111b at 112a.

heirs male" (not to be confused with the words necessary for a fee tail male, "to A and the heirs male *of his body*"[105]) would still give A a fee simple: the word "male" was ignored by the common law as being a limitation repugnant to the estate purported to be granted and therefore invalid.[106] It is important to note that the words of limitation must appear in the body of the deed, ie, in an appropriate operative part which by tradition is the *habendum*.[107] If the appropriate words are missing from there the deed will be ineffective to pass the fee simple and will not be saved by, eg, a definition or interpretation clause specifying that the word "purchaser" or "grantee" includes his "heirs".[108]

[4.026] It was important also to be clear whether the words in question were words of limitation or words of purchase.[109] In the standard formula "to A and his heirs," the words "to A" are the words of purchase only, ie, A only takes any estate in the land, in this case a fee simple. The words "and his heirs" are words of limitation only, delimiting A's estate; A's "heirs" take no estate at all. Even if at the time of conveyance there is someone who could be regarded as likely to be an "heir" of A, that person has at most a *spes successionis* only, ie, a hope of succeeding to A's estate should he die intestate as far as that estate is concerned. A's "heirs" or "heir" cannot be determined definitely until A dies. Until recently in Ireland this question of devolution was settled in accordance with the feudal law of primogeniture; A's heir was his eldest surviving son.[110] But the law on this subject has been changed by statute in both parts of Ireland, for the purposes of devolution on intestacy. "Heirs" for the purposes of devolution means the persons entitled to succeed on intestacy under Part VI of the Republic's Succession Act 1965, or Part II of the Administration of Estates Act (NI) 1955. These statutes, however, provide that the words "heir" or "heirs" used in any enactment, deed or instrument as words of limitation, before or after the enactment of the statutes, have the same effect as if the statutes had not been passed.[111] They also provide that where the words "heir" or "heirs" are used as words of purchase, they have the same effect in enactments and deeds, passed or executed before the passing of the statutes;[112] in the case of enactments and deeds passed or executed after the passing of the statutes they are to be construed to mean the person or persons entitled to succeed on intestacy (other than a creditor), unless a contrary intention appears.[113] An example of use of the word "heir" as a word of

---

[105] Para **[4.128]** *post*.
[106] *Idle v Cook* (1705) 1 P Wm 70 at 70. On the question of repugnancy generally, see para **[4.052]** *post*.
[107] See Wylie, *Irish Conveyancing Law* (2nd ed, 1996), para 18.86. *Cf Re Fayle and Irish Feather Co's Contract* [1918] 1 IR 13.
[108] *Re Ford and Ferguson's Contract* [1906] 1 IR 607. See also *Annesley v Annesley* (1873) 31 LR Ir 457; *Re Coleman's Estate* [1907] 1 IR 488.
[109] See para **[4.020]** *ante*.
[110] Ch 15, *post*.
[111] Succession Act 1965, s 15(1); Administration of Estates Act (NI) 1955, s 5(1).
[112] 1965 Act, s 15(2); 1955 Act (NI), s 5(2).
[113] 1965 Act, s 15(3); 1955 Act (NI), s 5(3).

purchase would be "to A's heir and his heirs".[114] If A was dead at the time of the conveyance, the fee simple went to his heir determined in accordance with the rules of primogeniture or, if the conveyance is after the statutes, his successors as determined under Part VI of the Republic's 1965 Act or Part II of Northern Ireland's 1955 Act. If A was alive at the time of the conveyance, the conveyance was void because it purported to convey the estate to someone not yet ascertained, so that an abeyance of seisin would occur which the common law would not allow.[115] Thus the recent statutory provisions on devolution on intestacy avoid upsetting the centuries-old practice of conveyancers in drafting documents of title.

Before leaving the distinction between words of limitation and words of purchase, it should be pointed out that there is one other important aspect of the distinction. This relates to the general principle known as the rule in *Shelley's Case* which we discuss below.[116]

(b) Corporations

[4.027] Corporations, whether created by charter or by or under statute, have a distinct legal personality of their own, so that they can own property and enter into contracts, and can sue or be sued in contract or tort as entities separate from individuals connected with them, such as directors or shareholders.[117] A corporation may be either a corporation aggregate made up of two or more individuals acting as a corporate body (eg, a limited company or a city corporation), or a corporation sole comprising one individual holding an office subject to perpetual succession (eg, Government Ministers in the Republic[118]). The law relating to words of limitation in conveyances to corporations is different from that relating to conveyances to individuals. So far as a corporation aggregate is concerned, it has long been settled at common law that a conveyance to the corporation by its corporate name gives it a fee simple without any need for words of limitation.[119] There is nothing surprising about this rule. A corporation is not like a natural person; it cannot die or have "heirs" in the way that a natural person can and it was for this reason that the feudal system, dependent upon revenue generated by deaths, disliked conveyances to corporations, hence the statutes on mortmain.[120]

[4.028] In the case of a corporation sole, however, a natural person is involved, who will die even though his office will continue. The rule here is that words of limitation must be used, in this case the words "and his successors".[121] Thus to give the Republic's

---

[114] It seems that to the same effect would be "to the heirs of A". See Megarry and Wade, *The Law of Real Property* (5th ed), p 50.

[115] Para **[5.013]** *post*.

[116] Para **[4.034]** *post*.

[117] See Keane, *Company Law in the Republic of Ireland* (2nd ed, 1991), Pts 1 and 3; Courtney, *The Law of Private Companies* (1994), Chs 2 and 3.

[118] Ministers and Secretaries Act 1924, s 2.

[119] *Re Woking UDC (Basingstoke Canal) Act 1911* [1914] 1 Ch 300 at 312 (*per* Swinfen Eady LJ).

[120] Para **[2.41]** *ante*, and para **[25.21]**, *post*.

[121] *Ex parte Vicar of Castle Bytham* [1895] 1 Ch 348 at 354 (*per* Stirling J).

Minister for Finance a fee simple the expression to be used is: "to the Minister for Finance and his successors". Failure to use these words of limitation would give the Minister a life estate only. A conveyance to the Minister "and his heirs" would also give him a fee simple, but in his private capacity and not as a corporation sole. It is not clear what the position is if a composite expression is used, eg, "to the Minister for Finance, his heirs and successors". It is a matter of construction whether the conveyance to the Minister is to him in his private or official capacity; use of his official title and of the words "and successors" would seem to suggest a conveyance to him in his official capacity. The question of construction would be more difficult in a case where his individual name was also given or even used without his official title.

(ii) By Statute

[4.029] This common law position as regards conveyances *inter vivos* of a fee simple has been modified by statute.[122] By the Conveyancing Act 1881,[123] the expression "in fee simple" may now be used to convey a fee simple; there is no need to use the older expression "and his heirs," though this expression is still commonly used by conveyancers. The 1881 Act merely provided an alternative form of words of limitation for a fee simple. It has been decided that the 1881 alternative will be construed just as strictly as the courts construed the expression "and his heirs". Thus it has been held that the expression "to A in fee" gives A a life estate only,[124] though it is possible that relief might be given by the court by way of rectification of the conveyance if it could be shown that a mistake had occurred in omitting the word "simple".[125] By its express terms s 51 of the 1881 Act seems to have provided an alternative to the common law formula "and his heirs" only, so that "and his successors" still has to be used to convey a fee simple to a corporation sole in his official capacity.[126]

[4.030] There is no equivalent in either part of Ireland of s 60(1) of the English Law of Property Act 1925, which abolished the necessity for words of limitation in the case of a fee simple. By that subsection the grantee of a deed of conveyance executed after 1925 takes the fee simple or other whole interest which the grantor had power to convey, unless a contrary intention appears in the conveyance. This reverses the common law position still prevailing in Ireland in respect of conveyances of unregistered land that, if appropriate words of limitation are not used, the smallest rather than the largest freehold estate is taken to pass to the grantee.[127] However, in respect of transfers of registered

---

[122] For modifications in the case of fee farm grants in Ireland, see paras **[4.057]** *et seq, post*.

[123] Section 51.

[124] *Re Ford and Ferguson's Contract* [1906] 1 IR 607 at 610 (see *A Casebook on Irish Land Law* (1984), p 115). See the comments on this case by Murray J in *Re Courtney* [1981] NI 58 at 63-5. See also the English case of *Re Ethel and Mitchells and Butlers' Contract* [1901] 1 Ch 945. *Cf Re Ottley's Estate* [1910] 1 IR 1.

[125] *Re Ottley's Estate* [1910] 1 IR 1. See also *Banks v Ripley* [1940] Ch 719.

[126] See Challis, *Law of Real Property* (3rd ed), pp 224-5.

[127] A provision similar to that in the English 1925 Act has been recommended for both the Republic, Law Reform Commission's *Report on Land Law and Conveyancing Law: (5) Further General Proposals* (LRC 44-1992), pp 6-7 and for Northern Ireland, *Survey of the Land Law of Northern Ireland* (HMSO, 1971), para 171. See also the Land Law Working Group's *Final Report* (HMSO, 1990), Vol 1, pp 105-6.

land, s 123 of the Republic's Registration of Title Act 1964, and s 35 of the Land Registration Act (NI) 1970, contain a provision similar to s 60(1) of the 1925 Act.[128]

2. *Gifts By Will*

(i) At Common Law

[4.031] It has already been stated that the courts took a more liberal approach to the interpretation of wills, so that the requirement of words of limitation was much less strict. Indeed, prior to 1838 all that was necessary was for the will to show an intention to create a fee simple. It was, therefore, a matter of construction whether the words of the will were sufficient to show such an intention, and it was likely that expressions such as "to A for ever" or "to A absolutely" created a fee simple. On the other hand, an expression such as "to A" was before 1838 unlikely to be enough and, without more, would pass a life estate only.

(ii) By Statute

[4.032] The position at common law was modified by the Wills Act 1837.[129] Under this Act, the fee simple or other whole interest of which the testator had power to dispose passed to the grantee under any will made or confirmed after 1837, unless a contrary intention was shown.[130] Thus since 1837 a devise "to A" would raise the presumption that A takes a fee simple. It should be noted, however, that this presumption only arose in respect of an estate or interest already held by the testator, which he was devising in his will. It did not arise where the testator was creating a new interest in his will, eg, a new rentcharge on land in favour of the devisee. If this was devised simply "to A", A would take a rentcharge for life only.[131] This remains the position in the Republic, but in Northern Ireland the 1837 presumption was extended by Article 18(2) of the Wills and Administration Proceedings (NI) Order 1994 to devises creating an estate "of any kind" in land.

3. *Equitable Gifts*

It has been a matter of some controversy over the years whether the rigours of the common law apply to gifts which are equitable only, eg, an estate conveyed to be held for the grantee under a trust. Here the grantee has an equitable interest only, for the legal estate is vested in the trustees.[132] One would have expected that since equitable estates and interests were originally recognised by the Court of Chancery only,[133] a relaxation

---

[128] Note that words of limitation are often still inserted in transfers of registered land in order to specify the estate passing in respect of which the statutory covenants for title will operate under s 7 of the Conveyancing Act 1991. Section 7 implies covenants only as regards the subject-matter "expressed" to be conveyed: see Wylie, *Irish Conveyancing Law* (2nd ed, 1996), para 21.11.

[129] Sections 28 and 34.

[130] This provision is to found now in s 94 of the Republic's Succession Act 1965 and Article 18 of the Wills and Administration Proceedings (NI) Order 1994. Thus the English Law of Property Act 1925, was merely extending the rule for wills to conveyances *inter vivos*, **[4.030]** *supra*. For a case showing a "contrary intention," see *Re Gannon* [1914] 1 IR 86.

[131] *Nichols v Hawkes* (1853) 10 Hare 342. On the subject of rentcharges generally, see paras **[6.131]** *et seq, post*.

[132] See, generally, Ch 9, *post*.

[133] See, generally, Ch 3, *ante*.

21

of the common law rules would be allowed as in the case of wills. Yet there are Irish authorities suggesting that this is not necessarily the case, so that an equitable fee simple requires the same words of limitation as a legal fee simple.[134] Later cases, however, seem to confine this rule to mean only that, if the settlor uses technical words in delimiting an equitable estate in land, those words will be treated as ordinary words of limitation and given their technical meaning under the common law.[135] Thus a conveyance "to A" would still give A an equitable life estate only. But if no technical words are used or it appears that the settlor is not using conventional conveyancing practice, it is arguable that the courts should give effect to what appears to be his intention, regardless of the technical requirement of words of limitation of common law.[136] The problem is determining when the settlor is not using technical words or conventional practice. Here there is a divergence between the views of the courts in the different parts of our islands.[137] For example, a conveyance "to A absolutely" could be construed as giving A an equitable fee simple, on the basis that the word "absolutely" is not a technical word of limitation at common law. This was the view taken by an English judge,[138] and accords with earlier Irish decisions.[139] It would also seem to accord with the views on the subject generally expressed by the Northern Ireland Court of Appeal.[140] However, in *Jameson v McGovern*,[141] the Republic's Supreme Court refused

---

[134] Eg, *Meyler v Meyler* (1883) 11 LR Ir 522; *Re Bennett's Estate* [1898] 1 IR 185; *cf, Re Murphy and Griffin's Contract* [1919] 1 IR 187; see Challis, *The Law of Real Property* (3rd ed), p 222. It should he noted, however, that equity may rectify a will or settlement on the ground of mistake (eg, words of limitation omitted); see *Ex parte Rice* (1896) 30 ILTR 57; *Fitzgerald v Fitzgerald* [1902] 1 IR 477 (see *A Casebook on Equity and Trusts in Ireland* (1985), p 279); *Re Davis's Estate* [1912] 1 IR 516.

[135] *Jameson v McGovern* [1934] IR 758 (see *A Casebook on Irish Land Law* (1984), p 116), explaining the English case, *Re Bostock's Settlement* [1921] 2 Ch 469. This seems to be an example of the maxim "equity follows the law"; see para **[3.047]** *ante*. See also the interpretation given in *Savage v Nolan* [1978] IR 758 (see *A Casebook on Irish Land Law* (1984), p 122), where Costello J held that "the decision of the Supreme Court in *Jameson v McGovern* can only be interpreted as meaning that an exception to the strict rule in *Bostock's Settlement* does not exist when the settlement being construed contains an agreement to settle the land referred to in the deed on the wife of the intended marriage absolutely. He then held that a remainder over to children of the intended marriage in a trust settlement vested in them the fee simple despite the absence of words of limitation, since the settlor intended that they should take absolutely. He then commented: "I accept that it is well established that the children of an intended marriage are within the consideration of the marriage and that accordingly the settlement constitutes an agreement which is enforceable by them by which they are entitled to absolute interests in the events that have happened." *Cf Re Hammersly's Estate* (1861) 12 Ir Ch R 319.

[136] *Re Houston* [1909] 1 IR 319; *Re Stinson's Estate* [1910] 1 IR 47; *Re Cross's Trusts* [1915] 1 IR 304; *Re Beer's Estate* [1925] NI 191. See also *Re Harte's Settlement* (1955) 89 ILTR 78, where it was held that an equitable fee simple was created under a trust which was declared by reference to a trust of personal property in the same settlement.

[137] See Keane, *Equity and the Law of Trusts in the Republic of Ireland* (1988), para 3.03-4.

[138] *Re Arden* [1935] Ch 326 (Clauson J).

[139] Eg, *Re Murphy and Griffins's Contract* [1919] 1 IR 187.

[140] *Re Beer's Estate* [1925] NI 191.

[141] [1934] IR 758.

to accept the trend of Irish decisions[142] and insisted that a conveyance of an equitable interest to a person "absolutely" would not pass the fee simple, whatever the intention of the grantor. In view of this firm ruling, it is difficult to see how the Republic's courts could now hold otherwise unless and until the Supreme Court itself reviews the matter and gives further guidance. On the other hand, it has been further suggested that the quantum of an equitable estate will not be affected by a failure to convey a legal estate of equal size to the trustees.[143] Thus a conveyance "to A and B on trust for C and his heirs" would still seem to give C an equitable fee simple even though A and B have a legal life estate only.

****

D. Classification

[4.043] There are several types of fee simple. These are usually divided for the purposes of analysis into two main categories: a fee simple absolute and a modified fee simple (often referred to by the shorthand description, a "modified fee"). As the term implies, a fee simple absolute forms one category on its own whereas the category of modified fees can be subdivided into several types of fee simple. In other words, by definition any fee simple other than a fee simple absolute is a modified fee.[144]

1. Fee Simple Absolute

[4.044] The expression "fee simple absolute" is not a term of art,[145] but in this context is usually taken to mean that the fee simple is held free of all restrictions other than those imposed by the general law, eg, as a matter of public policy,[146] or by statute, eg, planning legislation.[147]

---

[142] It took the view that decisions like *Re Murphy and Griffin's Contract* (fn 139 *supra*) and other cases referred to in fn 136 *supra* should be overruled, preferring the strict approach adopted in *Re Bostock's Settlement* (fn 135 *supra*), which had overruled an earlier decision of Joyce J in *Re Tringham's Trusts* [1904] 2 Ch 487. Joyce J's decision had certainly influenced the later Irish decisions overruled by the Supreme Court.

[143] *White v Baylor* (1846) 10 Ir Eq R 43 at 53 (*per* Smith MR).

[144] See Challis, *Law of Real Property* (3rd ed), pt III; Megarry and Wade, *Law of Real Property* (5th ed, 1984), pp 67-76. It should be noted, however, that the term "modified fee" is sometimes given a wider meaning so as to cover all fees other than a fee simple absolute, so as to include, eg, a fee tail: see Challis, *op cit*, p 62. And the terms "the fee" or "fee simple" are often taken to mean the fee simple absolute unless the contrary is indicated, Challis, *op cit*, p 438.

[145] *Cf*, the position in England where the term "fee simple absolute in possession" has a statutory definition, Law of Property Act 1925, ss 1(1)(*a*) and 7; Law of Property (Amendment) Act 1926, Sched. See *Re Clayton's Deed Poll* [1980] Ch 99. The term has been used recently in an Irish statute, see Land Development Values (Compensation) Act (NI) 1965, s 2 and more recently, in the Property (NI) Order 1997, Article 2(1) (definition of "fee simple"). See also *Survey of the Land Law of Northern Ireland* (HMSO, 1971), Ch 2 and the Land Law Working Group's *Final Report* (HMSO, 1990), Vol 1, pp 47-52.

[146] Para **[4.052]** *post*.

[147] Para **[1.077]** *ante*.

[4.045] In Northern Ireland the great bulk of agricultural land, which has been bought out under the Land Purchase Acts,[148] will probably be held by its owners in fee simple absolute once the land purchase annuities have been paid off.[149] This is because the statutory restrictions on sub-division and sub-letting on land bought out under the Acts[150] will last only as long as the annuities are being paid. Once these are paid off the land becomes free of such statutory incidents.[151] In the Republic, however, such statutory incidents remain attached to holdings bought out under the Land Purchase Acts after 1923, even when the annuities are paid off (except in the case of what has become or is near to urban land).[152] It is questionable, however, whether continuance of such restrictions after the ending of the land purchase annuity charges would prevent the estates in question from being regarded as held for fees simple absolute, within the above definition. Indeed, it is arguable that those charges themselves do not prevent the estates sold to tenant purchasers being regarded as fees simple absolute.[153]

In respect of urban land in Ireland, however, a fee simple absolute has, until recently, been rare. Here, as we shall see, many fees simple are held in fee farm, ie, subject to a perpetual rent and various rights and interests retained by the grantor,[154] and most Irish forms of fee farm grant come into the category of modified fees.[155] It should be noted, however, that fee farm grants are much more common in Northern Ireland than in the Republic of Ireland.

2. Modified Fees

(i) Determinable Fee

[4.046] A determinable fee is a fee simple which will determine automatically on the occurrence of an event which may or may not happen.[156] In other words, should the event in question occur the fee simple will definitely come to an end at that point in time; but it is not certain that the event in question will occur at any particular point in time or, indeed, ever occur at all.[157] In a sense all fees simple are determinable fees, at

---

[148] Para **[1.067]** *ante*.

[149] Para **[1.068]** *ante*.

[150] See Irish Land Act 1903, s 54(1). *Poe v Gillen* [1935] NI 1; *Moley's Case* [1957] NI 130.

[151] Leitch, 'Present-Day Agricultural Tenancies in Northern Ireland' (1965) 16 NILQ 491.

[152] See Land Acts 1923, s 65; 1927, ss 3 and 4; 1936, s 44; 1939, s 23; 1946, ss 3 and 6; 1965, ss 12 and 13. *McGillicuddy v Joy* [1959] IR 189; *Carew v Jackman* [1966] IR 177; *Horgan v Deasy* [1979] ILRM 71. See the discussion in Wylie, *Irish Conveyancing Law* (2nd ed, 1996), para 16.29 *et seq*. See further, para **[18.03]**, *post*.

[153] See Megarry and Wade, *op cit*, pp 142-4.

[154] Para **[4.059]**, *post*.

[155] *Cf*, the English form, Megarry and Wade, *op cit*, p 127.

[156] See, generally, Challis, 'Determinable Fees' (1887) 3 LQR 403; Farrer 'Reverter to Donor of Determinable Fee' (1935) 49 LQR 240, (1936) 50 LQR 33 and (1937) 51 LQR 361; Gray, 'Determinable Fees' (1887) 3 LQR 399; Hughes, 'Reverter to Donor of Determinable Fee' (1937) 51 LQR 347; Powell, 'Determinable Fees' (1923) 23 Col L Rev 237.

[157] Were this not so, the estate would not qualify as a "fee", ie, an estate which may last for ever, para **[4.004]**, *ante*.

least in Northern Ireland, because any fee simple may determine if the current holder dies intestate leaving no intestate successor.[158] But that is a rather special case, for here the determination is governed by the general law of intestate succession.[159] The point about a determinable fee, as that expression is usually used, is that the determining event is specified by the original grantor of the estate. Such an estate is similar to another kind of modified fee, a fee simple upon a condition, which is discussed below. Often it is a difficult matter of construction whether the estate is a determinable fee or a fee simple upon a condition. But whatever the questions of construction, the consequences and incidents of the estates are different, as we shall see.[160]

Examples of grants by way of determinable fee would be: "to A and his heirs so long as Northern Ireland remains part of the United Kingdom", "to B in fee simple until he qualifies as a solicitor".[161]

[4.047] There has been some controversy over the years whether a determinable fee could be validly granted, except under statute, since *Quia Emptores* 1290.[162] The basic argument against validity is that, unlike in the case of a fee simple absolute, the grantor of a determinable fee retains some interest in the property. His interest is called a *possibility of reverter*, ie, the possibility of acquiring an estate in the future.[163] It has been suggested that retention of such an interest meant that the grant was a form of subinfeudation, a practice prohibited by *Quia Emptores* in the case of a fee simple. Furthermore, a possibility of reverter has been likened to escheat between lord and tenant.[164] But the generally accepted view now is that *Quia Emptores* did not prohibit the creation of determinable fees.[165] First, it is questionable whether an interest like a possibility of reverter, the most ephemeral of interests in land, should be treated as an estate or interest in land sufficiently substantive as to allow the creation of tenure between the grantor and grantee. It is a mere possibility of an estate in land arising in future, not a present estate or interest.[166] Secondly, it is doubtful if a possibility of reverter has anything to do with the law of escheat: escheat was a general law relating to

---

[158] *Cf*, in the Republic, para **[4.021]**, *ante*.

[159] Ch 15, *post*.

[160] Paras **[4.049]**-**[4.055]**, *post*.

[161] See Challis, *Law of Real Property* (3rd ed), Ch XVII.

[162] Para **[2.042]** *ante*.

[163] This interest may, of course, be destroyed if the event in question becomes impossible, in which case the determinable fee becomes a fee simple absolute, eg, "a grant by G to A and his heirs until X becomes a solicitor"; if X dies without becoming a solicitor, A is left with a fee simple absolute and G is left with no interest at all in the land.

[164] See Gray, *Perpetuities* (4th ed, 1942), ss 31 *et seq* and 774 *et seq*; *Hopper v Liverpool Corporation* (1944) 88 Sol Jo 213.

[165] Morris and Leach, *The Rule Against Perpetuities* (2nd ed, 1962), pp 209-10; Megarry and Wade, *The Law of Real Property* (5th ed), p 68.

[166] *Att-Gen v Cummins* [1906] 1 IR 406 (see *A Casebook on Irish Land Law* (1984), p 131). In this case (heard in 1895) the Irish Court of Exchequer Division, through a judgment delivered by Palles CB, rejected the suggestion that the rule against perpetuities applied to possibilities of reverter, see para **[4.055]** *post*. Pettit, 'Determinable Interests and Rule Against Perpetuities' (1957) 21 Conv 213.

intestate succession applying to all grants; a possibility of reverter arises only in the special case of a determinable fee and then only by the draftsmanship of the particular grantor or his conveyancer.[167] Thirdly, it has been argued that *Quia Emptores* by implication applied to a fee simple absolute only in prohibiting future subinfeudation.[168] Apart from this, in practice most determinable fees derive from statute, eg, in respect of land acquired for public purposes, such as railways during the nineteenth century.[169]

(ii) Fee Simple Upon a Condition

[4.048] A fee simple upon a condition, often called a conditional fee,[170] is a fee simple to which is attached a condition subsequent, which may cause the estate to be brought to an end.[171] A condition *subsequent* must be distinguished from a condition *precedent*.[172] The latter is a condition which must be satisfied first before the estate or interest becomes vested in the grantee.[173] The former is a condition which may result in forfeiture of an estate already vested in the grantee.[174] Two examples should illustrate the distinction: "to A and his heirs if A reaches the age of 21" (condition precedent; A must become 21 before he gets his fee simple); "to A and his heirs provided A remains a

---

[167] *Cf*, Bennett V-C in *Hopper, op cit*; Megarry, (1948) 62 LQR 222.

[168] Challis, *Law of Real Property* (3rd ed), Appendix IV.

[169] See *Pickin v British Railways Board* [1974] AC 765. Note the special legislation enacted in England to deal with problems arising when such land ceased to be used for the public purposes in question, but it was by then unclear who was entitled on reverter: see Reverter of Sites Act 1987. Note also the School Sites (Ir) Act 1810, and Leases for Schools (Ir) Act 1881, which relate to leasehold land. See the Republic's Charities Act 1973, s 6.

[170] Unfortunately, this term is used in several senses; sometimes it covers both determinable fees and fees simple upon a condition (see, eg, Challis, *op cit*, pp 261-2); sometimes it refers to the special case of a fee tail, ie, a fee simple conditional upon birth of issue before the statute *De Donis*, 1285 (see para **[4.113]** *post*).

[171] See, generally, Benas, 'Conditions in Restraint of Religion' (1943) 8 Conv 6 and 66; Browder, 'Conditions and Limitations in Restraint of Marriage' (1949) 47 Mich L Rev 759; Delany, '"Name and Arms" Clauses' (1951) 17 Ir Jur 35; Maitland, 'Remainders After Conditional Fees' (1890) 6 LQR 22; Simes, 'Effect of Impossibility Upon Conditions in Wills' (1936) 34 Mich L Rev 909; Squibb, 'End of Name and Arms Clause' (1953) 69 LQR 219; Stone, 'Name Worship and Statutory Interpretation in the Law of Wills' (1963) 26 MLR 652; Williams, 'Conditions in Restraint of Marriage' (1896) 12 LQR 36.

[172] For discussion of the distinction, see the judgment of Hutton J (as he then was) in *Re Waring's Will Trusts* [1985] NI 105 (McCormack, (1986) 37 NILQ 175). See also *Re Richardson* [1988] NI 86.

[173] *Walker v Lenehan* (1852) 4 Ir Jur (os) 310; *Re Doherty* [1950] NI 83; *Re Blake* [1955] IR 89; *Kiersey v Flahavan* [1905] 1 IR 45; *Horrigan v Horrigan* [1904] 1 IR 271; *Fitzgerald v Ryan* [1899] 2 IR 637; *Re Callaghan* [1937] IR 84; *Re Tighe* [1944] 1 IR 166; *Re Mansfield* [1962] IR 454; *Re Hennessy* (1964) 98 ILTR 39; *Re Porter's Estate* [1975] NI 157; *McKillop v McMullan* [1979] NI 85; *Re Gault* [1982] NI 170; *Ulster Bank Ltd v McCullough* [1985] NI 288.

[174] *Re Fitzgibbon* [1993] 1 IR 520. The court has an inherent jurisdiction to grant relief against the forfeiture in appropriate cases (see *Re Porter* [1975] NI 157), but this does not apply where there is a gift over on failure to comply with the condition (see *Re Johnston* [1986] NI 229).

solicitor" (condition subsequent; A has the fee simple from the date of the conveyance but may lose it if he ceases to be a solicitor).[175]

Next the distinction must be drawn between a determinable fee and a fee simple upon a condition. There are two aspects of the distinction to be borne in mind: first, there is the question of how one can recognise which estate is created by the wording of a particular grant and, secondly, there are the different rules applying to the two types of fee simple.

(a) Creation

[4.049] Whether a particular conveyance creates a determinable fee or a fee simple upon a condition is largely a matter of the precise wording of conveyance. The theory on this matter is clear. In the case of a determinable fee the words describing the determining event are part of the words of limitation, ie, they delimit the estate granted.[176] In the case of a fee simple upon a condition, however, the words containing the condition are not part of the words of limitation, they are independent words of condition.[177] These words of condition confer a right of entry on the grantor or his successor, which must be exercised to determine the fee simple; a possibility of reverter becomes an actual reverter operating automatically when the specified event occurs, because the estate has thereby come to its natural determination according to the words of limitation. The problem in each case is to determine the effect of the particular words used and it is not always an easy problem to solve.[178] The courts have adopted over the years some "rules of thumb" whereby particular words or phrases are taken to indicate one type of estate rather than another. Thus words like "while," "during," "until" and "as long as" tend to be interpreted as words of limitation creating a determinable fee[179]; words like "provided that," "on condition that" and "but if" are usually taken to mean words of condition.[180] The point now seems to have been reached that it is the form that counts, not the substantive intention of the grantor, so that the following two conveyances would be interpreted as passing different estates: "to A and his heirs so long as he remains a solicitor" (determinable fee); "to A and his heirs provided that if he ceases to be a solicitor ..." (fee simple upon a condition). One Irish judge was moved to describe the distinction between the two types of fee simple as "little short of disgraceful to our jurisprudence".[181] In making this comment, the judge seems to have had in mind wills,

---

[175] In *Re Fitzgibbon* Carroll J held that where in a will there is a doubt as to whether the condition is a condition precedent or subsequent, the court would treat it as *prima facie* subsequent, applying a presumption in favour of early vesting.

[176] Challis, *The Law of Real Property* (3rd ed), pp 252-3, 260-1; *Re King's Trusts* (1892) 29 LR Ir 401 (see *A Casebook on Irish Land Law* (1984), p 137).

[177] Challis, *op cit*, pp 219-20, 260-1; *Re King's Trusts*, *op cit*.

[178] Megarry and Wade, *Law of Real Property* (5th ed), pp 69-70.

[179] Challis, *op cit*, pp 255-60; *Att-Gen v Cummins* [1906] 1 IR 406 (see *A Casebook on Irish Land Law* (1984), p 131).

[180] *Walsh v Wightman* [1927] NI 1.

[181] *Re King's Trusts* (1892) 29 LR Ir 401 at 410 (*per* Porter MR) (see *op cit*, p 137).

which the court usually interpret more liberally than conveyances *inter vivos*. He continued:

> "The distinction is intelligible to a lawyer; but no testator except a lawyer could be expected to understand it, much less to have regard to it in framing his will. We must, however, take the law as we find it."

But however nonsensical the distinction may appear to the layman the fact remains that much depends upon it. Our legal system has devised different rules with respect to the two estates, and some of these rules we now discuss.

(b) Determination

[4.050] In the case of a determinable fee, when the specified event occurs the fee simple comes to its natural determination according to the words of limitation, and the possibility of reverter takes effect automatically to confer the fee simple absolute on the grantor (or his successor if he has since died).[182] On the other hand, in the case of a fee simple upon a condition, the occurrence of the specified event, or satisfaction or breach of the condition, merely gives the grantor a right of entry so as to forfeit the grantee's estate.[183] Until that right is exercised, there is no forfeiture and the grantee continues to hold his estate.[184] Rights of entry and forfeiture arise in other areas of land law, and the courts have always been concerned to see that unfair advantage is not obtained through their invocation or exercise.[185] The courts' general approach to conditions subsequent we discuss below.[186]

(c) Alienation

[4.051] At common law a possibility of reverter and a right of entry for condition broken were descendible only, ie, they could be inherited. They were neither alienable *inter vivos* nor devisable by will.[187] The main reason for this rule seems to have been the fact that they did not belong to the category of estates in land, being mere rights or incidents attached to estates.[188] But that common law position has been changed by statute, at least as regards rights of entry for condition broken. Such rights of entry became devisable under the Wills Act 1837,[189] and alienable *inter vivos* under the Real Property Act 1845.[190] It was, and is still in Ireland, the case that a right of entry for condition broken could be limited only in a conveyance to the grantor "and his heirs".[191] This rule has been abolished in England by the Law of Property Act 1925 under which a conveyance may specify that such a right may he exercised by anyone and not merely

---

[182] Challis, *op cit*, pp 82-3. See also *Re Drought* (1967) 101 ILTR 1.
[183] Challis, *op cit*, p 219.
[184] *Ibid; Matthew Manning's Case* (1609) 8 Co Rep 94b at 95b.
[185] Note the jurisdiction to grant relief: see fn 212 *ante*.
[186] Para **[4.052]** *post*.
[187] Challis, *op cit*, pp 76-7, 176-7 and 228-9.
[188] Challis, *op cit*, pp 76-7.
[189] Section 3.
[190] Section 6.
[191] Challis, *op cit*, p 219.

the grantor and his successors in title.[192] Possibilities of reverter were also descendible at common law, but it has never been clear whether they were alienable *inter vivos* or devisable by will. [193] The probable rule is that they were not and never have become so because neither the Wills Act 1837, nor the Real Property Act 1845, applied to possibilities of reverter. They would seem to suffer from the same flaws as rights of entry in the eyes of the common law and no statute has been passed in Ireland to change that position. The position in England is not much clearer, though the generally accepted view seems to be that the Law of Property Act 1925 probably assimilated the position in this regard with rights of entry.[194] It is also the case still in Ireland that a possibility of reverter can exist only in the grantor and his heirs; it is a mere possibility of a future interest and, until it becomes an actuality, there is nothing left in the grantor after his conveyance of the fee simple to be disposed of to someone else.[195] There is one other matter about alienation to be mentioned. This is the extent to which the courts are prepared to allow grantors to impose restrictions on alienation of property in drafting their provisions about determining events or conditions subsequent. The courts have over the years adopted firm views on this subject as a matter of public policy and we discuss this matter next under the general heading of public policy.

(d) Public Policy

[4.052] There are several aspects to the courts' approach to determinable fees and fees simple upon condition in matters of public policy. To a large extent a more lenient approach has been taken in the case of determinable fees, no doubt because of the courts' general attitude of strict interpretation of clauses purporting to bring about forfeitures and to make estates and interests void [196]

(1) General

[4.053] First, the courts will treat as invalid any condition which is illegal, immoral, a violation of constitutional rights under the Republic's Constitution or which otherwise contravenes what they regard as public policy.[197] One of the most frequently litigated example of such conditions are those inserted in conveyances to restrain marriage.[198] Marriage is regarded as an institution essential to our society and so the courts will not allow grantors of property to prevent or discourage it by conditions inserted in their conveyances. It is a matter for the court in each case whether the particular condition will be declared void as contrary to public policy.[199] It seems clear that a total restriction

---

[192] Section 4(3). But such rights of entry are now subject to the rule against perpetuities, as are possibilities of reverter, para **[4.055]** *post.*

[193] Challis, *op cit*, pp 176-7 and 228-9.

[194] It depends on whether possibilities of reverter come within the expression "future equitable interest" in s 4(2)(*a*) of the 1925 Act. See Megarry and Wade, *Law of Real Property* (5th ed, 1984), p 75.

[195] *Cf*, Law of Property Act 1925, s 4(3).

[196] See articles cited in fn 209, para **[4.048]** *supra.*

[197] *Massy v Rogers* (1883) 11 LR Ir 409.

[198] *Duddy v Gresham* (1878) 2 LR Ir 442; *Re McLoughlin's Estate* (1878) 1 LR Ir 421; *Gray v Gray* (1889) 23 LR Ir 399. *Cf, Re Coghlan* [1963] IR 246 (see *A Casebook on Irish Land Law* (1984), p 141).

[199] *Ibid*. See also *Re Armstrong* (1968) 19 NILQ 215.

will be declared void, eg, "to A in fee simple but if A marries the grantor has a right to entry," unless the court concludes that the restriction was not intended to prevent A from marrying but was part of a genuine intention by the grantor simply to provide for A for a certain period, ie, while he remained single.[200] Indeed, in this case the grantor would have been better advised to frame his conveyance in the form of a determinable fee, eg, "to A in fee simple until he marries". The courts have a quite different approach to such conveyances and rarely hold them void as against public policy.[201] The limitation is regarded as coming to its natural determination and there is no question of a forfeiture.[202] Once again we see that the formula used in the conveyance can make all the difference to the validity of the grant. Difficult questions arise, however, where there is a partial restraint on marriage, eg, a prohibition against marrying a Protestant or a Catholic, without first obtaining someone else's consent.[203] It is a question of construction whether the particular restriction should be regarded as sufficiently in restraint of marriage (*in terrorem*) as to contravene public policy.[204] And there is always the possibility that a condition may be declared void for uncertainty.[205] Questions of uncertainty have frequently arisen where the condition has related to religious matters, eg, "practising the Roman Catholic religion,"[206] or bringing up children in the "Roman Catholic faith,"[207] or the taking of a particular name under a "name and arms" clause.[208] Similar problems over uncertainty have arisen over conditions requiring residence in a

---

[200] *Duddy v Gresham* (1878) 2 LR Ir 442; *McConnell v Beattie* (1904) 38 ILTR 133.

[201] *Re King's Trusts* (1892) 29 LR Ir 401 (see *A Casebook on Irish Land Law* (1984), p 137); *Oliver v Menton* [1945] IR 6; *Re Robson* [1940] Ir Jur Rep 72.

[202] *Ibid*; *Re Elliott* [1918] 1 IR 41; *Stewart v Murdoch* [1969] NI 78; *Re Dolan* [1970] IR 94.

[203] *Lowry v Patterson* (1874) IR 8 Eq 372; *White v McDermott* (1876) IR 7 CL 1; *Re McLoughlin's Estate* (1878) 1 LR Ir 421; *In b. Knox* (1889) 23 LR Ir 542; *Maguire v Boylan* (1870) IR 5 Eq 90; *Re Greene* [1895] 1 IR 130, 142; *Curran v Corbet* [1897] 1 IR 343; *Re Burchill's Contract* (1912) 46 ILTR 35; *Re McKenna* [1947] IR 277.

[204] *Greene v Greene* (1845) 8 Ir Eq R 473; *Alleyne v Alleyne* (1845) 8 Ir Eq R 493; *Duggan v Kelly* (1847) 10 Ir Eq R 295; *Hackett v Lord Oxmantown* (1948) 12 Ir Eq R 534; *Adams v Adams* (1858) 8 Ir Ch R 41; *Re Newcomens* (1865) 16 Ir Ch R 315; *Duddy v Gresham* (1878) 2 LR Ir 442; *Gray v Gray* (1889) 23 LR Ir 399.

[205] See, eg, *Re Coghlan* [1963] IR 245; *Re Hennessy* (1964) 98 ILTR 219. Also *McCausland v Young* [1949] NI 49; *Burke and O'Reilly v Burke and Quail* [1951] IR 216; *Re Blake* [1955] IR 89. *Cf, Duggan v Kelly* (1847) 10 Ir Eq R 295; *Re McKenna* [1947] IR 277; *Higgins v Walsh* (1948) 82 ILTR 10; *Re Parker* [1966] IR 309.

[206] *Burke and O'Reilly, op cit. Cf, McCausland v Young* [1949] NI 49 (see *A Casebook on Equity and Trusts in Ireland* (1985), p 27); *Re Vaughan* [1926] IR 67.

[207] *Re Blake, op cit; cf, Higgins v Walsh* (1948) 82 ILTR 10. See the discussion in *Blathwayt v Baron Cawley* [1976] AC 397; *Re Tuck's Settlement Trusts* [1978] Ch 49.

[208] *Re Montgomery* (1955) 89 ILTR 62; *Bevan v Mahon-Hagan* (1893) 31 LR Ir 342; *Miller v Wheatley* (1885) 28 LR Ir 144; *Vandeleur v Sloane* [1919] 1 IR 116; *Re Finlay* [1933] NI 89. *Cf, Re Talbot* [1932] IR 714; *Re Callaghan* [1937] IR 84; *Re De Vere's Will Trusts* [1961] IR 224. In *Kearns and McCarron v Manresa Estates Ltd* Unrep (HC, RI) 25 July 1975 (1974 No 193 Sp) (see *A Casebook on Irish Land Law* (1984), p 148), Kenny J held that a "name and arms" clause was void for uncertainty because it was impossible to state when the disuse or discontinuance of the name in question occurred. (contd.../)

particular property.[209] In several of these cases the courts have once again drawn a distinction between conditions precedent and conditions subsequent. In the case of the latter, because non-compliance will involve forfeiture of an already vested estate, the courts require sufficient certainty that it can be seen precisely and distinctly from the date of the condition coming into operation what events will cause a forfeiture.[210] This is sometimes referred to as "conceptual" as opposed to "evidentiary" certainty,[211] ie, if the condition is conceptually certain it will not be held invalid merely because of possible difficulties arising later in determining whether particular events trigger a forfeiture.[212] Such principles are not applied to a condition precedent.[213] Here the courts require only that the claimant establishes that he has met the condition, whatever uncertainty might arise in respect of other possible claimants.[214] If a condition subsequent is void for uncertainty, or as being contrary to constitutional rights or public policy, the fee simple becomes a fee simple absolute.[215] In other words, only the condition fails and the fee simple itself remains in effect, provided it is conveyed with the appropriate words of

---

[208] (\...contd) In so doing, he followed the *Montgomery* and *De Vere* cases in Ireland and declined to follow the English Court of Appeal decision in *Re Neeld* [1962] Ch 643 (upholding such a clause, and note that such a clause was also involved in the *Blathwayt* case, *supra*, and was, apparently, regarded as valid by the House of Lords). He was particularly critical of the English courts' use of the *de minimis* principle to justify disregard of "mistake or forgetfulness" or lapses in use:

> "But it is precisely the question as to what lapses are a disuse or a discontinuance that causes the difficulty for the court. How many deliberate or unintentional lapses bring the "*de minimis*" principle into operation? How many lapses are necessary so that it can be said that "*de minimis*" does not apply? I have the highest respect for any view expressed by Upjohn LJ (subsequently Lord Upjohn) but invoking the maxim of *de minimis* seems to me to be a way of avoiding difficulty. None of the judgments in *Re Neeld* deal with the question as to how the court is to decide that at any given moment of time (and that, as Mr Justice Fry pointed out [in *Re Exmouth* (1883) 23 Ch D 158], is the critical question) a person has disused or discontinued to use the surname which he is obliged to assume."

He also pointed out that, since the *Montgomery* and *De Vere* decisions, "titles to property included in the Vernon estate [at issue before him] and in other estates have been accepted on the basis that names and arms are void for uncertainty in Ireland. A decision now that the clauses involved were valid would render these titles bad. Although I am not bound by decisions of other judges of the High Court, the usual practice is to follow them unless I am satisfied that they were wrongly decided. I am not so satisfied: indeed I think that the reasoning of Mr Justice Dixon [in the *Montgomery* case] is unanswerable."

[209] *Atkins v Atkins* [1976-7] ILRM 62; *Re Waring's Will Trusts* [1985] NI 105; *Re Johnston* [1986] NI 229; *Re Fitzgibbon* [1993] 1 IR 520.

[210] *Moffat v McClearly* [1923] 1 IR 16; *Motherway v Coghlan* (1956) 98 ILTR 134; *Re Porter* [1975] NI 157; *Re Dunne's Estate* [1988] IR 155; *Re Fitzgibbon* [1993] 1 IR 520. See also *Clavering v Ellison* (1859) 7 HLC 707 at 725 (*per* Lord Cranworth).

[211] Note the criticism of such distinctions by Lord Denning MR in *Re Tuck's Settlement Trusts* [1978] Ch 49; Emery (1982) 98 LQR 551.

[212] *Re Johnston* [1986] NI 229; *Re Fitzsimons* [1992] 2 IR 295.

[213] *Re Waring's Will Trusts* [1985] NI 105. See also *Re Richardson* [1988] NI 86; *cf Re Tepper's Will Trusts* [1987] Ch 358.

[214] *Re Allen* [1953] Ch 810; *Re Abraham's Will Trusts* [1969] 1 Ch 463.

[215] *Re Coghlan* [1963] IR 246; *Re Hennessy* (1964) 98 ILTR 39. See also *Re Mulcair* [1960] IR 321.

limitation.[216] The contrary is the position in the rare case of a limitation in a grant of a determinable fee being held void as against public policy.[217] Here the words of limitation themselves are defective and so fail to pass the fee simple; the whole grant is ineffective and the grantee is left with nothing.[218] This position should not be confused with the situation where the possibility of reverter becomes impossible because it becomes clear that the determining event will never occur. For example, with a grant "to A and his heirs until B becomes a solicitor," it is possible that B may die without becoming a solicitor. If and when that happens as estate ceases to be a determinable fee and becomes a fee simple absolute.[219]

(2) Restrictions on Alienation

[4.054] It has been a matter of general policy of our land law from the earliest days that freehold land should be freely alienable.[220] As far as the fee simple is concerned, this general principle was enshrined *in Quia Emptores* 1290.[221] It is clear that an attempt to impose a condition in total restriction on alienation by the grantee of a fee simple is void.[222] Where the condition is not a total restriction, it is a question for the court as a matter of public policy whether it is so restrictive as to be void. In deciding this the court has to balance the competing interests of free disposition of property by grantors and the general policy of ensuring marketability of freehold land.[223] Thus a covenant by the grantee of a fee simple not to divide it into more than four lots without the consent of the grantor or his successors was held void.[224] A condition in a will devising property to four brothers in fee simple and to two other brothers *pur autre vie*, whereby no brother could sell his interest except to one of his brothers, was held void.[225] Also held void was a provision under which the grantee of a fee simple could not sell it unless all his

---

[216] *Re Porter* [1975] NI 157; *Re Fitzgibbon* [1993] 1 IR 520. See also *Re Dunne's Estate* [1988] IR 155, para **[4.054]** *infra*.

[217] Eg, *Re Moore* (1888) 39 Ch D 116 (a case of personalty).

[218] Note that this is not the case in NI where a possibility of reverter is void under the rule against perpetuities, as amended by the Perpetuities Act (NI), 1966, which in such a case renders the fee simple absolute, see para **[5.109]** *post*.

[219] Challis, *The Law of Real Property* (3rd ed), p 254.

[220] See Gray, *Restraints on the Alienation of Property* (2nd ed); Manning, 'Development of Restraints on Alienation Since Gray' (1935) 48 HLR 373; Smout, 'Racial and Religious Restraints on Alienation' (1952) 30 CBR 863; Sweet, 'Restraints on Alienation' (1917) 33 LQR 236 and 342. See discussion in *Re Congested Districts Board* [1919] 1 IR 146.

[221] Para **[2.46]** *ante*.

[222] *Byrne v Byrne* (1953) 87 ILTR 183; see also *Waugh v Harshaw* (1902) 36 ILTR 20; *Re Kelly-Kenny* (1904) 38 ILTR 163.

[223] *Re McDonnell* [1965] IR 354; *Martin v Martin* (1886) 19 LR Ir 72. These first four sentences of para **[4.054]** in the 2nd ed were quoted with approval by O'Hanlon J in *Re Dunne's Estate* [1988] IR 155.

[224] *Re Lunham's Estate* (1871) IR 5 Eq 170 (a case of a fee farm grant, see para **[4.110]** *post*).

[225] *Crofts v Beamish* [1905] 2 IR 349 (see *A Casebook on Irish Land Law* (1984), p 144). See also *Re Hennessy* (1964) 98 ILTR 39; *Re McDonnell* [1965] IR 354. *Cf*, the famous English case of *Re Macleay* (1875) LR 20 Eq 186, distinguished in *Re Brown* [1954] Ch 39.

brothers refused to buy it for £100.[226] On the other hand, in *Re Fitzsimons*,[227] where a devise of a farm was made conditional upon the devisee being the owner of lands transferred to him by the testator prior to his death, Keane J held that the condition was not repugnant to the fee simple devised. It did not prevent him from selling all or any part of the land devised.[228] It is important to remember that the underlying principles guiding the courts in these cases are based upon public policy. This was illustrated by *Re Dunne's Estate*,[229] where a testator left his freehold property to a couple subject to the condition that the house and lands, or any part thereof, should not "be sold or otherwise conveyed or transferred by them or either of them, their successors or assigns, to any member of the Meredith families of O'Moore's Forest, Mountmellick". O'Hanlon J held the condition void as inconsistent with public policy governing grants of freehold property, especially since "the obvious purpose" was "to perpetuate old resentments and antagonisms and bind the grantee or devisee to bear them in mind and give effect to them when contemplating any further disposition of the property".[230] It should, however, be noted that in Ireland a fee farm grant may contain a valid restriction on alienation, a subject to which we shall return.[231]

This general rule against inalienability applies in principle to other freehold estates like the fee tail and life estate. In the case of a life estate the courts have been more inclined to regard restrictions on alienation, and similar restrictions, with more leniency and to treat them like limitations rather than conditions. Thus it became common for the courts to recognise and enforce clauses determining life estates on alienation, or on bankruptcy.[232] Restraints upon anticipation so as to prevent married women from disposing of property were also enforced.[233] A restraint upon anticipation was a clause which prohibited a wife to whom a limited estate was given from anticipating the future income of the land. The result was, for example, that she could not mortgage it. The extent to which the courts would go to uphold such restrictions in the case of life estates was indicated by one Irish case in which land was devised to the testator's wife "on condition that she has no power to sign away or will said property to anyone but my brother John". Instead of construing this as a devise of a fee simple subject to a void

---

[226] *McGowan v Grimes* (1921) 55 ILTR 208.

[227] [1992] 1 IR 295.

[228] Keane J also rejected an argument that it was void for uncertainty: see para **[4.053]** *supra*.

[229] [1988] IR 155.

[230] *Ibid* p 157. He also held the condition void for uncertainty: see para **[4.053]** *supra*.

[231] Paras **[4.086]** and **[4.101]** *post*. Note also that a condition of inalienability is valid where the grantee is subject to such a statutory restriction, eg, the National Trust in NI: see *Re Richardson* [1988] NI 86.

[232] *Re Moore's Estate* (1885) 17 LR Ir 549; *Re Walsh's Estate* [1905] 1 IR 261. See para **[9.083]** *post*.

[233] *Re Dillon* (1916) 50 ILTR 144; *Re Taylor* [1914] 1 IR 111; *Re Keller's Estate* (1928) 62 ILTR 9. Such restraints were abolished in Northern Ireland by the Married Women (Restraint upon Anticipation) Act (NI) 1952 and in the Republic by the Married Women's Status Act 1957. See para **[25.14]** *post*.

restraint on alienation, the court construed it as one to the wife for life only, with a remainder to John.[234]

(3) Rule against Perpetuities

[4.055] It has been a matter of some controversy whether the rule against perpetuities (which we shall discuss in more detail later[235]) applied at common law to interests like a possibility of reverter or a right of entry for condition broken.[236] The position in England seemed to be that the rule applied at common law both to a possibility of reverter (at least in respect of land)[237] and to a right of entry for condition broken.[238] But whatever was the position in England at common law it has been put beyond doubt by statute that the rule applies now in both cases.[239] In Ireland, however, the courts have taken a contrary view of the common law. In *Att-Gen v Cummins*[240] the Irish Exchequer Division, led by Palles CB, held that the rule did not apply to possibilities of reverter, so that they could operate at any time in the future. In *Walsh v Wightman*[241] the Northern Ireland Court of Appeal refused to follow the English authorities and held that the rule did not apply to a right of entry for condition broken. This remains the position in the Republic, but Northern Ireland has since passed legislation to conform with English law.[242]

(iii) Base Fee

[4.056] A base fee is a special kind of determinable fee which can be created in connection with a fee tail estate. In view of this connection it will be discussed in the section dealing with the fee tail estate.[243]

IV. FEE FARM GRANTS

A. General

[4.057] A fee farm grant is a conveyance of a fee simple subject to payment by the grantee and his successors in title to the grantor and his successors in title of a perpetual rent.[244] The fee simple estate so conveyed exhibits the characteristics of the estate just described in the immediately preceding pages, but the significance of fee farm grants lies in the special features attached to that estate in the conveyances that have become so

---

[234] *Manning v O'Boyle* (1930) 64 ILTR 43.

[235] Paras **[5.056]** *et seq, post.*

[236] See, generally, Gray, *Rule Against Perpetuities* (4th ed, 1942); Morris and Leach, *The Rule Against Perpetuities* (2nd ed, 1962; Supp, 1964); Challis, *The Law of Real Property* (3rd ed), Ch XIV; Pettit, 'Determinable Interests and Rule Against Perpetuities' (1957) 21 Conv 213.

[237] *Hopper v Corporation of Liverpool* (1944) 88 Sol Jo 213 (Megarry, 62 LQR 222).

[238] *Re Hollis' Hospital* [1899] 2 Ch 540; *Cf Third Report of the Real Property Commissioners* (1832), pp 29 and 36.

[239] Perpetuities and Accumulations Act 1964, s 12.

[240] [1906] 1 IR 406 (see *A Casebook on Irish Land Law* (1984), p 131).

[241] [1927] NI 1.

[242] Perpetuities Act (NI) 1966, s 13 and see para **[5.108]** *post.*

[243] See especially para **[4.136]** *post.*

common in Ireland. These are significant because in many respects they are unique in the common law world. It is true that in a few areas of the North and South-West of England, particularly around Manchester and East Lancashire and the Bath, Bristol areas, fee farm grants of a particular type are quite common.[245] These are grants creating perpetual rentcharges which are a rare category in Ireland and which do not exhibit the striking features of other categories more common in Ireland.[246]

In view of the fact that the categories of grants in Ireland have widely divergent origins and characteristics, it is more convenient to discuss matters like their creation, words of limitation and rights of the parties separately in relation to each category. In doing so it must be emphasised that such grants will in due course cease to be a significant feature of the land law scene in both parts of Ireland because of the effect of recent legislation. This legislation is discussed at appropriate points in the ensuing paragraphs. For the moment it is important to emphasise that in the Republic it has probably[247] been impossible to create a fee farm grant in respect of a dwelling since 1978.[248] In Northern Ireland Article 28 of the Property (NI) Order 1997 makes it absolutely clear that on and after a day to be appointed "a fee farm grant is incapable of being made at law or in equity".[249] This applies generally in respect of any property.[250] Any agreement for or a conveyance purporting to create a fee farm grant will operate instead as an agreement for or conveyance of a fee simple[251] free from the fee farm rent and any covenants or other provisions connected with the rent or for the benefit of the grantor.[252]

B. Classification

[4.058] Fee farm grants fall into three main categories:[253] (1) those creating feudal tenure between the grantor and grantee; (2) those creating the modern landlord and tenant relationship between the grantor and grantee; (3) those creating the relationship

---

[244] Quoted with approval by Murray J in *Re Courtney* [1981] NI 58 at 62-3. Murray J's judgment contains an interesting discussion of several points relating to fee farm grants. See, generally, Mecredy, *The Law of Fee Farm Grants* (1877); Strahan and Baxter, *The Law of Real Property* (3rd ed, 1926); Stubbs and Baxter, *Irish Forms and Precedents*, pp 87-116; *Survey of the Land Law of Northern Ireland* (HMSO, 1971), Ch 20; Land Law Working Group's *Final Report* (HMSO, 1990), Vol 1, Pt 1; Montrose, 'Fee Farm Grants' (1938) 2 NILQ 194, (1939) 3 NILQ 40, 81 and 143, (1940) 4 NILQ 40 and 86; Wylie, 'Fee Farm Grants-Montrose Continued' (1972) 23 NILQ 285.

[245] See Megarry and Wade, *Law of Real Property* (5th ed, 1984), pp 125 and 820. See also the Law Commission's *Report on Rentcharges* (Law Com No 68, 1975) and the Rentcharges Act 1977; Bennett, 'Fee Farm Grants Purchased from the Crown' (1903) 19 LQR 417.

[246] See para **[4.104]** *post.*

[247] The point is not entirely clear: see paras **[4.076]** and **[4.092]** *post.*

[248] Landlord and Tenant (Ground Rents) Act 1978, s 2.

[249] Article 28(1).

[250] The Order's compulsory redemption procedures for ground rents apply to dwelling-houses only: see para **[4.077]** *post.*

[251] Ie a legal fee simple absolute in possession: see the definition in Article 2(2).

[252] Article 28(2). The fine (capital sum) payable by the grantee will remain payable, *ibid.*

[253] See Montrose, *op cit,* fn 282 *ante.*

of rentchargor and rentchargee between the grantor and grantee.[254] These categories are mutually exclusive in relation to the relationship created between the parties to the grants and their successors in title, though they do, of course, share some common features. The most obvious common features are that in every fee farm grant a fee simple estate is conveyed which, in each case, is subject to a perpetual rent.

1. Feudal Tenure

[4.059] Fee farm grants of this nature create the relationship of lord and tenant as it developed under the feudal system of landholding.[255] This sort of grant, therefore, involves the conveyancing process of "subinfeudation" which was prohibited for both England and Ireland by the statute *Quia Emptores* 1290.[256] Thus for any grant of this nature to exist in England today it would have had to have been created before 1290 and to have survived since then - a highly unlikely event.[257] But in Ireland the story has been somewhat different, at least since the seventeenth century. It has already been mentioned that during that century much Irish land was confiscated by the Crown and regranted to landowners owing allegiance to the Crown.[258] In making these regrants, usually by letters patent, it became the practice of the Crown to convey the land to the grantee to hold of the Crown subject to a chief rent, known as a "quit rent" in Ireland.[259] The letters patent then usually went on to grant a special dispensation from the statute *Quia Emptores* to the grantee so as to enable him to subinfeudate by way of fee farm grants "*non obstant Quia Emptores* or any other law or custom".[260] The Crown was not mentioned in *Quia Emptores* expressly or by necessary implication, so it was not bound by the statute and could freely make grants of the confiscated Irish land.[261] However, there was some doubt whether the Crown could grant a dispensation to its grantees to enable them to subinfeudate contrary to the statute. Judicial notice was taken of this point in some Irish cases but there seems to be no authoritative decision on the matter.[262] It is extremely doubtful whether it could be argued with much force today for at least two reasons. First, the Irish Parliament passed a series of statutes in the seventeenth century to resolve doubts about, and to quiet the titles to, lands conveyed in such *non*

---

[254] Montrose's series of articles (fn 282 *supra*) was never completed and does not cover this third category, but see Wylie (*ibid.*).

[255] Ch 2, *ante*.

[256] Para **[2.43]** *ante*.

[257] Megarry and Wade, *The Law of Real Property* (5th ed, 1984), pp 818 and 828.

[258] Paras **[1.029]-[1.034]** *ante*.

[259] See *Corporation of Dublin v Herbert* (1861) 12 ICLR 502; *Tuthill v Rogers* (1844 6 Ir Eq R 429; *Massy v O'Dell* (1859) 9 Ir Ch R 441; *Hatton v Waddy* (1834) Hay and Jon 601; *Re Maxwell's Estate* (1891) 28 LR Ir 356. Anon, 'A Notice on Quit Rents in Northern Ireland' (1952) 10 NILQ 30. See para **[6.009]** *post*.

[260] See, eg, the terms of the grant by Charles I to Viscount Montgomery of the Manor of Donaghadee in *Delacherois v Delacherois* (1864) 11 HLC 62.

[261] Para **[2.043]** *ante*. *Re Maxwell's Estate* (1891) 28 LR Ir 356, 358.

[262] *Delacherois v Delacherois, op cit*; *Verschoyle v Perkins* (1847) 13 Ir Eq R 72; *Butler v Archer* (1860) 12 ICLR 104.

obstante grants.[263] It may be argued that, while it is probable that these were primarily concerned with the original Crown grants, impliedly they confirmed sub-grants made under powers conferred by the original grants.[264] Secondly, whatever the technical doubts, the fact remains that many of the original Crown grantees exercised their powers of subinfeudation and executed a large number of fee farm grants which survive to this day. These grants, and subsequent sub-grants, have been acted upon by all concerned without challenge or question for two centuries. The current holders of land under such grants, and their predecessors before them, have long since acquired good "holding titles", based on adverse possession,[265] if nothing else.

[4.060] Feudal fee farm grants are more common in Northern Ireland than in the Republic of Ireland, for the powers of creating them were standard clauses in the grants made to the participants in the Ulster plantation.[266] It may be questioned whether many could survive after the land purchase operation, which involved the redemption of all superior rents and interests so as to ensure the vesting of a fee simple absolute in the tenant-purchaser (subject to the terminable land purchase annuity).[267] However, it must be remembered that a considerable proportion of the land originally subject to fee farm grants had ceased to be used for agricultural or pastoral purposes by the time of the land purchase scheme and so was outside its scope. This land is now to be found in the urban areas of Ireland that have developed since the seventeenth century and fee farm and sub-fee farm grants remain important links in the chains of title to that land.[268]

(i) Creation

[4.061] Feudal grants will have been created either before 1290 or under powers conferred in Crown grants of Irish land of the seventeenth century. The former type are unlikely to be met nowadays by practitioners; any made prior to 1290 would have long since ceased to have effect in view of the turbulent history of Irish land and the frequent changes in its ownership over the centuries since then.[269] As regards the latter any likely exercise of the powers conferred in the Crown grants will have long since been made. Indeed, most, if not all, feudal grants surviving in Ireland today would have been executed originally before 1845 so that the modern deed of conveyance introduced by

---

[263] Settlement of Ireland Acts 1634 (10 Chas 1, sess 1, c 3), 1639 (15 Chas 1, c 6), 1662 (14 & 15 Chas 2, sess 4, c 2), 1665 (17 & 18 Chas 2, c 3) and 1698 (10 Will 3, c 7). These statutes were all repealed in the Republic of Ireland by the Statute Law Revision (Pre-Union Irish Statutes) Act 1962. As regards NI, see the Property (NI) Order 1978, art 16(2) and Sched 2.

[264] For judicial discussion of these Settlement Acts, see *Delacherois v Delacherois, op cit; Little v Moylett* [1929] IR 439; *Moore v Att-Gen* [1934] IR 44. See also *Tuthill v Rogers* (1844) 6 Ir Eq R 429; *Tisdall v Parnell* (1863) 14 ICLR 1.

[265] Ch 23, *post*.

[266] Para **[1.030]** *ante*.

[267] Paras **[1.051]** *et seq, ante*.

[268] For further discussion of this subject, see paras **[4.179]** *et seq, post*.

[269] Ch 1, *ante*. The method of conveyance in such old grants would presumably have been by the old feudal mechanism, namely, feoffment with livery of seisin, para **[3.023]** *ante*.

the Real Property Act 1845 would not have been used.[270] The modes of conveyance used for such grants would have been those devised by the conveyancers after the Statute of Uses (Ireland) 1634, namely the bargain and sale and lease and release combined,[271] or a covenant to stand seised.[272] These were discussed in more detail in an earlier chapter.[273]

(ii) Words of Limitation

[4.062] A fee farm grant involves the conveyance of a fee simple and so the appropriate words of limitation would have to be used in the grant, in accordance with the rules discussed above.[274] However, it should be noted with respect to feudal grants that not all the modes of conveyance likely to be used in executing these involved a conveyance of the fee simple estate. A feoffment with livery of seisin, the oldest mode of conveyance, did involve such a conveyance and so would require use of appropriate words of limitation.[275] If a lease and release were used, the lease itself did not involve a conveyance of the fee simple and so no words of limitation were required. The release operated to extinguish the reversion on the lease rather than to convey it, so it seems that words of limitation were not required for it either.[276] As regards the bargain and sale and covenant to stand seised, these both raised uses recognised originally only by the Courts of Equity, and it is doubtful if words of limitation were any more necessary than in the case of wills.[277] or equitable interests,[278] though in these cases the uses were executed and created legal estates as a result of the Statute of Uses (Ireland) 1634.[279]

(iii) Fee Farm Rents

[4.063] Feudal grants create feudal tenure between the grantor and the grantee and so the rent is what is known as a rent service as opposed to a rentcharge or rent seck.[280] As part of the relationship of lord and tenant the obligation to pay the rent binds the successors in title of the grantee, and the right to receive it accrues to the successors in title of the grantor.

[4.064] As a rent service, the fee farm rent is recoverable by, in addition to an ordinary action for debt, the common law remedy of distress, irrespective of any express reservation of this right in the original or any subsequent grant. Distress was, in former times, the main remedy for the recovery of arrears of rent. The landlord entered on the land and seized cattle or other articles belonging to the tenant, which he could later sell

---

[270] Para **[3.026]** *ante.*
[271] See, eg, *Delacherois v Delacherois* (1864) 11 HLC 62.
[272] See, eg, *Re Sergie* [1954] NI 1 (see *A Casebook on Irish Land Law* (1984), p 70).
[273] Ch 3, *ante.*
[274] Para **[4.024]** *ante.*
[275] Para **[3.023]** *ante.*
[276] *Coke Upon Littleton* (19th ed, 1832), 193b. *Estoss's Case* (1597) 3 Dy 263a.
[277] Para **[4.031]** *ante.*
[278] Para **[4.033]** *ante.*
[279] Para **[3.024]** *ante.*
[280] See, generally, para **[6.132]** *post.*

and use the proceeds to pay the arrears. As we shall see in a later chapter, there have been many statutory provisions on the subject of distress.[281] In England, because *Quia Emptores* 1290 prohibited subinfeudation and thereby prevented the subsequent creation of tenure in a grant of a fee simple, a rent service and its attendant right of distress had come to be regarded as existing only where a lease was granted reserving a reversion to the landlord.[282] Irish seventeenth century feudal grants, however. pass a fee simple with no reversion at all left in the grantor, and so there are some doubts as to how many of the statutes relating to distress apply to feudal fee farm grantors. The matter is largely one of construction and the essential issue in each case is whether the particular statute is drafted widely enough to cover such fee farm grants or is confined in its application to the modern landlord and tenant relationship, which can also exist between fee farm grantors and grantees.[283] Thus it may be argued that the early feudal statutes relating to distress cover feudal fee farm grants, eg, Statute of Marlborough 1267[284]; Statute of Westminster I 1275[285]; Statute of Westminster II 1285[286]; Distress for Rent Acts (Ireland) 1634, 1695, 1712, 1721 and 1751.[287] Whether or not these Acts can be said to have impliedly applied to feudal fee farms grants, the Fee Farm Rents (Ireland) Act 1851,[288] expressly extended to "all Fee-farm Rents," where the persons to whom such rents were payable had no reversions, all the remedies for recovery of rent provided by ss 20 and 21 of the Renewable Leasehold Conversion Act 1849,[289] except actions of ejectment for non-payment of rent.[290] As regards the later statutes dealing with distress, it is probable that these were meant to be confined to the modern relationship of landlord and tenant and did not extend to feudal fee farm grants.[291] Finally, as regards Northern Ireland, it should be noted that distress as a remedy has been abolished and replaced by enforcement of a court judgment through the Enforcement of Judgments Office.[292]

---

[281] Para **[17.064]** *post.*

[282] Megarry and Wade, *The Law of Real Property* (5th ed, 1984), p 818.

[283] *Cf* Montrose, (1939) 3 NILQ 40 at 44 and at 150-1.

[284] Cc 1, 2, 4, 9, 15 and 22.

[285] Cc 16 and 17.

[286] Cc 2 and 37.

[287] Repealed by Deasy's Act 1860, only in so far as it related to the modern relationship of landlord and tenant dealt with by the 1860 Act.

[288] The 1851 Act was held to be retrospective in *Major v Barton* (1851) 2 ICLR 28.

[289] Ie, actions for debt and distress.

[290] Section 1. See Ch 17, *post.* On the 1851 Act, see *Butler v Archer* (1860) 12 ICLR 104.

[291] Eg, Ejectment and Distress (Ir) Act 1846; Landlord and Tenant (Ir) Act 1851; Landlord and Tenant Law Amendment Act Ireland 1860 (Deasy's Act), s 51; Law of Distress and Small Debts (Ir) Act 1888, and Law of Distress Amendment Act 1908, s 10. See para **[17.065]** *post.*

[292] Judgments (Enforcement) Act (NI) 1969, s 132, Sched 6. The 1969 Act has since been consolidated in the Judgments Enforcement (NI) Order 1981. See also the Judgments Enforcement (Amendment) (NI) Order 1986.

The other main remedy that a grantor might seek in relation to the fee farm rent would be forfeiture of the grant. The subject of forfeiture generally is, perhaps, one of the most difficult aspects of feudal fee farm grants and it is to this subject that we now turn.

(iv) Forfeiture

[4.065] It was a general principle of early feudal law that, if the tenant did anything which could be regarded as a denial of his lord's title, his lord had the right to forfeit the tenant's holding, because this amounted to a breach of the basic duty of homage underlying the feudal tenurial relationship.[293] Then the Statute of Gloucester 1278[294] expressly provided that a lord who "let his land in fee-farm" and later found that, because of his tenant's mismanagement, there was nothing to distrain for non-payment of the rent, could, after a period of two years, bring an action to demand the land back, "by writ out of the Chancery".[295] The Statute of Westminster II 1285, provided that such "writs of entry" could be obtained by heirs of the grantor against heirs and alienees of the grantee.[296] Despite these provisions, however, there grew up amongst conveyancers a practice of inserting express provisions with respect to forfeiture in feudal grants and a general body of law evolved governing these provisions at common law.

[4.066] It became a general rule that, before a grantor could rely on the terms of his grant for his right of forfeiture, he had to prove that either the agreement which he claimed had been broken by the grantee had been expressly drafted as a condition of the grantee's holding the land, or, if it had been drafted simply as a covenant by the grantee, that there had been included in the grant a separate forfeiture clause, reserving to the grantor the express right of forfeiture for breach of any of the grantee's covenants. This rule was later applied to leases so as to govern the modern relationship of landlord and tenant.[297]

[4.067] With respect to feudal fee farm grants, it would seem that this general rule about covenants and conditions governs forfeiture both for non-payment of rent and for breach of any other grantee's obligation in the grant. Apart from the very early thirteenth century statutes mentioned above, there would seem to be no later statutes on the matter of non-payment of rent. Certainly the eighteenth and nineteenth Irish statutes governing the action of ejectment for non-payment of rent did not apply.[298] These were confined in scope to the modern relationship of landlord and tenant. Thus the Fee Farm Rents (Ireland) Act 1851, also mentioned above, in extending ss 20 and 21 of the Renewable Leasehold Conversion Act 1849, to all fee farm rents, and other rents payable to

---

[293] This right should not be confused with the King's right of forfeiture for treason, see para **[2.23]** *ante*.

[294] C 4.

[295] The statute provided that the tenant could keep the land if he tendered the arrears and any damages due. This action was one of the old real actions (para **[4.008]**, *ante*), and c 4 was repealed by the Statute Law Revision (Ir) Act 1872.

[296] C 21.

[297] Megarry and Wade, *The Law of Real Property* (5th ed, 1984), pp 670-73. See also *Croker v Orpen* (1847) 9 Ir Eq R 563.

[298] See generally, para **[17.098]** *post*.

grantors with no reversion, expressly excluded "the remedy by ejectment for non-payment of rent".[299] This was a special remedy introduced by the Irish Parliament for landlords in Ireland and was governed by statutes designed to get rid of the formalities of the common law of England relating to forfeitures for non-payment of rent. The English position was later consolidated in the Common Law Procedure Act 1852,[300] but this did not apply to Ireland. The Common Law Procedure Amendment (Ireland) Act 1853, which corresponded to the English 1852 Act, did not contain provisions relating to forfeiture for non-payment of rent, though it did contain some references to ejectment actions. Thus there seems to be no legislation to cover forfeiture for non-payment of rent by feudal fee farm grantees and common law rules will apply, such as the rule that the grantor must first make a formal demand for the rent before exercising his right of forfeiture and re-entering.[301] The grantee has, however, an equitable right to relief against forfeiture.[302]

[4.068] This leaves the question whether later statutes, governing the exercise of a right of forfeiture for breach of obligations other than those relating to rent, apply to feudal fee farm grants. Once again there is a problem of construction caused by the fact that these statutes are English statutes drafted primarily with the English position in mind, namely, that no freehold subinfeudation could occur after 1290 and the only rights of forfeiture likely to exist were those of landlords in the modern sense. However, while the Conveyancing Acts 1881 and 1892 (governing forfeiture for breach of covenants other than those relating to rent) speak in terms of "leases", s 14(3) of the 1881 Act expressly defines "lease" to include a "grant at a fee farm rent". The question of construction remains whether this provision includes feudal fee farm grants creating feudal tenure as opposed to the modern landlord and tenant relationship usually found in leases. There seems to be no authority on the point and one can only state that it would be more convenient and desirable if s 14 were given an interpretation wide enough to cover feudal grants. If it were not given this interpretation, there would seem to be no other statutory provisions to control the grantor's exercise of his right of re-entry or forfeiture. He would not have to comply with any formalities, such as the requirement of serving a notice on the grantee specifying the breach complained of and requesting compensation.[303] Perhaps even more serious, the grantee would appear otherwise to have no claim to equitable relief against forfeiture in such cases, because of the attitude of the courts to relief in cases other than non-payment of rent. In the latter case the courts were always ready to furnish relief in appropriate cases, but in the former case it became the settled rule that relief would not ordinarily be granted.[304] This relief is now grounded entirely on statute law, namely the Conveyancing Acts.[305]

---

[299] Section 1.

[300] Megarry and Wade, *op cit*, pp 676-8.

[301] This view of the law was accepted as correct in relation to leases by Carroll J in *Re Erris Investments Ltd* [1991] ILRM 377. See paras **[17.091]** and **[17.098]** *post*.

[302] *Ibid*.

[303] 1881 Act, s 14, and 1892 Act, ss 2 and 4.

[304] Megarry and Wade, *op cit*, pp 675-83. See discussion in *Whipp v Mackey* [1927] IR 372.

[305] Paras **[17.088]**-**[17.091]** *post*.

(v) Covenants

[4.069] The law relating to covenants in feudal fee farm grants is very obscure in several respects. The reason is that most of the learning relating to freehold covenants is confined to the usual situation in England where the freehold is conveyed without creating any form of tenure between the grantor and the grantee;[306] tenure is created only by leases and the law relating to leasehold covenants is a different subject altogether.[307] It is submitted that Irish feudal fee farm grants which involve the conveyance of a fee simple estate, a freehold, should be governed by the law of freehold covenants rather than that of leasehold covenants. It is difficult, however, to be dogmatic in view of the almost complete absence of authority on the point.[308]

[4.070] A first question that may be raised in this context is whether there are restrictions on the type of covenants that could be inserted in a feudal fee farm grant. In particular, when the Crown granted dispensations to its grantees from *Quia Emptores* 1290, did this cover all aspects of that statute's provisions? We have already seen that another important principle of our land law, apart from the prohibition of further subinfeudation of freehold land, enshrined in the statute was the right of all free tenants in fee simple to alienate without their lords' consent.[309] This provision established what came to be known as the rule against inalienability, which provides that the grantor of a freehold estate cannot impose restrictions in the grant substantially prohibiting or excessively restricting the grantee's right of alienation.[310] It is submitted that this rule applies to feudal fee farm grants; the fee simple remains a fee simple even though there exists a relationship of lord and tenant between the grantor and grantee. The Crown dispensations of *Quia Emptores* should be regarded as designed only to get round the prohibition against subinfeudation and to facilitate the making of further grants by Crown grantees. They should not be regarded as changing the nature of the estates contained in those grants, which are otherwise governed by the general law relating to freehold estates or by statutes, such as *Quia Emptores* itself. In this sense the dispensations merely conferred powers of granting estates already known to the law. Some support for this view may be gleaned from Irish cases. In *Re Lunham's Estate*,[311]

---

[306] See Elphinstone, *Covenants Affecting Land* (1946); Preston and Newsom, *Restrictive Covenants Affecting Freehold Land* (8th ed, 1991). Also Ch 19, *post*.

[307] Megarry and Wade, *op cit*, Ch 14; also Ch 19, *post*. Note, however, the radical change to NI introduced by Article 34 of the Property (NI) Order 1997: see para **[19.48]** *et seq, post*.

[308] Montrose seems to have taken the same view, see (1939) 3 NILQ 42-4 and 150-1; (1940) 4 NILQ 40. One doubt might be raised on the basis that a right of distress lies in the grantor of a fee farm grant which is a remedy more commonly associated with a lessor. This, however, is an ancient remedy, which did originally belong to freehold feudal lords and which later was extended to landlords in the modern sense. In other words part of freehold law became leasehold law also; in the case of covenants, however, no such development took place and the two laws remained divergent on fundamental principles, see Ch 19 *post*.

[309] Para **[2.46]**, *ante*. The Crown could annex a condition against alienation in its grant of a fee simple, *Fowler v Fowler* (1865) 16 Ir Ch Rep 507.

[310] See paras **[5.033]** *et seq*.

[311] (1871) IR 5 Eq 170.

Flanagan J held that a covenant in a fee farm grant prohibiting assignment and subletting without consent, if this would entail the property being split into more than four divisions or lots, was void and inoperative "as repugnant to the power of alienation necessarily implied in a fee farm grant". It is true that the learned judge decided that the grant in that case created a rentcharge, ie, that it belonged to the third category of grants found in Ireland,[312] but the implication, and it is no more than that, seems to be that in any grant not creating the modern relationship of landlord and tenant, the second category,[313] such a covenant would be void under the usual law relating to freeholds. A similar implication may be found in some of the second category cases, namely those relating to conversion grants which have special statutory provisions applying to them.[314] The point at issue in these cases seems to stem partly from the view that, but for those special statutory provisions, the covenants in question would be void in fee farm grants as repugnant to the fee simple estates granted.[315]

[4.071] Another question with respect to covenants which may be raised relates to what other covenants, apart from those relating to the fee farm rent, may be inserted in feudal grants. By the seventeenth century there were few vestiges of the feudal system remaining in Ireland and the Tenures (Abolition) Act (Ireland) 1662 abolished most services and incidents of feudal tenure, other than monetary ones like fixed rents. Yet it is the case that other covenants were commonly inserted in Irish feudal grants, particularly covenants restricting the user of the land.[316] No doubt these covenants were enforceable as between the original grantor and grantee on the basis of privity of contract, but how far does the benefit and burden of covenants in feudal fee farm grants run with the land and rent so as to bind successors in title of the original grantor and grantee? What significance in this context has the fact that these grants created feudal tenure between the parties?

[4.072] This brings us to the medieval law of covenants, which all the authorities categorise as thoroughly unclear.[317] This law was based on the ancient law of warranty,[318] under which an express or implied warranty of title was given by the grantor to the grantee. If his title was impeached, the grantee could "vouch to warranty" the grantor and call for a conveyance of lands of equal value or, later in history, damages for breach of warranty through the old writ of covenant. This law developed into the modern law of covenants for title (relating to a right to convey and for quiet enjoyment), and there grew up alongside it a body of law relating to other covenants contained in

---

[312] Para **[4.104]** *post.*

[313] Para **[4.078]** *post.*

[314] *Ibid.*

[315] Eg, *Re McNaul's Estate* [1902] 1 IR 114 (see *A Casebook on Irish Land Law* (1984), p 41). See paras **[4.085]-[4.086]** *post.*

[316] See the covenants in the *Delacherois* case (1864) 11 HLC 62 (eg, obligation to grind corn in the manor mills).

[317] See, eg, Holmes, *The Common Law* (1968; ed Howe), Ch XI.

[318] Milsom, *Historical Foundations of the Common Law* (1969), pp 108-9 and 147-8; Bailey, 'Warranties of Land in the Thirteenth Century' (1942-4) 8 CLJ 274 and (1945-7) 9 CLJ 82.

conveyances of freehold land. It was eventually resolved that, while the benefit of covenants could be annexed to the land so as to run with the land in favour of successors in title of the grantor,[319] the burden would not run so as to bind successors in title of the grantee.[320] The classic statement of this common law position was given by the English Court of Appeal in *Austerberry v Corporation of Oldham*.[321] Then the modification in the common law position was established in equity to the effect that the burden of a restrictive covenant would run with the land so as to bind successors in title of the grantee, provided the covenant "touched and concerned" the land.[322] This rule of equity came to be known as the rule in *Tulk v Moxhay*.[323]

[4.073] In conclusion, then, it is submitted that covenants in Irish feudal fee farm grants are governed by the general law relating to freehold covenants. The benefit runs at common law so long as the covenant touches and concerns the land and the benefit is annexed to the legal estate of the covenantee; the burden runs in equity only in respect of restrictive covenants attached to the covenantor's land. Thus a *bona fide* purchaser of the legal estate without notice of such a restrictive covenant theoretically could take the land free of it. It must be mentioned, however, that this is rarely likely to occur in Ireland because of the Registry of Deeds system which was introduced by the Registration of Deeds Act (Ireland) 1707. As we shall see, while registration itself does not fix subsequent purchasers with actual notice, it is necessary to secure priority for the covenantee against subsequent purchasers of the covenantor's land.[324]

(vi) Redemption

Various provisions have been enacted over the years to provide for redemption of fee farm rents and the discharge of covenants and conditions contained in grants, so as to leave the current grantee with a fee simple absolute title. Once again there is the problem of construction as to whether these statutes apply to feudal fee farm grants.

(a) Chief Rents Redemption (Ireland) Act 1864

[4.074] This Act provided for voluntary redemption as between the fee farm grantor and grantee through an application to the court. It seems fairly clear from its terminology that the Act was meant to cover all types of fee farm grant including feudal grants.[325] The Act seems to have been invoked rarely and seems to have long since fallen into disuse. Indeed, the advantages of such a statute are doubtful; if the grantor and grantee are agreed voluntarily upon having redemption, why should they incur the trouble and

---

[319] Bailey, 'The Benefit of a Restrictive Covenant' (1938) 6 CLJ 339; *Report of the Committee on Positive Covenants Relating to Land* (1965; Cmnd 2719); Preston and Newsom, *Restrictive Covenants Affecting Freehold Land* (8th ed, 1991).

[320] *Ibid*. Also para **[19.21]** *post*.

[321] (1885) 29 Ch D 750.

[322] See generally, Ch 19, *post*.

[323] (1848) 2 Ph 774.

[324] See paras **[3.069]**-**[3.079]**, *ante* and para **[19.45]**, *post*.

[325] By s 1, it applied to "*Any* lands or tenements held in Fee Farm, or for Lives renewable for ever ..." (italics added).

expense of an application to the court? If they cannot agree upon a price for redemption, they might as well arrange their own arbitration rather than submit to the court which has no power under the Act to coerce either party to agree to its award.[326] The 1864 Act will be repealed in Northern Ireland by the Property (NI) Order 1997.[327]

(b) Redemption of Rent (Ireland) Act 1891

[4.075] This Act was part of the land purchase scheme and so applied only to fee farm grants of agricultural land being bought out under that scheme.[328] It was used extensively in respect of fee farm grants at the end of the last century,[329] but the question whether it applied to feudal grants caused the courts some difficulty. The reason was that the Act, being linked closely to the land purchase scheme for agricultural tenants, seemed to be more properly confined to the modern relationship of landlord and tenant.[330] It might have been questioned as a matter of policy why a distinction should have been drawn between one type of fee farm grant and another, once the decision had been taken to extend the land purchase scheme to any type of grant at all. Indeed, no less an authority than Palles CB stated, albeit *obiter*, in *Adams v Alexander* that in his view "grants of lands in old manors" were within the 1891 Act.[331] But the majority view amongst Irish judges seems to have been that feudal grants did not come within the 1891 Act, on the ground that it should be read as being in *pari materia* with the Land Law and Land Purchase Acts and thereby confined to grants creating the modern relationship of landlord and tenant. There is not an authoritative decision on the point, but the better view is that a fee farm grant creating the modern relationship of landlord and tenant was a prerequisite to application of the 1891 Act.[332] The point is, of course, largely academic

---

[326] *Survey of the Land Law of Northern Ireland* (HMSO, 1971), para 472.

[327] Article 53(2) and Sch 5.

[328] See also the Purchase of Land (Ir) Act 1985, s 10; Land Law (Ir) Act 1887, ss 15 and 16; Purchase of Land (Ir) Act 1891, s 20; Land Law (Ir) Act 1896, ss 31, 33 and 37; Irish Land Act 1903, ss 61-64. See also the Republic's Land Acts 1923, s 38; 1931, s 44; 1933, s 42; 1936, s 43; 1939, ss 47-9; 1950, ss 21 and 23. *Re Clements's Estate* [1924] 1 IR 165; *Eustace-Duckett v Thompson* (1938) 72 ILTR 226; *Re Keyser's Estate* [1938] IR 326.

[329] *Re Pentland's Estate* (1888) 22 LR Ir 649; *O'Hea v Morrison* (1892) 30 LR Ir 651; *Merry v Irwin* (1894) 28 ILTR 59; *Gaffney v Trumbull* (1895) 29 ILTR 129; *Cowell v Buchanan* [1898] 2 IR 153; *Mairs v Lecky* [1895] 2 IR 475; *Glenny v Bell* [1898] 2 IR 233; *Wynne v Wilson* (1901) 35 ILTR 152; *Cowell v Buchanan* [1903] 1 IR 58; *Shiel v Irvine* (1903) 37 ILTR 92; *Re Barry's Estate* [1917] 1 IR 11; *Re Greene's Estate* [1929] IR 615.

[330] The Land Law (Ireland) Act 1896, s 14 (*b*) seemed to confirm this by providing that with respect to the 1891 Act "a person shall be a lessee or a grantee under a fee farm grant within the meaning of the said Acts [Land Law Acts], notwithstanding that the instrument under which he holds, *though purporting to create the relation of landlord and tenant*, is dated before the first day of January one thousand eight hundred and sixty-one, and by reason of its date does not create *the relation of landlord and tenant* between him and the person to whom money is payable thereunder in respect of the holding, and that person shall be a lessor or grantor in like manner as if the instrument were executed on or after the above-mentioned day" (italics added). The date mentioned relates to the operation of s 3 of Deasy's Act 1860, as to which see para **[4.091]** *post*.

[331] [1895] 2 IR 363, 372; *cf* Barry LJ at p 383.

[332] Eg, *Christie v Peacocke* (1892) 30 LR Ir 646; *Kelly v Rattey* (1893) 32 LR Ir 445; *Gormill v Lynne* (1894) 28 ILTR 44; *Hamilton v Casey* [1894] 2 IR 224.

nowadays as most agricultural land has been bought out under the land purchase schemes in both parts of Ireland, and the fee farm rents and other superior interests have been redeemed.[333]

(c) Landlord and Tenant (Ground Rents) Act 1967 and (No 2) Act 1978 (RI)

[4.076] These Acts in the Republic confer on certain lessees the right to acquire the fee simple by enabling them to invoke statutory procedures for buying out superior rents and interests.[334] The 1967 Act defined "fee simple" as not including the estate of a person holding under a fee farm grant,[335] so that enfranchisement by lessees under that Act and the 1978 Act necessarily entails redemption of superior fee farm rents and other interests held under fee farm grants of any kind. Whether fee farm grantees in occupation of the land can redeem on their own is not entirely clear since it could be argued that a fee farm grantee who, *ex hypothesi*, already holds the fee simple ought not to be able to take advantage of legislation relating to "acquisition of the fee simple".[336] However, the right to acquire the fee simple is conferred on various "leases" and a "lease" is defined in the legislation as *including* a "fee farm grant".[337] This suggests that a fee farm grantee can invoke the acquisition procedures to redeem the fee farm rent and to get rid of other interests like covenants and conditions contained in the grant and any superior grants.[338]

(d) Leasehold (Enlargement and Extension) Act, (NI) 1971 and Property (NI) Order 1997

[4.077] A right of enfranchisement was introduced for long lessees in Northern Ireland by the Leasehold (Enlargement and Extension) Act, (NI) 1971, which adopted many of the provisions of the Republic's 1967 Act. In particular, in adopting a similar definition of "fee simple,"[339] it indicated that enfranchisement by lessees in Northern Ireland also involved redeeming any superior fee farm rents. Once again this presumably covered feudal grants, as there seems to be no reason why enfranchisement should have a more limited scope. One curious feature of the Northern Ireland Act is, however, that, unlike

---

[333] Paras **[1.065]**-**[1.068]** *ante*; see also *O'Hea v Morrison* (1892) 30 LR Ir 651. On the post-1920 legislation in the Republic in relation to fee farm rents, see, however, *Re Clements's Estate* [1924] 1 IR 165; *Re Greene's Estate* [1929] IR 615; *Re Radcliff's Estate* [1939] IR 213.

[334] The 1967 Act was based on the recommendations of the Ground Rents Commission's *Report on Ground Rents* (1964; Pr 7783). The 1978 Act, which was amended by the Landlord and Tenant (Amendment) Act 1980, added new categories of lessees entitled to buy the fee simple (see ss 10, 11, 12 and 26).

[335] Section 2(1).

[336] See ss 3-5 of the 1967 Act and Pt II of the 1978 (No 2) Act (as amended by ss 70-73 of the Landlord and Tenant (Amendment) Act 1980). See generally Wylie, *Irish Landlord and Tenant Law,* Ch 31 and para **[18.26]** *et seq, post*.

[337] 1978 Act (No 2), s 3.

[338] An argument to the contrary was rejected in an oral judgment by Keane J in *Arch Properties Ltd v Lambert Jones Estates Ltd* High Court, unrep, 1 June 1984. See Wylie, *Irish Landlord and Tenant Law,* para 4.044.

[339] Section 33.

the Republic's 1967 Act, the 1971 Act's long title stated that another purpose of the Act was to enable "grantees of certain fee farm grants to redeem their fee farm rents". The implication seems to be that fee farm grantees in occupation of the land could so redeem under the Act, hence the definition of "lease" to include a fee farm grant.[340] Whatever the position under the 1971 Act, it is of little practical significance since its provisions have been rarely invoked.[341] Much more comprehensive provisions for redemption of ground rents were proposed by the Land Law Working Group in 1990[342] and effect will be given to those by Part II of the Property (NI) Order 1997.[343] The Order is discussed later,[344] but for the moment it should be noted that it provides a comprehensive scheme for redemption of "ground rents". This will operate *compulsorily* on a "pre-sale" basis in respect of any sale after the appointed day of land comprising a "dwelling-house", but the statutory procedure may also be used *voluntarily* by a landowner not intending to sell but holding property subject to a ground rent. "Ground Rent" includes a "fee farm grant",[345] which means a rent payable under a "fee farm grant", ie, "a grant of a fee simple reserving or charging a perpetual rent (whether or not the relation of landlord and tenant subsists between the person entitled to receive the rent and the person liable to pay it) and includes a sub-fee farm grant".[346] In other words it clearly covers all types of fee farm grant created in Ireland, including feudal grants.

[4.078] We come now to a unique feature of Irish land law - a fee farm grant which creates the modern relationship of landlord and tenant between the parties. In other words, this is a grant of a freehold estate which creates leasehold tenure. To the English conveyancer this seems to be a contradiction in terms, which breaches the fundamental principles of real property law.[347] Yet in Ireland this category is the most common of fee farm grants, largely due to nineteenth-century legislation which applied to Ireland only. The explanation for these grants' prevalence in Ireland lies, therefore, in special statute law rather than in any revolution in the development of the common law.

The first point to be made about these grants is that they fall into two sub-categories. One sub-category consists of "conversion" grants made under statutes like the Renewable Leasehold Conversion Act 1849, and certain private Acts. This sub-category is dealt with in the next section. The other sub-category relates to grants creating the relationship of landlord and tenant within the meaning of s 3 of the Landlord and Tenant

---

[340] *Ibid*. See, generally, Wylie, 'Leasehold (Enlargement and Extension) Act (NI) 1971 - A Critique' (1971) 22 NILQ 389.

[341] See the Land Law Working Group's Interim Report (*Ground Rents and Other Periodic Payments*) (1983), Ch 4. See para **[18.40]** *post*.

[342] *Final report* (HMSO, 1990) Vol 1, Pt 1.

[343] The Order will not come into force until appointed days are specified and is likely to be phased in as recommended by the Working Group: see *ibid* para 1.3.19 (voluntary redemption first and then compulsory redemption). Note that the 1971 Act will then cease to apply to any land coming within the 1997 Order, Article 33.

[344] Paras **[4.183]** and **[18.43]** *et seq, post*.

[345] Article 3(1)(a).

[346] See the definitions of "fee farm grant" and "fee farm rent" in Article 2(2).

[347] See paras **[4.007]**-**[4.009]** *ante*.

Law Amendment Act, Ireland 1860, sometimes known as "Deasy's Act grants". This second sub-category will be discussed after the next section of this chapter.

2. Landlord and Tenant Conversion Grants

(i) Creation

Conversion fee farm grants have all arisen out of leases as a result of statutory provisions.

(a) Church Temporalities Acts

[4.079] By statutory provisions of the seventeenth century the powers of bishops and other ecclesiastical persons to grant leases of lands belonging to the Church of Ireland (then the established Church) were limited.[348] Generally, such persons could not alienate church land except by lease for a period up to 21 years in respect of agricultural land, and up to 40 years for houses in cities and towns.[349] These "bishops' leases," as they were called, became quite common in Ireland and the practice developed of inserting in them covenants for renewal, subject to payment of renewal fines.[350] It was also common to have a *toties quoties* covenant for renewal inserted in sub-leases of lands held under bishops' leases, specifying that, every time the lessee under the head-lease obtained a renewal of the head-lease, he would grant a renewal of the sub-lease.[351] Then the Church Temporalities Act 1833,[352] gave tenants holding under bishops' leases the right to purchase the fee simple subject to a fee farm rent.[353] The fee farm rent was to be basically the old leasehold rent plus the average annual value of renewal fines due under the old lease, calculated in accordance with the Act.[354] In the case of a sub-lease, if the sub-lessor obtained a fee farm grant he could under the Act compel the sub-lessee to contribute to its purchase price. In that case the sub-lessee became entitled to a sub-fee farm grant.[355] These conversion fee farm grants were, under the 1833 Act, to be subject to the same uses and trusts as the old leases, and the fee farm rents were to be recoverable by the same means as ordinary rents under a lease were recoverable by a landlord.[356] However, the Act disestablishing the Church of Ireland, the Irish Church

---

[348] Ecclesiastical Lands Act (Ir) 1634, as amended by the Ecclesiastical Lands Act (Ir) 1795.

[349] 1634 Act, ss 2 and 3. Leases of up to 60 years might be granted under licence from the Lord Deputy, *ibid*, s 3.

[350] *Brabazon v Lord Lucan* (1849) 12 Ir Eq R 432.

[351] *Dockrill v Dolan* (1841) 3 Ir Eq R 552; *Bleakely v Collum* (1863) 14 Ir Ch R 375; *Pilson v Spratt* (1889) 25 LR Ir 5.

[352] See also the Church Temporalities (Ireland) Acts, 1834, 1836 and 1860.

[353] Section 210. *Clarke v Staples* (1843) 5 Ir Eq R 246; *Hilhouse v Tyndall* (1849) 13 Ir Eq R 209; *Campbell v Ross* (1856) 7 Ir Ch R 222; *Courtenay v Parker* (1864) 16 Ir Ch R 20.

[354] Section 128. *Betty v Ecclesiastical Commissioners* (1843) 2 Con & L 520; *Brabazon v Lord Lucan* (1849) 12 Ir Eq R 432; *Re Jackson* (1861) 11 Ir Ch R 145. In the absence of special circumstances the landlord was not entitled to compensation for mere conversion of his reversion into a fee farm rent, *Re Lawless* (1854) 4 Ir Ch R 230; *Thackwell v Jenkins* (1854) 4 Ir Ch R 243.

[355] *Poirez v Collum* [1907] 1 IR 5; *Carson v Jameson* [1908] 2 IR 308.

[356] Section 146. *Courtenay v Parker* (1864) 16 Ir Ch R 320.

Act 1869, prohibited any further conversion grants after January 1 1874.[357] The main reason for this was that the 1869 Act was, in effect, the first of the Land Purchase Acts, under which eventually most tenants of agricultural land were to buy out the unencumbered fee simple of their land, including redemption of any fee farm rents. The Church Temporalities Commissioners established under the 1869 Act, who replaced the Ecclesiastical Commissioners who had operated the earlier 1833 and later Acts, were instructed to sell the unencumbered fee simple of lands still subject to unconverted leases in January 1874.[358] The position is, therefore, that this category of conversion grant would have had to have been created between 1833 and 1874. Furthermore, as we shall see in a moment, it seems clear that these grants came within the scope of the Land Purchase Acts and the Redemption of Rent (Ireland) Act 1891, so that most of them would probably have been subject to redemption under the land purchase scheme.[359] The few that are likely to survive today are probably conversion grants relating to former church property in the urban areas of Ireland.

(b) Trinity College, Dublin, Leasing and Perpetuity Act 1851

[4.080] By the nineteenth century, Trinity College, Dublin owned large estates in many parts of Ireland, but its powers of disposition were limited by statute just as bishops' powers were. The restrictions on the leasing powers of bishops applied also to masters or governors and fellows of colleges,[360] and a similar practice developed of inserting covenants for renewal in college leases.[361] Then the 1851 Act (a local and personal Act) was passed to provide tenants of the College with the right to require the College, at any time within four years of the passing of the Act, to grant them "leases in perpetuity" at a rent.[362] These, in effect, formed another type of conversion fee farm grant.

(c) Renewable Leasehold Conversion Acts

[4.081] During the eighteenth and nineteenth centuries there developed in Ireland the practice of large landowners granting leases for lives (usually three) renewable for ever. The lease contained a covenant for renewal by grant of a lease for a new life whenever one of those for whose life the original lease was granted died, subject, of course, to payment of a fine to the landlord. This practice is discussed in more detail later in this chapter.[363] For the moment it may be said that the significance of these leases was that they were also the subject of legislation in the nineteenth century providing for conversion into fee farm grants. The Renewable Leasehold Conversion Act 1849[364] gave lessees of such leases (and leases for years with a covenant for perpetual

---

[357] Section 31. See also the Irish Church Act 1869, Amendment Act 1872, s 12.

[358] Section 34. *Bernard v Hungerford* [1902] 1 IR 89; *McSweeney v Drapes* [1905] 1 IR 186.

[359] Para **[4.088]** *post*.

[360] See statutes cited in fn 386, para **[4.079]** *supra*.

[361] *Orr v Littlewood* (1859) 8 Ir Ch R 348; *Re Conolly's Estate* (1869) IR 3 Eq 339.

[362] Section 3. The College was also given a discretion to grant leases for 99 years (s 1), and to make perpetuity grants at any time before the expiry of an existing 21 year lease (s 2).

[363] Paras **[4.167]** *et seq, post*.

[364] See also the Renewable Leaseholds Conversion (Ireland) Act 1868.

renewal[365]) the right to obtain a fee farm grant from the lessor, subject to a fee farm rent.[366] The fee farm rent was to be the old leasehold rent plus an estimated sum based on the average annual value of renewal fines.[367] Perhaps even more important was the fact that the 1849 Act went on to say that all future purported leases for lives renewable for ever (or for perpetually renewable years) were to operate automatically as fee farm grants, subject only to the condition that the purported lessor had power to convey a fee simple.[368] It has been stated that not as many lessees as might have been expected took advantage of the 1849 Act,[369] and it is impossible to estimate how many grants have come into operation since 1849 under the automatic conversion provisions. However, note that s 74 of the Republic's Landlord and Tenant (Amendment) Act 1980 now provides that, as from the commencement of the Act, the holder of an interest in land originating under a lease for lives renewable for ever created prior to 1849, and not converted into a fee farm grant under the 1849 Act, holds the land in fee simple, which in this case means one which does *not* include "interest in land of person holding land under a fee farm grant". Thus, whatever it does, s 74 does not convert the landowner's interest into one held under a fee farm grant, as the 1849 Act did (see the definition in s 2(1) of the Landlord and Tenant (Ground Rents) Act 1967, and s 3(1) of the Landlord and Tenant (Ground Rents) (No 2) Act 1978, which was incorporated by s 1(2) of the 1980 Act). At first sight the application of the definition of "fee simple" might be taken to imply that the fee simple is no longer subject to rent, but, in the absence of any provision for compensation to the rentowner, it is highly unlikely that this was intended. Furthermore, s 74 provides that the estate so held "shall be deemed to be a graft upon the previous interest and shall be subject to any rights or equities arising from its being such a graft". This suggests that the section creates a new statutory fee simple held subject to the old rent and other covenants and conditions in the lease for lives renewable forever.[370] In Northern Ireland, Article 36 of the Property (NI) Order 1997, in addition to prohibiting the future creation of perpetually renewable leases,[371] provides for automatic conversion on an appointed day of every subsisting perpetually renewable

---

[365] See definition of "lease in perpetuity" in s 38. *Cf* the definition in Article 36(1) of the Property (NI) Order 1997: *infra* and para **[4.176]** *post*.

[366] Section 1. *Ex parte Waldron* (1850) 1 Ir Ch R 269; *Ex parte Barlow* (1852) 2 Ir Ch R 272; *Re Gore* (1858) 8 Ir Ch R 589; *Palmer v Slaney* (1863) 14 Ir Ch R 540; *Ex parte Murray* (1872) IR 6 Eq 534; *Ex parte Guerin* (1870) IR 4 Eq 467; *Ex parte Walsh* (1874) IR 8 Eq 146; *Ex parte Quinn* [1895] 1 IR 187. It seems that some landlords procured private legislation conferring powers to make fee farm grants to tenants on their estates, see *Layard v Donegal* (1861) 8 HLC 460. The Act also applied, at least as regards post-1849 leases, to leases for years (as opposed to lives) renewable for ever, see s 37.

[367] Section 2. *Ex parte Keatinge* (1867) IR 2 Eq 26; *Ex parte Hutchinson* (1871) IR 6 Eq 34; *Ex parte Scott* [1906] 1 IR 159; *Fitzpatrick v Warren* [1917] 1 IR 156.

[368] Section 37. *Forde v Brew* (1865) 17 Ir Ch R 1; *Sheridan v Nesbitt* (1896) 30 ILTR 39.

[369] *Report of the Committee on Registration of Title to Land in Northern Ireland* (1967; Cmd 512), para 123.

[370] Wylie, *Irish Landlord and Tenant Law*, para 4.045 and pp 1181-81; Laffoy, *Irish Conveyancing Precedents*, Precedent E.1.12.

[371] See para **[4.167]** *post*.

lease[372] into a fee farm grant, provided the rent is still being paid under the lease.[373] Like the Republic's 1980 Act, the 1997 Order provides that the new grant is subject to the same covenants, conditions and other provisions of the old lease[374] but, unlike the 1980 Act, the 1997 Order also contains detailed provisions for adjustment of the rent to compensate for loss of renewal fines.[375]

(ii) Words of Limitation

[4.082] It seems to be settled law that, despite the fact that a conversion grant involves the conveyance of a fee simple estate which would normally require the use of appropriate words of limitation, such words are not necessary in grants purporting to operate under the relevant statutory provisions. It was held in *Re Johnston's Estate*[376] that a conversion grant purporting to have been executed under the Renewable Leasehold Conversion Act 1849 passed a fee simple despite the absence of any words of limitation. This decision may be taken as indicative of a general judicial attitude to conversion grants to the effect that they are special creatures of statute law and, as such, should not necessarily be subjected to the common law rules relating to conveyances of freehold estates in general, or of a fee simple estate in particular.[377] We shall see that this attitude has come to light in other contexts in Irish cases.

(iii) Fee Farm Rents

[4.083] The various statutes dealing with conversion of leases into fee farm grants usually provided as part of the process of conversion that the fee farm rent was to be recoverable by the same remedies as the old leasehold rents.[378] In other words the fee farm grantor, as he became under the conversion, had the remedies of a landlord, in particular the right of distress and ejectment for non-payment of rent.[379] Thus ss 20 and 21 of the Renewable Leasehold Conversion Act 1849, provided that the fee farm rents were to be recoverable by a landlord's normal remedies for recovery of a rent service.[380] And in Ireland this included the special statutory remedy of ejectment for non-payment of rent.[381]

---

[372] Both leases for lives and for years, and combinations of these, renewable forever: Article 36(1). *Cf* s 74 of the 1980 Act.

[373] It does not matter that lives have not been renewed or renewal fines have not been paid: Article 36(9).

[374] But *not* those relating to renewal fines nor provisions prohibiting alienation or otherwise repugnant to a fee simple: Sch 2, para 1(1).

[375] Sch 1, para 7-8,

[376] [1911] 1 IR 215.

[377] Murray J quoted this sentence as "helpful" in *Re Courtney* [1981] Nl 58 at 65.

[378] See, eg, as regards converted bishops' leases, the Church Temporalities Act 1833, s 14.

[379] See, generally, Ch 17, *post*; *Re Hassett's Estate* (1898) 32 ILTR 115.

[380] *Att-Gen v Wilson* (1893) 31 LR Ir 28 at 48-53 (*per* Palles CB).

[381] Para **[17.098]** *post*.

(iv) Forfeiture

[4.084] As regards non-payment of rent, it was unlikely that a conversion fee farm grantor would concern himself with forfeiture since he had the statutory right of ejectment for non-payment of rent. However, there was nothing to prevent reservation of a right of forfeiture in the conversion grant and, indeed, one of the standard precedents included such a right.[382] As has been mentioned earlier,[383] there seems to be no statute law in Ireland governing exercise of a right of forfeiture for non-payment of rent such as that contained in the English Common Law Procedure Act 1852.

As regards forfeiture for breach of obligations other than those relating to the fee farm rent, it seems clear that conversion fee farm grants come within s 14 of the Conveyancing Act 1881 as amended by ss 2 and 5 of the Conveyancing Act 1892. These provisions govern the exercise by the grantor of any powers of re entry reserved in the grant for breach of the grantee's obligations.[384] A conversion fee farm grant, creates the modern relationship of landlord and tenant between the grantor and grantee and so would clearly seem to come within the definition of a lease (as including a fee farm grant) in s 14(3) of the 1881 Act.[385]

(v) Covenants

[4.085] It has been a matter of some controversy whether the ordinary common law with respect to covenants attached to a fee simple estate applies to conversion fee farm grants. The majority view amongst Irish judges has been that these grants are statutory creations to which the common law rules should not necessarily be applied; in particular, they are conversions of leases and this factor should be borne in mind in construing the relevant statutory provisions. Since these provisions usually stated that the covenants contained in the converted lease were to continue in force to the same extent when the conversion to the fee farm grant occurred, the result of the cases has been generally to apply the law of leasehold covenants rather than freehold covenants to conversion grants.[386] The Church Temporalities Act 1833 specified that the fee simple conveyed in the conversion grant was to be vested in the grantee "for the like estate, estates or interests, and to and upon the same uses, trusts, intents and purposes respectively (or as near thereto as the nature of each case and the difference of interest will admit)".[387] It is questionable whether the qualification in brackets would prevent the application of the law of leasehold covenants to Church Temporality grants. The judges tended, in construing this provision, to put emphasis on what the position of the lessee was under the unconverted lease and, then, to strive to assimilate his position as grantee after the conversion to that as far as possible.[388]

---

[382] Stubbs and Baxter, *Irish Form and Precedents* (1910), Precedent No 1, p 121.

[383] Paras **[4.065]-[4.068]** *ante.*

[384] Para **[17.087]** *et seq, post.*

[385] Para **[4.068]** *ante.* For s 14's application to a lease for lives renewable for ever, see *Ruttledge v Whelan* (1882) 10 LR Ir 263; to a fee farm grant, *Walsh v Wightman* [1927] NI 1.

[386] See Ch 19, *post.*

[387] Section 148. See *Dockrill v Dolan* (1841) 3 Ir Eq R 552; *Clarke v Staples* (1843) 5 Ir Eq R 246; *Hilhouse v Tyndall* (1849) 13 Ir Eq R 209.

[388] See, eg, *Campbell v Ross* (1856) 7 Ir Ch R 222; *Re Dane's Estate* (1871) IR 5 Eq 498; *Re Dane's Estate* (1876) IR 10 Eq 207.

[4.086] Section 1 of the Renewable Leasehold Conversion Act 1849 stated that a conversion grant made under the Act was to be subject to the same "covenants, conditions, exceptions, and reservations" as the lease before conversion (other than, of course, the covenant for renewal).[389] Section 7 stated that the fee simple was to be subject to the same "uses, trusts, provisos, agreements ... charges, liens, incumbrances, and equities" as the lease before conversion.[390] Section 10 provided that the benefit and burdens of all covenants implied in leases under the general law of landlord and tenant, and all covenants to be contained in grants under the Act, were to run with the land as if the fee farm grantee were the lessee or his assignee and the grantor the lessor or his assignee.[391] Questions arose over these provisions whether they should be interpreted widely to mean that covenants usual and valid when contained in leases could continue as valid and enforceable in the conversion grants of the fee simple, even though under the general common law they could not be attached to a freehold estate. For example, a covenant prohibiting alienation (assignment, subletting or otherwise parting with possession), or restricting it to occasions when the landlord gave consent, was a common clause in a lease, but would usually be invalid in a conveyance of a freehold as infringing the rule against inalienability and, in the case of a fee simple, as being repugnant to the nature of the estate granted.[392] The general judicial view seems to have been that these clauses would continue as valid and enforceable in conversion grants. This was certainly the view of the Court of Appeal in *Re McNaul's Estate*,[393] where the converted lease had contained a covenant by the lessee to pay a higher rent if he alienated without the lessor's consent to someone other than a child or grandchild of the lessor. This covenant was held to be valid in the conversion grant. The court did indicate that it was open to doubt whether such a covenant was properly regarded as a restriction on alienation at all[394] or, if it was, whether it was a sufficient restraint as to be void even in a conveyance of a fee simple at common law.[395] However, an earlier case, *Billing v Welch*,[396] which had held that, if a covenant would be void if contained in an ordinary grant in fee simple, it should be also held void when inserted in a fee simple grant under

---

[389] *Mahony v Tynte* (1851) 1 Ir Ch R 577; *Kent v Stoney* (1858) 9 Ir Ch R 249; *Gore v O'Grady* (1867) IR 1 Eq 1; *Quinn v Shields* (1877) IR 11 CL 254; *Fishbourne v Hamilton* (1890) 25 LR Ir 483.

[390] Thus a conversion fee farm grant has been held not to be a good root of title, *Dawson v Baxter* (1886) 19 LR Ir 103; *Re Carew's Estate* (1887) 19 LR Ir 483; *Maconchy v Clayton* [1898] 1 IR 291; *Smyth v Shaftesbury* (1901) 1 NIJR 34; *Re Garde Browne* [1911] 1 IR 205; *cf McClenaghan v Bankhead* (1874) IR 8 CL 195. *Quaere* whether this is still good law, see Wylie, *Irish Conveyancing Law* (1978), paras 13.11 and 13.56.

[391] *Re Quin* (1858) 8 Ir Ch Rep 578; *Dooner v Odlum* [1914] 2 IR 411. See discussion of parties' position after a grant under the Act by Barry J in *Morris v Morris* (1872) IR 7 CL 295, 297-9.

[392] Para **[4.051]** *ante*. See *Re Lunham's Estate* (1871) IR 5 Eq 170.

[393] [1902] 1 IR 114 (see *A Casebook on Irish Land Law* (1984), p 41).

[394] Thus FitzGibbon LJ stated that in the court's opinion it was "not a covenant prohibiting alienation - on the contrary, it permitted alienation on the terms of paying the additional rent." *Ibid*, p 125. *Cf*, Walker LJ at p 133.

[395] Thus Holmes LJ stated that the "restraint of alienation is of a limited and partial character." *Ibid*, p 137.

[396] (1871) IR 6 CL 88. *Cf Re Quin* (1858) 8 Ir Ch R 578; *Ex parte Raymond* (1874) IR 8 Eq 231.

the Renewable Leasehold Conversion Act,[397] was expressly overruled by the Court of Appeal in *McNaul's* case in so far as it held void such covenants "upon the ground of repugnancy to a common law estate in fee".[398] As has been stated earlier,[399] the Court of Appeal were agreed that the 1849 Act created a special statutory fee simple estate to which were annexed incidents generally recognised as attaching to leasehold estates only.[400] It would seem that the same principle would apply to the fee simple estate vested by s 74 of the Republic's Landlord and Tenant (Amendment) Act 1980 in a person holding under a pre-1849 lease for lives renewable for ever and not converted into a fee farm grant under that Act. As we saw earlier,[401] that estate is deemed to be a graft upon the previous (leasehold) interest and is subject to "any" rights or equities arising from its being such a graft. However, it does *not* apply to the fee simple subject to a fee farm rent into which perpetually renewable leasehold interests are converted under Article 31 of Property (NI) Order 1997.[402] Although that fee simple is also generally "subject to the same conditions, covenants, exception and reservations as in the lease"[403] and "is for all purposes a graft on the estate created by the lease and is subject to any rights or equities arising from its being such a graft", expressly excepted from these provisions are those "prohibiting or restricting assignment, sub-demise or parting with possession"[404] or "any other provisions that are repugnant to a fee simple".[405] It is clear, therefore, that such statutory fee farm grants, notwithstanding their leasehold origin, are governed by the principles relating to freehold estates, such as the rule against inalienability[406] and general law of repugnancy on grounds of public policy.[407]

---

[397] *Per* O'Brien J, *ibid*, p 103.

[398] *Per* FitzGibbon LJ, *op cit*, p 124, who had earlier stated that the court held, in general, "that the doctrine of repugnancy applicable at common law to an estate in fee is modified, in the case of fee-farm grants founded on renewable leases." *Cf Bell v Belfast Corporation* [1914] 2 IR 1, where the court held that a grantee under a conversion grant was not liable for waste for which a lessee would ordinarily have been liable, para **[17.058]** *post*.

[399] Para **[4.082]** *ante*.

[400] See *op cit*, p 124 (FitzGibbon LJ) and p 133 (Walker LJ). It may be noted that the Irish Land Act 1903, s 70, provided that no restraint on alienation contained in any fee farm grant was to impede a sale under the Land Purchase Acts, whether or not the restraint was valid. For sales under the Land Purchase Acts, with redemption of fee farm rents, see *Re Leader's Estate* [1904] 1 IR 368; *Re O'Donoghue's Estate* (1912) 46 ILTR 83; *Re Dawson's Estate* (1912) 46 ILTR 288; *Colles v Hornsby* [1913] 2 IR 210; *Re Foley* (1912) 46 ILTR 96; *McCarthy v Anderson* (1912) 46 ILTR 96; *Re Briscoe's Estate* (1913) 47 ILTR 64.

[401] Para **[4.081]** *ante*.

[402] See *ibid*.

[403] Sch 2, para 1(2).

[404] *Ibid* para 1(2)(b).

[405] *Ibid* para 1(2)(c).

[406] Para **[4.051]** *ante*.

[407] Para **[4.052]** *et seq, ante*.

(vi) Redemption

(a) Chief Rents Redemption (Ireland) Act 1864

[4.087] Although by its terms this Act seems to apply to all fee farm grants, it may be doubted whether it was envisaged by its draftsmen that it would extend to special statutory conversion grants. There is no authority at all on the point which must be regarded as unsettled. However, it is no longer of practical importance in view of later legislation.

(b) Redemption of Rent (Ireland) Act 1891

[4.088] It has been settled that this Act did apply to fee farm conversion grants so as to facilitate redemption of fee farm rents as part of the land purchase scheme for agricultural holdings. Thus Bewley J held in *Hamilton v Casey*[408] that a sub-grant under the Church Temporalities Act 1833 was a fee farm grant within the 1891 Act,[409] and the same was held with respect to a grant under the Trinity College Act 1851 in *Gormill v Lyne*.[410] It has similarly been held that conversion grants operating under the Renewable Leasehold Conversion Act 1849 came within the 1891 Act.[411] It is easy to understand these decisions in view of the amount of agricultural land which used to be held under leases for lives renewable for ever and which would probably have become land held under converted fee farm grants.[412] It was important to the land purchase scheme that as much agricultural land as possible should come within its scope.[413]

(c) Landlord and Tenant (Ground Rents) Act 1967 and (No 2) Act 1978 (RI)

[4.089] It seems clear, for the reasons given earlier,[414] that a tenant purchasing the fee simple under these Acts would have to redeem any fee farm rents in the chain of title to the fee simple.

(d) Leasehold (Enlargement and Extension) Act (NI) 1971 and Property (NI) Order 1997

[4.090] It also seems clear, again for the reasons given earlier,[415] that the 1971 Act provided for redemption of fee farm rents as part of the enfranchisement process by urban tenants, and also that it probably provided for redemption by fee farm grantees in occupation of land independent of enfranchisement by "ground" lessees. It is certainly

---

[408] [1894] 2 IR 224.

[409] See also Palles CB in *Adams v Alexander* [1895] 2 IR 363 at 372.

[410] (1894) 28 ILTR 44.

[411] *Gun-Cunningham v Byrne* (1892) 30 LR Ir 384; *Sheridan v Nesbitt* (1896) 30 ILTR 39; *Langtry v Sheridan* (1896) 30 ILTR 64. See also Palles CB in *Adams v Alexander, op cit.*

[412] The Devon Commission (para **[1.041]** *ante*) reported that about 1/7th of the land in Ireland was held under perpetually renewable leaseholds in the mid-nineteenth century.

[413] See also s 14 of the Land Law (Ireland) Act 1896, fn 368, para **[4.075]** *ante*.

[414] Para **[4.076]** *ante*.

[415] Para **[4.077]** *ante*.

the case that redemption of ground rents under the 1997 Order includes redemption of a fee farm rent.[416]

3. Deasy's Act Grants

[4.091] Perhaps the most significant development in the growth of fee farm grants in Ireland was the passing of Deasy's Act - the Landlord and Tenant Law Amendment Act, Ireland 1860.[417] The reason was the wording of s 3 of that Act -

> The relation of landlord and tenant shall be deemed to be founded on the express or implied contract of the parties, and not upon tenure or service, *and a reversion shall not be necessary to such relation*, which shall be deemed to subsist in all cases in which there shall be an agreement by one party to hold land from or under another in consideration of any rent.[418]

[4.092] The operation of this section on the general law of landlord and tenant will be more fully discussed in a later chapter.[419] For the moment its significance lies in the fact that it facilitated, from 1 January 1861 onwards,[420] the making of fee farm grants creating the full relationship of landlord and tenant between the grantor and grantee. In other words, the grantor and grantee of such a grant were to be treated almost exactly as if the former were a landlord and the latter a tenant as regards their rights and duties and the remedies for enforcement of these.[421] This construction of s 3 obviously had a revolutionary effect on the law of estates in land in Ireland, because the 1860 Act was of general application and not confined to special situations as in the case of conversion grants. For this reason there were some doubts expressed about the application of s 3 to grants of a fee simple, especially since *Quia Emptores* was not included in the repeal schedule of Deasy's Act.[422] This, however, seems to confuse once again the feudal relationship of lord and tenant with the modern relationship of landlord and tenant; *Quia Emptores* did not apply to the latter and s 3 was simply extending its range.[423] The confusion from the common lawyer's point of view is, of course, perfectly understandable because the extension was so revolutionary. It involved an invasion of the territory of the old feudal law (freehold tenure and estates) by modern landlord and tenant law. The wording of s 3, however, seems clearly wide enough to support this

---

[416] See the definition of "ground rent" in Article 3(1), *ibid*.

[417] See, generally, Ch 17, *post*.

[418] Italics added. Prior to the Act the common law position had been confirmed in Ireland that a reversion in the landlord was a prerequisite of the relationship, see *Pluck v Digges* (1828) 2 Hud & Br 1; *Porter v French* (1844) 9 Ir LR 514. Also *Fawcett v Hall* (1833) Alc & Nap 248.

[419] Ch 17, *post*.

[420] The date of operation of the Act was fixed by s 105. It was held in *Chute v Busteed* (1865) 16 ICLR 222 (see *A Casebook on Irish Land Law* (1984), p 155) that s 3 was not retrospective in operation; see also *McAreavy v Hannan* (1861) 13 ICLR 70.

[421] See, generally, Ch 17, *post*. Limitations on this statement are considered below, paras **[4.097]** *et seq*, *post*.

[422] See eg, remarks by Christian J in *Chute v Busteed*, *op cit*, p 246; also Stubbs and Baxter, *Irish Forms and Precedents* (1910), p 89.

[423] Para **[4.064]** *ante*.

broad view of its effect and the fact remains that this view has been generally accepted by Irish conveyancers ever since its enactment. Thus Christian J in *Chute v Busteed*[424] commented on the effect of s 3:

> "I think it might fairly be argued that an instrument executed after this statute had been passed ought to be construed with reference to the new law founded by the statute; and that if worded as this deed is, like an ordinary lease, it should be held to embody an agreement that the new statutable relation of landlord and tenant should exist -a relationship discharged of the element of tenure and reversion, and resting exclusively on contract."[425]

Numerous grants purporting to operate under Deasy's Act have been made and acted upon without question for decades. The only limitation recognised by the legal profession has been that special care should be taken in drafting the wording of such grants, a matter to which we now turn. Before doing so it may be queried whether the future creation of fee farm grants has been curtailed in the Republic by the Landlord and Tenant (Ground Rents) Act 1978. Section 2(1) of this Act renders void a "lease" of "dwellings" only if the "lessee" could, apart from the Act, have the right to acquire the fee simple under s 3 of the Landlord and Tenant (Ground Rents) Act 1967 (since replaced and extended by Part II of the Landlord and Tenant (Ground Rents) (No 2) Act 1978).[426] But, as mentioned earlier,[427] a "lease" for these purposes is defined as including a "fee farm grant" (see now s 3 of the Landlord and Tenant (Ground Rents) (No 2) Act 1978)[428] it is arguable that a fee farm grantee who already holds the fee simple can be regarded as having the right to invoke the acquisition procedures contained in the legislation. Of course, the most that he could achieve would be redemption of the fee farm rent so as to leave him with an unencumbered fee simple[429] and it is not clear whether the legislation applies to such a limited exercise. It certainly seems to be stretching the language to breaking-point to call "redemption of fee farm rents" the "enlargement of [the fee farm grantee's] interest into a fee simple" (s 3 of the Landlord and Tenant (Ground Rents) Act 1978), or to speak of conveying to or vesting in the grantee an estate which he already holds. If the matter is looked at in terms of the policy of the Landlord and Tenant (Ground Rents) Act 1978, in prohibiting future creation of ground rents, it can be said, on the one hand, that a fee farm grantee does not suffer from the lack of security of tenure and in particular the danger of losing a home he or his predecessors built at their own expense that a lessee does. And it may be argued that it is these inequities that the legislation is primarily aimed at; on the other hand, a fee farm grantee, like a lessee, is subject to the burden of a form of "ground" rent and, of course, to the grantor's remedy of forfeiture or ejectment for non-payment,

---

[424] (1865) 16 ICLR 222.

[425] *Op cit*, p 246. See also *Kelly v Rattey* (1893) 32 LR Ir 445, especially Walker C at p 449; *Adams v Alexander* [1895] 2 IR 363, especially Barry LJ at p 383.

[426] See Wylie, *Irish Landlord and Tenant Law*, Ch 31.

[427] Para **[4.076]** *ante*.

[428] The two 1978 Acts are to be construed together, 1978 (No 2) Act, s 1(2).

[429] This was the view of Keane J in the *Arch Properties* case, para **[4.076]** fn 376 *ante*.

and it may be argued that it was also the intention of the legislators to remove such burdens from the Irish scene. In Northern Ireland the position is much clearer under the Property (NI) Order 1997. Articles 28-31 give effect to the policy espoused by the Land Law Working Group[430] of prohibiting the future creation of ground rents of most kinds.[431] Article 28, as we saw earlier,[432] prohibits, as from a day to be appointed, the creation of fee farm grants of any kind in respect of any type of property.

(i) Creation

[4.093] From what has already been said, and especially in view of the doubts about the precise effect of s 3, a fee farm grant purporting to operate under Deasy's Act must indicate an intention to create the "relation of landlord and tenant" between the parties.[433] As s 3 says, this may be founded on the "express or implied contract of the parties," and the practice has been adopted by Irish conveyancers of drafting these fee farm grants along the lines of a lease, with appropriate modifications.[434] The precedents for such a grant most commonly used contain a recital which states expressly something like "Whereas the parties hereto have agreed that a contract of tenancy and the relation of landlord and tenant shall be created between them ..."[435]

[4.094] As regards the instrument of conveyance, a deed is in practice always used for a fee farm grant, as it is for any lease for a substantial term of years. Theoretically there would seem to be no more need for a deed in the case of a grant than in the case of a lease operating under Deasy's Act. Under s 4 of the Act:

> Every lease *or contract* with respect to lands whereby the relation of landlord and tenant is intended to be created for *any freehold estate or interest*, or for any definite period not being from year to year or any lesser period, shall be by deed executed, *or note in writing* signed by the landlord or his agent thereunto lawfully authorised in writing.[436]

Deasy's Act does expressly amend the Real Property Act 1845 (s 2 of which introduced the deed as an alternative mode of conveyance for freehold land), so far as s 3 related to the relationship of landlord and tenant in Ireland.[437] So a written instrument in writing

[430] *Final Report* (HMSO 1990), Ch 1.6.

[431] Various exceptions apply in the case of long lease, Article 30 and see *ibid* para 1.6.3.

[432] Para **[4.057]** *ante*.

[433] Indeed, it has been suggested that some conveyancers attempted to avoid interpretation problems with such grants by deliberately drafting instead a perpetually renewable lease, which would operate automatically as a fee farm grant under s 37 of the Renewable Leasehold Conversion Act 1849 (para **[4.081]** *ante*), see Stubbs and Baxter, *Irish Forms and Precedents* (1910), p 90. In view of the general acceptance now of the validity of Deasy's Act grants this is rarely, if ever, done today. See Wylie, *Irish Conveyancing Law* (2nd ed, 1996), para 19.37 *et seq*.

[434] Eg, the parties are usually referred to as the "grantor" and "grantee", rather than as the "lessor" and "lessee".

[435] See, eg, Stubbs and Baxter, *op cit*, Precedent 2, p 122. But such a recital is not, apparently, strictly necessary, see *Re Courtney* [1981] NI 58 at 63 (*per* Murray J).

[436] Italics added. And s 1 defines "lease" as meaning "any instrument in writing, whether under seal or not, containing a contract of tenancy in respect of any lands, in consideration of a rent or return."

[437] Schedule B.

not under seal would seem to suffice for a Deasy's Act fee farm grant despite its granting of a fee simple estate, unless a deed is necessary for some special reason, eg, reservation of an easement.[438]

(ii) Words of Limitation

[4.095] It has been suggested that another effect of s 3 of Deasy's Act was that a fee farm grant executed under it could operate without any of the words of limitation requisite at common law in a conveyance of a fee simple.[439] The reasoning is that, since s 3 rests the matter entirely upon the express or implied contract of the parties, all that is necessary is that the particular instrument should indicate an intention to create the relationship of landlord and tenant for an estate in fee simple. Thus, the reasoning continues, a clause such as "to A for ever" would be sufficient in a fee farm grant without any further words of limitation. The only real authority on the point seems to be *Twaddle v Murphy*,[440] which does not support the reasoning. That case involved a deed which granted and demised land to "A and B, *their heirs and assigns*, for the lives of C, D and E, or for 999 years, *or for ever*, whichever should last longest".[441] The court held that this was a fee farm grant, the largest estate (fee simple) absorbing the inferior estates.[442] It is true that the court laid some stress on the words "for ever" as an indication of intention in relation to the question of construction of the wording of the grant,[443] but it did not decide that these words were sufficient in themselves to allow the conveyance to operate as a fee farm grant. The fact is that the conveyance in this case did contain appropriate words of limitation for an ordinary conveyance of a fee simple - the words "heirs and assigns". The standard formula in practice used by conveyancers in Ireland for Deasy's Act grants is an *habendum* as follows: "To hold the said premises unto the grantee his heirs and assigns for ever".[444]

[4.096] Apart from *Twaddle v Murphy*, it is suggested that, as a matter of principle, Deasy's Act does not dispense with the necessity for words of limitation in a fee farm grant. The crucial point is once again the operation of s 3.[445] The better view is that the section should be regarded only as extending the scope of the relationship of landlord and tenant to cover estates and interests that would not come within that relationship at

---

[438] See *Re Courtney* [1981] NI 58 at 67 (*per* Murray J - deed unnecessary for a conveyance of land held under a fee farm grant). As regards reservation of easements, see para **[6.056]** *et seq, post*.

[439] See, eg, Cherry, *Irish Land Law and Land Purchase Acts* (3rd ed, 1903), p 5, fn c, citing *Twaddle v Murphy* (1881) 8 LR Ir 123 and a dictum of Palles CB in *Hodges v Clarke* (1883) 17 ILTR 82 at 84: "When we are obliged to determine for what period a tenant holds, we are bound to look to the agreement of the parties."

[440] (1881) 8 LR Ir 123 (see *A Casebook on Irish Land Law* (1984), p 113).

[441] Italics added.

[442] Para **[4.025]** *ante*.

[443] See May CJ, *op cit*, p 127.

[444] Stubbs and Baxter, *Irish Forms and Precedents* (1910), Precedent 2, p 123. *Cf* a conversion grant, Precedent 1, p 120. The reasoning in this and the next paragraph was adopted expressly by Murray J in *Re Courtney* [1981] NI 58 at 65-6. See also Wylie, *Irish Conveyancing Law* (2nd ed, 1996), para 19.42.

[445] See discussion in Montrose, 'Fee Farm Grants' (1939) 3 NILQ 143; (1940) 4 NILQ 40 and 86.

common law. That does not mean that the section goes further and alters the nature of the estate and abolishes all its normal incidents. It should be regarded only as doing this where other provisions in Deasy's Act make it clear. Section 3 says only that a reversion is no longer necessary and that the relationship of landlord and tenant can arise when the appropriate intention is shown. Section 4 goes on to talk of an intention to create that relationship "for any freehold estate or interest," but does not say how such an estate is to be created. The implication would seem to be that intention to create a particular estate should be indicated in the same way as before the Act; in other words, by the words of limitation appropriate for that estate.[446] As one learned writer on the subject concluded with respect to leases for a term of years, on the one other hand, executed under Deasy's Act:

> "There is no complete assimilation of the two, no radical change. The creation of the relation of landlord and tenant in fee farm grants means only that certain incidents of leases for years become also incidents of fee farm grants."[447]

It may be convenient then at this point to consider other aspects of Deasy's Act grants in an attempt to clarify the extent of assimilation with leases for years.

(iii) Fee Farm Rents

[4.097] Since a Deasy's Act grant creates *ex hypothesi* the relationship of landlord and tenant, a grantor has all the usual remedies of a landlord for recovery of his fee farm rent - action for debt, distress[448] and ejectment for non-payment of rent. These remedies are covered by several other provisions in Deasy's Act itself (it was essentially a consolidating Act for most of the earlier legislation on landlord and tenant).[449] Section 52 of the Act specifically refers to application of the statutory action of ejectment for non-payment of rent, dealt with in it and subsequent sections, to "any fee farm, grant".[450] The word "any" would seem to be misleading; this section, like all of Deasy's Act, is confined to grants creating the relationship of landlord and tenant.[451]

---

[446] For some *dicta*, not always very helpful, on this subject, see *Chute v Busteed* (1862) 14 ICLR 115 at 130 (Fitzgerald B), (1865) 16 ICLR 222 at 230 (O'Hagan J), at 244 (Christian J) (see *A Casebook on Irish Land Law* (1984), p 155); *Gordon v Phelan* (1878) 12 ILTR 70 (Fitzgerald B); *Hodges v Clarke* (1883) 17 ILTR 82 at 84 (Palles CB); *Seymour v Quirke* (1884) 14 LR Ir 455 (CA); *Donelly v Galbraith* (1884) 18 ILTR 54 (Bewley J); *O'Sullivan v Ambrose* (1893) 32 LR Ir 102 (Madden J); *Re Maunsell's Estate* [1911] 1 IR 271 (Ross J).

[447] Montrose, (1940) 4 NILQ 86, 91. On the basis of this reasoning Murray J held that words of limitation are necessary in a conveyance of land held under a fee farm grant, even though, in the case of a Deasy's Act grant, s 9 of Deasy's Act renders a deed unnecessary. See *Re Courtney* [1981] NI 58 and para **[17.029]** *post*.

[448] Abolished now in Northern Ireland, para **[17.066]** *post*. See *Irish Land Commission v Holmes* (1898) 32 ILTR 85.

[449] Discussed in more detail in Ch 17, *post*.

[450] On s 52, see *Chute v Busteed* (1862) 14 ICLR 115, (1865) 16 ICLR 222; *Mennons v Burke* (1890) 26 LR Ir 193; *Eustace-Duckett v Thompson* (1938) 72 ILTR 226. The comma is presumably a draftsman's error or idiosyncrasy.

[451] *Cf*, the Fee Farm Rents (Ireland) Act 1851, which expressly excluded the remedy of ejectment for non-payment of rent, para **[4.064]** *ante*, and which was not expressly amended by Deasy's Act.

(iv) Forfeiture

[4.098] Once again, the law relating to landlord and tenant applies. The remedy of ejectment for non-payment of rent may be invoked by the fee farm grantor. The grant may also include an express right of re-entry for non-payment of rent,[452] in which case the grantor may invoke this remedy instead of his statutory action of ejectment. It has already been stated that there appear to be no statutory restrictions on the exercise of such a right of re-entry in Ireland.[453]

As regards forfeiture for breach of covenants other than those relating to rent, Deasy's Act grants would clearly seem to come within s 14 of the Conveyancing Act 1881, which does certain restrictions on the grantor's exercise of rights under any forfeiture clause relating to such covenants.[454]

(v) Covenants

[4.099] Deasy's Act contains various provisions relating to covenants. Section 41 specifies covenants or agreements to be implied in every "lease" on behalf of the "landlord" (for good title and quiet enjoyment[455]) and s 42 covenants or agreements to be implied on behalf of the "tenant" (to pay the rent and taxes, keep in repair and give up peaceable possession on determination of the lease).[456] "Lease" is defined by the Act to mean "any instrument in writing ... containing a contract of tenancy"; "landlord" is defined as including the person entitled to the landlord's interest "under any lease or other contract of tenancy ... and whether he has a reversion or not"; "tenant" is defined as meaning "the person entitled to any lands under any lease or other contract of tenancy".[457] This wording would seem to be wide enough to cover fee farm grants coming within the Act, so as to assimilate them with leases for the purposes of implied covenants. There seems to be no authority on the point which, in practice, is of academic interest only. Invariably, most fee farm grants, like most leases, have express covenants inserted in them by their draftsmen, who are usually loath to leave such matters to the general law.[458]

[4.100] Sections 12 and 13 of Deasy's Act provide for the running of the benefit and burden of landlords' and tenants' covenants or agreements "contained or implied" in "any lease or other contract of tenancy" so as to bind successors in title of both parties.[459] Once again the wording seems to be wide enough to cover fee farm grants operating under the Act. Clearly this was the assumption of the court in *Chute v*

---

[452] Thus the precedent in Stubbs and Baxter, *Irish Forms and Precedents* (1910), does contain one, see p 124.

[453] Para **[4.067]** *ante*.

[454] Para **[4.068]** *ante*, and see para **[17.087]** *et seq, post*. See also *Walsh v Wightman* [1927] NI 1; *Whipp v Mackey* [1927] IR 372.

[455] See *Riordan v Carroll* [1996] 2 ILRM 263.

[456] On these covenants generally, see para **[17.040]** *et seq, post*.

[457] Section 1.

[458] See Precedent No 2 in Stubbs and Baxter, *Irish Forms and Precedents* (1910) pp 122-3.

[459] See, generally, para **[17.071]**, *et seq, post*.

Busteed,[460] where the Court of Exchequer held that, since s 3 was not retrospective, the provisions of Deasy's Act relating to covenants did not apply to a fee farm grant executed in 1826.[461]

[4.101] Some controversy has arisen, however, in academic circles whether s 10 of Deasy's Act applied to fee farm grants within the Act.[462] This section specified that, if any lease contained an agreement restraining or prohibiting assignment, it was not "lawful" to assign contrary to such agreement without the consent in writing of the landlord or his agent.[463] The question was raised whether this section also applied to fee farm grants, and whether such an agreement in a grant would have been valid generally in the light of *Quia Emptores*. Some have argued that a negative reply should be given to this question, on the ground that the estate granted remained a fee simple and *Quia Emptores* was not expressly repealed by Deasy's Act. It has been argued that the general principle should be maintained that Deasy's Act does not alter the nature of the estate granted and does not decree that a freehold estate should assume the characteristics of a leasehold estate for all purposes. It has been further suggested that s 10 should be read as presupposing that such an "agreement" would have been valid anyway, ie, judged according to the law before Deasy's Act. This construction, however, is difficult to reconcile with the courts' attitude to other sections in the Act, such as ss 12 and 13.[464] In *Chute v Busteed*, the court discussed *Quia Emptores* in relation to Deasy's Act, and one is left to consider the effect of Christian J's dictum that "it might fairly be argued that an instrument executed after this statute had been passed ought to be construed with reference to the new law founded by the statute."[465] This could be regarded as an indication that fee farm grants operating under Deasy's Act should be treated in the same way as conversion grants, ie, creating a special statutory fee simple to which the usual common law characteristics should not necessarily be attached.[466]

(vi) Redemption

(a) Chief Rents Redemption (Ireland) Act 1864

[4.102] As a matter of literal construction, the wide wording of this Act would seem to cover Deasy's Act grants.[467] It might be questioned, though, whether an Act passed only

---

[460] (1865) 16 ICLR 222 (see *A Casebook on Irish Land Law* (1984), p 155).

[461] The successor in title of the original grantor was held not able to enforce (against the successor of the original grantee) a covenant to keep and deliver up in good repair a wall.

[462] See also para **[17.035]** *et seq, post.*

[463] See *Craigdarragh Trading Co Ltd v Doherty* [1989] NI 218. Section 10 was repealed in the Republic by s 35(1) of the Landlord and Tenant (Ground Rents) Act 1967. See Wylie, *Irish Landlord and Tenant Law*, para 21.08 *et seq.*

[464] *Cf*, the question of the necessity for words of limitation, paras **[4.095]**-**[4.096]** *supra.*

[465] Para **[4.092]**, *supra. Cf*, Bewley J in *Donelly v Galbraith* (1894) 28 ILTR 54; *Re McClatchie and Smyth's Contract* (1904) 38 ILTR 35.

[466] Para **[4.086]** *ante. Cf*, Montrose, (1940) 4 NILQ 86; Stubbs and Baxter, *Irish Forms and Precedents* (1910), p 109.

[467] Note that the Act will be repealed in NI by the Property (NI) Order 1997, Article 53(2) and Sch 5.

some four years later was intended to allow redemption in the case of grants that could be created only from 1860 onwards. There is no authority on the point.

(b) Redemption of Rent (Ireland) Act 1891

[4.103] This Act, especially in view of the amendment contained in s 14(b) of the Land Law (Ireland) Act 1896,[468] applied to Deasy's Act grants of agricultural land in order to facilitate redemption as part of the land purchase scheme. Deasy's Act grants create *ex hypothesi* the relationship of landlord and tenant and this, as s 14(b) clearly presupposes and the judges confirmed, was the essential prerequisite for the application of the 1891 Act.[469]

(c) Landlord and Tenant (Ground Rents) Act 1967 and (No 2) Act 1978 (RI)

It would seem that these Acts apply to Deasy's Act grants as much as they do to other fee farm grants.[470]

(d) Leasehold (Enlargement and Extension) Act (NI) 1971 and Property (NI) Order 1997

The 1971 Act would also seem to have applied as much to Deasy's Act grants as to other fee farm grants.[471] The 1997 Order redemption procedures certainly apply to Deasy's Act grants.[472]

4. Rentcharges

[4.104] We come now to the third category of fee farm grant to be found in Ireland. This is a grant which creates no form of "tenure," feudal or leasehold, between the grantor and the grantee. These grants are probably more common in England,[473] but it is clear that some are to be found in Ireland.[474] All that is created by the grant is a perpetual rentcharge on the land granted.[475] It is doubtful if many grants of this nature have been created since Deasy's Act 1860, because the rights of a grantor under a Deasy's Act

---

[468] See fn 368, para [4.075] *ante.*

[469] *Kelly v Rattey* (1893) 32 LR Ir 445; *Adams v Alexander* [1895] 2 IR 365; *Wynne v Wilson* (1901) 35 ILTR 152; *Barton v Fisher* [1901] 1 IR 453; *Sheil v Irvine* (1903) 37 ILTR 92; *Re Maunsell's Estate* [1911] 1 IR 271.

[470] See para [4.076] *ante.*

[471] See para [4.077] *ante.*

[472] *Ibid.*

[473] Para [4.057] *ante.*

[474] For examples, see *Brady v Fitzgerald* (1848) 12 Ir Eq R 273; *Smith v Smith* (1855) 5 Ir Ch R 88; *Delacherois v Delacherois* (1864) 11 HLC 62. *Re Lunham's Estate* (1871) IR 5 Eq 170; *Re Maunsell's Estate* [1911] 1 IR 271. Note that in England the creation of many such grants is prohibited by the Rentcharges Act 1977, which also contains various provisions for redemption or discharge of existing ones. Once again it is doubtful whether the Republic's Landlord and Tenant (Ground Rents) Act 1978, applies to such grants (see para [4.092] *ante*). Indeed, it is even more doubtful in this case since there is no landlord and tenant relationship between the rentchargor and rentchargee as there is in the case of a Deasy's Act grant.

[475] The subject of rentcharges is dealt with generally in Ch 6, *post.*

grant are more extensive than those of a perpetual rentchargor. Rentcharge grants in Ireland are usually pre-1860 grants, which were neither executed under a Crown patent dispensing with *Quia Emptores*[476] nor operating under conversion statutes, or post-1860 grants not purporting to create the relationship of landlord and tenant within s 3 of Deasy's Act. So far as the Republic is concerned, it is probably the case that it has not been possible to create such a fee farm grant in respect of dwellings since 1978, as a result of the provisions of s 2 of the Landlord and Tenant (Ground Rents) Act 1978.[477] In Northern Ireland the Property (NI) Order 1997 makes the position absolutely clear. Article 28 prohibits the creation from a day to be appointed of any fee farm grant[478] in respect of any kind of property.[479]

(i) Creation

[4.105] So far as fee farm grants are concerned, a perpetual rentcharge is created by the grant of a fee simple in which a rent is reserved to the grantor and charged on the land. The interest so created is in fact an incorporeal hereditament, a legal interest which will bind all successors to the land.[480] The common law rule was that it had to be created *inter vivos* by deed.[481]

(ii) Words of Limitation

[4.106] A rentcharge is governed by the general law, as amended by statute, as to words of limitation in so far as the transfer of an existing rentcharge is concerned.[482] In the case of a fee farm grant annexing the rentcharge to a fee simple, the appropriate words of limitation for a fee simple will have to be used. It has been held that s 28 of the Wills Act 1837 does not apply to the creation of a new rentcharge, so that the full words of limitation would have to be used in a grant by will.[483]

(iii) Fee Farm Rents

[4.107] At common law, a rentcharge could be enforced by an action for the rent as a debt.[484] The action lay against the person known as the "terre tenant," ie, the *freehold*

---

[476] An interesting feature of the *Delacherois* case, *op cit*, is that the original Crown grant by letters patent did contain the standard dispensation clause conferring a licence to make grants in fee simple "the statute *Quia Emptores* or any other law notwithstanding". But the House of Lords eventually held that the subsequent grants in question were not an exercise of this power; as Lord St. Leonards stated: "There is not that of which the statute *Quia Emptores* complained, that grants were made to hold of the feoffors, and not of the superior Lords". *Op cit*, p 100.

[477] See paras **[4.057]** and **[4.076]** *ante*.

[478] Note the definition in Article 2(2): see para **[4.077]** *ante*.

[479] Note also the prohibition on rentcharges (subject to certain exceptions) in Article 29: see para **[6.132]** *et seq, post*. For these purposes a "rentcharge" does *not* include a fee farm rent because of the separate prohibition on the latter in Article 28: see the definition in Article 2(2).

[480] Ch 6, *post*.

[481] Megarry and Wade, *The Law of Real Property* (5th ed, 1984), p 822.

[482] *Re Bennett's Estate* [1898] 1 IR 185; see also *Plunket v Reilly* (1852) 2 Ir Ch R 585.

[483] *Nicols v Hawkes* (1853) 10 Hare 342.

[484] Megarry and Wade, *op cit*, p 823.

tenant for the time being of the land, who is the fee farm grantee or his successor in title.[485] The interesting feature of this remedy is that it was a descendant of one of the old real actions and thereby confined to persons seised of the land, so that a lessee in occupation of the land could not be sued for the rent.[486] In this respect such a rentcharge should not be confused with indemnity "rentcharges" which commonly arise as a result of the sub-division of leasehold land and consequent apportionment of head-rents between the sub-divided parts of the land.[487] However, under the common law a rentcharge, or a rent seck (dry rent) as it used to be called, had to be distinguished from a rent service created along with tenure, feudal or otherwise. A rent service had certain incidents automatically annexed to it, including the remedy of distress for rent. The owner of a rentcharge did not have this remedy unless it was expressly reserved in the grant.[488] However, statute law has changed this position. First, the Distress for Rent Act (Ireland) 1712 conferred a statutory right of distress in respect of all rents reserved "upon any grant ... where no reversion is retained," to be annexed "to the estate in the rent".[489] Then the Fee Farm Rents (Ireland) Act 1851 extended all the remedies of a landlord for recovery of rent, except ejectment for non-payment of rent, to all fee farm rents and other rents with no reversion retained.[490] This Act clearly covered perpetual rentcharges, and it was held to be retrospective in operation.[491]

[4.108] Finally, s 44 of the Conveyancing Act 1881 also contains statutory remedies for recovery of rentcharges, which apply unless they are expressly excluded in the grant.[492] There is an obvious element of duplication here for Ireland so far as fee farm grants are concerned (the 1881 Act also applied to England where it was then the only legislation[493]), as occurs with other provisions of the 1881 Act. Section 44 provides the remedy of distress where the rentcharge is 21 days in arrears,[494] a right of entry into

---

485 See discussion in *Swift v Kelly* (1889) 24 LR Ir 478, espec. at 481 and 485-6 (Palles CB); *Sligo, Leitrim and Northern Rly Co v Whyte* (1893) 31 LR Ir 316; *Odlum v Thompson* (1893) 31 LR Ir 394.

486 But see the Fee Farm Rents (Ireland) Act 1851, *infra*.

487 Para **[6.136]** *post*. For an example in relation to a conversion grant, see *De Vesci v O'Connell* [1908] AC 298.

488 It was in the fee farm grant considered in the *Delacherois* case, (1864) 11 HLC 62. As Lord St. Leonards put it: "The rent is reserved, not as incident to tenure, but with an express power of distress." *Op cit*, p 101. See also *Pennefather v Stephens* (1847) 11 Ir Eq R 61; *Brady v Fitzgerald* (1848) 12 Ir Eq R 273.

489 Section 7. Replaced as far as the relationship of landlord and tenant was concerned by Deasy's Act 1860, Sched B, and repealed altogether in Northern Ireland with the abolition of the remedy of distress by the Judgments (Enforcement) Act (NI) 1969. Para **[17.066]** *post*.

490 Section 1.

491 *Major v Barton* (1851) 2 ICLR 28.

492 Section 44(5). The Act applies only to instruments coming into effect after the Act, s 44(6); for before the Act, see *Smith v Smith* (1855) 5 Ir Ch R 88.

493 Note that s 45, relating to discharge of rentcharges, did not apply to Ireland, see s 45(7).

494 Section 44(2), which, of course, no longer applies in Northern Ireland: fn 527, *supra*.

possession if the rentcharge is 40 days in arrears[495] and, also in the latter case, a power to demise the land to a trustee for a term of years on trust to raise the money due, with all costs and expenses.[496]

(iv) Forfeiture

[4.109] It is quite common in a rentcharge grant for an express forfeiture clause to be inserted, reserving to the grantor a right of re-entry for non-payment of the rent or breach of any other obligation. Since it is contained in what is otherwise an ordinary conveyance of the fee simple, none of the legislation relating to forfeiture by a landlord applies in this case.[497] In the Republic of Ireland, this right is not confined to the perpetuity period,[498] but in Northern Ireland it is not exercisable after the end of that period.[499]

(v) Covenants

[4.110] The law applicable to covenants contained in a rentcharge fee farm grant is that applicable generally to freehold covenants.[500] Annexing a rentcharge does not in this regard attach any special characteristics to the conveyance of the fee simple. On the same reasoning, *Quia Emptores* clearly applies, and any attempt to prohibit or unduly restrict alienation by the grantee will be void.[501] Thus a covenant restricting alienation in an 1858 fee farm grant, to which neither the conversion statutes nor Deasy's Act applied, was held void as repugnant to the free power of alienation necessarily implied in the grant. In this case, *Re Lunham's Estate*,[502] Flanagan J described the grant thus: "In legal effect, it is simply a grant of certain premises from Mr Stokes to Mr Lunham in fee simple, and a re-grant of a rent-charge of £400 a year out of these premises".[503]

(vi) Redemption

(a) Chief Rents Redemption (Ireland) Act 1864

[4.111] The wide wording of this Act would seem to cover rentcharge fee farm grants.[504]

---

[495] Section 44(3). A right of *entry*, conferring power to take possession and receive the profits of the land until the debt is paid, should not be confused with a right of *re-entry* which effects a forfeiture of the estate granted and determines the grantee's interest in the land as soon as it is exercised, subject to equitable relief against forfeiture, see discussion in *Brady v Fitzgerald* (1847) 11 Ir Eq R 55, (1848) 12 Ir Eq R 273. See also para **[6.142]** *post*.

[496] Section 44(4). These remedies were excepted from the rule against perpetuities, Conveyancing Act 1911, s 6(1), and also Perpetuities Act (NI) 1966, s 12.

[497] *Stevelly v Murphy* (1840) 2 Ir Eq R 448. See also para **[17.087]**, *post*.

[498] Para **[5.105]** *post*.

[499] Perpetuities Act (NI) 1966, s 13(1)(a), reversing *Walsh v Wightman* [1927] NI 1. See para **[5.110]** *post*.

[500] See Ch 19, *post*. Also *Stevelly v Murphy* (1840) 2 Ir Eq R 448.

[501] Para **[4.070]** *ante*.

[502] (1871) IR 5 Eq 170.

[503] *Ibid*, p 171.

[504] Para **[4.074]** *ante*. Note that the 1864 Act will be repealed in NI by the Property (NI) Order 1997, Article 53(2) and Sch 5.

(b) Redemption of Rent (Ireland) Act 1891

This Act did not apply to rentcharge fee farm grants because they do not purport to create the relationship of landlord and tenant which is the prerequisite for the Act's application.[505]

(c) Landlord and Tenant (Ground Rents) Act 1967 and (No 2) Act 1978 (RI)

These Acts, however, would seem to apply to rentcharge grants to the same extent as they apply to other fee farm grants.[506]

(d) Leasehold (Enlargement and Extension) Act (NI) 1971 and Property (NI) Order 1997

The same would seem to have applied to the 1971 Act. There seems to be no good reason for distinguishing between one type of fee farm grant and another for the purposes of that Act.[507] There is no doubt that the redemption procedures of the Property (NI) Order 1997 will apply to all kinds of fee farm grant.[508]

V. FEE TAIL

A. General

[4.112] The fee tail estate derives essentially from the early statute *De Donis Conditionalibus* 1285. This statute was passed at the instigation of landowners who found their settlements being frustrated by the interpretation of the judges. The statute succeeded in the sense that the estate became the cornerstone of the complex system of land settlements which conveyancers in England and Ireland built up over the centuries and which remains in existence in modern times.[509] Although it is an estate which belongs to a different age, and would be highly unlikely to be created nowadays, it remains possible to create one in the Republic. The Law Reform Commission considered recommending its abolition but, in the end, concluded that it does no harm and should remain available to use by those who might so wish.[510] A recommendation for its abolition was made in Northern Ireland several years ago[511] and this was supported by the Land Law Working Group.[512]

---

[505] Paras **[4.075]** and **[4.088]** *ante. Christie v Peacocke* (1892) 30 LR Ir 646; *Kelly v Rattey* (1893) 32 LR Ir 445; *Alexander v Mackey* (1893) 32 LR Ir 485.

[506] Para **[4.076]** *ante.*

[507] Para **[4.077]** *ante.*

[508] *Ibid.*

[509] See further on settlements, Ch 8, *post.*

[510] *Report on Land Law and Conveyancing Law: (1) General Proposals* (LRC 30-1989) paras 13-15. The Commission did, however, recommend replacement of the requirement of enrolment of disentailing assurances in the High Court: see para **[4.123]** *post.*

[511] *Survey of the Land Law of Northern Ireland* (HMSO, 1971), paras 44-47.

[512] *Final Report* (HMSO, 1990), Vol 1, para 2.1.28. In England the Law Commission made a similar recommendation, *Transfer of Land: Trusts of Land* (Law Com No 181), para 16.1 and this was put into effect as from 1 January 1997 by the Trusts of Land and Appointment of Trustees Act 1996, Sch 1, para 5.

1. Conditional Fee

[4.113] In very early feudal law two freehold estates only were recognised, the fee simple and life estate. But the practice arose of conveying land in fee simple with conditions attached, which attempted to vary the usual mode of descent for a fee simple, ie, inheritance by general heirs, including collaterals.[513] One form of conveyance subject to a condition was the *maritagium*,[514] usually a conveyance of land by a father to his daughter and her husband "and the heirs of their bodies". In this case, and other similar conveyances, the courts interpreted the words in quotation marks as imposing a condition on the grantees that they must have issue born to them before the fee simple would vest in them.[515] The courts held, however, that, if issue of the marriage was born, the condition was fulfilled and the grantees took a fee simple which they could transfer. Thus the grantor's right to get the land back, when there was a subsequent failure of issue, was defeated and the right of the issue to inherit disappeared. In other words, the conveyance was subject to a condition precedent, which had to be met before the grantee took his estate and could freely alienate it. If no alienation took place the estate was inheritable by the issue, but once the grantee and his issue died the land reverted to the grantor. Such a conditional fee must, therefore, be distinguished from a determinable fee and a fee simple upon a condition, both described earlier.[516] A conditional fee was like a determinable fee in that it could determine on a future event, but that event would not necessarily determine it if the fee had been alienated in the meantime, whereby the alienee took a fee simple absolute free of any future interest of the grantor or of the grantee's issue. This fact is what gave rise to much of the criticism by landowners of the courts' interpretation and resulted in the passing of *De Donis*. A conditional fee was like a fee simple upon a condition in that they were both subject to a condition, but in the former case the condition was a condition precedent while in the latter it was a condition subsequent.[517] One governed the vesting of the fee simple in the grantee in the first place, the other governed the grantor's right of forfeiture of the fee simple which had already been vested in the grantee.

2. De Donis Conditionalibus 1285

[4.114] *De Donis*[518] was passed to modify the courts' interpretation of conveyances creating a conditional fee. It recorded that lands were many times "given upon condition" and yet, through alienation by the donee after birth of issue, the land did not revert to the grantor or his heirs due to death of the donee without heirs of his body. This, the Act went on, "seemed very hard ... to the givers and their heirs, that their will being expressed in the gift, was not heretofore, nor yet is observed". Such alienation so

---

[513] Para **[4.006]** *ante*.

[514] See Megarry and Wade, *The Law of Real Property* (5th ed, 1984), pp 76-77.

[515] See, generally, Challis, *The Law of Real Property* (3rd ed), Ch XVIII. Until the condition was satisfied the grantees took at most a life estate only.

[516] Paras **[4.046]-[4.055]** *ante*.

[517] Note the early version of a conditional fee granted in Ireland discussed in (1967) 18 NILQ 347-8.

[518] Statute of Westminster II, 13 Edw 1, c 1.

as to deprive the grantor of his reversion and the issue of their inheritance was "contrary to the minds of the givers, and contrary to the form expressed in the gift".[519] The statute provided the remedy and enacted that "the will of the giver, according to the form in the deed of gift manifestly expressed, shall be henceforth observed; so that they to whom the land was given under such condition, shall have no power to aliene the land so given, but that it shall remain unto the issue of them to whom it was given after their death, or ... unto the giver or his heirs, if issue fail".[520]

[4.115] Thus the courts' attempt to reinforce the fundamental principle of free alienation of land received a set-back, which was to remain effective for a couple of centuries. As a result of *De Donis*, the conditional fee ceased to be a category of the fee simple estate and really became a separate category of freehold estate. It was an estate of less value than the fee simple, hence the name "fee tail" - "taillé" or "cut down". It was cut down because, while like the fee simple and unlike the life estate it was an estate of inheritance,[521] the heirs capable of inheriting were a limited class, ie, the legitimate issue of the grantee. Just as significant was the fact that these heirs of the body would always inherit whatever the grantee did with the land. In the case of a fee simple, the grantee's heirs would succeed only if he died without having alienated the land. If the grantee of a fee simple alienated his estate, his heirs had no claim to inheritance; that passed to the alienee's heirs until he in turn alienated and so on. With a fee tail, if the original grantee purported to alienate after *De Donis*, the alienee took an estate *pur autre vie* only,[522] ie, an estate which would last only for the life-time of the original grantee. On that grantee's death, his issue inherited the land regardless of any claim by the grantee's alienee. This rule applied also to cases where the grantee's interest was determined not by voluntary alienation but by some other means, for the claims of the issue could not be defeated by acts causing an escheat or forfeiture of the grantee's estate.[523] To this extent the statute also modified the feudal incidents normally attaching to freehold estates.[524]

[4.116] *De Donis* thus established the basis of the complex system of family settlements of land which was to develop over the centuries and, indeed, despite further reforms facilitated both by the courts and legislatures, has survived down to modern times. It provided the conveyancers with the key instrument by which to ensure that family land and estates were kept within the family.[525] In an age which knew nothing about the modern sources of wealth, government securities and stocks and shares, the desire

---

[519] *Ibid.*

[520] *Ibid.* Writs of "formedon" were provided to enable the donee's issue, reversioners and remaindermen to claim the land back if necessary: see Brand, 'Formedon in the Remainder before "De Donis"'(1975) 10 Ir Jur (ns) 318; Milsom, 'Formedon Before De Donis' (1956) 72 LQR 391.

[521] Para **[4.006]** *ante.*

[522] Para **[4.160]** *post.*

[523] Paras **[2.023]**-**[2.024]** *ante.*

[524] Entails became subject to forfeiture by the High Treason Act 1534, 26 Hen 8, c 13, s 5, extended to Ireland by the Treason Act (Ir) 1537, 28 Hen 8, c 7 (Ir), s 6.

[525] This subject is pursued in greater detail in Ch 8, *post.*

amongst landowners for such a system was manifold. Yet it had many vices,[526] not the least of which was the fact that it breached completely the fundamental principle of feudal land law that the land should be as freely alienable as possible. As custodians of the common law, it was to be expected that the courts would once again seek ways of curtailing the powers given to landowners and their conveyancers by *De Donis*.

3. Fines and Recoveries

[4.117] The task facing property lawyers was to find a method of circumventing *De Donis* which the courts could and would enforce. It was clear what their landowner clients wanted. They wanted to be able to sell their entailed land free from restrictions and limitations imposed by the existence of future rights to the land resting in their issue and in reversioners or remaindermen. The courts could not disregard the Act directly, but they might be persuaded to recognise a mechanism which, though it did not directly contravene the Act, did circumvent it indirectly and give the landowners substantially what they wanted. The mechanism devised by the lawyers was the "collusive action," ie, an action brought against a defendant with his consent - essentially a piece of procedural chicanery but none the less effective at that. Two types of collusive action were devised for tenants in tail, one which was a set of proceedings known as "suffering a recovery" and another known as "levying a fine".[527]

(i) Common Recovery

[4.118] The leading authority on this action was an English case decided in the late fifteenth century, usually known as *Taltarum's Case*.[528] The nature of the proceedings was that a stranger to the settlement of the land was persuaded to bring an action claiming the land. The tenant in tail offered no defence to this action, admitted to the court that he had no good title to the land and thereby allowed judgment to be given against him - he suffered a recovery of the land.[529] This judgment would clearly bind the tenant in tail and probably also his issue as claimants through him.[530] It would not on its own bar claimants to the land whose rights did not derive through the tenant in tail, but derived independently from the settlor through the terms of his original settlement. It would not bind, therefore, reversioners (the original settlor and his successors) or remaindermen who would otherwise take the land on failure of the tenant in tail's issue. To achieve this another piece of medieval procedural law was employed, namely, "vouching to warranty".[531] It has already been mentioned that in early feudal law it was the practice for a grantor of land to warrant his title to the land and to undertake to compensate the grantee with lands of equal value should that title subsequently turn out

---

[526] See further Ch 8, *post*.

[527] Challis, *op cit*, Ch XXVII.

[528] 12 Edw 4, pl 25, f 19a (YB), translated in Kiralfy, *Source Book of English Law* (1957), p 86. See *Houlditch v Wallace* (1838) 5 Cl & F 629.

[529] See *Morrison v Heath* (1818) Rowe 552; *Murphy d. Wray v Humes* (1829) 2 Hud & Br 395; *Ellis v Mahony* (1834) 3 Law Rec (NS) 25.

[530] Megarry and Wade, *op cit*, p 79.

[531] *Fitzgerald v Roddy* (1854) 4 ICLR 74.

to be bad.[532] Using this principle, the tenant in tail suffering the recovery vouched to warranty some friend or a "man of straw" (any person selected by the parties and accepted without question by the court), who alleged that he had previously conveyed the land to the tenant with the usual warranty of good title. Then, when the tenant in tail disclosed his bad title to the court and suffered the recovery, his "common vouchee"[533] in turn suffered a judgment to be entered against him to make compensation with other land.[534] This judgment was worthless in real terms since it was based entirely on fictitious proceedings, but it had the vital technical function of barring any further claims of reversioners or remaindermen to the land originally conveyed to the tenant in tail and now passing to the person in whose favour the common recovery was suffered. These claims were now supposed to be satisfied out of the judgment given against the common vouchee.[535]

[4.119] The result of this collusion, to which the court was an open party, was that the person in whose favour the recovery judgment was given obtained the fee simple absolute in the land. Thus the tenant in tail gained full powers of alienation, subject only to any fee or bribe necessary to secure the co-operation of the other parties to the court action and to the time and trouble involved in the action itself. There was also the limitation that, since the court action was essentially one for the recovery of land, it could be brought only against a person currently seised of the land.[536] A common recovery was effective only if brought against a tenant in tail in possession; if a tenant currently holding only an estate in tail in remainder wished to initiate such proceedings, he would have to enlist the co-operation of the freeholder currently in possession, who would have been seised. It was this limitation which led to the second collusive action for barring entails, the fine.

(ii) Fine

[4.120] In this context a fine meant a compromise of an action before any judgment was given by the court, a compromise that was worked out by the parties, approved by the court and then registered in the court's records. The use of such a device to bar entails had been expressly prohibited by *De Donis* itself.[537] However, later legislation reversed this provision, in particular the Fines Act (Ireland) 1634,[538] which provided that all fines

---

[532] Para [4.072] *ante.*

[533] So-called because the practice developed of some court official acting as the man of straw for any parties requiring him, Challis, *op cit*, p 311. *Fitzgerald v Roddy* (1854) 4 ICLR 74 (see also 6 HLC 823).

[534] *Hume v Burton* (1784) 1 Ridgw PC 16.

[535] Being a man of straw, he never appeared in court again and so any action to recover against him was doomed from the beginning, Challis, *ibid.*

[536] Para [4.018] *ante. William v Notley* [1913] 2 IR 281 (see *A Casebook on Irish Land Law* (1984), p 170).

[537] C 1 - "And if a fine be levied hereafter upon such lands, it shall be void in the law".

[538] 10 Chas 1, sess 2, c 8 (Ir). The English equivalent was the Fines Act 1540 (32 Hen 8, c 36) which was considered to confirm the courts' interpretation of an earlier Fines Act of 1489, see Challis, *op cit*, pp 306-7; Megarry and Wade, *op cit*, p 80.

levied by tenants in tail in possession, reversion or remainder were "to all intents and purposes" sufficient to bar the entail.

[4.121] The significant point about this type of action was that not only a tenant in tail in possession could use it. A tenant in tail in remainder could enter into a compromise agreement with respect to the land, though he could not be sued for recovery of the land itself because he had no seisin.[539] He had no need to get the consent of the tenant in possession who was seised. Yet herein lay the weakness of the device. The tenant in tail's agreement could bind only himself and those claiming through him, his issue; it could not bind reversioners or remaindermen unless they were also made parties to the agreement.[540] If they were not, the stranger who was the other party to the compromise did not obtain a fee simple absolute but instead what was known as a "base fee".[541] This was in substance a determinable fee simple, a fee which would last only until the tenant in tail and his issue died out, at which time the reversion or remainder would take effect.

[4.122] To sum up, then, the early law relating to fines and recoveries, they both involved fictitious actions in court to circumvent the clear policy of *De Donis*, which was that the tenant in tail should not be able to bar the entail so as to defeat the future interests in the land of the issue in tail and reversioners or remaindermen to take after them. The common recovery could be used less frequently, since it was confined to tenants in tail in possession. It was also a more complicated and probably more expensive action, though it had a more extensive effect in producing a fee simple absolute. The fine could be used much more frequently by tenants in tail in possession or remainder, and even with contingent interests only. It was a less complicated action, since it did not proceed to judgment, but it had the less extensive effect of producing a base fee only. Both actions exhibited the ingenuity and enterprise of property lawyers and the determination of the courts to abide by the fundamental principles of feudal land law, contrary to the spirit of legislation if necessary. The actions also illustrated some of the striking features of the early common law - the use of legal fictions and the twisting of procedure to provide substantive rights. That substantive rights had been created was made clear by the courts' insistence that any attempt by settlors expressly to exclude the power to suffer recoveries or levy fines was void as being repugnant to the very nature of a fee tail estate. Such a restriction was regarded by the courts as being as much repugnant to the fee tail estate as a prohibition against alienation was with respect to the fee simple estate. It was essential, however, that the tenant in tail or life tenant in possession should consent to these procedures and he would usually consent only if those entitled on his death settled the land by a resettlement in favour of the family. Thus each generation ensured that the land passed to the next generation as life tenants or tenants in tail and so family estates were preserved.[542] As the common law developed,

---

[539] *Jones v Inman* (1794) Ir Term Rep 433.
[540] *Carhampton v Carhampton* (1795) Ir Term Rep 567.
[541] Discussed more fully, para **[4.136]** *post*.
[542] See further, Ch 8, *post*.

it was only a matter of time before legislation would be introduced to get rid of the more absurd aspects of the law of fines and recoveries.

4. Fines and Recoveries (Ireland) Act 1834

[4.123] The Fines and Recoveries (Ireland) Act 1834[543] abolished fines and recoveries as methods of barring entails and replaced them with a single and much more simple method, ie, execution by the tenant in tail of a "disentailing assurance".[544] This means in effect the execution of a conveyance using words which, if executed by the fee simple owner, would convey the fee simple.[545] Failure to execute such a deed meant that the fee tail was not enlarged into a fee simple and what was created was a base fee only,[546] defined by the Act as "that estate in fee simple into which an estate tail is converted where the issue in tail are barred, but persons claiming estates by way of remainder or otherwise are not barred".[547] This was the usual type of base fee, which would arise if the tenant in tail failed to obtain the consent of the protector where necessary.[548] However, it seems that the courts also recognised a more narrowly defined base fee, sometimes referred to as a *voidable* base fee.[549] This has been held to arise where the defect in the disentailing assurance was of a more formal or technical nature. For example, the Act provided that to be effective the disentailing assurance had to be enrolled within six calendar months of its execution in court.[550] Failure to comply with these statutory requirements results, it seems, in the creation of a base fee determinable or voidable by entry of the issue in tail.[551]

---

[543] The English equivalent was the Fines and Recoveries Act 1833, parts of which did also apply to Ireland.

[544] Sections 2 and 12. *Re Skerrett's Trusts* (1884) 15 LR Ir 1; *Re Gosford's Estate* (1910) 44 ILTR 234; *Gaussen and French v Ellis* [1930] IR 116; *Re Ottley's Estate* [1910] 1 IR 1; *Bank of Ireland v Domvle* [1956] IR 37 (see *A Casebook on Irish Land Law* (1984), p 178). (Note that in places the Report of the last case mistakenly refers to the date of the 1834 Act as "1894", see the headnote and p 43; *cf*, pp 52 and 58-9.) For the Act's effect on fines and recoveries levied before the Act, see *Davies v D'Arcy* (1853) 3 ICLR 617.

[545] Section 38. *Nelson v Agnew* (1871) IR 6 Eq 232.

[546] 1834 Act, ss 12, 38 and 39. See *Re Knox* [1912] 1 IR 288.

[547] Section 1.

[548] As in the case of a fine levied before the Act, the tenant in tail would have to get the consent of the freeholder in possession, para **[4.121]** *ante*. For "protector", see para **[4.124]** *infra*.

[549] See Challis, *The Law of Real Property* (3rd ed), pp 322 and 330.

[550] Section 39. Now in the High Courts of the Republic of Ireland and of Northern Ireland. *Peyton v Lambert* (1858) 8 ICLR 485 (see *A Casebook on Irish Land Law* (1984), p 253); *Bank of Ireland v Domvile* [1956] IR 37 (see *ibid*, p 178). The Republic's Law Reform Commission took the view that this requirement was "excessive" and should be replaced by a requirement that the disentailing deed should be registered in either the Registry of Deeds or the Land Registry, according to whether the land was unregistered or registered: see *Report on Land Law and Conveyancing Law: (1) General Proposals* (LRC 30-1989), para 14. This recommendation has not been acted upon.

[551] *Re St George's Estate* (1879) 3 LR Ir 277; *Witham v Notley* [1913] 2 IR 281 (see *A Casebook on Irish Land Law* (1984), p 170). The distinction between the usual base fee and a voidable base fee has been given statutory recognition in New Zealand's Property Law Act 1952, s 16, see *Survey of the Land Law of Northern Ireland* (HMSO, 1971), para 46.

[4.124] The Act recognised, however, one of the features of the previous law, namely, the necessity for consent by the freeholder in possession to a recovery suffered by a tenant in tail in remainder so as to bar the entail effectively. The Act provided that in this case there was to be a person known as the "protector of the settlement," who would have to give his consent to the disentailing assurance. A disentailing assurance executed without his consent created a base fee only.[552] The protector could generally use his discretion about giving consent, but he could not bind himself by agreement to withhold consent in the future.[553] The protector was either the person who would have had to give his consent to a recovery before the Act,[554] or any special protector appointed as such expressly by the settlor, as he was empowered to do by the Act.[555] It was also provided that the protector retained his powers even though he might subsequently part with his own estate.[556]

[4.125] The result of this Act was that a tenant in tail in possession acquired the power to dispose of the fee simple estate, provided he followed the procedures laid down. He could either sell it to a third party or enlarge his own previous entailed estate into a fee simple by conveying it to his own use.[557] This disposition had to be by an assurance operating *inter vivos*; it was too late to do it by will. Otherwise, the tenant in tail enjoyed most of the rights and privileges of the fee simple owner. Thus he was not liable for waste, whereas the owner of a mere life estate was.[558] It is true that his ability to grant lesser estates and interests out of his entailed estate, which would be binding on his issue or remaindermen, was curtailed[559] until later settlements legislation radically altered the law in this regard.[560] One further restriction may be noted, which relates to rentcharges held in entail.[561] If a rentcharge already in existence (*in esse*) and held in fee simple were conveyed in fee tail, the tenant in tail could bar the entail by a disentailing assurance under the Act and thereby create a rentcharge in fee simple, for himself or his assignee.[562] Where however the rentcharge had been created for the first time (*de novo*) by the conveyance to the tenant in tail, so that the rentcharge was limited in duration initially to the entailed estate, any assurance under the Act would create a base fee

---

[552] Section 32. As to the type of base fee, see para **[4.121]** *ante*.

[553] Sections 34 and 35.

[554] Section 28. Here the protector was usually the tenant in tail or life tenant in possession of the land, para **[4.121]** *ante*.

[555] Section 30, which provided that more than one but not more than three persons could be appointed protectors.

[556] Section 19.

[557] This method of conveyance was explained earlier, para **[3.019]** *ante*.

[558] Para **[4.149]** *post*.

[559] The Leases Act (Ir) 1634, 10 Chas 1, sess 3, c 6 (Ir), enabled the tenant in tail to grant leases for not more than 21 years or a period of 3 lives binding on the issue in tail, though not remaindermen. This Act was replaced by the Settled Estates Act 1856, s 35 which was in turn replaced by the Settled Estates Act 1877 and the Settled Land Acts 1881-92. See Ch 8, *post*.

[560] Ch 8, *post*.

[561] See, generally, paras **[6.131]** *et seq*, *post*.

[562] *Re Franks's Estate* [1915] 1 IR 387.

barring the issue in tail only but not remaindermen.[563] Remaindermen would have been barred, however, if the original conveyance creating the rentcharge had given it in remainder in fee simple to some other party, whom the tenant in tail could bar by enlarging his entailed estate into a fee simple.[564]

B. Creation and Transfer

[4.126] Like the fee simple estate, a fee tail has usually been created by deed since the Real Property Act 1845.[565] A transfer of the estate and its effect is governed by the Fines and Recoveries (Ireland) Act 1834, which has been discussed.

C. Words of Limitation

[4.127] As a freehold estate of inheritance, a fee tail must be created by appropriate words of limitation. Again, as in the case of a fee simple, the law has developed different sets of rules governing the words of limitation according to whether they are contained in a conveyance *inter vivos* or in a will. In the case of a fee tail there is a further complication. A fee simple is an estate which could be inherited by the heirs general, whereas a fee tail is an estate inheritable by heirs special. The point is, however, that there can be degrees of speciality and different words have to be used to indicate what degree of speciality in the heirs is required, if any. This problem does not arise in the case of a fee simple where there can be no question of degree in this sense.[566]

1. Conveyances Inter Vivos

(i) At Common Law

[4.128] The general rule for a fee tail is that the heirs special are always limited to descendants of the holder of the entail. Thus, while the word "heirs" was essential at common law to indicate that the estate granted was a freehold estate of inheritance, that word had to be qualified by additional words indicating that the inheritance was confined to descendants, if it was to create a fee tail. The standard words of limitation for a conveyance *inter vivos* at common law were: to A "and the heirs of his body". Other qualifications of the word "heirs" to the same effect would suffice, eg, to A "and the heirs of his flesh".[567] Formulae which omitted the vital word "heirs" generally were insufficient in an *inter vivos* conveyance, so that a conveyance to A "and his issue" would not create a fee tail, probably only a joint life estate in A and those of his issue alive at the date of execution of the conveyance.[568] This was the position for a fee tail

---

[563] *Pinkerton v Pratt* [1915] 1 IR 406.

[564] *Re Franks's Estate, op cit*; Challis, *The Law of Real Property* (3rd ed), pp 327-28.

[565] Para **[4.023]** *ante*.

[566] *Cf* the classification of fees simple, para **[4.043]** *ante*, with the classification of fees tail, para **[4.135]** *post*.

[567] *Cf, Re Smith's Estate* (1891) 2 LR Ir 121. Note that now heirs for the purposes of creation of a fee tail may include illegitimate children: see the RI Status of Children Act 1987, s 27 and Children (NI) Order 1995, Sch 6, para 2(2) (*cf* Article 4(3) of the Family Law Reform (NI) Order 1977, which is repealed).

[568] *Cf*, the case of a will, para **[4.130]** *post*.

general, where descendants of every kind could inherit. It was quite possible, however, to restrict the class of descendants further, so as to create a fee tail *special*.[569] Thus a fee tail male could be created by the words "and the heirs male of his body," a fee tail female by the words "and the heirs female of his body". In the former case, the entail could last only as long as it could descend through an unbroken line of male descendants; in the latter, it could descend only through an unbroken line of female descendants. Even further restriction could be made by specifying that the heirs of the body could be begotten of one particular spouse only, eg, to A "and the heirs male of his body begotten upon Mary". Here only male descendants of A and Mary could inherit the fee tail.

(ii) By Statute

[4.129] The Conveyancing Act 1881 provided alternative formulae for the creation of fees tail. Section 51 provided that for a fee tail general the words "in tail" were sufficient, for a fee tail special the words "in tail male" and "in tail female". It may be noted that the word "fee" was not mentioned in the section, but there seems to be no reason why "to A in fee tail" should not also create a fee tail.[570]

2. Gifts by Will

(i) At Common Law

[4.130] In accordance with the courts' generally more liberal approach to the interpretation of wills,[571] the rule was, and is, that any words sufficient to show an intention on the part of the testator to create a fee tail will suffice.[572] There is, therefore, no need to use technical words and the omission of the word "heirs" will not invalidate the grant. There have been numerous cases holding that expressions like "to A and his issue" or "to A and his descendants" create a fee tail in a will.[573] These expressions indicate that inheritance by a line of descendants is intended.[574] More difficulty was

---

[569] Sometimes this label is confined to the case of an even further restriction, ie, to the heirs of the body of a specified spouse, see Megarry and Wade, *The Law of Real Property* (5th ed, 1984), p 55 and s 95(1) of the Republic of Ireland's Succession Act 1965, quoted para **[4.131]** *post*.

[570] *Cf Twaddle v Murphy* (1881) 8 LR Ir 123 (a case involving a fee farm grant) (see *A Casebook on Irish Land Law* (1984), p 113) where the court held that superadded words would not prevent the operation of an otherwise effective conveyance, para **[4.095]** *ante*. *Cf Roche v O'Brien* (1852) 13 Ir LR 253; *Kempster v Maher* (1903) 37 ILTR 29.

[571] Para **[4.031]** *ante*.

[572] *Cf Atkins v Atkins* [1976-7] ILRM 62, where the testator's will initially purported to create a fee tail in favour of his nephew but contained a later provision to the effect that every nephew was to be a tenant for life. Kenny J took the latter provision as an indication of the testator's intention, to which effect should be given, and found support for this holding in the well-established rule of construction of wills that a later part prevails over an earlier part. See Brady, *Succession Law in Ireland* (2nd ed, 1995), paras 5.41-43.

[573] *Mandeville v Earl of Carrick* (1795) 3 Ridgw PC 352; *Bower v Eccles* (1815) Rowe 466; *Manning v Moore* (1832) Alc & Nap 96; *Blackwell v Hale* (1850) 1 ICLR 612.

[574] Thus it seems that even an expression like "to A and his heirs" (which would normally create a fee simple) might as a matter of construction in a particular case be taken to create a fee tail, see, eg, *Re Waugh* [1903] 1 Ch 744.

caused by an expression like "to A and his children" which tended to suggest that inheritance was confined to the first generation only. The courts devised a special principle for this sort of case, known as the rule in *Wild's Case*.[575] According to this principle, if A had no children when the will was made,[576] the words "and his children" were construed as words of limitation and A took a fee tail.[577] The theory was that giving A a fee tail was the only way the testator could have intended to benefit A's children, though A could always prevent this by barring the entail. If, however, A did have children living when the will was made; the words "and his children" were construed as words of purchase and A took jointly with all his children living at the testator's death.[578]

(ii) By Statute

[4.131] The above common law position remains the law in Northern Ireland, until recommendations for abolishing the fee tail estate altogether have been acted upon.[579] In the Republic of Ireland the common law position for wills, including the rule in *Wild's Case*, has been reversed by s 95 of the Succession Act 1965, which reads:

(1)   An estate tail (whether general, in tail male, in tail female or in tail special) in real estate may be created by will only by the use of the same words of limitation as those by which a similar estate tail may be created by deed.

(2)   Words of limitation contained in a will in respect of real estate which have not the effect of creating an estate in fee simple or an estate tail shall have the same effect, as near as may be, as similar words used in a deed in respect of personal property.

[4.132] These provisions, which may be contrasted with provisions introduced in England in 1925,[580] and which have given rise to considerable controversy there,[581] make the position for entails created by will much stricter than the common law. Subsection (1) means that, if a testator in the Republic wishes nowadays to create a fee tail in his will, he must use the technical expressions required for conveyances *inter vivos* at common law or under the Conveyancing Act 1881, s 51. These expressions have been discussed above.[582] If a testator fails to use such an expression he fails to

---

[575]   (1599) 6 Co Rep 16b. *Cf re* personalty, *Heron v Stokes* (1842) 4 Ir Eq R 284.

[576]   It is arguable that this was an exception to the general rule, enshrined in s 24 of the Wills Act 1837, that a will speaks from the death of the testator, which is the date at which to judge the validity of limitations operating under it, para **[14.042]** *post.*

[577]   *Clifford v Koe* (1880) 5 App Cas 447.

[578]   *Re Moyles' Estate* (1878) 1 LR Ir 155. *Cf, Ward v Ward* [1921] 1 IR 117.

[579]   *Survey of the Land Law of Northern Ireland* (HMSO, 1971), paras 44-7; Land Law Working Group's *Final Report* (HMSO, 1990) Vol 1, para 2.1.28.

[580]   Law of Property Act 1925, ss 130(1) and (2), though note that other provisions for estates tail were introduced by this Act for England, eg, making them subsist as equitable estates only after 1925. Note, however, that estates tail are abolished by the Trusts of Land and Appointment of Trustees Act 1996, Sch 1, para 5; para **[4.112]** *ante.*

[581]   See Bailey, (1938) 6 CLJ 67; (1947) 9 CLJ 185; Megarry, (1947) 9 CLJ 46; Morris, (1947) 9 CLJ 190.

[582]   Paras **[4.025]-[4.030]** *ante.*

create a fee tail; that much at least is clear from subs (1). What he does create is governed by subs (2), which is not so clear. The subsection clearly presupposes that the testator has used words of limitation of some sort[583] and these have to be construed so as to have the same effect as in a transfer *inter vivos* of *personal* property, with appropriate allowance made for the different nature of the property transferred. In other words, the subsection applies to what would previously have been regarded as words of limitation, but which now cease to be effective by virtue of subs (1) so far as an estate tail is concerned. More difficulty arises with respect to words of limitation not creating an estate in fee simple in a will, because, even before the Wills Act 1837, any words indicating an intention to create a fee simple were sufficient and nothing in the Succession Act 1965 seems to change this common law position. The subsection would seem to have in mind expressions which were more likely to be regarded as intended to create a fee tail, if any freehold estate, rather than a fee simple, because what was at least clear was that the inheritance was intended to be restricted to a class narrower than heirs general. The subsection seems to apply, therefore, to wills using expressions like "to A and his issue," "to A and his descendants" or "to A and his children". What the effect of such expressions is in a transfer *inter vivos* of personal property is a matter of construction and, in applying this construction to a will, presumably regard should be had to the intention of the testator. Furthermore, s 95 should be read in conjunction with s 89 of the Succession Act 1965, which reiterates the statutory rule that a will speaks from death.[584] Thus "to A and his issue" or "to A and his children" could be construed as an absolute gift jointly to A and any of his issue or children living at the testator's death (when the will takes effect). If there are no such issue or children then living, it could be construed as a gift to A absolutely, ie, in fee simple where land is concerned, if the testator has power to transmit this.

3. Equitable Gifts

[4.133] The same rules would seem to apply here as in the case of a fee simple estate. In other words, if a settlor purports to use technical words of limitation in delimiting an equitable fee tail, they will be given their usual meaning under the common law, as amended by statute. If he does not purport to use technical words, the courts will strive to give effect to what appears to have been his intention, by construing them regardless of the usual requirements as to words of limitation, if necessary.[585]

---

[583] Otherwise the fee simple or other whole estate or interest the testator had power to dispose of by will would pass under the general provision in s 94 of the 1965 Act: para **[4.032]** *ante*.

[584] Wills Act 1837, s 24 (re-enacted in NI in Article 17 of the Wills and Administration Proceedings (NI) Order 1994). Note that s 89 of the 1965 states that this rule of construction (it is subject to a contrary intention appearing from the will) applies not only with reference to all the estate comprised in the will (*cf* s 24 of the 1837 Act and Article 17(1) of the 1994 Order - "with reference to the property referred to in it"), but also to "every devise or bequest contained in it". This emphasises that the size of a devisee's estate is governed by the position at the time of the testator's death.

[585] See para **[4.033]** *ante*, and the authorities therein cited. Also *Crumpe v Crumpe* [1900] AC 127; *The Land Purchase Trustee, Northern Ireland v Beers* [1925] NI 191.

4. Rule in Shelley's Case

[4.134] The rule in *Shelley's Case*, which was discussed earlier in relation to the fee simple estate,[586] applies equally to the fee tail estate. Thus a conveyance "to A for life, remainder to the heirs of his body" creates a fee tail in A, the remainder being taken, in accordance with the rule, to contain words of limitation only. The same rules apply as in the case of a fee simple estate and there is no need to repeat them here. It may be noted in particular with respect to wills, that, where a testator uses words that are not the normal words of limitation, eg, "to A for life, remainder to his successors," the general principle is that it is a matter of construction whether the testator meant by that the whole inheritable issue (ie, the heirs of the body) or *personae designatae*.[587] Thus in *Finch v Foley*,[588] a devise "to A and his first and other sons successively in remainder one after another according to their respective seniorities in tail male" was held to give A a fee tail. Yet in England a similar devise "to A during his life with ... remainder to the use of his first and other sons successively according to seniority in tail male" was held not to be a case for the application of *Shelley's Case*.[589] The English judge thought that such a limitation was a common form of settlement designed to convey a life estate, followed by estates tail in succession to *personae designatae*. Yet the fact is that that form covers the persons who would inherit under a fee tail, and the judge interpreted Lord Macnaghten's statement in *Van Grutten v Foxwell*[590] as meaning that this fact was not conclusive of the question of construction as to what the testator intended.[591] Finally, it may be noted that the rule in *Shelley's Case* was abolished in England in 1925,[592] but this step has not yet been taken in either part of Ireland.[593]

D. Classification

1. Fees Tail General and Special

[4.135] The distinction between a fee tail general and a fee tail special (which may be one of several kinds) has already been discussed.[594] It should also be noted that in theory there is no reason why a fee tail, general or special, may not be subjected to further restrictions like a fee simple. Thus it may be made determinable or subject to a condition precedent or subsequent.[595]

---

[586] Paras **[4.034]** *et seq, ante*.

[587] Para **[4.041]** *ante. Re Bishop and Richardson's Contract* [1899] 1 IR 71; *Re Keane's Estate* [1903] 1 IR 215; *Re Taylor's Trusts* [1912] 1 IR 1; *Ward v Ward* [1921] 1 IR 117.

[588] [1949] Ir Jur Rep 30 (Kingsmill Moore J).

[589] *Re Williams* [1952] Ch 828 (Roxburgh J).

[590] [1897] AC 659.

[591] *Op cit*, pp 833-4.

[592] Law of Property Act 1925, s 131. See Adams, 'The Doctrine of Very Heir' (1973) 37 Conv 113; Farrer, 'Law of Property Act, s 131' (1937) 53 LQR 371; Hargreaves, 'Shelley's Ghost' (1938) 54 LQR 70; Megarry, 'Shelley's Case and the Doctrine of Very Heir' (1943) 59 LQR 272; 'Shelley's Ghost' (1944) 60 LQR 222.

[593] See, however, *Survey of the Land Law of Northern Ireland* (HMSO, 1971), paras 274-5.

[594] Para **[4.128]** *ante*.

[595] Paras **[4.046]** *et seq, ante. Magee v Martin* [1902] 1 IR 367; *Re Elliot* [1916] 1 IR 30; *cf Re Talbot* [1932] IR 714.

2. Base Fee

[4.136] A base fee is essentially a fee simple liable to determine on failure of the heirs of the body of the tenant in tail creating the base fee. This is the usual case which arises where the tenant in tail fails to bar the entail effectively, ie, so as to bar reversioners or remaindermen due to take the land after failure of the issue of the tenant in tail. The most common occasion for the creation of such a base fee is where a tenant in tail not in possession executes a disentailing assurance without the consent of the protector.[596] There is also the rarer case when the base fee can be determined by entry of the issue in tail, which arises where the failure to bar the entail is caused by a more formal or technical flaw, such as failure to enrol the disentailing assurance within six months of its execution.[597]

[4.137] A base fee can be created by the tenant in tail either in some other person in favour of whom the disentailing assurance is executed or in the tenant in tail himself.[598] This sort of estate, however, was obviously an unsatisfactory one, since neither the tenant in tail nor any purchaser from him could be sure when it would end. This made it an extremely unattractive commercial asset. So the law permitted the enlargement of a base fee into a fee simple absolute, thereby producing the same result as a fully effective barring of the entail. Prior to the Fines and Recoveries (Ireland) Act 1834, this could have been achieved for the owner of the base fee by the tenant in tail suffering a recovery.[599] The 1834 Act, however, abolished recoveries.[600] Since 1834, a base fee can be enlarged by the tenant in tail who created it, if the tenant executes another disentailing assurance either with the consent of the protector this time or after the protectorship has ceased to exist.[601] Thus the tenant in tail could do this on the death of the freeholder in possession, if he had been the protector.[602] If the tenant in tail had died first, the new disentailing assurance could be executed by whoever would have succeeded to the entail (eg, his eldest son), but it has been held in England that any purchaser to whom the base fee may have been conveyed cannot so enlarge it.[603]

[4.138] A base fee may also be enlarged by its current owner, including, therefore, any purchaser from the tenant in tail, buying out the immediate fee simple remainder or reversion. In this case, s 37 of the 1834 Act specifically provides that the base fee will not merge into the fee simple, for otherwise it would have been subject to any charges or incumbrances attaching to the fee simple.[604] Instead, s 37 provides that the base fee "shall be *ipso facto* enlarged into as large an estate as the tenant in tail, with the consent

---

[596] Para **[4.124]** *ante.*

[597] Para **[4.123]** *ante.*

[598] By using an executed use, see paras **[3.019]**-**[3.020]**, *ante.*

[599] Para **[4.118]**, *ante.* See Challis, *op cit*, pp 335-8.

[600] Section 2.

[601] Section 16; see also s 33. *Bank of Ireland v Domvile* [1956] IR 37 (see *A Casebook on Irish Land Law* (1984) p 178).

[602] Para **[4.124]** *ante.*

[603] *Bankes v Small* (1887) 36 Ch D 716.

[604] As to the law of merger, see Ch 24, *post. Re Wallace's Estate* [1907] 1 IR 91.

of the protector, if any, might have created by any disposition under this Act, if such remainder or reversion had been vested in any other person". In other words, the base fee is enlarged into a fee simple absolute free of all claims by the issue in tail or any reversioners or remaindermen taking after them.[605]

[4.139] Lastly, the current holder of a base fee may enlarge it into a fee simple by acquiring a title to the latter by adverse possession,[606] ie, by remaining in possession of the land for 12 years after the protectorship has ceased. The original period laid down for this automatic enlargement was twenty years' possession,[607] but this was reduced later to twelve years,[608] which has remained the period in the modern statutes of limitations in both the Republic and Northern Ireland.[609]

3. Entails After Possibility

[4.140] Where there is a fee tail special of the kind limiting inheritance to the issue of a specified spouse,[610] the tenant in tail is put in a restricted position if that spouse predeceases him, leaving no such issue. The tenant becomes a tenant in tail "after possibility of issue extinct".[611] Section 15 of the Fines and Recoveries (Ireland) Act 1834 provided that such a tenant could not bar the entail by executing a disentailing assurance under the Act.[612] Thus the reversion or remainder is bound to take effect on his death, when there will also, *ex hypothesi*, be a failure of the issue in tail. Because his estate is, therefore, really no more than a life estate, a tenant in tail after possibility, like a tenant for life[613] but unlike most tenants in tail,[614] may be liable for waste, at least to some extent. He is probably not liable for voluntary waste,[615] but may be liable for equitable waste, ie, wanton destruction.[616]

4. Other Unbarrable Entails

[4.141] Apart from the special case of an entail after possibility of issue extinct, there are several other kinds of unbarrable entails - despite the general principle that any contract, covenant or other restriction purporting to prevent a tenant in tail from barring the entail is void as repugnant to the nature of an estate in fee tail.[617] In England, for

---

[605] Section 12.

[606] As to which, generally, see Ch 23, *post*.

[607] Real Property Limitation Act 1833, s 23.

[608] Real Property Limitation Act 1874, s 6; *Bank of Ireland v Domvile* [1956] IR 37 (see *A Casebook on Irish Land Law* (1984), p 178).

[609] Statute of Limitations 1957, s 19 (RI); Statute of Limitations (NI) 1958, s 23 (see now the Limitation (NI) Order 1989, Article 21).

[610] Para **[4.128]** *ante*.

[611] See *Re Toppin's Estate* [1915] 1 IR 330.

[612] Note, however, that he does have the powers of a tenant for life under the Settled Land Acts, see Settled Land Act 1882, s 58(1)(vii), and also para **[8.021]** *post*.

[613] Para **[4.149]** *post*.

[614] Para **[4.125]** *ante*.

[615] Challis, *op cit*, p 292.

[616] Megarry and Wade, *op cit*, p 91.

[617] Para **[4.122]** *ante*.

example, certain entails were made expressly unbarrable by statute. Thus entails created by the Crown in lands settled on grantees in recognition of services to the Crown, where the reversion was in the Crown, were unbarrable.[618] But these statutory provisions did not apply to Ireland,[619] so that a reversion in the Crown did not prevent the barring of entails here. Some entails in England were also made unbarrable specifically by special Acts of Parliament, such as those given to the first Duke of Marlborough and Duke of Wellington for public services.[620] There would seem to be no such entails in Ireland.[621]

[4.142] Finally, it may be noted that certain persons may be under a disability which prevents them from barring the entails. This is really part of the general law relating to persons under a disability, such as minors, married women and persons suffering from mental disorder. This will be discussed in general in a later chapter,[622] so little need be said here. There is nothing in the Fines and Recoveries (Ireland) Act 1834 to prevent a minor executing a disentailing assurance, but this would seem to be subject to the general law relating to conveyances and other transactions executed by minors. In other words, the assurance would be valid unless and until revoked by the minor on reaching full age.[623] Restraints on anticipation with respect to a married woman have gone in Ireland and she may now act like a *feme sole* in this regard.[624] Other persons, while they may not act themselves, may have someone else act for them, eg, the Official Assignee or a trustee in bankruptcy could bar a bankrupt's entail.[625]

5. Quasi-Entail

This subject is discussed below in relation to life estates.[626]

---

[618] Feigned Recoveries Act 1542, 34 & 35 Hen 8, c 20; Fines and Recoveries Act 1833, s 18. See Challis, *op cit*, pp 323-4.

[619] Section 15 of the Fines and Recoveries (Ireland) Act 1834, which was the equivalent of s 18 of the English 1833 Act, did not contain the relevant provisions referred to here. Holders of these unbarrable entails were, however, given the powers of a tenant for life under the Settled Land Act 1882, s 58(1)(i), para **[8.021]** *post*.

[620] 6 Anne, c 6, 1706, s 5; 6 Anne, c 7, 1706, s 4; 54 Geo 3, c 161, 1814, s 28.

[621] Land Law Working Group's *Final Report* (HMSO, 1990), Vol 1, para 2.1.28. The holders of such entails purchased by Parliament in England for public services were not given the powers of a tenant for life under the Settled Land Act 1882, s 58(1)(i); see *Re Duke of Marlborough's Parliamentary Estates* (1891) 8 TLR 179; *Re Duke of Marlborough's Blenheim Estates* (1892) 8 TLR 582. *Cf*, the English Settled Land Act 1925, s 20(1)(i) and 23(2).

[622] Ch 25, *post*.

[623] Para **[25.06]** *post*.

[624] As to the Republic of Ireland, see Married Women's Status Act 1957; for Northern Ireland, see Law Reform (Miscellaneous Provisions) Act (NI) 1937; Married Women (Restraint upon Anticipation) Act (NI) 1952, and Law Reform (Husband and Wife) Act (NI) 1964.

[625] See now the Republic's Bankruptcy Act 1988: Sanfey and Holohan, *Bankruptcy Law and Practice in Ireland* (1991); Insolvency (NI) Order 1989: Hunter, *Northern Ireland Personal Insolvency* (1992).

[626] Para **[4.165]** *post*.

VI. LIFE ESTATE

A. General

[4.143] The life estate is the third category of freehold estate, though, unlike the other two categories, the fee simple and fee tail, it is not an estate of inheritance.[627] There are two main types of life estate, one being an estate for the life of the tenant himself and the other being an estate for the life or lives of some person (or persons) other than the life of the tenant holding the estate. The latter is known as an estate *pur autre vie*, and varieties of it were, and still are, extremely common in Ireland, notably the lease for lives renewable for ever and the lease for lives combined with a term of years.[628] These estates in Ireland are somewhat complex in nature because they combine aspects of both freehold estates and leasehold estates. Thus, while they could be discussed in the chapter relating to landlord and tenant,[629] they will be discussed here in view of their close connection with freehold estates. First, however, the discussion will be confined generally to the life estate and estate *pur autre vie*, apart from the Irish variations.

B. Creation and Transfer

[4.144] An ordinary life estate or estate *pur autre vie* would, as a freehold estate, be created or transferred by a deed of conveyance under s 2 of the Real Property Act 1845,[630] or by a will executed in accordance with the statutory provisions.[631]

C. Words of Limitation

1. Conveyances Inter Vivos

[4.145] A life estate, or estate *pur autre vie*, may be created directly by a conveyance using words of limitation such as to A "for life" or "for the life of X". On the other hand, a life estate can be created indirectly by the use of words insufficient to create a fee simple.[632] Thus the courts have held that expressions like "to A" simply, or "to A for ever," in a conveyance *inter vivos* created a life estate only in A.[633] In England this position has been reversed because, under the Law of Property Act 1925, the whole estate which the grantor had power to convey is presumed to pass unless a contrary intention is shown.[634] No such provision exists in either part of Ireland.[635] An estate *pur*

---

[627] Para [4.006], *ante*.

[628] Paras [4.167] *et seq, ante*.

[629] Ch 17, *post*.

[630] Para [3.026] *ante*.

[631] Now the Republic's Succession Act 1965 and the Wills and Administration Proceedings (NI) Order 1994, both of which replaced the Wills Act 1837: Ch 14 *post*.

[632] It is unlikely, therefore, that an estate *pur autre vie* could be created indirectly in this way.

[633] *Jameson v McGovern* [1934] IR 758 (see *A Casebook on Irish Land Law* (1984), p 116). See also *Re Courtney* [1981] NI 58.

[634] Section 60(1).

[635] Except in respect of transfers of *registered* land, see para [4.030] *ante*. But see the Republic's Law Reform Commission's *Report on Land Law and Conveyancing Law: (5) Further General Principles* CLRC 44-1992), pp 6-7; Land Law Working Group's *Final Report* (HMSO, 1990), Vol 1, paras 2.5.28-30.

autre vie can be created indirectly by the tenant of a life estate (for his own life) alienating his estate to someone else. All the tenant has to convey is an estate to last for his own life and so his alienee takes an estate *pur autre vie*, the *cestui que vie*[636] being the original tenant.

2. Gifts by Will

(i) At Common Law

[4.146] The rule at common law for wills was a modification of the rule for conveyances *inter vivos*. The testator might not have to use the technical words of limitation for a fee simple or a fee tail, but he did have to use words showing an intention to create one or other of these freehold estates of inheritance. If he failed to show this intention as a matter of construction, then once again all that would pass to the devisee would be a life estate.[637]

(ii) By Statute

[4.147] The Wills Act 1837 modified the common law in both parts of Ireland by providing that the fee simple or other whole estate of the testator passes unless a contrary intention is shown.[638] So since 1837 a life estate in a will must, in effect, be created expressly or directly rather than indirectly.

D. Classification

1. Life Estate

[4.148] The courts developed some special rules to govern the position of a tenant for life to take account of two things. First, there was the fact that his occupation of the property was bound to be for a limited time, so that those taking the property after him should have their interests protected during his tenancy. Secondly, his interest was of uncertain duration, so that he should not be deterred from making the best and fullest use of the property by the fear that he would die before he could enjoy the fruits of his labour. To a large extent, of course, the settlements legislation of the second half of the nineteenth century made the tenant's position much more secure and gave him vastly increased powers in relation to the land. Thus these common law rules are not as significant as they were and some of the statutory modifications have been replaced by the settlements legislation.[639]

(i) Waste

[4.149] The law of waste is that which restricts an owner of a limited interest in land from damaging it so as to prejudice those who will take the land after him, whether by way of reversion or remainder. Thus it covers the case of a tenant for life and a tenant

---

[636] Ie, the person by whose life the duration of the estate is measured. For problems of proof *re* existence of lives, see para **[4.170]** *post*.

[637] Para **[4.031]** *ante*.

[638] Sections 28, 30 and 31, replaced in the Republic of Ireland by the Succession Act 1965, s 94 and in NI by Article 18 of the Wills and Administration Proceedings (NI) Order 1994.

[639] This legislation is discussed in detail in Ch 8, *post*.

holding for a term of years under a lease or tenancy agreement. The law of waste as regards landlords and tenants forms a separate subject now in view of statutory modifications,[640] though the general principles as to what constitutes waste remain those fashioned at common law by the courts.

The general rule is that the reversioner or remainderman may in certain circumstances apply to the court for an injunction to restrain waste being committed by the tenant for life.[641] He may also be able to claim damages if he has suffered loss as a result of the waste[642] or ask the court to order the tenant to account for any profits he has made from the waste.[643] The courts have come to recognise four main types of waste: ameliorating, permissive, voluntary and equitable.[644] In each case the land occupied by the tenant for life has been altered by the waste, but to varying degrees and so his liability varies.

(a) Ameliorating

[4.150] In a sense this type seems to be a contradiction in terms. The act complained of so far from damaging the property actually benefits or improves it. The element of waste seems to exist in the fact that the nature of the property has been changed, eg, from residential to business use, however much this may have increased its value from a purely commercial point of view.[645] Not surprisingly, perhaps, the courts have shown little enthusiasm for actions complaining about this sort of waste.[646] It is unlikely that any substantial damages would be granted because no damage has been suffered. Usually the reverse is the case, and so the courts are loath to grant an injunction to prevent such waste. As Lord O'Hagan said in an appeal from Ireland:

> "[T]he waste with which a Court of Equity, or your Lordships acting as a Court of Equity, ought to interfere, should not be ameliorating waste, nor trivial waste. It must be waste of an injurious character - it must be waste of not only an injurious character, but of a substantially injurious character, and if either the waste be really ameliorating waste

---

[640] As to which, see para **[17.057]**, *post*.

[641] *Coppinger v Gubbins* (1846) 9 Ir Eq R 304; see also *Davies v Davies* (1840) 2 Ir Eq R 414.

[642] *Re Dilapidations of the Deanery-house of St. Patrick's, Dublin* (1864) 10 Ir Jur (NS) 38; *Minister for Local Government and Public Health v Kenny* (1941) 75 ILTR 26; *Ellis v Dublin Corporation* [1940] IR 183.

[643] *Crampton v Bishop of Meath* (1837) s & Sc 297.

[644] *Cf*, the concept of "wilful" waste in s 55(*b*) of the Republic's Landlord and Tenant Act 1931, discussed in *Gilligan v Silke* [1963] IR 1 and *O'Reilly v East Coast Cinemas Ltd* [1968] IR 56. Section 55(*b*) of the 1931 Act has been replaced by s 65(3) (which retains the concept of "wilful" waste) of the Republic's Landlord and Tenant (Amendment) Act 1980. See further on s 55 of the 1931 Act, *Taylor v Moremiles Tyre Services Ltd* (1978) Unrep (HC, RI), 6 June 1978 (1975 No 2646P); Wylie, *Irish Landlord and Tenant Law*, paras 15.30-31.

[645] *Cf, Brooke v Kavanagh* (1888) 23 LR Ir 97 (erection of buildings on a cultural land).

[646] See, generally, *Doherty v Allman* (1878) 3 App Cas 709 (see *A Casebook on Irish Land Law* (1984), p 201); *Belton v Nicholl* [1941] IR 230. Also *Palmer v McCormick* (1890) 25 LR Ir 110; *Grand Canal Co v McNamee* (1892) 29 LR Ir 131; Bathurst, 'Strict Common Law Rules of Waste' (1949) 13 Conv 278; Yardley, 'Ameliorating Waste in England and the United States' (1956) 19 MLR 150.

- that is a proceeding which results in benefit and not in injury - the Court of Equity, and your Lordships acting as a Court of Equity, ought not to interfere to prevent it."[647]

That case involved the conversion of store buildings that had become dilapidated into dwelling-houses and it was held a proper exercise of the court's discretion to refuse an injunction.[648] In another case, it was held that erecting a large spirit grocery immediately beside a villa residence, in what had since become an urbanised area, was not waste, though it clearly altered the character of that residence.[649]

(b) Permissive

[4.151] Permissive waste is the failure to do that which ought to be done, such as failure to repair property.[650] The general rule is that a tenant for life is not liable for such waste unless an express obligation to this effect has been imposed upon him, ie, he has been made impeachable for waste.[651] A tenant for life is rarely made so impeachable but the reverse is the case with a tenant holding under a lease or tenancy agreement.[652]

(c) Voluntary

[4.152] This is the opposite of permissive waste and is the doing of that which ought not to be done - positive acts as opposed to negative omissions. The general rule is that a tenant for life is liable for voluntary waste unless expressly made unimpeachable for waste. Thus removing earth or clay from the land would be voluntary waste,[653] as would be cutting down hedges so that they would not grow again or grubbing up the thorns forming the base of the hedge.[654] A common form of waste committed in Ireland was the burning of land and the legislature stepped in to make it an offence for the tenant or occupier of land to burn the surface of land.[655] Under the common law, a tenant for life

---

[647] *Doherty v Allman, op cit,* p 724. *Cf,* Lord Cairns LC, who said about ameliorating waste - "Now there again the course which the Court of Chancery ought undoubtedly to adopt would be to leave those who think they can obtain damages at common law to try what damages they can so obtain. Certainly, I think here again, the Court of Chancery would be doing very great injury to the one side for the purpose of securing to the other, that slightest possible sum which would at common law be considered the full equipment to which he was entitled." *Op cit,* p 723. For the distinction between common law and equitable remedies, see para **[3.050]** *ante.*

[648] In fact the case did not involve a life estate, but a long lease. The same principles apply, however, see para **[17.057]** *post.* See also *Belton v Nicholl* [1941] IR 230.

[649] *Craig v Greer* [1899] 1 IR 258 (see *A Casebook on Irish Land Law* (1984), p 616). *Cf, Palmer v McCormick* (1890) 25 LR Ir 110 (ploughing pasture land held to be beneficial); *Murphy v Daly* (1860) 13 ICLR 239 (ploughing ancient meadow land held to be voluntary waste); *Bobbett v Kennedy* (1916) 50 ILTR 171 (ploughing injurious).

[650] *Cf, White v McCann* (1850) 1 ICLR 205 (accidental fire not due to negligence by the lessee held not to be permissive waste). See also *Hughes v Sullivan* (1829) Hay & Jon app xliv; *Shee v Poor Law Commrs* (1852) 4 Ir Jur (os) 346.

[651] *Re Cartwright* (1889) 41 Ch D 532; see also *Davies v Davies* (1840) 2 Ir Eq R 414.

[652] Para **[17.045]** *post.*

[653] *Templemore v Moore* (1862) 15 ICLR 14; *Shaftesbury v Wallace* [1897] 1 IR 381.

[654] *Dunn v Bryan* (1872) IR 7 Eq 143.

[655] See Burning of Land Acts (Ireland) 1743, 17 Geo 2, c 10 (Ir); 1763, 3 Geo 3, c 29 (Ir); 1765, 5 Geo 3 c 10 (Ir); 1800, 40 Geo 3, c 24 (Ir). These Acts were replaced as regards tenants holding under leases or tenancy agreements by Deasy's Act 1860, s 30.

could not cut down timber on the land except to the extent that he was entitled to reasonable *estovers*. The right to estovers allowed the tenant to cut down suitable timber for such purposes as his own personal fuel, repairing his house or fences and making or repairing farm implements.[656] The tenant was not entitled to cut down more timber than was strictly necessary and suitable for this purpose, nor could he sell such timber for profit, unless he happened to occupy a timber estate on which the cutting and selling of timber was part of the annual income of the occupier.[657] However, the common law position was radically altered by statute.[658] A series of Irish Timber Acts were passed to promote the cultivation of trees in Ireland to replace the numerous forests destroyed over the centuries as a result of the constant changing of ownership of the land and plantation of settlers.[659] These Acts, for example, empowered tenants for life or lives to register by affidavit with the clerk of the peace of the county trees planted by them, whereby they became entitled to cut and sell those trees.[660] Failure to register prevented the tenant from asserting the right to cut down the trees,[661] and, until cut down, the trees remained part of the land and passed with it.[662] So far as tenants holding under leases were concerned, this right was withdrawn by an Act of 1791,[663] which made it an offence to cut down any tree or wood[664] growing on the land, unless authorised by the terms of the lease or agreement or with the consent in writing of the landlord.[665] Then, nineteenth century settlements legislation provided that, even if a tenant for life is impeachable for waste, he may cut and sell timber ripe and fit for cutting, provided he gets the consent of the trustees of the settlement or an order of the court.[666] Three-quarters of the proceeds are set aside as capital and the tenant for life may keep the remaining one-quarter as income.[667] Finally, it should be noted that nowadays the State

---

[656] As regards a tenant for life of land containing a turf bog, see *Jones v Meany* [1941] Ir Jur Rep.

[657] *The Fishmongers' Company v Beresford* (1818) Beat 607; *Gilmore v The O'Connor Don* [1947] IR 462 (see *A Casebook on Irish Land Law* (1984), p 212). See also *Simpson v Simpson* (1879) 3 LR Ir 308; *Marquis de la Bedoyère v Nugent* (1890) 25 LR Ir 143.

[658] See, however, *Kirkpatrick v Naper* (1945) 79 ILTR 49 (see *op cit*, p 225), where it was held that the common law notion of timber (ie, oak, ash and elm) was also relevant to the Irish Timber Acts.

[659] Timber Acts (Ireland) 1698, 10 Will 3, c 12 (Ir); 1705 4 Ann, c 9 (Ir); 1710, 9 Ann, c 5 (Ir); 1721, 8 Geo 1, c 8 (Ir). Land Improvement Acts (Ireland) 1735, 9 Geo 2, c 7 (Ir); 1765, 5 Geo 3, c 17 (Ir); 1767, 7 Geo 3, c 20 (Ir); 1776, 15 & 16 Geo 3, c 26 (Ir); 1784, 23 & 24 Geo 3, c 39 (Ir). See discussion in *Kirkpatrick v Naper* (1945) 79 ILTR 49.

[660] *Mountcashel v O'Neill* (1857) 5 HLC 937; see also *Standish v Murphy* (1852) 2 Ir Ch R 264; *Pentland v Somerville* (1851) 2 Ir Ch R 289.

[661] *RCB v Robinson* (1922) 56 ILTR 123; see also *Re Moore's Estate* (1902) 36 ILTR 14.

[662] *Alexander v Godley* (1857) 6 ICLR 445; *Galway v Baker* (1840) 7 Cl & F 379.

[663] 31 Geo 3, c 40 (Ir), which excepted leases for lives renewable for ever (see para **[4.167]** *post*) and rights of tenants with respect to trees already registered under the earlier Acts.

[664] Excepting "willows, osiers or sallows".

[665] See now Deasy's Act 1860, s 31, para **[17.058]**, *post*.

[666] Settled Land Act 1882, s 35(1), para **[8.088]** *post*.

[667] *Ibid*, s 35(2).

may impose restrictions on the felling, uprooting or otherwise damaging of trees, as part of its general protection of the environment and public amenities, such as forests.[668]

[4.153] As regards mines and minerals, the rule at common law was that it was voluntary waste for a tenant for life to open and work an unopened mine, whereas it was not waste to continue working a mine already opened on the land.[669] Substantially the same position was enacted by various Irish statutes[670] in respect of mines and quarries for tenants holding under leases and tenancy agreements. As regards tenants for life a series of statutes were passed enabling them to grant mining leases whether or not a mine was already open and whether or not the tenant was impeachable for waste.[671] Now a tenant for life may grant a mining lease for a term of up to 60 years.[672] If the tenant is impeachable for waste, three-quarters of the rent must be set aside as capital, in other cases one quarter only, and the residue he can keep as rents and profits.[673] Most mining and mineral rights are nowadays subject to State ownership and control, so that the law of waste has been largely superseded in this respect.[674]

(d) Equitable

[4.154] The courts took the view that, even though a tenant for life was made expressly unimpeachable for waste, he ought not to be allowed to commit acts of wanton destruction.[675] This would be too inequitable as regards the reversioner or remainderman, who could ask the court for an injunction to prevent such acts.[676] Equitable waste has been defined as "that which a prudent man would not do in the management of his own property".[677] To escape liability for such acts, the tenant for life would have to prove not only that he was made expressly "unimpeachable for waste" (which would cover voluntary waste only) but for "equitable" waste as well.[678]

---

[668] Eg, Forestry Act 1946 (RI), s 37, which makes it an offence to uproot any tree over ten years old or to cut down trees other than those specified in the section, without first giving notice to the Gardaí.

[669] *Elias v Snowdon Slate Quarries Co* (1879) 4 AC 454. *Cf, re* quarries, *Mansfield v Crawford* (1846) 9 Ir Eq R 272.

[670] See Mines Act (Ir) 1723, 10 Geo 1, c 5 (Ir), ss 4-7; Mines (Ir) Act 1806, ss 2 and 3, replaced by Deasy's Act 1860, ss 25-8, para **[17.058]**, *post*.

[671] Mines Acts (Ir) 1723, 10 Geo 1, c 5 (Ir); 1741, 15 Geo 2, c 10 (Ir); Mining Leases Act (Ir) 1749, 23 Geo 2, c 9 (Ir); Mines (Ir) Act 1806; Mining Leases (Ir) Act 1848.

[672] Settled Land Act 1882, s 6.

[673] *Ibid*, s 11. See, generally, para **[8.075]** *post*.

[674] See Minerals Development Acts 1940 and 1979 (RI) and Petroleum and other Minerals Development Act 1960 (RI); Mineral Development Act (NI) 1969.

[675] *Cf*, as regards tenants holding under leases or tenancy agreements, "fraudulent or malicious" waste in s 25 of Deasy's Act 1860, and "wilful waste in s 55(*b*) of the Republic's Landlord and Tenant Act 1931. Note again that s 55(*b*) of the 1931 Act has been replaced by s 65(3) of the Republic's Landlord and Tenant (Amendment) Act 1980. See para **[4.149]** fn 682 *ante*.

[676] Para **[3.136]** *ante*.

[677] *Turner v Wright* (1860) 2 De GF & J 234, 243.

[678] Judicature (Ir) Act 1877, s 28(3). In Northern Ireland, s 28(3) of the 1877 Act has been replaced by s 90 of the Judicature (Northern Ireland) Act 1978 (see para **[3.136]** *ante*).

(ii) Fixtures

[4.155] This is another subject which has relevance in the area of landlord and tenant law, where it has been dealt with by some special legislative provisions.[679] In each case the problem concerns the position of someone who has been in occupation of property for a substantial period of time and who has, during that period, attached fixtures to the land or to buildings on the land. The question is whether those fixtures have been so attached that they become part of the land or buildings and pass with the land or buildings when the tenant for life or years ceases his occupation.[680] Many of the general principles are common to tenants for life and tenants for years and they will be discussed in greater detail later.[681] The general rule as regards tenants for life is that items properly regarded as fixtures, according to the rules governing the degree and purpose of annexation, do pass with the land to the remainderman or reversioner. Certain items have, however, come to be excepted from this general rule, notably trade, ornamental and domestic fixtures.[682] This matter is governed entirely by case law; there is no legislation such as that which governs landlords and tenants.[683]

(iii) Emblements

[4.156] Another problem which can arise with respect to an occupier of land for a limited, but uncertain period, whether because his estate is for the period of a life or for a term of years fixed as to maximum duration but determinable within that period,[684] is that the tenant may find that the determination comes unexpectantly. In the case of agricultural land, this could be a serious problem where the tenant has sown crops and his tenancy determines before harvest time. The law dealt with this problem by giving such a tenant a right to *emblements*, ie, a right in the tenant, or his personal representatives (in the case of a tenant for life), to enter upon the land after the determination of the tenancy and to reap the crops sown during its currency.[685] This right related to cultivated crops only, like corn, wheat and flax,[686] and arose only in the case of a determination beyond the control of the tenant, such as the tenant's own death or the death of the *cestui que vie* in an estate *pur autre vie*. It would not apply where the tenant brought it upon himself, by serving a notice to determine the tenancy or bringing about

---

[679] Para **[17.060]** *post.*

[680] Amos, *The Law of Fixtures*; Bingham, 'Some Suggestions Concerning the Law of Fixtures' (1907) 7 Col L Rev 1; Guest and Lever, 'Hire-Purchase Equipment Leases and Fixtures' (1963) 27 Conv 30. McCormack, 'Hire-Purchase, Reservation of Title and Fixtures' [1990] Conv 275; Bennett, 'Fixtures, Purchase Money Security Interests and Dispositions of Interests in Land' (1994) 110 LQR 448.

[681] Para **[17.060]** *post.* See also as regards mortgagors and mortgagees, para **[13.010]** *post.*

[682] As to which, see para **[17.060]** *post.* See *Shinner v Harman* (1853) 3 ICLR 243; *Deeble v McMullen* (1857) 8 ICLR 355.

[683] Para **[17.060]** *post.* See also Wylie, *Irish Landlord and Tenant Law*, Ch 9.

[684] Para **[4.010]** *ante.*

[685] *Short v Atkinson* (1834) Hay & Jon 682; *O'Connell v O'Callaghan* (1841) Long & Town 157; *Lalor v Netterville* (1854) 6 Ir Jur (os) 261. See Cherry, *Irish Land Law and Land Purchase Acts* (3rd ed, 1903), p 67; De Moleyns, *Landowners' and Agents' Practical Guide* (8th ed, 1899), Ch 24.

[686] *Flanagan v Seaver* (1858) 9 Ir Ch R 230; see also *Rodwell v Phillips* (1840) 9 M & W 501.

an event operating to determine his tenancy (eg, breaking a condition relating to marriage or bankruptcy).[687]

(iv) Curtesy and Dower

[4.157] Rights of curtesy and dower were special kinds of life estate devised by the early common law. The need for them arose from the fact that, under early feudal law, a landowner was not allowed to make a will leaving his land to those members of his family, or in such shares, as he chose. The law of intestate succession or inheritance, as it was then called, was governed by the principle of *primogeniture*, ie, the eldest son succeeded to all estates and interests in the land.[688] This was felt to be rather harsh on the surviving spouse of the deceased landowner and rights of curtesy and dower were the common law's solution. These rights have been abolished in relation to those dying after 1955 in Northern Ireland and 1966 in the Republic of Ireland, but the philosophy of ensuring proper provision for certain members of the family lives on.[689]

[4.158] Curtesy was the right of a widower to a life estate in the *whole* of the real property of his deceased wife. Dower was the right of a widow to a life estate in *one-third*[690] of the real property of her deceased husband. In each case, the wife or husband must have been entitled during the marriage to a freehold estate of inheritance - there could only be curtesy or dower out of a fee simple or fee tail, not a life estate or leasehold.[691] In each case, the husband or wife must have been seised of the land or entitled in possession to an equitable interest, and no claim could be made if it had been held in a joint tenancy, since the right of survivorship in the other tenant or tenants was inconsistent with curtesy or dower.[692] A husband could not claim curtesy unless issue of the marriage capable of inheriting the land had been born alive, whereas the widow could claim dower if birth of such issue had been *possible*, even if none had in fact been born. A husband could not claim curtesy if his wife had disposed of her land *inter vivos* or by will, to the extent she could do this.[693] As regards dower, the Dower Act 1833 provided that a widow could not claim it out of any land disposed of by her husband *inter vivos* or by will, or where it had been barred by the husband so declaring by deed or in his will under the Act.[694]

[4.159] As mentioned above, however, rights to curtesy and dower have been abolished as to the persons dying after 1966 in the Republic of Ireland, by the Succession Act 1965,[695] and after 1955 in Northern Ireland by the Administration of Estates (NI)

---

[687] *Kelly v Webber* (1860) 11 ICLR 57.

[688] See further on intestate succession, Ch 15, *post*.

[689] Ch 15, *post*.

[690] *Murland v Despard* [1956] IR 170.

[691] *Loyd v Loyd* (1842) 2 Con & L 592; *Kernaghan v McNally* (1859) 11 Ir Ch R 52.

[692] Ch 7, *post*.

[693] Para **[25.10]**, *post*.

[694] Sections 4, 6 and 7. *Gurly v Gurly* (1840) 2 Dr & Wal 463; *Fyan v Henry*, (1840) 2 Dr & Wal 556; *Killen v Campbell* (1848) 10 Ir Eq R 461; *Cooper v Cooper* (1856) 1 Ir Jur (ns) 370; *Re Dwyers* (1862) 13 Ir Ch R 431.

1955.[696] These statutes introduced a new law of intestate succession to land whereby the various members of the deceased's family, including a widower or widow, receive specified shares of the estate, real and personal.[697]

2. Estate Pur Autre Vie

[4.160] The main attributes to this type of life estate have already been mentioned,[698] and it shares many of the features discussed above in relation to the ordinary life estate.[699] At common law, a tenant *pur autre vie* could freely alienate his estate *inter vivos* and it seems that, when he did so, no special words of limitation were necessary to pass the whole of his estate to his assignee.[700] Though there was nothing to prevent the tenant of an estate *pur autre vie* conveying it with an express limitation for life, ie, the life of the grantee.[701] There are, however, some special features with respect to the estate *pur autre vie*, which arise from the fact that the life determining the duration of the estate is not that of the holder of the estate itself.

(i) Occupancy

[4.161] An obvious question that arises is what happens when the holder predeceases the person for whose life the estate was granted. The converse case causes no problems because in that case the estate simply comes to its natural determination while the grantee is still alive. Under early law, a tenant *pur autre vie* could not make a will leaving his estate to someone else in the event of his dying before the expiry of the life in question. Indeed, the early legislation relating to wills of land did not apply to such estates.[702] The common law had to formulate some rules to govern this situation. These rules made up the law of *occupancy*.[703] The general theory of this law was that the estate was succeeded to by the first person to enter and become seised of the land after the death of the tenant. This person did not take as heir, because an estate *pur autre vie* was not an estate of inheritance like a fee simple or fee tail.[704] He took only as the appropriate successor under the peculiar law of occupancy. Originally a distinction had to be made between *general* occupancy and *special* occupancy.

---

[695] Section 11(2).

[696] Section 1(4).

[697] See, generally, Ch 15, *post*.

[698] Paras **[4.143]**-**[4.145]** *ante. Brenan v Boyne* (1864) 16 Ir Ch R 87; see also *Tisdall v Tisdall* (1839) 2 Ir LR 41.

[699] Eg, the law of waste, para **[4.149]** *ante*, fixtures, para **[4.155]** *ante*, and emblements, para **[4.156]** *ante*.

[700] *McClintock v Irvine* (1860) 10 Ir Ch R 480; *Re Bayley's Estate* (1863) 16 Ir Ch R 215; *Brenan v Boyne* (1864) 16 Ir Ch R 87; *Currin v Doyle* (1878) 3 LR Ir 265; *Horan v Horan* [1935] IR 306. *Cf, Dawson v Dawson* (1852) 13 Ir LR 472; *Barron v Barron* (1858) 8 Ir Ch R 366.

[701] *Mitchell v Coulson* (1827) 1 Hud & Br 210; *Ryan v Cowley* (1835) L1 & G *temp*. Sug 7; *Crozier v Crozier* (1843) 3 Dr & War 373; *Dawson v Dawson* (1852) 13 Ir LR 472; *Rotheram v Rotheram* (1884) 13 LR Ir 429.

[702] Eg, the Statute of Wills (Ir) 1634.

[703] Challis, *The Law of Real Property* (3rd ed), pp 358-62. *Horan v Horan* [1935] IR 306.

[704] Para **[4.006]** *ante*.

(a) General Occupancy

[4.162] If an estate *pur autre vie* had been granted without any reference to the grantee's heirs or successors in the conveyance, the law of general occupancy applied.[705] Literally the first person to enter upon the land after the grantee's death succeeded to it and remained entitled to it until the estate came to an end with the death of the *cestui que vie*. This rule was connected with the common law's abhorrence of any gap in the seisin and its desire to see that someone, even if a complete stranger to the land, should always be seised at any particular point in time.[706] It may be noted that the general occupant was not liable for any of the grantee's debts.[707]

[4.163] It was not a very satisfactory system of devolution to have strangers taking over the ownership of land, and so it is not surprising that legislation abolished general occupancy. The Statute of Frauds (Ireland) 1695 provided that where there was no special occupant, so that normally general occupancy rules would have applied, the estate *pur autre vie* was to descend to the grantee's personal representative for distribution like personalty.[708] The statute provided that in all cases the land so succeeded to was liable for payment of the deceased grantee's debts.[709]

(b) Special Occupancy

[4.164] Under this law, if the estate *pur autre vie* had been conveyed to the grantee "and his heirs," the heirs (determined under the rules of inheritance) succeeded as special occupant, not by way of inheritance.[710] Thus until the passing of the Statute of Frauds (Ireland) the land so taken by the heir was not liable for the deceased's debts.[711]

(c) Statute of Frauds (Ireland) 1695

By s 9[712] of this statute a tenant *pur autre vie* became entitled to dispose of his estate by will, thereby displacing the law of occupancy.

(d) Administration of Estates Act (NI) 1955

Section 1(3) of this Act abolished the law of special occupancy for the purposes of devolution on intestacy after 1955. Since then, on death of a tenant *pur autre vie*

---

[705] Challis, *op cit*, p 359.

[706] Challis, *ibid*. And see on the common law seisin rules, para **[5.012]** *post*.

[707] Megarry and Wade, *The Law of Real Property* (5th ed, 1984), p 94.

[708] Section 9 replaced by the Wills Act 1837, s 2 (see also ss 3 and 6); *cf*, the English Statute of Frauds 1677, s 12. *Plunket v Reilly* (1852) 1 Ir Ch R 585; *Mountcashell v More-Smyth* [1896] AC 158; *Re King* [1899] 1 IR 30; *Re Murray* [1916] 1 IR 302. See also Deasy's Act 1860, s 9. Para **[17.029]** *post*.

[709] *Ibid*.

[710] *Dowell v Dignan* (1826) Batty 698. See also *Kelly v Coote* (1857) 2 Ir Jur (NS) 195.

[711] The heir still succeeded even if executors and administrators were also referred to in the conveyance. The latter took as special occupants only if the heir or heirs were not referred to. Challis, *op cit*, pp 359-61; *Wall v Byrne* (1845) 7 Ir Eq R 578; *Croker v Brady* (1879) 4 LR Ir 653; *Whitehead v Morton* (1887) 19 LR Ir 435; *Horan v Horan* [1935] IR 306.

[712] Replaced by ss 2 and 6 of the Wills Act 1837.

intestate, his land devolves like any other land, other than entailed land.[713] In other words, it devolves on the personal representatives to be administered by them with the rest of the estate in accordance with the Act.[714]

(e) Succession Act 1965 (RI)

Section 11(1) of this Act similarly abolished devolution by special occupancy in the Republic with respect to devolution since 1967. On death of a tenant *pur autre vie* intestate, his land devolves on his personal representatives for distribution with the rest of his estate, real and personal.

(ii) Quasi-Entails

[4.165] An estate *pur autre vie* could be conveyed to someone else so as to give him an entailed interest. This estate was not an estate of inheritance and so was outside the scope of *De Donis* 1285.[715] The courts held that such a conveyance created what was called a *quasi*-entail in the assignee, ie, the estate would pass to the heirs of the body of the assignee in the same way as an entail, for so long as the life determining the estate assigned lasted.[716] It was a "quasi" entail only because the successors were not taking by way of inheritance but, in effect, as special occupants. Apart from this, however, the courts strove to apply and develop the rules applying to quasi-entails as closely as possible to those relating to entails.[717] Thus the rights of the heirs as occupants, or of reversioners or remaindermen, could be barred by the quasi-tenant in tail executing a conveyance *inter vivos*.[718] It seems this could be done even before the Fines and Recoveries (Ireland) Act 1834, so that there was no need to enrol the deed before or after the Act, which applies only to disentailing deeds operating under it.[719] If the quasi-tenant in tail was not in possession he would need the consent of the tenant in possession,[720] and it seems that, as in the case of entails, a quasi-entail could not be barred by will. There was some doubt about this point on the argument that, when estates *pur autre vie* themselves became devisable by will, quasi-entails of them could be similarly barred.[721] This would seem to be a fair argument so far as barring the heirs

---

[713] Para **[15.013]** *post.*

[714] Chs 15 and 16, *post.*

[715] Para **[4.114]** *ante.*

[716] Challis, *op cit*, pp 362-3. *Allen v Allen* (1842) 2 Dr & War 307; *Batteste v Maunsell* (1876) IR 10 Eq 314; *Re McNeale's Estate* (1858) 3 Ir Jur (NS) 310; *Lynch v Nelson* (1870) IR 5 Eq 192; *Walsh v Studdert* (1873) IR 7 CL 482; *MacAndrew v Gallagher* (1874) IR 8 Eq 490; *Betty v Humphreys* (1872) IR 9 Eq 332; *Blackhall v Gibson* (1878) 2 LR Ir 49; *Re Carew's Estate* (1887) 19 LR Ir 483.

[717] For the application of the rule in *Shelley's Case* to estates *pur autre vie*, see *Crozier v Crozier* (1843) 3 Dr & War 373, espec. at 381-2 (*per* Sugden LC); *Colclough v Colclough* (1870) IR 4 Eq 263; *Macnamara v Dillon* (1883) 11 LR Ir 29.

[718] Para **[4.123]** *ante.*

[719] Megarry and Wade, *op cit*, p 95. It was held in *Morris v Morris* (1872) IR 7 CL 295 that a fee farm grant executed under the Renewable leasehold Conversion Act 1849 (para **[4.081]** *ante*) barred a quasi-entail. See also *Batteste v Maunsell* (1876) IR 10 Eq 314; *Blackhall v Gibson* (1878) 2 LR Ir 49.

[720] *Allen v Allen* (1842) 2 Dr & War 307, espec. at 324-38 (*per* Sugden LC). Para **[4.124]** *ante.*

[721] Challis, *op cit*, p 363.

otherwise succeeding as occupants was concerned, but the Irish courts have consistently questioned the argument and have insisted that at least quasi-remainders over after the quasi-entail could not be so barred.[722]

[4.166] As a result of the Administration of Estates Act (NI) 1955, and the Republic's Succession Act 1965, the law relating to quasi-entails has rapidly become obsolete, being applicable now only to estates created before the operation of the Acts. Both Acts abolished all rules, modes and canons of descent and of devolution by special occupancy with a saving only for descent of an estate tail.[723] This saving does not cover quasi-entails because the succession in these cases by the heirs of the body is not by descent or inheritance, but by occupancy.[724]

3. Lease for Lives Renewable for Ever

[4.167] One of the most common methods of holding land in Ireland has been the lease for lives renewable for ever.[725] This sort of grant has rarely occurred on the other side of the Irish Sea, if ever, though a lease for years perpetually renewable was quite common until all such leases were converted into leases for 2,000 years by the Law of Property Act 1922.[726] A "lease" for lives renewable for ever is a curious mixture of land law concepts. It creates leasehold tenure between the parties to the lease, but the estate granted to the lessee is a freehold estate.[727] It is in effect an estate *pur autre vie*, though in this case there are usually three lives named in the lease. The Irish courts have held that in a conveyance *inter vivos* strict words of limitation are not necessary to pass the entire estate of the lessee in a lease for lives renewable for ever. It is sufficient if other words are used indicating such an intention.[728]

[4.168] The origin of such leases has been a matter of some controversy over the centuries.[729] One theory is that they gained popularity because those participating in land settlements in the seventeenth century, particularly the Ulster plantation,[730] were

---

[722] *Allen v Allen, op cit*; *Campbell v Sandys* (1803) 1 Sch & Lef 281, espec. at 294-5 (*per* Lord Redesdale); *Dillon v Dillon* (1809) 1 Ba & B 77, espec at 95 (*per* Lord Manners); *Hopkins v Ramage* (1826) Batty 365; *Kelly v Kelly* (1901) 35 ILTR 215. Lyne, *Leases for Lives Renewable for Ever* (1837), pp 24-6.

[723] 1955 Act, s 1(3); 1965 Act, s 11(1).

[724] Para **[4.165]** *supra*.

[725] See, generally, Lyne, *Leases for Lives Renewable for Ever* (1837); Furlong, *Law of Landlord and Tenant as Administered in Ireland* (2nd ed, 1869), bk 2, Ch 4; Finlay, *Law of Renewals in Respect of Leases for Lives Renewable for Ever* (1829).

[726] Section 145 and Sched 15. See *Survey of the Land Law of Northern Ireland* (HMSO, 1971), paras 61-9; Land Law Working Group's *Discussion Document No. 2* ('Estates and Interests and Family Dealings in Land') (HMSO, 1981), pp 17-21. Also *Re Hopkins' Lease* [1972] 1 WLR 372.

[727] Paras **[4.003]**-**[4.012]** *ante*.

[728] *McClintock v Irvine* (1860) 10 Ir Ch R 480; *Re Bayley's Estate* (1863) 16 Ir Ch R 215; *Brenan v Boyne* (1864) 16 Ir Ch R 87; *Betty v Elliott* (1865) 16 Ir Ch R 110; *Currin v Doyle* (1878) 3 LR Ir 265; *Horan v Horan* [1935] IR 306.

[729] See, eg, Lyne, *op cit*, pp 1-7.

[730] Para **[1.30]**, *ante*.

given express power to grant leases for lives renewable for ever.[731] Some landowners were given powers by private Acts of Parliament.[732] These leases afforded all the advantages of the relationship of landlord and tenant, especially the extensive landlord's remedies available in Ireland,[733] yet they also gave the tenants a major estate in the land. Indeed, as we shall see, the estate came to be regarded almost as equivalent to a fee simple, and ultimately the legislature recognised this in passing the Renewable Leasehold Conversion Act 1849.[734] Unlike a fee farm grant, which produced a perpetual fixed annual income in the shape of the fee farm rent, a lease for lives renewable for ever had the advantage of producing additional periodic income in the shape of the fines (sums of money) to be paid to the landlord every time one of the three lives had to be renewed. Such a lease also had the advantage for the landlord over an ordinary lease for a term of years in that the freehold estate carried the parliamentary vote, in the days when this was a qualification, and the landlord could usually expect his tenants to vote for himself or his nominees.[735]

[4.169] Whatever the reasons for their creation, there is no doubt that leases for lives renewable for ever became an extremely popular form of tenure in Ireland. So much so that during the nineteenth century it was estimated that up to one-seventh of the entire soil of Ireland was held under such leases.[736] The standard form of lease consisted of a conveyance to the tenant for the lives of three specified persons, with a covenant for perpetual renewal of these lives on payment to the landlord of a specified fine on each renewal.[737] Otherwise, the conveyance took the form of an ordinary lease for years, with various covenants and conditions inserted governing the relationship of the landlord and the tenant. The landlord had all the usual remedies for enforcement of the tenant's obligations, actions for debt, distress and ejectment for non-payment of rent.[738] Yet the fact remained that, although leasehold tenure existed between the parties, the tenant had a freehold estate, an estate *pur autre vie*. Thus succession to his estate, which could be perpetual as new lives were added on each appropriate occasion, was governed by the general law of succession relating to such a freehold estate, ie, the law of occupancy.[739] It also became very common to make settlements of these estates, which was not surprising in view of the perpetual nature of the estates and of the amount of land in

---

[731] See the discussion in *Bateman v Murray* (1785) 1 Ridgw PC 187. The settlers' powers of making fee farm grants have already been discussed, para **[4.060]** *ante*.

[732] Eg, the second Duke of Ormonde, see 7 Will 3, c i (Ir). See *Sweet v Anderson* (1788) 2 Bro PC 256; *Boyle v Lysaght* (1787) 1 Ridgw PC 384.

[733] Ch 17, *post*.

[734] Paras **[4.081]** *ante* and **[4.176]** *post*.

[735] See also para **[1.035]** *ante*.

[736] Lyne, *op cit*, p 1.

[737] See Stubbs and Baxter, *Irish Forms and Precedents* (1910); see also Edge, *Forms of Leases and Other Forms Relating to Land in Ireland* (1884).

[738] For statutory provisions dealing with such remedies against tenants *pur autre vie*, see the Arrears of Rent Act (Ir) 1634, 10 Chas 1, sess 2, c 5 (Ir), s 3; Distress for Rent Act (Ir) 1710, 9 Ann, c 8 (Ir), s 7; Landlord and Tenant Act (Ir) 1784, 23 & 24 Geo 3, c 46 (Ir), s 2.

[739] See paras **[4.161]**-**[4.164]** *ante*.

Ireland held subject to them. The effect of limiting a lease for lives to A "and the heirs of his body" was, of course, to create a quasi-entail, a subject we have discussed above.[740] In *Morris v Morris*[741] it was held that a fee farm conversion grant executed under the Renewable Leasehold Conversion Act 1849[742] barred a quasi-entail. Not all the law relating to estates *pur autre vie*, however, was strictly applied, for some account had to be taken of the potentially perpetual nature of the tenant's estate. This had more of the attributes of a fee simple, with no reversion or remainder to be protected, than of a life estate. In particular, the law of waste was modified with respect to leases for lives renewable for ever. Thus s 1 of the Land Improvement Act (Ireland) 1765[743] specified that tenants for lives renewable for ever were not impeachable for waste in respect of timber planted by them or their predecessors in title.[744] This was held to apply whether or not the trees had been registered under the Timber Acts (Ireland).[745] Such tenants were excepted from the statutory provisions prohibiting tenants for lives or years from cutting down trees under the guise of *estovers*, unless expressly authorised in the lease or by licence from the landlord.[746] They were also excepted from statutory provisions prohibiting assignment or subletting without licence or consent from the landlord.[747]

[4.170] The Irish courts recognised that the estate given to the tenant was potentially perpetual. It is true that the Irish Parliament had in the early days favoured the landlords in passing the Life Estates Act (Ireland) 1695.[748] Section 1 of this Act provided that persons for whose lives estates were granted, who remained "beyond the seas" or absented themselves from Ireland for seven years, were to be presumed dead for the purpose of any action by a lessor or reversioner for recovery of possession of the land.[749] The courts took the view, however, that the estate granted to the tenant was intended to be perpetual, so that not only would the landlord be compelled to perform specifically

---

[740] Para **[4.165]** *ante*.

[741] (1872) IR 7 CL 295. See also *Batteste v Maunsell* (1876) IR 10 Eq 314; *Blackhall v Gibson* (1878) 2 LR Ir 49.

[742] Para **[4.176]** *post*.

[743] 5 Geo 3, c 17 (Ir), one of the Irish Timber Acts (see para **[4.152]** *ante*).

[744] See now Deasy's Act 1860, s 25. Para **[17.058]**, *post*.

[745] *Pentland v Somerville* (1851) 2 Ir Ch R 289; *Ex parte Armstrong* (1857) 8 Ir Ch R 30; *Re Moore's Estate* (1902) 36 ILTR 14.

[746] Landlord and Tenant Act (Ir) 1791, 31 Geo 3, c 40 (Ir); see now Deasy's Act 1860, s 31. Para **[17.058]** *post*.

[747] Assignment and Subletting of Land (Ir) Act 1826, 7 Geo 4, c 29; see also the Assignment of Leases (Ir) Act 1832, 2 & 3 Will 4, c 17. See now Deasy's Act 1860, s 10, still in force in Northern Ireland, but repealed in the Republic by the Landlord and Tenant (Ground Rents) Act 1967, s 35(1). *Craigdarragh Trading Co Ltd v Doherty* [1989] NI 218 and para **[17.035]** *et seq*.

[748] 7 Will 3, c 8 (Ir). See *Aldworth v Allen* (1865) 11 HLC 549; *Secretary of State for War v Booth* [1901] 2 IR 692.

[749] Section 3 provided that, if it was later proved that the "lives" were not dead at the time of the action, the lessee could re-enter and recover as damages the full profits received by the lessor in the meantime, plus interest.

the covenant to renew the lease at the appropriate times, but relief would be granted in equity against forfeiture by him of the lease for mere lapse of time by the tenant in claiming his renewals on the dropping of the lives in question.[750] The courts developed what was known as the "old equity of the country".[751] This was a general principle that a lessee for lives renewable for ever could always obtain a renewal of his lease even though all the lives had long since died, provided there was no fraud or other misconduct on his part[752] and that he was prepared to compensate the landlord for the arrears in renewal fines which the landlord would have been entitled to had the renewals been obtained when the lives had dropped.[753] Great consternation was caused in Irish legal circles when some members of the House of Lords, notably Lords Mansfield and Thurlow, seemed to call in question the activities of the Irish courts in this regard towards the end of the eighteenth century.[754] The Irish Parliament reacted swiftly and passed the Tenantry Act (Ireland) 1779.

---

[750] *Lennon v Napper* (1802) 2 Sch & Lef 682; *Butler v Mulvihill* (1819) 1 Bligh 137.

[751] *Sweet v Anderson* (1722) 2 Bro PC 256; *Worsop v Rosse* (1740) 1 Bro PC 281.

[752] *Lennon v Napper* (1802) 2 Sch & Lef 682.

[753] *Sweet v Anderson* (1722) 2 Bro PC 256.

[754] See *Kane v Hamilton* (1784) 1 Ridgw PC 180 (action begun in Ireland in 1768); *Bateman v Murray* (1785) 1 Ridgw PC 187 (action begun in 1765). In the latter, Lord Thurlow stated that a court of equity would "never assist" a lessee "where he has lost his right by his own gross laches or neglect". Note that these cases were reported long after the passing of the Tenantry Act (Ir) 1779, which resulted directly from them.

Chapter 6

INCORPOREAL HEREDITAMENTS

IV. EASEMENTS AND PROFITS

[6.022] We now begin more extended treatment of those incorporeal hereditaments which are of practical significance in Ireland today. One of the most common categories is that concerning two very similar interests in land, an easement and a profit *à prendre*. Indeed, much land in both parts of Ireland is subject to interests of this nature, for they include such common matters as rights of way, of light and of support and mining, quarrying fishing and gaming rights.

A. Nature

[6.023] Though easements and profits have many similar characteristics, there are important points of distinction which should be emphasised. Furthermore there are several other interests in land which are neither easements nor profits. In the next few pages we consider first the nature of easements and profits and then compare them with similar concepts recognised by our land law.

1. Easements

[6.024] Case law has settled that there are four essential features of an easement.[1]

(i) Dominant and Servient Tenement

[6.025] The first essential feature of an easement is that it can exist only if it is *appurtenant* (annexed) to some piece of land, ie, so as to benefit that land.[2] An easement, unlike a profit *à prendre*,[3] cannot exist *in gross*, ie, independently of a piece of land which is benefited by it.[4] Although it has been queried from time to time whether this requirement is strictly necessary it is probably too late now to question it and has recently been reaffirmed by the English courts.[5] The result is, therefore, that the concept of an easement involves the existence of two pieces of land, usually called the *dominant* and *servient* tenements.[6] The dominant tenement is the land benefited by the easement

---

[1] See, generally, Morris, *Outline of the Law of Easements* (1869); Gale, *Law of Easements* (14th ed, 1972); Jackson, *The Law of Easements and Profits* (1978). See also *Re Ellenborough Park* [1956] Ch 131.

[2] Hence the argument that an easement was not properly regarded as an incorporeal hereditament but rather a mere right appurtenant or incident to a corporeal hereditament, see Challis, *Law of Real Property* (3rd ed, 1911), pp 51-2 and 55-6. See also *Associated Properties Ltd v Representatives of Nolan* (1951) 85 ILTR 86.

[3] Para **[6.038]** *post*.

[4] *Hawkins v Rutter* [1892] 1 QB 668.

[5] *London and Blenheim Estates Ltd v Ladbroke Retail Parks Ltd* [1993] 4 All ER 157. Followed in *Voice v Bell* [1993] EGCS 128.

[6] See the discussion in *Scott v Goulding Properties Ltd* [1972] IR 200 (see *A Casebook on Irish Land Law*, (1984), p 299).

and the servient tenement is the land over which the easement exists, eg, X, the owner of Blackacre, has a right of way over Whiteacre, which is owned by his neighbour Y.[7] It is wise to specify the dominant tenement clearly in the deed, otherwise there is the danger that, although the courts are often willing to imply rights in the nature of easements,[8] the court may construe the dominant tenement more narrowly than was intended by the parties.[9]

(ii) Accommodation of Dominant Tenement

[6.026] It is not enough that the easement benefits the owner of the dominant land in his personal capacity, it must benefit the land he owns, as the dominant land. The question in each case is whether or not the alleged easement improves the land in some way, whether in terms of amenity, utility or convenience.[10] For example, a right of light may be necessary to make a building serviceable[11] or a diminution in the amount of light previously coming to a building may make it less convenient to use or enjoy.[12] It follows from this that the servient tenement must be in sufficient proximity to the dominant tenement to confer a practical benefit on it. This does not mean that the two tenements must be contiguous, but they must be neighbouring lands.[13] A farmer as owner of land in Cork cannot have a right of way over land in Galway.

[6.027] A right which confers a personal advantage only on the owner for the time being of the dominant land is not an easement. Thus a grant of the sole and exclusive right of putting pleasure-boats on a canal to a lessee of land on the canal's bank was held to confer a licence only.[14] In *Ackroyd v Smith*[15] it was held that a grant of a right of way "for all purposes" to the tenant of an estate and his successors in title permitted the right to be used for purposes not necessarily connected with that estate and so it failed to create an easement.[16]

(iii) Ownership or Occupation by Different Persons

[6.028] The general rule is that the dominant and servient tenements must be held under separate ownership. An easement, like other incorporeal hereditaments, is essentially an interest held by one person over another person's land.[17] However, this rule is subject to

---

[7]   See *Gaw v CIE* [1953] IR 232 (see *ibid*, p 622).
[8]   See para **[6.060]** *et seq, post.*
[9]   See, eg, *Nickerson v Barraclough* [1981] Ch 426.
[10] *Scott v Goulding Properties Ltd* [1972] IR 200.
[11] *Annally Hotel Ltd v Bergin* (1970) 104 ILTR 5.
[12] *McGrath v Munster and Leinster Bank Ltd* [1959] IR 313; *Scott v Goulding Properties Ltd* [1972] IR 200.
[13] *Bailey v Stephens* (1862) 12 CB (ns) 91 at 115.
[14] *Hill v Tupper* (1863) H & C 121. *Cf Moody v Steggles* (1879) 12 Ch D 261. See further on licences, para **[6.049]** *post.*
[15] (1850) 10 CB 164.
[16] *Cf Gaw v CIE* [1953] IR 232 at 243 (*per* Dixon J) (see *A Casebook on Irish Land Law* (1984), p 622).
[17] Para **[6.003]** *ante.* See also *Re Flanagan and McGarvey and Thompson's Contract* [1945] NI 32 (see *ibid*, p 317).

the substantial qualification that an easement may exist in the case of a common "owner" of the two tenements provided the occupation of them is not common. The obvious example, which was extremely common in Ireland,[18] though not, perhaps, so common nowadays,[19] is where the dominant and servient tenements are owned by a common landlord but one or other of them or both are occupied by tenants.[20] It is settled that a tenant may have an easement in respect of other land occupied by his own landlord or occupied by another tenant of the same landlord.[21]

[6.029] One further point should be noted in this context. While, in general, a landowner cannot have an easement over his own land, his habitual exercise of rights over part of his land does have some significance in our land law. As we shall see later in this chapter,[22] rights so exercised, which would be easements if the other part were owned or occupied by another person, are called "quasi-easements" and may become full easements if the land is subsequently divided into separate parcels in terms of either ownership or occupation.

(iv) Subject-matter of a Grant

[6.030] The fourth essential feature of an easement is that the alleged right in any particular case must be capable of forming the subject-matter of a grant. The general rule is that all easements "lie in grant,' ie, must be created by deed, and so every purported easement must belong to categories of property rights which have over the centuries come to be regarded as capable of being conveyed from one person to another.[23] Thus the following have been recognised as established easements: rights of way,[24] light,[25] support,[26] and water.[27] It must be emphasised that these categories or "heads" of easements are very wide ones and numerous kinds of rights may be subsumed within them.[28] Furthermore it is doubtful whether the categories or list of easements recognised by our law should be regarded as closed, for, as Lord St Leonards

---

[18] See Chua, 'Easements: Termors in Prescription in Ireland' (1964) 15 NILQ 489; Delaney, 'Lessees and the Doctrine of Lost Grant' (1958) 74 LQR 82. See further para **[6.078]** *post.*

[19] Due to the disappearance of agricultural tenancies under the Land Purchase Acts, Ch 18 *post.*

[20] Of course, the tenants are also "owners" of the land in that they hold leasehold estates in the land, as opposed to the freehold estate of the landlord, para **[4.007]** *ante.*

[21] *Hanna v Pollock* [1900] 2 IR 664 (see *A Casebook on Irish Land Law* (1984), p 329); *Flynn v Harte* [1913] 2 IR 322; *Tallon v Ennis* [1937] IR 549. There has, however, been much controversy in Ireland and England over the question of acquisition of easements by *prescription* in the case of leasehold land, see paras **[6.078]** - **[6.079]** *post.*

[22] Para **[6.061]** *post.*

[23] Para **[6.002]** *ante.*

[24] *Gaw v CIE* [1953] IR 232 (see *A Casebook on Irish Land Law* (1984), p 622).

[25] *Tisdall v McArthur & Co (Steel and Metal) Ltd* [1951] IR 228 (see *ibid,* p 357); *Annally Hotel Ltd v Bergin* (1970) 104 ILTR 65; *Scott v Goulding Properties Ltd* [1972] IR 200 (*ibid,* p 299).

[26] *Latimer v Official Co-Operative Society* (1885) 16 LR Ir 305 (*ibid,* p 293); *Green v Belfast Tramways Co* (1887) 20 LR Ir 35; *Gateley v Martin* [1900] 2 IR 269.

[27] *McCartney v Londonderry and Lough Swilly Rly Co* [1904] AC 301; *Kelly v Dea* (1966) 100 ILTR 1.

[28] See further on the various categories of easements, paras **[6.107]** *et seq, post.*

once remarked: "The category of servitudes and easements must alter and expand with the changes that take place in the circumstances of mankind".[29]

[6.031] The courts have, however, over the years also taken the view that there must be limits to the rights recognised as easements. They do not look with favour upon novel rights which do not seem to conform with the general nature of easements. This is particularly so where the easement claimed is "negative", ie it prevents the servient owner from doing something on his *own* land which he would otherwise be entitled to do, rather than "positive", ie, it allows the dominant owner to do something on the *servient owner's* land (such as exercising a right of way over it. Thus it has been held in Ireland that there is no such easement as a right to "shade and shelter" from a hedge,[30] just as in England it was more recently held that there was no such easement as a right, in respect of a wall of a house, to protection from weather by an adjoining house.[31] Such easements, if recognised, would have prevented the servient owner from removing the hedge or demolishing the house on his own land. For some time it was thought that a right to use a path or garden for taking walks or wandering around could not be an easement, being a mere *jus spatiandi*.[32] However, it now seems to be recognised that such a right may properly form the subject-matter of any easement in particular cases, eg, when annexed to a housing estate adjoining parks and gardens.[33] In *Middleton v Clarence*,[34] an Irish court held that the right to throw quarry refuse on another person's land was a proper easement. Both these easements were positive in the sense given above. However, an easement is an *incorporeal* hereditament[35] and so a right which confers on the dominant owner occupational or possessory rights over the servient tenement to the exclusion of the servient owner cannot be an easement[36] and must be created by a lease or licence arrangement.[37]

---

[29] *Dyce v Lady James Hay* (1852) 1 Macq 305 at 312-3. *Cf* the discussion of ancient lights by the Republic Supreme Court in *Scott v Goulding Properties Ltd* [1972] IR 200 (*ibid*, p 299).

[30] *Cochrane v Verner* (1895) 29 ILT 571.

[31] *Phipps v Pears* [1965] 1 QB 76, followed in *Giltrap v Busby* (1970) 21 NILQ 342 and by the Republic's Supreme Court in *Treacy v Dublin Corporation* [1993] 1 IR 305. Of course, an owner whose property is damaged by the activities of an adjoining owner may have a remedy in tort, for negligence or nuisance. Furthermore, as the *Treacy* case illustrates there may be statutory protection - in that case where a sanitary authority was exercising its power to demolish premises under the Local Government (Sanitary Services) Act 1964.

[32] See *Henry Ltd v McGlade* [1926] NI 144 (see *A Casebook on Irish Land Law* (1984), p 324, see also *International Tea Stores Co v Hobbs* [1903] 2 Ch 165, espec at 172.

[33] *Re Ellenborough Park* [1956] Ch 131. *Cf Henry Ltd v McGlade* [1926] NI 144 (man carrying pole advertising licensed premises).

[34] (1877) IR 11 CL 499. *Cf Wright v Macadam* [1949] 2 KB 744 (right to store coal in a shed held to be an easement); *Copeland v Greenhalf* [1952] Ch 488 (right of a wheelwright to stand an unlimited number of vehicles on a strip of neighbouring land held not to be an easement).

[35] Para **[6.003]** *ante*.

[36] See *Copeland* case *supra. Cf Grigsby v Melville* [1972] 1 WLR 1355 (upheld on other grounds [1974] 1 WLR 80). *Cf* a right to store or to park items (eg cars) in no particular part of the servient tenement: see *Att-Gen of Southern Nigeria v John Holt & Co (Liverpool) Ltd* [1915] AC 599; *London and Blenheim Estates Ltd v Ladbroke Retail Parks Ltd* [1993] 1 All ER 307, 314-16 (*per* Judge Paul Baker QC) (aff'd on other grounds [1993] 4 All ER 157).

[37] See Chs 17 and 20 *post*.

[6.032] It is part of the principle under discussion that the alleged easement should be capable of precise definition, so that it can, if necessary, be described accurately in a conveyance. It is for this reason that many alleged easements of light fail.[38] Such an easement can be claimed only in respect of a particular window in a building receiving a defined amount of light and there can be no general right to a view.[39] If such less well-defined rights are sought, the only way to secure them is by a special contract for their protection, which may be drafted in the form of a restrictive covenant.[40]

[6.033] Finally, the principle requiring that an easement be capable of forming the subject-matter of a grant implies that there must also be a capable grantor and grantee of the easement. This may give rise to difficulties in a particular case, eg, where a corporation is involved and it has no power to deal with land.[41]

2. Profits à Prendre

[6.034] A profit *à prendre*, as the name implies, is a right to take something from another person's land. The general rule is that the something must be a part of the land itself, eg, minerals[42] or turf,[43] or creatures living naturally on the land which, when taken, are capable of being owned, eg, wild game[44] or fish.[45]

[6.035] The nature of a particular profit *à prendre* depends to some extent on the category of profits to which it belongs. Three categories at least have been recognised over the years.

(i) Appurtenant

[6.036] A profit may be created appurtenant to a dominant tenement, like an easement. In such a case the profit must in general comply with the four features necessary for an easement discussed above. It seems that such a profit must be confined to the needs of the dominant tenement, in the absence of a provision to the contrary in the grant.[46]

---

[38] See Bodkin, 'Easements and Uncertainty' (1971) 35 Conv 324.

[39] See the distinction drawn by the Republic's Supreme Court between obstruction of "ancient lights" and reduction of light to "modern" windows in *Scott v Goulding Properties Ltd* [1972] IR 200 (Walsh J, *dissentiente*) (see *A Casebook on Irish Land Law* (1984), p 299). See also *McGrath v Munster and Leinster Bank Ltd* [1959] IR 313; *Annally Hotel Ltd v Bergin* (1970) 104 ILTR 65. Hudson, 'Parasitic Damages for loss of Light' (1975) 39 Conv 116.

[40] Para **[6.046]** and Ch 19 *post*.

[41] Para **[25.21]** *post*.

[42] *Fishbourne v Hamilton* (1890) 25 LR Ir 483; *Earl of Antrim v Dobbs* (1891) 30 LR Ir 424; *Staples v Young* [1908] 1 IR 135.

[43] *Convey v Regan* [1952] IR 56; *Re Bohan* [1957] IR 49. See also *Lowry v Crothers* (1871) IR 5 CL 98; *Westropp v Congested Districts Board* [1919] 1 IR 224.

[44] *Finlay v Curteis* (1832) Hayes 496; *Radcliff v Hayes* [1907] 1 IR 101.

[45] *Toome Eel Fishery (Northern Ireland) Ltd v Cardwell* [1966] NI 1. See also *Kerry CC v O'Sullivan* [1927] IR 26; *Moore v Att-Gen* [1934] IR 44 (see *A Casebook on Irish Land Law* (1984), p 5).

[46] *Harris v Earl of Chesterfield* [1911] AC 623. See also *Cronin v Connor* [1913] 2 IR 119. In *Anderson v Bostock* [1976] Ch 312, Blackett-Ord VC, applying *Harris v Earl of Chesterfield*, held that an exclusive unlimited right to grazing could not exist as a profit appurtenant and, indeed, was a right unknown to the law.

(ii) Appendant

[6.037] A profit appendant is a profit annexed to land by operation of law, as opposed to act of the parties. The most common example was the ancient feudal right of common pasturage, under which a freehold grantee of arable manor land had as appendant to that land a right to pasture certain animals on manor waste land.[47] The right was confined to animals necessary for ploughing (horses and oxen) and manuring (cows and sheep) the arable land granted and the number was limited to that which the dominant land could maintain during winter.[48] However, such a grant of freehold land within a manor amounted to subinfeudation and so no new profits appendant of this nature could be created after *Quia Emptores* 1290.[49] For this reason, it is doubtful if any survive in Ireland today.

(iii) In Gross

[6.038] Unlike an easement, a profit can also be enjoyed quite independently of any dominant tenement, ie, in gross. It is nevertheless regarded as an interest in land and is as much an incorporeal hereditament as a profit appurtenant.[50]

3. Similar Concepts

There are several other concepts recognised by our land law which share many of the characteristics of easements and profits, but which must be distinguished from them.

(i) Natural Rights

[6.039] Natural rights, which are essentially rights protected by the law of torts,[51] are very like certain easements. There is, however, one major point of distinction. An easement must be acquired whereas a natural right, as the name indicates, exists automatically in respect of the land. This means, of course, that a plaintiff's task in court is considerably easier if he can base his claim on a natural right instead of having to establish an easement. One common natural right is a right of support which can also be acquired as an easement.[52] The natural right of support, which is a right not to have support removed by a neighbour, is confined to support for land in its natural state.[53] No

---

[47] *Doyle's Case* (1833) Alc Reg Cas 36. See also *Bennett v Reeve* (1740) Willes 227; *Earl of Dunraven v Llewellyn* (1850) 15 QB 791. Note the other form of common of pasturage, *pur cause de vicinage*, see Megarry and Wade, *Law of Real Property* (5th ed, 1984), p 910.

[48] *Robertson v Hartopp* (1889) 43 Ch D 484.

[49] Para **[2.44]** *ante*. See also *Baring v Abingdon* [1892] 2 Ch 374.

[50] Note that there can be a letting of an incorporeal hereditament, eg, a several fishery, *Bayley v Conyngham* (1863) 15 ICLR 406 (see *A Casebook on Irish Land Law* (1984), p 311). Paras **[6.116]** - **[6.117]** *post*.

[51] See McMahon and Binchy, *Irish Law of Torts* (2nd ed, 1990), Ch 23.

[52] See the discussion in the leading case of *Dalton v Angus & Co* (1881) 6 App Cas 740, applied in *Latimer v Official Co-Operative Society* (1885) 16 LR Ir 305 (see *A Casebook on Irish Land Law* (1984), p 293). Garner, 'Rights of Support' (1948) 12 Conv 280. Para **[6.111]** *post*.

[53] *Latimer v Official Co-Operative Society* (1885) 16 LR Ir 305.

natural right of support exists in respect of buildings on the land; such a right in respect of buildings must be acquired as an easement.[54]

[6.040] Another common natural right is the right to water flowing in a defined channel, eg, the rights enjoyed by the owners of land on the banks of a river or stream.[55] Such riparian owners, as they are called, may sue to protect their natural rights if the river or stream is dammed or diverted.[56] On the other hand, there is no natural right to water not flowing through a defined channel, eg, water percolating underground.[57] Rights to water are, however, commonly acquired as easements,[58] even in respect of artificial watercourses.[59]

(ii) Public Rights

[6.041] Certain public rights are very similar to rights also recognised as easements or profits. For example, there can be a public right of way over land. The essential difference between such a right and an easement is that the public right of way can be invoked by any member of the public regardless of his ownership of any dominant land.[60] At common law, a public right of way was known as a "highway" and could be created by "dedication and acceptance",[61] ie, the owner of the land dedicates the way to the public which then accepts that dedication. The dedication is usually made informally and the acceptance inferred from long usage by the public.[62] For the user to raise a

---

[54] *Green v Belfast Tramways Co* (1887) 20 LR Ir 35; *Gateley v Martin* [1900] 2 IR 269. *Cf Treacy v Dublin Corporation* [1993] 1 IR 305. See further, para **[6.111]** *post*. Also Bodkin, 'Rights of Support for Buildings and Flats' (1962) 26 Conv 210.

[55] *Thompson v Horner* [1927] NI 191. Brett, 'Right to Take Flowing Water' (1950) 14 Conv 154; Fiennes, 'Right to Take Water on the Land of Another' (1938) 2 Conv 203.

[56] *McClone v Smith* (1888) 22 LR Ir 559; *Massereene v Murphy* [1931] NI 192. Note, however, that a riparian owner's *corporeal* rights in respect of the bed and soil of a river or lake to a median line out from his bank should be distinguished from *incorporeal* rights in the nature of a profit (such as fishing rights in the river or lake) which may be held by a third party: see *Tennent v Clancy* [1987] IR 15; see also *Gannon v Walsh* Unrep (HC, RI), 20 June 1996.

[57] *Black v Ballymena Township Commrs* (1886) 17 LR Ir 459; *cf Ewart v Belfast Poor Law Commrs* (1881) 9 LR Ir 171.

[58] *Wilson v Stanley* (1861) 12 ICLR 345; *Pullan v Roughfort Bleaching and Dying Co Ltd* (1888) 21 LR Ir 73; *Craig v McCance* (1910) 44 ILTR 90.

[59] *Hanna v Pollock* [1900] 2 IR 664 (see *A Casebook on Irish Land Law* (1984), p 329); *Kelly v Dea* (1966) 100 ILTR 1.

[60] *Att-Gen (Cork CC) v Perry* [1904] 1 IR 247; *Healy v Bray UDC* [1962-63] Ir Jur Rep 9. *Cf Antrim CC v Trustees of Gray* (1930) 64 ILTR 71.

[61] *Fitzpatrick v Robinson* (1828) 1 Hud & Br 585; *Early v Flood* [1953-54] Ir Jur Rep 65; *Browne v Davis* (1959) 93 ILTR 179. See also *O'Keefe v Dromey* (1898) 32 ILTR 47; *Smith v Wilson* [1903] 2 IR 45; *Giant's Causeway Co v Att-Gen* (1905) 5 NIJR 301. Property dedicated to public use has long been exempt from rates: see Poor relief (Ir) Act 1838, s 63 (proviso); *Dublin County Council v Westlink Toll Bridge Ltd* Unrep (SC, RI) 13 February 1996.

[62] *Browne v Davis, op cit*. See also *Fitzpatrick v Robinson* (1828) 1 Hud & Br 585; *Reilly v Thompson* (1877) IR 11 CL 238; *Neill v Byrne* (1878) 2 LR Ir 287; *O'Connor v Sligo Corp* (1901) 1 NIJR 116; *Bruen v Murphy* Unrep (HC, RI), 11 March 1980 (1978 No 5085P). *Cf* where the alleged right is linked to a commercial operation, eg, use of a towpath running along the banks of a canal: see *Scarff v Commissioners of Public Works* Unrep, (HC, RI), 15 March 1995 (1994/3444P).

presumption of a public right of way, the user must have been open, "as of right" and without interruption.[63] Apart from creation of a public right of way at common law, a public road may, of course, nowadays be adopted by a local authority under statutory powers.[64] The law of nuisance may be invoked to protect public rights of way.[65]

[6.042] So far as profits *à prendre* are concerned, perhaps the most obvious analogous public right is the right of the public to fish in the sea and all tidal rivers and waters.[66] In strict theory, this fishing right belonged ultimately to the Crown and now, in the Republic of Ireland, the State.[67] It has now been settled in a series of cases concerning some of the main rivers of Ireland[68] that, while the Crown was free to grant individual or several fishery rights to specified parts of tidal and navigable waters prior to Magna Carta 1215,[69] that charter prohibited the granting of any new fisheries thereafter.[70] It

---

[63] *Cf* the requirements for acquisition of an easement by prescription, para **[6.075]** *post*. Hence the common practice of landowners, who, as a matter of indulgence, allow members of the public to use roads or pathways running through their land, of closing the road or pathway once a year to prevent a public right of way arising: see Samuels, 'Annual Closure of a Right of Way' [1986] Conv 161.

[64] See the Republic's Local Government Acts 1925, s 25 and 1953, s 2; Roads (NI) Order 1993, Article 68. See also *City Brick and Terra Cotta Co Ltd v Belfast Corp* [1958] NI 44.

[65] *Healy v Bray UDC* [1962-63] Ir Jur Rep 9; *Cunningham v MacGrath Bros* [1964] IR 209; *Kelly v Mayo CC* [1964] IR 315; *Wall v Morrissey* [1969] IR 10.

[66] *Cf* non-tidal waters, *Bloomfield v Johnston* (1867) IR 8 CL 68; *Pery v Thornton* (1889) 23 LR Ir 402. See also *Murphy v Ryan* (1868) IR 2 CL 143; *Whelan v Hewson* (1871) IR 6 CL 283.

[67] See especially the detailed discussion of the subject by Kennedy CJ in *R (Moore) v O'Hanrahan* [1927] IR 406 and Gavan Duffy P in *Foyle and Bann Fisheries Ltd v Att-Gen* (1949) 83 ILTR 29.

[68] *Malcolmson v O'Dea* (1863) 10 HLC 593 (Shannon); *Neill v Duke of Devonshire* (1882) 8 App Cas 135 (Blackwater); *R (Moore) v O'Hanrahan* [1927] IR 406 (Erne); *Moore v Att-Gen* [1934] IR 44 (Erne) (see *A Casebook on Irish Land Law* (1984) p 5); *Cooper v Att-Gen* [1935] IR 425 (Ballisodare); *Little v Cooper* [1937] IR 1 (Moy); *Foyle and Bann Fisheries Ltd v Att-Gen* (1949) 83 ILTR 29 (Foyle).

[69] Ie, a franchise, para **[6.020]** *ante*.

[70] C 16. The reported statements of the Irish judges in the case of *The Royal Fishery of the Banne* (1610) Dav 149 seem to have been made in ignorance of *Magna Carta* and are, therefore, wrong, see *Moore v Att-Gen* [1934] IR 44 (see *A Casebook on Irish Land Law* (1984), p 5); also *Duke of Devonshire v Hodnett* (1827) 1 Hud & Br 322. One of the issues also in dispute in these cases was to what extent the Ulster plantation patent grants and seventeenth-century Acts of Settlement (paras **[1.31]**-**[1.33]** *ante*) could be regarded as overruling *Magna Carta* on this point and the general view of the judges seems to have been that they should not be so construed. See *Moore v Att-Gen* [1934] IR 44; *Foyle and Bann Fisheries Ltd v Att-Gen* (1949) ILTR 29. *Cf Little v* Moylett [1929] IR 439; *Cooper v Att-Gen* [1935] IR 425. Note also subsequent private Acts conferring private fisheries, eg, the "Cooper Act" of 1837, subsequently incorporated in the Fisheries (Ir) Act 1842. For litigation on this private legislation, see *Cooper v Att-Gen* [1935] IR 425; *Att-Gen (Mahony) v Cooper* [1956] IR 1.

was, however, accepted that those fisheries existing before Magna Carta, whose survival in private hands could be established,[71] remain valid to this day.[72]

(iii) Local Customary Rights

[6.043] Local customary rights differ from easements in that they are not necessarily annexed to any dominant tenement.[73] They can be invoked by all who come within the custom of the locality regardless of ownership of other land, eg, the right of parishioners to use a path to their church.[74] Such rights differ from public rights, on the other hand, because they are confined to members of a local community, eg, the inhabitants of a particular town or village, the fishermen of a port or the tenants of an estate.[75]

[6.044] Such local customary rights are recognised at common law provided they satisfy the four basic requirements of being ancient, certain, reasonable and continuous.[76] Being ancient means in theory dating back to or before the beginning of legal memory, ie 1189,[77] but in practice courts are prepared to presume such an ancient origin provided long enjoyment of 20 to 40 years is shown and no proof of a later origin is forthcoming.[78]

[6.045] It seems that at common law the courts were reluctant to accept customary rights analogous to profits on the ground that, to allow a fluctuating body of persons to take things from the land, might result after a short time in little of the subject-matter of the profit being left.[79] However, the courts have had to recognise that many customary rights regularly invoked and exercised in certain localities for centuries take the form of

---

71 This is a particular problem with respect to those parts of Ireland, eg, the North West, which did not come under the influence of the English feudal system introduced by the Normans until the late sixteenth or early seventeenth century, paras **[1.27]**-**[1.28]** *ante*. Until then the system of law in force in the North West of Ireland was the brehon system, which does not seem to have recognised private property rights in several fisheries, though this is a matter of dispute amongst Irish scholars. Note the evidence given by scholars of ancient Irish law in *R (Moore) v O'Hanrahan* [1927] IR 406; *Moore v Att-Gen* [1934] IR 44 (see *A Casebook on Irish Land Law* (1984), p 5); *Foyle and Bann Fisheries Ltd v Att-Gen* (1949) 83 ILTR 29.

72 The court was satisfied as to proof of ownership of a several fishery in the River Moy in counties Mayo and Sligo prior to *Magna Carta* in *Little v Cooper* [1937] IR 1. *Cf* a fishery in the river Erne in Co Donegal (the ancient Irish territory in Tirconnaill) in *Moore v Att-Gen* [1934] IR 44 (see *A Casebook on Irish Land Law* (1984), p 5). See also *Little v Wingfield* (1859) 11 ICLR 63; *Allen v Donnelly* (1856) 5 Ir Ch R 452; *Ashworth v Browne* (1860) 10 Ir Ch R 421.

73 *Cf Re Pews of Derry Cathedral* (1864) 8 Ir Jur (ns) 115.

74 *Cf* a right to use a pew in a church, see *Re Pews of Derry Cathedral, op cit*.

75 *Abercromby v Fermoy Town Commissioners* [1900] 1 IR 302 (see *A Casebook on Irish Land Law* (1984), p 294); *Daly v Cullen* (1958) 92 ILTR 127.

76 *Daly v Cullen* (1958) 92 ILTR 127.

77 Fixed by the Statute of Westminster I, 1275, c 39. See further para **[6.081]** *post*.

78 Para **[6.081]** *post*.

79 See, eg, the remarks of Lord Campbell CJ in *Race v Ward* (1855) 4 E & B 702 at 709. *Cf* Chatterton VC in *Hamilton v Att-Gen* (1881) 5 LR Ir 555 at 576.

profits and have enforced them.[80] In fact, in Ireland many such customary rights can be traced to Crown grants resulting from the numerous confiscations and resettlements of Irish land.[81] The Irish courts have often been prepared to explain and elaborate the general words of Crown patents or grants according to the evidence of long user and enjoyment of claimed rights.[82]

(iv) Restrictive Covenants

[6.046] As we shall see later,[83] restrictive covenants are very similar to certain easements. The main similarity lies in the feature of both concepts that allows the owner to restrict another person in the use of his land. Thus rights in respect of light, water, air and support may either be acquired as easements[84] on or secured by imposing restrictive covenants[85] on the servient land. The existence of dominant and servient tenements is another common feature of the two concepts.[86]

[6.047] There are, however, also distinctions of a fundamental nature. Easements have been recognised by the common law from the earliest stages of development of our land law system. They are usually *legal* interests[87] in land which bind all successors in title to the land. Restrictive covenants relating to freehold land[88] became recognised as part of land law only during the early part of the nineteenth century and then as interests enforceable against third parties in equity only.[89] This remains the position in the Republic of Ireland. Creating an equitable interest only, a restrictive covenant is often a less secure interest in land because its enforceability may be defeated by the claim of a bona fide purchaser of the legal estate in the land without notice of the covenant.[90] Its enforceability is also based on equitable principles and a court always has a discretion to refuse to grant the equitable remedy usually sought in such cases, namely an

---

[80] In England, the courts have been prepared to presume incorporation of a body of persons as recipients of a Crown grant, *Re Free Fishermen of Faversham* (1887) 36 Ch D 329, or even to presume a charitable trust or condition binding corporate grantees in favour of the claimants of the customary right, *Goodman v Mayor of Saltash* (1882) 7 App Cas 633. See Megarry and Wade, *Law of Real Property* (5th ed, 1984), pp 854-5. *Cf* on the *Saltash* principle, *Tighe v Sinnott* [1897] 1 IR 140.

[81] There has been much litigation concerning grants made under the Ulster plantation with respect to fishing rights, *Allen v Donnelly* (1856) 5 Ir Ch R 452; *Moore v Att-Gen* [1934] IR 44 (see *A Casebook on Irish Land Law* (1984), p 5); *Foyle and Bann Fisheries Ltd v Att-Gen* (1949) 83 ILTR 29; *Toome Eel Fishery (Northern Ireland) Ltd v Cardwell* [1966] NI 1.

[82] See, eg, *Hamilton v Att-Gen* (1881) 5 LR Ir 555; *Stoney v Keane* (1903) 37 ILTR 212.

[83] Ch 19 *post.*

[84] Paras **[6.108]-[6.111]** *post.*

[85] Ch 19 *post.*

[86] Ie, if a restrictive covenant is to be enforceable against third parties.

[87] They may, of course, like most legal estates and interests also exist in equity, Ch 4 *ante.*

[88] *Cf* covenants contained in leases: see para **[19.03]** *et seq, post.*

[89] Ch 19 *post.*

[90] In practice, however, this claim will rarely succeed in Ireland, paras **[3.069]** *et seq, ante* and Ch 22 *post.*

injunction.[91] This was also the position in Northern Ireland, but that will change dramatically under the Property (NI) Order 1997. Under Article 34 the rules of the common law and equity relating to the enforceability of freehold covenants are replaced by its statutory provision, under which most such covenants will fully bind successors in title. Thus freehold covenants contained in deeds executed from and after the appointed day[92] will have the characteristics of legal interests, akin to easements.[93]

[6.048] A restrictive covenant, as the name indicates, confers a purely negative right[94] whereas an easement can have a positive nature, eg, a right to draw water.[95] Finally, apart from such fundamental points of difference, there are also important differences in detail between the two concepts, eg, an easement can be acquired through long enjoyment (prescription)[96] whereas a restrictive covenant cannot be so acquired.

(v) Licences

[6.049] Licences have really come to be recognised as sometimes creating interests in land only during the past few decades. As we shall see later,[97] there are still several unresolved aspects of their precise status in the sphere of land law, but for the moment it may be said that a degree of similarity with the concept of an easement exists in that a licence can confer rights over another person's land, such as user of a path or driveway. There are, however, as in the case of restrictive covenants, fundamental differences in the nature of the two concepts. To the extent that a licence creates an interest in land, it seems clear from the case law that often the interest is equitable only.[98] On the other hand, a licence may be created very informally[99] and may exist in gross, independent of any dominant tenement.[100] A licence may also confer a general right to occupation, indeed exclusive possession of, the servient tenement and in this respect is more like a corporeal hereditament,[101] than an incorporeal one,[102] such as an easement.

---

[91] Para **[3.050]** *ante* and Ch 19 *post*.

[92] Article 34(2)(a).

[93] See also Article 45 (enforcement of covenants).

[94] See further Ch 19 *post*.

[95] Para **[6.110]** *post*.

[96] Para **[6.073]** *post*.

[97] Ch 20 *post*.

[98] *Ibid*.

[99] Para **[20.03]** *post*.

[100] In this respect a licence, *vis-à-vis* third parties, differs also from a restrictive covenant, Ch 19 *post*.

[101] Ie, it may appear to confer rights very similar to those granted to a tenant under a tenancy agreement, Ch 17 *post*.

[102] Para **[6.003]** *ante*. Cf *Judge v Lowe* (1873) IR 7 CL 291; *Atkinson v King* (1877) IR 11 CL 536; *Stanley v Riky* (1893) 31 LR Ir 196; *Radcliff v Hayes* [1907] 1 IR 101; *Whipp v Mackey* [1927] IR 372. Note also the RI Supreme Court's decision in *Telecom Éireann v Commissioners of Valuation*, fn 11, para **[6.003]** *ante*.

B. Acquisition

There are four ways in which an easement or profit can be acquired: by statute, express grant or reservation, implied grant or reservation and presumed grant (prescription).

1. Statute

[6.050] Rights in the nature of easements or profits were conferred by statute on private individuals more commonly in past eras. In Ireland, this was particularly the case during the many land disturbances which took place in the seventeenth century and resulted in the confiscation of so much of the land and its re-granting by the English Crown. These Crown grants were confirmed by various Acts of Settlement which, *inter alia*, were designed to confirm the grantees' titles and the rights conferred by them.[103] There were also many private and local Acts of Parliament passed as late as the nineteenth century conferring easements and profits, eg, free fishing rights.[104]

[6.051] In more modern times, it has become extremely common for statutory rights equivalent or analogous to easements and profits to be conferred on, or the power of compulsory acquisition to be given to, public and State bodies charged with execution of public undertakings, eg, in relation to gas, water and electricity supply.[105] In some cases, easements or profits have been expressly conferred on or vested in state bodies by statute.[106] In all cases where easements, profits and similar rights are created under statute, the method of creation is governed by the statute in question, so that if the statute authorises a body to create such rights it may permit this to be done in a way not permissible under the general law governing creation of easements and profits.[107]

---

[103] Paras **[1.29]** - **[1.33]** *ante*. See the discussion of these Acts of Settlement in *Little v Moylett* [1929] IR 439; *Moore v Att-Gen* [1934] IR 44 (see *A Casebook on Irish Land Law* (1984), p 5).

[104] See the "Cooper Act" of 1837 relating to a several fishery held by one, Joshua Edward Cooper, in the Ballisodare River Estuary. The 1837 Act was amended by the Fisheries (Ir) Act 1842. See the discussion in *Cooper v Att-Gen* [1935] IR 425; *Att-Gen (Mahony) v Cooper* [1956] IR 1. See also *Foyle and Bann Fisheries Ltd v Att-Gen* (1949) 83 ILTR 29.

[105] The right to lay pipes, wires, cables and the like in, over, or under land is usually known as a *"wayleave"*. See also re private rights *Telecom Éireann v Commissioner of Valuation* [1994] 1 IR 67 (pay phones installed in shopping centre). Garner, 'Statutory Easements' (1956) 20 Conv 208.

[106] Eg, fishing rights in rivers vested in the Republic's Electricity Supply Board, see Shannon Fisheries Act 1938, Pt II; Electricity (Supply) (Amendment) Act 1961, ss 9 and 10; *Daly v Quigley* [1960] Ir Jur Rep 1; *ESB v Gormley* [1985] ILRM 494. *Cf* as regards minerals and mining rights, Minerals Development Acts 1940 and 1979, Minerals Exploration and Development Company Act 1941, and Minerals Company Acts 1945, 1947 and 1950 (RI); *Tara Prospecting Ltd v Minster for Energy* [1993] ILRM 771; Mineral Development Act (NI) 1969. In the Republic, mines and minerals not being worked in 1922 were vested in the State by the 1922 Constitution, Article 11; see now Article 10 of the 1937 Constitution and Hogan & Whyte, *Kelly: The Irish Constitution* (3rd ed, 1994), pp 71-75.

[107] See *Dublin County Council v Westlink Toll Bridge Ltd* Unrep (SC, RI), 13 February 1996 (right to collect motorway tolls could be created by agreement, without using a deed).

2. Express Grant or Reservation

[6.052] Easements and profits may be created expressly by the parties to a land transaction. For example, if X, the owner of Blackacre, sells a part of Blackacre to Y, retaining the other part, he may, as part of the sale, confer on Y various easements (eg, a right of way) and profits (eg, fishing rights) to be enjoyed by Y over the part of Blackacre retained by X. In other words, the part sold to Y becomes the dominant tenement and the part retained by X the servient tenement. Quite independently of this transaction, X could grant other profits to be enjoyed in gross, ie, without any dominant tenement, to other persons (eg, a right of turbary[108] to Z, who lives in a village some miles away). Both these cases involve an express grant of the easement or profit by X, and it should be noted that a grant of an easement or profit may be made on its own, ie, independently of any conveyance of either the dominant or servient tenement.

[6.053] Alternatively, when selling part of Blackacre to Y, X could reserve easements (eg, support for farm buildings on the boundary line between the part sold and the part retained) and profits (eg, quarrying rights) to be enjoyed by him over the part of Blackacre sold to Y. Here the dominant tenement is the part of Blackacre retained by X and the servient tenement is the part sold to Y. The transaction involves an express reservation of easements and profits rather than an express grant.

(i) Grant

[6.054] The usual method of expressly granting an easement or profit is by deed.[109] In practice the grant or reservation is usually only part of a larger land transaction being executed by that deed. Caution dictates that appropriate words of limitation be used to make it clear for what estate the easement or profit is given. This point is by no means settled in Ireland for there seems to be no authority on it and the controversy which existed in England prior to the 1925 legislation[110] has not yet died down.[111] Such English authority as there was about the pre-1926 position[112] suggests that the appropriate words of limitation for an *inter vivos* conveyance ought to be used, otherwise the grantee may be held to acquire an easement or profit for life only.[113] The need for words of limitation was, of course, abolished in both parts of Ireland in respect of transfers of registered

---

[108] Ie to cut and take away turf, para **[6.114]** *post*.

[109] Since s 2 of the Real Property Act 1845 introduced the deed of grant as an alternative to older methods of conveyance, such as feoffment with livery of seisin and the bargain and sale, para **[3.026]** *ante*. See the discussion by Monahan CJ in *Bayley v Conyngham* (1863) 15 ICLR 406 (see *A Casebook on Irish Land Law* (1984), p 311). *Cf the Westlink Toll Bridge* case fn 199 *supra*.

[110] See, eg, Sweet, 'True Nature of an Easement' (1908) 24 LQR 259; Underhill, 'Words of Limitation and Easements' (1908) 24 LQR 199; Williams, 'Creation of Easements' (1908) 24 LQR 264.

[111] Megarry and Wade, *Law of Real Property* (5th ed, 1984) p 856.

[112] *Hewlins v Shippam* (1826) 5 B & C 221 at 228-9 (*per* Bayley J).

[113] This passage was quoted with approval by Keane J in *Gannon v Walsh* Unrep (HC, RI), 20 June 1996. See also Laffoy, *Irish Conveyancing Precedents,* Precedent E.8.1, p E1040; para **[4.025]** *ante*. Note that in NI the need for words of limitation for *creation* of rights like an easement or rentcharge by *will* was removed expressly by Article 18(2) of the Wills and Administration Proceedings (NI) Order 1994: see para **[6.139]** *post*.

land,[114] but, as a consequence of the particular wording of the legislation in question, this would *not* seem to apply to most *incorporeal* hereditaments where words of limitation would appear still to be necessary. Section 123 of the Republic's Registration of Title Act 1964 refers to a transfer of "registered land" which is defined in s 3(1) as "land of which an owner is or is deemed to be registered" under the Act. The Act provides for registration of land comprising incorporeal hereditaments held *in gross*[115] (eg, certain profits *à prendre*[116]), but all easements and many profits are not held *in gross*, but rather are appurtenant rights.[117] Thus an assurance creating or transferring such rights is not a transfer of registered land, but rather of rights appurtenant to such land. Similar provisions exist in Northern Ireland.[118] There is also another major point to note about Irish law in this context. The word "lands" is defined in the basic statute dealing with the relation of landlord and tenant in Ireland, Deasy's Act,[119] as including "houses, messuages, and tenements of every tenure, whether corporeal or *incorporeal*".[120] There can, therefore, be lettings of easements and profits (and they are very common) the formalities of which are governed by Deasy's Act. This means that in most cases writing only is necessary, not a deed (under seal), and, where the letting is at a rent or other return for a period "from year to year or any lesser period", the creation may be oral, with no formalities at all.[121] Thus in *Bayley v Conyngham*[122] a letting by parol of fishing rights in land for a year was upheld as a valid tenancy, creating the relation of landlord and tenant between the grantor and grantee.[123]

[6.055] Even if the requisite formalities for creation of a legal easement or profit are not met, an easement or profit may come into force in equity. Any written document not under seal may be construed as a contract for the grant of an easement or profit and may be enforced in equity through a decree of specific performance.[124] Even an oral agreement for consideration may be enforced in equity, provided there is a sufficient act

---

[114] See para **[4.030]** *ante*.

[115] Section 8(b)(i).

[116] See paras **[6.025]** and **[6.038]** *ante*.

[117] Which should be noted only as burdens on the servient registered land under s 69 of the 1964 Act and may be registered as appurtenances to the dominant registered land under s 82: see paras **[21.33]** and **[21.36]** *post*.

[118] Land Registration Act (NI) 1970, ss 10 (registration of incorporeal hereditaments held in gross), 35 (transfer of registered freehold estate), 51 (appurtenant rights) and Sch 6, Pt I (burdens).

[119] Landlord and Tenant Law Amendment Act, Ireland 1860. See, generally, Ch 17 *post*.

[120] Section 1 (italics added).

[121] Section 4. See further para **[17.012]** *post*.

[122] (1863) 15 ICLR 406.

[123] "It occurs to me, and to the majority of the court, that if we are at liberty to give any effect to the glossary of the Act, the word 'lands' embraces incorporeal hereditaments, and that it was the intention of the legislature to place lands and incorporeal hereditaments on the same footing, so far as relates to landlord and tenant; and that therefore whatever is sufficient to create the relation of landlord and tenant in corporeal, is sufficient also with respect to incorporeal hereditaments." *Per* Monahan CJ, *ibid*, p 412.

[124] Para **[3.144]** *ante*.

of part performance to prevent the case coming within the Statute of Frauds (Ireland) 1695.[125]

(ii) Reservation

[6.056] A reservation of an easement or profit is also usually contained in a deed. However, there was a problem about this at common law because of the basic rule that a grantor of land could not make a simple reservation to himself. The common law allowed a grantor only to *except* from his grant a part of the land itself or a pre-existing right over it. Things like mines and minerals, stones and quarries are commonly the subject-matter of exceptions.[126] We are considering here the creation of easements or profits for the first time and they *ex hypothesi* could not form the subject-matter of an exception - they come into operation only when the grant of the land is made.[127] The common law did allow some new rights to be reserved, but only if they were to issue out of the land granted, eg, X in selling Blackacre to Y could reserve to himself a rentcharge of £100 per annum charged on Blackacre.[128] The question, however, is how X could reserve to himself easements and profits over the part of Blackacre sold to Y and to be enjoyed by X as owner of the part of Blackacre retained after that sale to Y.

[6.057] In Ireland this object may be achieved in two ways. First, Y could execute the conveyance from X to Y of the part of Blackacre in question. The common law took the view that a conveyance containing a reservation in favour of the grantor and executed by the grantee had a dual operation. The conveyance was regarded as a grant of the land to the grantee followed by a regrant of the reserved right (easement or profit) by the grantee to the grantor.[129] Secondly, since 1881, the grantor may use the Statute of Uses (Ireland) 1634.[130] X could convey the part of Blackacre to Z and his heirs to the use that X should have the easements and profits and, subject to that provision, to the use of Y and his heirs. Prior to 1882, this mechanism did not work[131] because the Statute of Uses (Ireland) 1634, like the English 1535 Statute, applied only where one person (Z in our example) was seised of land to the use of another person.[132] Once again we are

---

[125] Para **[3.149]** *ante*. See again the discussion in *Bayley v Conyngham* (1863) 15 ICLR 406 (see *A Casebook on Irish Land Law* (1984), p 311).

[126] *Coke upon Littleton*, 47a. *McDonnell v Kenneth* (1850) 1 ICLR 113; *Quinn v Shields* (1877) IR 11 CL 254. See also *McDonnell v McKinty* (1847) 10 Ir LR 514.

[127] Prior to that the rights in question could exist as quasi-easements only, paras **[6.029]** *ante* and **[6.061]** *post*. See the discussion in *O'Donnell v Ryan* (1854) 4 ICLR 44, espec at 59-60 (*per* Ball J).

[128] *Coke upon Littleton*, 143a. See further on rentcharges, para **[6.131]** *post*.

[129] *Durham & Sutherland Rly v Walker* (1842) 2 QB 940, espec at 967. In the case of a transaction for value the grantor would have an equitable right to seek specific performance against the grantee, to compel him to execute the conveyance, and in the meantime would have an equitable easement or profit, paras **[3.038]** *ante* and **[9.061]** *post*.

[130] See further, paras **[3.015]** *et seq*, *ante*.

[131] It did, of course, in equity and, if for value (unlikely in the case of a mere conveyancing device), X could enforce the use against Z, para **[9.061]** *post*.

[132] Section 1. Para **[3.019]** *ante*.

considering the creation of easements and profits for the first time and Z, the feoffee to uses, could not be seised of them unless they already existed before the feoffment or grant of them to the use of another person.[133] This difficulty was, however, removed by the Conveyancing Act 1881, s 62(1) of which applies the following provision to conveyances made after the Act:

> A conveyance of freehold land to the use that any person may have, for an estate or interest not exceeding in duration the estate conveyed in the land, any easement, right, liberty, or privilege in, or over, or with respect to that land, or any part thereof, shall operate to vest in possession in that person that easement, right, liberty, or privilege, for the estate or interest expressed to be limited to him; and he, and the persons deriving title under him, shall have, use and enjoy the same accordingly.[134]

In other words, by virtue of the 1881 Act the use in favour of X relating to the easements and profits would be "executed" so as to vest the legal title to them in X.[135]

(iii) Construction of Grants and Reservations

[6.058] The precise effect of a purported grant or reservation of easements or profits is, of course, to a large extent a matter of construction of the particular conveyance. In such questions of construction two principles are most relevant, namely that a grant is in general construed against the grantor and that a man may not derogate from his grant. The first principle means that, in cases of doubt (eg, over the exact scope of the easement or profit), a grant of an easement or profit will be construed against the grantor in favour of the grantee, whereas a reservation, being treated as a regrant by the grantee,[136] will be construed against him in favour of the grantor.[137] The underlying philosophy is that the person who is in a position to dictate the terms of a transaction, by making the grant, cannot complain if a dispute subsequently occurs and he is not given the benefit of the doubt. Reservations in respect of new easements or profits were

---

[133] *Ibid.* The 1634 Statute could operate, of course, to transfer an existing easement or profit.

[134] In England, the 1881 Act, like the Statute of Uses 1535, has been replaced by the Law of Property Act 1925, s 65 of which now provides that a reservation of a legal estate or interest is effective at law with any execution of the conveyance by the grantee. A similar provision has been recommended for Northern Ireland, see *Survey of the Land Law of Northern Ireland* (HMSO, 1971), paras 40 and 175; Land Law Working Group's *Final Report* (HMSO, 1990) Vol 1, para 2.5.32.

[135] Para **[3.016]** *ante.*

[136] Para **[6.057]** *supra.*

[137] See the discussion in *Neill v Duke of Devonshire* (1882) 8 App Cas 135, espec at 149 (*per* Lord Selborne LC). This remains the rule in England despite s 65 of the Law of Property Act 1925 (fn 226 *supra*), see *Bulstrode v Lambert* [1953] 1 WLR 1064; *Johnstone v Holdway* [1963] 1 QB 601; *St. Edmundsbury and Ipswich Diocesan Board of Finance v Clark (No 2)* [1975] 1 WLR 468; Wade (1954) CLJ 191. The NI Land Working Group have recommended the reversal of this construction, see *Final Report* (HMSO, 1990) Vol 1, para 2.5.32.

treated as a special case[138] because of the common law's view that they should be regarded as regrants by the grantee.[139]

[6.059] As regards the rule that a man may not derogate from his grant, the philosophy here is that, when a man transfers his land to another person, knowing that it is going to be used for a particular purpose, he may not do anything which is going to defeat that purpose and thereby frustrate the intention of both parties when the transfer is made.[140] Usually application of this principle creates property rights in favour of the grantee which take the form of restrictions enforceable against the grantor's land. In this respect the rights are similar to restrictive covenants though, it must be emphasised, the principle has nothing to do with the law relating to such covenants. On the other hand, the principle is not confined to the area of easements and profits and may create rights which do not conform strictly with the requirements of easements and profits.[141] Finally, when considering the effect of the wording of an express grant, the provisions of s 6 of the Conveyancing Act 1881, must be borne in mind. This is a subject we discuss below.[142]

3. Implied Grant or Reservation

Even if a particular conveyance does not mention the creation of easements or profits expressly, they may be created by implication on a true construction of the deed. Once again a distinction has to be drawn between grants in favour of the grantee and reservations in favour of the grantor.[143]

(i) Grant

[6.060] The general rule is that a grant is construed in favour of the grantee and this results frequently in the creation of implied easements and, sometimes, implied profits *à prendre*. The following are the main circumstances in which implied grants are construed as taking place.

---

[138] Thus, at common law, exceptions and other reservations (eg of rent) were construed in the normal way against the grantor making them, *Lofield's Case* (1612) 10 Co Rep 106a. Bigelow and Madden, 'Exception and Reservation of Easements' (1924) 38 HLR 180.

[139] This paragraph was quoted with approval by Keane J in *Gannon v Walsh* Unrep (HC, RI) 20 June 1996. See also *Connell v O'Malley* Unrep, (HC, RI), 20 July 1983 (1979/8260P); Lyall, 'Non-derogation from Grant' (1988) 6 ILT 143.

[140] "A grantor having given a thing with one hand is not to take away the means of enjoying it with the other." *Per* Bowen LJ in *Birmingham, Dudley & District Banking Co v Ross* (1888) 38 Ch D 295 at 313; *cf Lyttleton Times Co Ltd v Warners Ltd* [1907] AC 476 at 481 (*per* Lord Loreburn LC). See also *Griffin v Keane* (1927) 61 ILTR 177; *Kennedy v Elkinson* (1937) 71 ILTR 153.

[141] See the discussion in *Cable v Bryant* [1908] 1 Ch 259; *Browne v Flower* [1911] 1 Ch 219. Elliott, 'Non-Derogation from Grant' (1964) 80 LQR 244.

[142] Para **[6.066]** *post.*

[143] Stroud, 'Implied Grant and Reservation of Easements' (1940) 56 LQR 93.

(a) Easements of Necessity

Where X grants part of Blackacre to Y and the only means of access to Y's part is through the part of Blackacre retained by X, then an easement or way of necessity over X's retained land will be implied in favour of Y.[144] This topic is discussed in more detail in relation to implied reservations which is, perhaps, the case more commonly litigated.[145]

(b) Intended Easements

Easements which are necessary to carry out the common intention of the parties to the grant will be implied, particularly in favour of the grantee. It is, of course, essential to establish such a common intention, but this can often be inferred from the circumstances of the case,[146] eg, a sale of one of two attached houses will usually involve an implication of an easement of support for the house sold by the house retained.[147]

(c) Rule in Wheeldon v Burrows

[6.061] The rule in *Wheeldon v Burrows*[148] is an example of the more general principle that a man may not derogate from his grant.[149] It is important to realise the limits to the rule enunciated in that case. First, the rule is confined to cases of implied grant; there can be no application of the rule in cases of implied reservation.[150] Secondly, the rule is confined to cases of creation of easements, and possibly profits,[151] for the first time and does not relate to transfer of easements already existing. In fact, the rule is confined to cases of *quasi*-easements, ie, rights exercised by the grantor in respect of the land granted, while it was in his common ownership, which have the potential to become full easements on sale of that part of the land to another person.[152]

---

[144] *Donnelly v Adams* [1905] 1 IR 154. See also *Browne v Maguire* [1922] 1 IR 23; *McDonagh v Mulholland* [1931] IR 110; *B & W Investments Ltd v Ulster Scottish Friendly Society* (1969) 20 NILQ 325.

[145] Para **[6.070]** *post*.

[146] *Gogarty v Hoskins* [1906] 1 IR 173. *Cf Annally Hotel Ltd v Bergin* (1970) 104 ILTR 65 (doctrine of estoppel also invoked).

[147] *Cf Latimer v Official Co-Operative Society* (1885) 16 LR Ir 305 (see *A Casebook on Irish Land Law* (1984), p 293).

[148] (1879) 12 Ch D 31. For discussion of the rule in Ireland, see *Donnelly v Adams* [1905] 1 IR 154; *McDonagh v Mulholland* [1931] IR 110; *Re Flanagan and McGarvey and Thompson's Contract* [1945] NI 32 (see *ibid*, p 317).

[149] Para **[6.059]** *supra*. See also *Griffin v Keane* (1927) 61 ILTR 177.

[150] In fact, this is the actual *ratio decidendi* of *Wheeldon v Burrows* since it concerned a claim that the easements in question were impliedly reserved. See also para **[6.069]** *post. Wheeldon v Burrows* did not establish the rule either; it merely enumerated principles established by earlier decisions.

[151] It is not clear to what extent, if at all, the rule applies to profits *à prendre* appurtenant, a point on which there is little authority. It is arguable that quasi-profits would not satisfy the test of being "continuous and apparent" in relation to the servient tenement, para **[6.062]** *infra*. See Megarry and Wade, *The Law of Real Property* (5th ed, 1984), p 865.

[152] Para **[6.029]** *ante*.

[6.062] The rule in *Wheeldon v Burrows* lays down that, on the grant of part of land owned by the grantor, there pass to the grantee as easements all rights in the form of quasi-easements over the land retained by the grantor which satisfy three tests, namely, rights which (1) were "continuous and apparent", (2) were necessary to the reasonable enjoyment of the part of the land granted to the grantee and (3) had been, and still were at the time of the grant, used by the grantor for the benefit of the part granted. What is not clear from *Wheeldon v Burrows* itself is the precise relationship between these three tests, in particular whether they are three quite independent tests, each of which must be satisfied for the rule to apply. The first test has given rise to some controversy and it has even been suggested that it was an alien concept imported into the common law from French law.[153] It is also not clear to what extent the first test should be regarded only as all alternative to the second test.[154] The two seem to involve a considerable amount of overlapping when applied to particular cases. Bearing these points in mind, the three tests may be considered in a little more detail.

[6.063] With respect to the first, it seems that the grantor need not have exercised the quasi-easement continuously in the strict sense.[155] It has been argued that in this context the word "continuous" is used not in the sense of incessant user but rather in the sense of the regular user characteristics of permanent as opposed to temporary rights.[156] Furthermore, while there is some suggestion in the cases that the rule is confined to passive rights, ie, rights which do not require the dominant owner to do some acts (eg, light or support to buildings),[157] there have been cases where this notion has been ignored, eg, where a right of way, whose exercise necessarily involves positive action, has been held to be created by implied grant under the rule.[158] As regards the requirement of "apparent", this seems to confine the rule to cases where the rights claimed were clearly being exercised over the servient tenement.[159] The courts have taken this to mean that, if the existence of the easement on the servient land cannot be seen or be discovered by a careful inspection of the land, it does not satisfy the test.[160] It is on these grounds primarily that it is argued that the rule in *Wheeldon v Burrows*

---

[153] Note the remarks of Lord Westbury in *Suffield v Brown* (1864) 4 De GJ & S 185 at 195 and Lord Blackburn in *Dalton v Angus & Co* (1881) 6 App Cas 740 at 821, cited by Barton J in *Donnelly v Adams* [1905] 1 IR 154 at 165-6. See also Gale, *Law of Easements* (1st ed, 1839), p 53; *Ward v Kirkland* [1967] Ch 194; Simpson (1967) 83 LQR 240.

[154] *Cf* Harpum [1977] Conv 425.

[155] *Suffield v Brown* (1864) 4 De GJ & S 185 at 199.

[156] Gale, *Law of Easements* (1st ed, 1839), p 53.

[157] *Worthington v Gimson* (1860) 2 E & E 618; *Polden v Bastard* (1865) LR 1 QB 156.

[158] *Clancy v Byrne* (1877) IR 11 CL 355; *Donnelly v Adams* [1905] 1 IR 154; *Head v Meara* [1912] 1 IR 262; *McDonagh v Mulholland* [1931] IR 110. See also *Brown v Alabaster* (1887) 37 Ch D 490; *Borman v Griffith* [1930] 1 Ch 493.

[159] *McDonagh v Mulholland* [1931] IR 110. See also *Pyer v Carter* (1857) 1 H & N 916 (water from eaves of house running into underground drain); *Watts v Kelson* (1870) 6 Ch App 166 (watercourse running through visible pipes).

[160] Thus the rights of way cases have generally been confined to rights over made roads or worn tracks, see cases cited in fn 250 *supra*.

cannot apply to profits *à prendre*. Profits necessarily involve positive acts on the part of the dominant owner; they are rarely, if ever, exercised continuously[161] and often their exercise is not apparent on the servient land.[162]

[6.064] As regards the second test, it is important not to confuse this with the requirements of an easement of necessity. For an easement of necessity to be established it must be one without which the land in question cannot be enjoyed at all,[163] whereas the rule in *Wheeldon v Burrows* simply requires that reasonable enjoyment of the land cannot be had without the rights in question.[164]

[6.065] The third test is a straightforward requirement that the rights should not only have been enjoyed right up to the time of the grant,[165] but also have been enjoyed in respect of the part of the land sold. In other words, the rights in question must have the potential to satisfy the normal requirements of easements (ie, be quasi-easements in the technical sense), so that, for example, there must be a dominant and servient tenement with the rights, which must accommodate the dominant tenement.[166]

(d) Conveyancing Act 1881, s 6

[6.066] Section 6 of the Conveyancing Act 1881[167] is important in the present context because, to some extent, it can perform the same function as the rule in *Wheeldon v Burrows*, in that it may create easements out of quasi-easements. From the outset, however, it must be emphasised that the section does so through giving an extended meaning to general words in an express grant,[168] rather than by way of an implied grant, and the section can bring into operation a much wider range of rights than the rule in *Wheeldon v Burrows*.

Section 6 (1) provides as follows:

> A conveyance of land shall be deemed to include and shall by virtue of this Act operate to convey, with the land, all buildings, erections, fixtures, commons, hedges, ditches, fences, ways, waters, watercourses, liberties, privileges, easements, rights, and advantages whatsoever, appertaining or reputed to appertain to the land, or any part thereof, or at the time of the conveyance demised, occupied, or enjoyed with, or reputed or known as part or parcel of or appurtenant to the land or any part thereof.[169]

---

[161] They can, however, be just as permanent in nature as easements, para **[6.054]** *ante*.

[162] *Cf* however, mining, quarrying and turbary rights with fishing and sporting rights, paras **[5.113]**-**[5.119]** *post*.

[163] Para **[6.070]** *post*.

[164] See *Borman v Griffith* [1930] 1 Ch 493; *cf Goldberg v Edwards* [1950] Ch 247. See also *Wheeler v JJ Saunders Ltd* [1995] 2 All ER 697; *Millman v Ellis* (1995) 71 P & CR 158.

[165] The English courts seem to allow some flexibility on this point: see *Costagliola v English* (1969) 210 Est Gaz 1425.

[166] Paras **[6.025]**-**[6.026]** *ante*.

[167] *Henry Ltd v McGlade* [1926] NI 144 (see *A Casebook on Irish Land Law* (1984) p 324). For England, see now s 62 of the Law of Property Act 1925.

[168] Para **[6.052]** *ante*. See also *Geoghegan v Fegan* (1872) IR 6 CL 139; *Head v Meara* [1912] 1 IR 262.

[169] *Jeffers v Odeon (Ireland) Ltd* (1953) 87 ILTR 187. Similar provisions for conveyances of land with "houses or other buildings" and "manors" (now obsolete) are contained in s 6(2) and (3).

This provision applies only to conveyances executed since 1881[170] and in this context a conveyance includes, *inter alia*, an assignment, appointment, lease, settlement and other assurance.[171] It also applies if and so far only as a contrary intention is not expressed in the conveyance and is subject to the terms of the conveyance and its provisions.[172]

[6.067] So far as creation of easements and profits is concerned, the following points about s 6 should be noted. First, the section has a much wider scope than the rule in *Wheeldon v Burrows*. It is capable of applying to all kinds of quasi-easements and profits as well as other liberties and privileges.[173] Secondly, the section is not subject to the requirements of *Wheeldon v Burrows*, such as that the quasi-easements must be "continuous and apparent"[174] and must be reasonably necessary to the enjoyment of the land granted. All the section requires is that the rights in question were, or were reputed to be, appertaining to or enjoyed with the land granted.[175] A common example of the operation of the section is where a landlord grants a renewal of a lease and the new lease operates to convert into easements or profits licences or privileges which the landlord previously permitted the tenant to enjoy.[176] Thirdly, it seems clear that s 6 cannot convert into an easement or profit a right which does not comply with the essential requirements of easements and profits. The section is a purely technical conveyancing device intended to shorten conveyances; it is not intended to alter substantive rights or to extend the categories of rights or interests recognised by the law.[177] Fourthly, since the section operates by way of express grant, it cannot create rights which the grantor has no power to grant.[178] Fifthly, and this appears to be a considerable restriction on the section's operation, it has been held that the section operates only where there has been a diversity of ownership, or at least of occupation (eg, as between landlord and tenant), of the dominant and servient tenements prior to the conveyance.[179] In other words, it

---

[170] 1881 Act, s 6(6).

[171] 1881 Act, s 2(v).

[172] 1881 Act, s 6(4). *Steele v Morrow* (1923) 57 ILTR 89.

[173] *Henry Ltd v McGlade* [1926] NI 144 (see *A Casebook on Irish Land Law* (1984), p 324) (right to advertise café by having man stand with pole at entrance to arcade). See also *White v Williams* [1922] 1 KB 727 (quasi-profit of a sheepwalk).

[174] *Cf Titchmarsh v Royston Water Co Ltd* (1899) 81 LT 673; *Long v Gowlett* [1923] 2 Ch 177 at 202-4. See also *Ward v Kirkland* [1967] Ch 194.

[175] Eg, rights acquired by encroachment or adverse possession over a strip of adjoining land: see *Creavin v Donnelly* Unrep (HC, RI), 25 June 1993 (1992/6523P). See further on such acquisition Ch 23 *post*.

[176] *Wright v Macadam* [1949] 2 KB 744; *Goldberg v Edwards* [1950] Ch 247; *Rye v Rye* [1962] AC 496. See also *Jeffers v Odeon (Ireland) Ltd* (1953) 87 ILTR 187.

[177] *International Tea Stores Co v Hobbs* [1903] 2 Ch 165; *Regis Property Co Ltd v Redman* [1956] 2 QB 612; *Phipps v Pears* [1965] 1 QB 76; *Crow v Wood* [1971] 1 QB 77. *Cf* the controversy over the effect of s 5 of the Real Property Act 1845 and s 56 of the Law of Property Act 1925, see *Beswick v Beswick* [1968] AC 58, espec at 102 (*per* Lord Upjohn). Paras **[3.041]** *ante* and **[19.16]** *post*.

[178] Note also the saving in s 6(5)of the 1881 Act. *Quicke v Chapman* [1903] 1 Ch 659.

[179] *Long v Gowlett* [1923] 2 Ch 177. *Cf Head v Meara* [1912] 1 IR 262 at 264-5 (*per* Ross J); also *Wright v Macadam* [1949] 2 KB 744 (*per* Jenkins LJ); *Ward v Kirland* [1967] Ch 194. (contd.../)

seems that the section cannot be invoked in, perhaps, the most common case for the application of the rule in *Wheeldon v Burrows*, where a common owner of quasi-dominant and servient tenements sells the quasi-dominant tenement to another person. The argument in support of this contention is that the section passes rights only in the nature of "liberties", "privileges" and "easements", which are more appropriate expressions for rights over other people's property rather than expressions normally used to describe rights which a common owner has over his own property. Yet, the section does also refer to "ways" and "watercourses" and to "rights" and "advantages", which seem equally appropriate in the case of a common owner[180] and it should be noted that the courts have said that the restriction relating to common ownership or occupation does not apply in the case of a right of light.[181] On the other hand, the section appears to be confined to a "conveyance" of existing rights, ie, it does not apply to the "creation" of rights not already in existence.[182]

[6.068] One further point should be mentioned with respect to both the rule in *Wheeldon v Burrows* and s 6 of the 1881 Act. Both operate with respect to a grant or conveyance of land and have nothing to do with the interpretation of any prior contract for such grant or conveyance.[183] The rule in *Wheeldon v Burrows* is based on the principle that a man may not derogate from his grant and so can be involved only after a grant has been made. Section 6 relates only to interpretation of general words in a "conveyance", which, though widely defined in s 2(v) of the 1881 Act, does not include a contract. Yet it is important to realise that in most cases of a grant or conveyance of land there is initially in force a contract for the sale of the land and questions of its interpretation may arise. What is included in the contract is largely a matter of the intention of the parties as to its scope. It may well be that the contract is intended to include quasi-easements and this may be implied from the circumstances of the case.[184] But neither the rule in *Wheeldon v Burrows* nor s 6 of the 1881 Act have any direct relevance to this matter.

---

[179] (\...contd) Hargreaves, (1952) 15 MLR 265. *Long v Gowlett* was approved by the House of Lords in *Sovmots Investments Ltd v of Secretary of State for the Environment* [1977] 2 WLR 951; see *ibid*, pp 958 (*per* Lord Wilberforce), 965, (*per* Lord Edmund-Davies) and 973 (*per* Lord Keith of Kinkel). Note the controversy provoked by this aspect of the decision between Harpum, 'Easements and Centre Point: Old Problems Resolved in a Novel Setting' (1977) 41 Conv 415 and 'Long v Gowlett: a Strong Fortress' [1979] Conv 113 and Smith, 'Centre Point: Faulty Towers with Shaky Foundations' [1978] Conv 449.

[180] See *Head v Meara* [1912] 1 IR 262.

[181] *Broomfield v Williams* [1897] 1 Ch 602. See also *Long v Gowlett* [1923] 2 Ch 177 at 200 - 3. Note also, however, that a right of light is a somewhat special case in the law of easements generally, para **[6.097]** *post*.

[182] Yet it does apparently apply to *enlarge* existing rights, by, eg, converting what was previously a privilege or bare licence into an easement: see the second point made above.

[183] See discussion in *Re Flanagan and McGarvey and Thompson's Contract* [1945] NI 32 at 40-1 (*per* Black J) (see *A Casebook on Irish Land Law* (1984), p 317); also *Borman v Griffith* [1930] 1 Ch 493.

[184] *McDonagh v Mulholland* [1931] IR 110 at 122 (*per* Kennedy CJ); *Re Flanagan and McGarvey and Thompson's Contract* [1945] NI 32 at 40-1 (*per* Black J). See also *Re Peck and the School Board for London's Contract* [1893] 2 Ch 315; *Re Walmsley and Shaw's Contract* [1917] 1 Ch 93; *Borman v Griffith* [1930] 1 Ch 493.

Furthermore, if the prior contract contained restrictions as to what was to pass with the land, but the subsequent conveyance is drafted in unrestricted form so that, under the rule in *Wheeldon v Burrows* or s 6 of the 1881 Act or both, various rights would be created, it would always be open to the parties to seek rectification of the conveyance in equity on the ground of common mistake.[185] Alternatively, if the purchaser seeks a decree of specific performance against the vendor in relation to the contract, the court will at most oblige the vendor to transfer only those rights which he contracted to sell.[186] The contract may include rights which would pass under the conveyance by virtue of the rule in *Wheeldon v Burrows* or s 6 of the 1881 Act and it may not. In the end of the day, it is entirely a question of the intention of the parties to the contract and the search for this should not be confused by reference to rules or statutory provisions relating to grants or conveyances.

(ii) Reservation

[6.069] It is the corollary of the rules just discussed that few easements arise by implied reservation. Since a grant is generally construed against the grantor, he should, if he wishes to reserve easements for himself, do so expressly. However, the courts have been prepared to relax this general rule and to permit easements to arise by implication in at least two cases.

(a) Easements of Necessity

[6.070] If, on making a grant of part of his land, a grantor cuts himself off from part of his land retained, eg, it becomes landlocked,[187] there will be implied in his favour a way of necessity.[188] The grantor is given the right to choose a convenient means of access and must thereafter stick to it.[189] Such means of access must be a necessity at the date of the grant[190] and no implied right will arise if there is an alternative route available to the grantor.[191] The grantor will succeed in establishing a way of necessity in the last situation only if he can show that the alternative route is not really open to him, because he has no legal right to it as opposed to permission or a licence which may be revoked at any time, or he has not even permission to use it.[192] The grantor will certainly not succeed if he can show only that the alternative route is inconvenient.[193] The view has

---

[185] Para **[3.162]** *ante*.

[186] Paras **[3.144]** and **[3.155]** *ante*.

[187] *Maude v Thornton* [1929] IR 454. See also *Nickerson v Barraclough* [1981] Ch 426.

[188] *Nugent v Cooper* (1854) 7 Ir Jur (os) 112; *Geraghty v McCann* (1872) IR 6 CL 411; *Clancy v Byrne* (1877) IR 11 CL 355; *Browne v Maguire* [1922] 1 IR 23. See also the remarks of Black J in *Re Flanagan and McGarvey and Thompson's Contract* [1945] NI 32 at 42 (see *A Casebook on Irish Land Law* (1984), p 317).

[189] *Cf Donnelly v Adams* [1905] 1 IR 154 (case of implied grant).

[190] *Geraghty v McCann* (1872) IR 6 CL 411; *Browne v Maguire* [1922] 1 IR 23.

[191] *Nugent v Cooper* (1854) 7 Ir Jur (os) 112.

[192] See *Barry v Hasseldine* [1952] Ch 835.

[193] *Manjang v Drammeh* (1990) 61 P & CR 194. *Cf MRA Engineering Ltd v Trimster Co Ltd* (1987) 56 P & CR 1.

been taken in England that a claim to an easement of necessary must be based upon the presumed intention of the parties and not on public policy.[194]

[6.071] Ways of necessity are by far the most common case of easements arising by implied reservation, but there is no reason why other easements of necessity cannot be established, eg, an easement of support without which the land or buildings retained could not be enjoyed at all.[195] In each case the grantor has to prove the necessity.[196] Whether the easement ceases to exist subsequently when the necessity ceases, eg, when an alternative means of access to landlocked property is acquired, is a moot point. There is some authority for saying that the easement does cease[197] but it has been criticised.[198] It is arguable that once the easement comes into existence it cannot be destroyed except in accordance with the usual rules for determination of easements.[199]

(b) Intended Easements

[6.072] There is some authority for saying that the courts will imply in favour of the grantor easements required to give effect to the common intention of the parties to the grant. The most commonly cited example is the case of a sale of one of two adjoining houses where the parties can he taken to intend that there should be mutual rights of support.[200] To some extent there seems to be an overlap with cases of necessity, but intended easements may include a wider category.[201] It can be stated with more certainty that the burden of proof on the grantor in such cases is considerable.[202]

4. Presumed Grant or Prescription

[6.073] The basis of prescription is the presumption by the courts, on being given evidence of long enjoyment of a right in the nature of an easement or profit, that the right had a lawful origin.[203] In this respect the courts acknowledge the theory that easements lie in grant[204] but in practice they recognise the existence of rights without

---

[194] *Nickerson v Barraclough* [1981] Ch 426 (CA reversing Megarry VC [1980] Ch 325).

[195] *Union Lighterage Co v London Graving Dock Co* [1902] 2 Ch 557, at 573 (*per* Stirling LJ).

[196] See discussion in *Donnelly v Adams* [1905] 1 IR 154 at 161 (*per* Barton J).

[197] *Holmes v Goring* (1824) 2 Bing 76. *Cf Mulville v Fallon* (1872) IR 6 Eq 458 (substituted way and implied release of old one). See also *Clancy v Byrne* (1877) IR 11 CL 355.

[198] *Barkshire v Grubb* (1881) 18 Ch D 616 at 620. See also Garner, 'Ways of Necessity' (1960) 24 Conv 208; Grundes, 'Right of Way: Ways of Necessity' (1939) 3 Conv 425; Simonton, 'Ways of Necessity' (1925) 25 Col L Rev 571.

[199] *Cf Stevenson v Parke* [1932] LJ Jr 228. Note also the comments of Meredith J in *Maude v Thornton* [1929] IR 454 at 458 (implied reservation of way of necessity, not simply a licence irrevocable so long as the necessity continues).

[200] *Cf Gogarty v Hoskins* [1906] 1 IR 173. See also *Richards v Rose* (1853) 9 Exch 218 at 221.

[201] *Jones v Pritchard* [1908] 1 Ch 630; *Cory v Davies* [1923] 2 Ch 95. *Cf Shubrook v Tufnell* (1882) 46 LT 886; *Pwllbach Colliery Co Ltd v Woodman* [1915] AC 634; *Re Webb's lease* [1951] Ch 808; *Wong v Beaumont Property Trust Ltd* [1965] 1 QB 173.

[202] *Richards v Rose* (1853) 9 Exch 218.

[203] This is one point of distinction between prescription and the doctrine of adverse possession, Ch 23 *post*.

[204] Para **[6.030]** *ante*.

requiring direct documentary evidence of their creation.[205] The underlying policy is that of "quieting men's titles", a policy that is the foundation of other principles of our land law system.[206]

[6.074] Three methods of prescription have come to be recognised over the centuries, namely, prescription at common law, under the doctrine of lost modern grant and by statute.[207] Each of these methods is considered in detail below, but first we must examine certain conditions which must be met for any of those methods to be applicable.

(i) Conditions

The following are the main conditions which must be satisfied for a claim of acquisition of an easement or profit by prescription to succeed.[208]

(a) User as a Right

[6.075] The claimant by prescription must show that he has used or enjoyed the easement or profit "as of right", ie, as if he were entitled to it.[209] This principle follows from the theory that the court makes a presumption on the basis that the right claimed had a lawful origin. If the claimant has acted in a manner to suggest that his right did not have such an origin, then this destroys the theory upon which the court acts and so the claim must fail.[210] On this point the courts have adopted the terminology of Roman law and have reiterated that the user must have been *nec vi, nec clam* and *nec precario*, ie, without force, without secrecy and without permission.[211] This shows that the claimant must prove not only that he has used or enjoyed the right in question but also that the servient owner acquiesced in that user or enjoyment,[212] as he would in respect of an established right.[213] What is not so clear is what the effect is of a mistake made by the parties. In particular, if the claimant has mistakenly believed that he has an easement or

---

[205] See the discussion in *Timmons v Hewitt* (1888) 22 LR Ir 627. See also Anderson, 'Easement and Prescription - Changing Perspectives in Classification' (1975) 38 MLR 64.

[206] Eg, the doctrine of adverse possession, see Wallace, 'Limitation, Prescription and Unsolicited Permission' (1994) 58 LQR 156 and Ch 23 *post. Cf* the equitable doctrine of laches, para **[3.066]** *ante*. Note that in NI the Land Law Working Group recommended phasing out of acquisition of profits by prescription and replacement of the law relating to acquisition of easements by a new statutory scheme of prescription: see *Final Report* (HMSO, 1990) Vol 1, para 2.7.32 *et seq*.

[207] Ie, the Prescription Act 1832, as applied to Ireland by the Prescription (Ir) Act 1858.

[208] Note, however, the special position of rights of light, para **[6.097]** *post*.

[209] See the discussion in *Hanna v Pollock* [1900] 2 IR 664 (see *A Casebook on Irish Land Law* (1984), p 329).

[210] *Wilson v Stanley* (1861) 12 ICLR 345.

[211] *Coke on Littleton* (19th ed, 1832), 114a.

[212] It follows that "tolerance" by the servient owner of the claimant's user is not usually a defence to a prescriptive claim - it will only amount to this if it destroys "user as of right", eg, by amounting to permission. See the discussion in *Mills v Silver* [1991] Ch 271.

[213] See *Annally Hotel Ltd v Bergin* (1970) 104 ILTR 65. Also *Deeble v Linehan* (1860) 12 ICLR 1. *Cf Beggan v McDonald* (1877) 2 LR Ir 560. Para **[6.091]** *post*.

profit, does this prevent him from establishing a claim by prescription?[214] The English Court of Appeal has held that it does not unless the mistake has in some way contributed positively to mislead the servient owner, ie, it may affect the way in which user is conducted by the claimant or the way in which it is perceived by the servient owner.[215] The mistake may, therefore, in a particular case mean that the user was not "as of right", but not necessarily so.[216]

[6.076] If the claimant has had user through force or violence on his part only, or the servient owner has permitted user after protest or objection only,[217] it is clear that a claim cannot be established "as of right".[218] Similarly, for the servient owner to acquiesce in the user, he must have knowledge of it and secret user, eg, in the form of claimed support for a building where the servient owner is unaware that he is providing such support, will not be enough to establish a claim.[219] For this reason also claims in respect of subterranean water often fail.[220] Finally, the claimant cannot succeed in establishing user "as of right" if, on the contrary, the user has been made under an agreement with or licence from the servient owner.[221] In such a case the position of the claimant is governed by the terms of the agreement or licence and not by the law of prescription.[222]

(b) Continuous User

[6.077] It is also a settled principle that the user or enjoyment must be continuous for a claim by prescription to succeed.[223] In the case of certain easements, eg, a right of way, this has been interpreted as requiring regular user as opposed to intermittent user.[224]

---

[214] See Hudson, 'Mistake and Prescription' (1989) 40 NILQ 64; Kodilyne, 'Prescription under Mistake' [1989] Conv 261.

[215] *Bridle v Ruby* (1988) P & CR 155 at 162 (*per* Gibson LJ). See also *Earl de la Warr v Miles* (1881) 17 Ch D 535; *cf Lyell v Lord Hothfield* [1914] 3 KB 911

[216] See *Dawson v McGreggan* [1903] 1 IR 92 (prescriptive claim to right to cut turf upheld despite claimant's mistaken belief that such a right was granted by an existing lease, a mistake apparently shared with the servient owner).

[217] The fact that the objection or protest may be mistaken or transient or fluctuating does not render it ineffective to prevent "user as of right": see *Newnham v Willison* (1988) 56 P & CR 8.

[218] *Eaton v Swansea Waterworks Co* (1851) 17 QB 267.

[219] *Gateley v Martin* [1900] 2 IR 269.

[220] *Ewart v Belfast Poor Law Commrs* (1881) 9 LR Ir 172. *Cf Black v Ballymena Township Commrs* (1886) 17 LR Ir 459. It seems that the servient owner may not succeed on this ground by simply "turning a blind eye" to the user in question, see *Union Lighterage Co v London Graving Dock Co* [1902] 2 Ch 557, espec at 571 (*per* Romer LJ); also *Lloyds Bank Ltd v Dalton* [1942] Ch 466.

[221] *Arkwright v Gell* (1839) 5 M & W 203.

[222] However, prescription may become relevant if the right continues to be enjoyed after the contract or licence ends, *Gaved v Martyn* (1865) 19 CB (ns) 732.

[223] *Cf* the concept of "without interruption" under the Prescription Act 1832, para **[6.093]** *post*.

[224] *Hollins v Verney* (1884) 13 QBD 304; *Cf* abandonment through disuse or substitution of an alternative, *Mulville v Fallon* (1872) IR 6 Eq 458; *Stevenson v Parke* [1932] LJ Ir 228.

(c) Leasehold Property

[6.078] In England it has long been a settled principle that the doctrine of prescription is generally confined to freehold property.[225] The theory applied by the English courts seems to have been that prescription involves the notion of a permanent right created at some unspecified date in the past and that this is inconsistent with acquisition in respect of leasehold property.[226] Thus the English Courts have held: (1) there can be no prescription against a landowner who holds a limited freehold estate[227] or a leasehold estate only;[228] (2) where the claimant is himself a limited owner or lessee, he can claim easements by prescription on behalf of the fee simple owner or his landlord only, and so cannot prescribe against other land held by the fee simple owner or the landlord;[229] (3) on the same ground as in (2), one tenant cannot prescribe against another tenant of the same landlord.[230]

[6.079] The Irish courts have taken a quite different approach to this subject,[231] which may be partly due to the fact that there was a time when so much of the land in what is still a predominantly agricultural island was subject to tenancies.[232] Furthermore, many of these tenancies were and still are in areas which have since become urbanised, for very substantial periods, eg, 999 and 10,000 years,[233] which for practical purposes seem little different than grants in fee simple so far as the long enjoyment or permanent user of the rights in question is concerned. The result of the Irish courts' reaction to the English decisions[234] is as follows: (1) Prescription against a limited owner or tenant can

---

[225] Indeed, confined to the fee simple estate, *Bright v Walker* (1834) 1 Cr M & R 211; *Gayford v Moffat* (1868) 4 Ch App 133. See also *Simmons v Dobson* [1991] 4 All ER 25.

[226] *Wheaton v Maple & Co* [1893] 3 Ch 48 at 63 (*per* Lindley LJ). The English courts have, however, accepted that easements or profits could be acquired in respect of leasehold property by express grants, *Kilgour v Gaddes* [1904] 1 KB 457 at 460 or where the tenants had the right to enlarge their leases into a fee simple; *Bosomworth v Faber* (1992) 69 P & CR 288. See also Kiralfy, 'Position of Leaseholder in Law of Easements' (1948) 13 Conv 104; Sparkes, 'Establishing Easements against Leaseholds' [1992] Conv 167.

[227] *Barker v Richardson* (1821) 4 B & Ald 579; *Roberts v James* (1903) 89 LT 282. Note, however, that the Settled Land Act 1882, s 3(i) empowered a tenant for life to grant easements in fee simple, Ch 8 *post*.

[228] *Daniel v North* (1809) 11 East 372.

[229] In effect the argument is essentially that the landlord cannot, through his tenant, claim a right against himself, *Gayford v Moffat* (1868) 4 Ch App 133.

[230] *Kilgour v Gaddes* [1904] 1 KB 457.

[231] See Chua 'Easements: Termors in Prescription in Ireland' (1964) 15 NILQ 489; Delaney 'Lessees and Doctrine of Lost Grant' (1958) 74 LQR 82.

[232] Ch 18 *post*. See also the remarks of Dodd J in *Flynn v Harte* [1913] 2 IR 322 and the discussion by the Court of Appeal in *Hanna v Pollock* [1900] 2 IR 664 (see *A Casebook on Irish Land Law* (1984), p 329).

[233] Note also leases for lives renewable for ever, Ch 4 *ante*.

[234] Especially *Bright v Walker* (1834) 1 Cr M & R 211 and *Gayford v Moffat* (1868) 4 Ch App 133.

be claimed under the Prescription Act 1832,[235] and the doctrine of lost modern grant.[236] There is no authority on whether such a claim can be established at common law.[237] (2) A tenant can probably prescribe against other land held by his own landlord under the Prescription Act 1832,[238] but not under the doctrine of lost modern grant.[239] Once again there is no authority on the position at common law, but it is likely that a claim would fail as in the case of a claim based on lost modern grant. (3) A tenant can prescribe against another tenant holding under the same landlord under the Prescription Act 1832,[240] probably also under the doctrine of lost modern grant[241] and possibly even at common law.[242]

[6.080] We must now turn to the three methods of prescription recognised by our law. At the outset it must be emphasised that all three methods can still be invoked today and it is usual to plead more than one in a particular case in the hope that the court will find that at least one method is applicable.[243]

---

[235] But in the case of 40 years' enjoyment only, *Wilson v Stanley* (1861) 12 ICLR 345; *Beggan v McDonald* (1877) 2 LR Ir 560, espec at 570-1 (*per* May CJ) (holding this remained the case despite the servient tenant's landlord's absence of knowledge of or non-acquiescence in the enjoyment during the tenancy). In the case of 20 year's enjoyment only, it must be "as of right" under the 1832 Act and this seems to preclude a claim against the tenant so as to bind his landlord, *Wilson v Stanley, op cit*. *Cf* if the claim is for an easement for the period of the servient owner's tenancy only, fn 328 *infra*.

[236] Provided sufficient evidence of the landlord's knowledge of and acquiescence in the enjoyment is shown, *Deeble v Linehan* (1860) 12 ICLR 1. It is, of course, possible to argue that in certain cases the easement is to attach to, and to last for, the term of the servient owner's tenancy only, see *O'Kane v O'Kane* (1892) 30 LR Ir 489 at 494 (*per* O'Brien CJ).

[237] Where the point has been raised, the courts have tended to decide the issue on other grounds, eg, by holding an easement arose by *implied* grant, see *Timmons v Hewitt* (1887) 22 LR Ir 627. Also *Clancy v Byrne* (1877) IR 11 CL 355.

[238] Again limited to cases of 40 years' enjoyment *Fahey v Dwyer* (1879) 4 LR Ir 271. *Cf Clancy v Byrne* (1877) IR 11 CL 355.

[239] *Macnaghten v Baird* [1903] 2 IR 731.

[240] *Fahey v Dwyer* (1879) 4 LR Ir 271.

[241] *Hanna v Pollock* [1900] 2 IR 664 (see *A Casebook on Irish Land Law* (1984), p 329); *Flynn v Harte* [1913] 2 IR 322; *Tallon v Ennis* [1937] IR 549; *Tisdall v McArthur & Co (Steel and Metal) Ltd* [1951] IR 228 at 240-1 (*per* Kingsmill Moore J) (see *ibid*, p 357). Once again the grant may be presumed to relate only to the period of the servient owner's tenancy and not to bind the common landlord, *O'Kane v O'Kane* (1892) 30 LR Ir 489. The courts may also invoke the doctrine of implied grant and hold that the common landlord impliedly granted the easement when demising the dominant tenement, *Timmons v Hewitt* (1887) 22 LR Ir 627 at 637 (*per* Palles CB).

[242] *Timmons v Hewitt* (1887) 22 LR Ir 627. See also *Clancy v Byrne* (1877) IR 11 CL 355.

[243] For reasons which should become clear from the ensuing discussion, it is usual to plead in the order, first the Prescription Act, second, at common law and third the doctrine of lost modern grant. However, practices varied over the years and there was a time when judges were less reluctant to adopt the doctrine of a lost grant. Indeed, the doctrine seems to have made something of a "come-back" in recent times in England: see *Bridle v Ruby* [1989] QB 169; *Mills v Silver* [1991] Ch 271; *Simmons v Dobson* [1991] 4 All ER 25.

(ii) At Common Law

[6.081] At common law the courts were prepared to presume that a grant of the easement or profit claimed had been made if user as of right could be shown to have continued from time immemorial,[244] ie, "from time whereof the memory of men runneth not to the contrary".[245] In fact, the date fixed as the limit of legal memory was 1189,[246] so that a claimant under common law in theory has to establish that he and his predecessors in title have enjoyed the easement or profit continuously since 1189.[247] This clearly would be impossible in most, if not all, cases and so the courts for centuries have been prepared to presume such continuous user where a claimant has user for a substantial time immediately prior to his action. In practice the courts have been prepared to make this presumption on production of evidence showing 20 years' continuous user,[248] or, sometimes, user since living memory.[249] This reduced considerably the burden of proof on the claimant at common law but there remain two major difficulties in establishing prescription at common law.

[6.082] First, the theory of continuous user since 1189 is still the basis of a claim to prescription at common law and the court's presumption in this regard on being shown 20 years' user can easily be rebutted by showing that user was not possible since 1189. Even if the defendant cannot establish exactly the date after 1189 when user began,[250] he can often show that it must have been some time after that date, eg, where an easement of light is claimed for a building clearly not eight centuries old.[251] Secondly, a claim at common law can also be defeated by showing that at some date since 1189 there has been unity of possession,[252] ie, that the dominant and servient tenements have been owned and occupied by the same person.[253] It was in an effort to cure these difficulties at common law, especially the first, that the courts devised the second method of prescription, the doctrine of lost modern grant.[254]

(iii) Lost Modern Grant

[6.083] Under this doctrine the courts are prepared to indulge in an alleged fiction that the easement or profit claimed was the subject of a grant executed since 1189 but before

---

[244] *Craig v McCance* (1910) 44 ILTR 90. See also *Daly v Cullen* (1958) 92 ILTR 127.

[245] *Coke on Littleton* (19th ed, 1832), 170.

[246] So fixed by the Statute of Westminster I, 1275, c 39.

[247] *Abercromby v Fermoy Town Commissioners* [1900] 1 IR 302 (see *A Casebook on Irish Land Law* (1984), p 294). See also *Craig v McCance* (1910) 44 ILTR 90; *Carroll v Sheridan* [1984] ILRM 451.

[248] *McCullagh v Wilson* (1838) 1 Jebb & Sym 120; *O'Brien v Enright* (1867) IR 1 CL 718; *Powell v Butler* (1871) IR 5 CL 309; *Timmons v Hewitt* (1887) 22 LR Ir 627.

[249] *Clancy v Whelan* (1958) 92 ILTR 39. See also *Daly v Cullen* (1958) 92 ILTR 127.

[250] *Hanna v Pollock* [1900] 2 IR 664 (see *A Casebook on Irish Land Law* (1984), p 329).

[251] *Duke of Norfolk v Arbuthnot* (1880) 5 CPD 390.

[252] *Wilson v Stanley* (1861) 12 ICLR 345.

[253] Para **[6.106]** *post*.

[254] Described by Lush J as a "revolting fiction" in *Angus & Co v Dalton* (1877) 3 QBD 85 at 95, but considered at length and approved in the same case by the House of Lords, *sub nom, Dalton v Angus & Co* (1881) 6 App Cas 740.

the action brought by the claimant, and that the deed of grant has been lost and so cannot be produced in evidence.[255] In earlier days juries were instructed to find as a fact that such a grant had been made if they were satisfied that sufficient evidence of long user or enjoyment had been shown,[256] and so the presumption arose that user from living memory or a period of 20 years prior to the action established the existence of a lost grant.[257] Since the doctrine is based on the theory of a grant at some unspecified date in the past, there is no need to prove continued user since 1189. The "fiction" has never been carried to the lengths of requiring findings as to the details of the grant, such as the date of its execution and the names of the parties to it.[258] An interesting point which never seems to have been addressed by the Irish courts is how the doctrine relates to the registration of deeds system, whereby a deed must be registered to secure priority over a subsequently registered deed.[259] It has been suggested that the only way to reconcile the doctrine of lost grant with the registration system is to presume not only the existence of the lost deed but also that it was registered in the Registry of Deeds.[260] Although the lost modern grant doctrine may resolve some of the problems in making a claim of prescription under the common law, there are, however, difficulties even with respect to this second method of prescription.

[6.084] First, the court will refuse to make the presumption of a lost grant if it can be established that during the period when the grant could have been made eg, during the lifetime of the building to which the easement relates, a grant was impossible because of some technicality, such as the servient owner being under a disability, like mental incapacity, or was a corporation prohibited by its articles of association from dealing in land.[261] To this extent, at least, the courts have not treated the matter as being wholly one of fiction. Secondly, even the Irish courts have made it clear in landlord and tenant cases that a grant cannot be presumed in favour of a tenant against his own landlord,[262] though

---

[255] See the discussion in *Hanna v Pollock* [1900] 2 IR 664. Also *Ingram v Mackey* [1898] 1 IR 272; *Whelan v Leonard* [1917] 2 IR 323.

[256] *Deeble v Linehan* (1860) 12 ICLR 1; *O'Kane v O'Kane* (1892) 30 LR Ir 489.

[257] *Deeble v Linehan, op cit*; *O'Kane v O'Kane, op cit*; *Flynn v Harte* [1913] 2 IR 322; *Tisdall v McArthur & Co (Steel and Metal) Ltd* [1951] IR 228 (see *A Casebook on Irish Land Law* (1984), p 357); *Scott v Goulding Properties Ltd* [1972] IR 200 (*ibid*, p 299).

[258] *Palmer v Guadagni* [1906] 2 Ch 494. *Cf Dunne v Molloy* [1976-7] ILRM 266 (claim failed where only persons who could have made the grant were living and in court where no evidence to support it was given).

[259] See para [3.084] *et seq, ante*.

[260] See Dowling, 'Lost Grants and Registered Deeds' (1992) 43 NILQ 53.

[261] *Rochdale Canal Co v Radcliffe* (1852) 18 QBD 287. See also *Neaverson v Peterborough RDC* [1902] Ch 557; *Oakley v Boston* [1976] QB 270.

[262] *Macnaghten v Baird* [1903] 2 IR 731, applying the principle laid down by Lord Cairns in *Gayford v Moffat* (1868) 4 Ch App 133 at 135: "... the possession of the tenant of the demised close is in the possession of his landlord, and it seems to be an utter violation of the first principles of the relation of landlord and tenant to suppose that the tenant, whose occupation of a close A was the occupation of his landlord, could by that occupation acquire an easement of close B, also belonging to his landlord ...". (contd.../)

it seems that the courts are prepared to allow the doctrine of lost modern grant to operate as between tenants, even though holding under the same landlord.[263]

[6.085] The difficulties over a claim based on prescription at common law and under the doctrine of lost modern grant prompted the enactment of the Prescription Act 1832. This Act did not apply originally to Ireland but was extended *en bloc* to Ireland by the Prescription (Ireland) Act 1858, from 1 January 1859.[264]

(iv) Prescription Act 1832

[6.086] Though the 1832 Act did reduce many of the difficulties relating to the concept of prescription as developed by the courts, it has created its own difficulties for, as it was once put in an oft-quoted statement, it is notorious as "one of the worst drafted Acts on the Statute Book".[265] The following is a summary of the Act's main provisions and, at the outset, it should be noted that the Act contains special provisions for rights of lights, which are discussed at the end of this section. As in the case of the other two methods of prescription, the Act applies to profits *à prendre* as well as to easements, though there are some differences in detail in its application to the two kinds of incorporeal hereditament. These differences are noted in the following passages of this chapter.

(a) Prescription Periods of User

[6.087] Sections 1 and 2 of the 1832 Act lay down two periods of user whereby easements and profits may be acquired by prescription under the Act. In a case of the shorter period only being shown, namely 20 years' user of an easement (other than of light)[266] and 30 years' user of a profit,[267] the Act simply provides that the easement or profit claimed cannot be defeated by showing only that it was first enjoyed at any time prior to the 20 or 30-year period.[268] In other words, where the shorter period of user only can be shown by a claimant, all the Act does is to prevent his claim being defeated by one of the main defences to a claim at common law, ie, proof that user began after 1189 and so has not continued since time immemorial.[269] In this respect the Act aids a claim to prescription at common law only.[270]

---

[262] (\...contd) However, the Irish courts have suggested that a tenant may acquire an easement against his landlord under the doctrine of implied grant. *Timmons v Hewitt* (1887) 22 LR Ir 627 at 637 (*per* Palles CB). See fn 333, para **[6.079]** *ante*.

[263] *Hanna v Pollock* [1900] 2 IR 664 (see *A Casebook on Irish Land Law* (1984), p 329). See also *Flynn v Harte* [1913] 2 IR 322 at 326 (*per* Dodd J); *Tisdall v McArthur & Co (Steel and Metal) Ltd* [1951] IR 228 at 240-1 (*per* Kingsmill Moore J) (see *ibid*, p 357).

[264] 1858 Act, s 1. Following the English 1832 Act, the 1858 Act's short title stated that it was an Act "for shortening the Time of Prescription in certain cases in Ireland".

[265] See the English Law Reform Committee's 14th Report *Acquisition of Easements and Profits by Prescription* (1966; Cmnd 3100), para 40.

[266] Section 2.

[267] Section 1. *Doyle's Case* (1833) Alc Reg Cas 36.

[268] Sections 1 and 2.

[269] Para **[6.082]** *ante*. Thus it is expressly provided in the case of a claim based on one of the shorter periods of user that "such claim may be defeated in any other way by which the same is now liable to be defeated" - see ss 1 and 2 of the Act.

[6.088] Where, however, a claimant can show the longer period of user, namely 40 years for an easement (other than of light)[271] and 60 years for a profit,[272] the Act is more positive and provides that the easement or profit is to be "deemed absolute and indefeasible",[273] unless it has been enjoyed by written consent.[274] It is upon the basis of this difference in operation of the Act in the case of user for the longer period that the Irish courts have been prepared to hold not only that prescription under the Act may operate against a tenant so as to bind even his landlord's reversionary estate in certain circumstances,[275] but also that one tenant can prescribe under the Act against another tenant of the same landlord[276] and possibly even directly against his own landlord.[277]

[6.089] It must be emphasised again that the 1832 Act provides an *additional* basis for a claim to an easement or profit by prescription and does not exclude the pleading also of the other two alternatives of prescription at common law or acquisition under the doctrine of lost modern grant.[278] Indeed, it is common to plead at least two of the methods of prescription, if not all three, as the Irish cases show.[279] Usually a claim based on the Prescription Act is easier to establish (which is precisely what the Act intends[280]), but it may happen that such a claim fails on a technicality based on other provisions in the Act[281] and so one has to fall back on the other methods of prescription.[282] However,

---

[270] This seems to have been one of the reasons why the Irish courts have argued that a claim to prescription under the 1832 Act, based on the shorter periods of 20 or 30 years, cannot be made by or against a tenant, see *Wilson v Stanley* (1861) 12 ICLR 345; *cf Beggan v McDonald* (1877) 2 LR Ir 560.

[271] Section 2.

[272] Section 1. See *Doyle's Case* (1833) Alc Reg Cas 36. *Lowry v Crothers* (1871) IR 5 CL 98 (profits *à prendre*).

[273] Sections 1 and 2.

[274] Discussed further, para **[6.091]** *post*.

[275] Ie, if the landlord does not resist the claim within 3 years of determination of the tenant's tenancy under s 8 of the 1832 Act. See discussion in *Beggan v McDonald* (1877) 2 LR Ir 560, espec at 570-1 (*per* May CJ). Also *Wilson v Stanley* (1861) 12 ICLR 345 at 355 (*per* Pigot CB).

[276] *Fahey v Dwyer* (1879) 4 LR Ir 271; *Hanna v Pollock* [1900] 2 IR 664 (see *A Casebook on Irish Land Law* (1984), p 329); *Flynn v Harte* [1913] 2 IR 322; *Tallon v Ennis* [1937] IR 549.

[277] *Ibid*. *Cf Timmons v Hewitt* (1887) 22 LR Ir 627 at 635 (*per* Palles CB).

[278] The suggestion in England that lost modern grant can no longer be raised in respect of an easement of light (see, eg, *Tappling v Jones* (1865) 11 HLC 290) had been doubted in Ireland, see *Tisdall v McArthur & Co (Steel and Metal) Ltd* [1951] IR 228 at 235 and 240-1 (*per* Kingsmill Moore J) (see *A Casebook on Irish Land Law* (1984), p 357). See also *Scott v Goulding Properties Ltd* [1972] IR 200 (*ibid*, p 299).

[279] Eg *Wilson v Stanley* (1861) 12 ICLR 345 (Prescription Act and lost modern grant); *Timmons v Hewitt* (1887) 22 LR Ir 627 (Prescription Act, common law and lost modern grant); *Hanna v Pollock* [1900] 2 IR 664 (see *A Casebook on Irish Land Law* (1984), p 329) (Prescription Act, common law and lost modern grant).

[280] See its short title, fn 356, para **[6.085]** *ante*. Thus the Act is usually pleaded first, then prescription at common law, so that a request to the court to adopt a "fiction" is put last. See the remarks of Lord Macnaghten in *Gardner v Hodgson's Kingston Brewery Co Ltd* [1903] AC 229 at 240.

[281] Eg, consent or interruption, see paras **[6.091]** and **[6.093]** *infra*.

[282] *Hanna v Pollock* [1900] 2 IR 664 (see *A Casebook on Irish Land Law* (1984), p 329).

the Act provides expressly that user for less than the statutory period is not to give rise to any presumption in favour of the claim in question,[283] though it has been stated that a lost grant may still be presumed from user for less than the statutory period, provided there is some other item of evidence to support that presumption.[284]

(b) Claim by Litigant

[6.090] It is essential to realise that the Act's provisions are expressly confined to cases where "some suit or action wherein the claim or matter to which such period [of user] may relate shall have been or shall be brought into question".[285] To establish an easement or profit under the Act, the claimant must bring an action for infringement of the alleged right[286] or, if the claimant does not wish to wait for such infringement,[287] he may apply to the court for a declaration that he is entitled to the easement or profit in question.[288] Furthermore, the Act also provides that, when a suit or action is brought the vital period of user to be considered by the court is the period "next before" that suit or action. In other words, the claimant must not only show the statutory period of user but also show that user took place immediately prior to his suit or action.[289]

(c) User as of Right

[6.091] The Act contains the same basic requirement which applies to the other two methods of prescription, namely that the user made by the claimant to the easement or profit was "as of right",[290] ie, *nec vi, nec clam* and *nec precario*.[291] This general principle at least holds good so far as the shorter periods in the Act are concerned, but there is one problem relating to the longer periods whereby easements or profits are deemed absolute and indefeasible. The Act expressly provides that this applies only if the easement or profit was not enjoyed "by some consent or agreement expressly made or given for that purpose *by deed or writing*".[292] Under the common law rules, however, even oral consent or permission will prevent the user from being "as of right" and so the implication seems to be that, under the Act, this does not apply in the case of a claim

---

[283] Section 6.

[284] *Hanmer v Chance* (1865) 4 De GJ & S 626 at 631.

[285] Section 4. "The important point is that the fruits of the Act can be reaped only by a litigant." Megarry and Wade, *Law of Real Property* (5th ed, 1984), p 880.

[286] *Tisdall v McArthur & Co (Steel and Metal) Ltd* [1951] IR 228 (see *A Casebook on Irish Land Law* (1984), p 357).

[287] Eg, he may wish to establish the existence of the right prior to selling or otherwise dealing with the dominant land.

[288] *Gaw v CIE* [1953] IR 232 (see *A Casebook on Irish Land Law* (1984), p 622).

[289] *Parker v Mitchell* (1840) 11 Ad & El 788. The law is not so strict where a claim is based on the common law or doctrine of lost modern grant: see *Tehidy v Minerals Ltd v Norman* [1971] 2 QB 528; *Mills v Silver* [1991] Ch 271.

[290] See ss 1 and 2 (which refer to any person "claiming right thereto") and 5(which states that in the pleadings it is sufficient "to allege the enjoyment thereof as a right").

[291] Para **[6.075]** *ante*.

[292] Sections 1 and 2 (italics added). See *Lowry v Crothers* (1871) IR 5 CL 9.

based on user for one of the longer periods. Yet the Act still requires that (and this applies equally to claims based on the longer periods of user) the claimant should claim "right" to the easement or profit and allege in the pleadings enjoyment "as of right".[293] The House of Lords has suggested[294] that the way to reconcile the apparent conflict between the various provisions of the Act is to hold that, in the case of the longer periods, oral consent or permission will defeat a claim only if it is given during the statutory period of user, or is renewed during that period. Consent given at the beginning of the period only, even if intended to apply throughout, must be in writing.

[6.092] It seems to be clear that the consent or permission sufficient to prevent acquisition by prescription may be given by whoever is the current occupier of the servient tenement, whether owner of the fee simple, tenant for life or for years or even a squatter.[295] The same applies to acknowledgement of no rights by the occupier of the dominant tenement, so that a tenant may prevent his landlord from acquiring an easement or profits by prescription.[296]

(d) Without Interruption

[6.093] The Act also provides that the user by the claimant must have been "without interruption".[297] This concept should not be confused with user by consent or permission which also prevents acquisition by prescription under the Act. In the case of user by consent or permission, the user *ex hypothesi* continues, as, indeed, it does where the user is subject to protest.[298] An interruption, on the other hand, involves interference with the enjoyment of the right, if not actual cessation of the enjoyment.[299] The interruption or obstruction may be caused by acts of the servient owner[300] or a stranger,[301] or may be due to natural causes, such as a stream drying up.[302]

[6.094] However, the Act goes even further than this and requires that the interruption, to be effective in preventing acquisition of rights by prescription under it, must be "submitted to or acquiesced in for one year after the party interrupted shall have had or shall have notice thereof, and of the person making or authorising the same to be

---

[293] See fn 382 *supra*.

[294] See the discussion in *Gardner v Hodgson's Kingston Brewery Co Ltd* [1903] AC 229. Also *Gaved v Martyn* 19 CB (ns) 732; *Ward v Kirland* [1966] 1 WLR 601.

[295] See the discussion in *Lowry v Crothers* (1871) IR 5 CL 98.

[296] See the discussion in *Hyman v Van den Bergh* [1907] 2 Ch 500 at 531 (*per* Parker J) on appeal [1908] 1 Ch 167 at 179 (*per* Farwell LJ).

[297] Sections 1-3. See the discussion in *Tisdall v McArthur & Co (Steel and Metal) Ltd* [1951] IR 228 (see *A Casebook on Irish Land Law* (1984), p 357).

[298] See the discussion in *Reilly v Orange* [1955] 1 WLR 616.

[299] *Barry v Lowry* (1877) IR 11 CL 483.

[300] *Hanks v Cribbin* (1857) 7 ICLR 489 (see also (1859) 9 ICLR 312n): *Claxton v Claxton* (1873) IR 7 CL 23; *Geoghegan v Henry* [1922] 2 IR 1; *Scott v Goulding Properties Ltd* [1972] IR 200 (see *A Casebook on Irish Land Law* (1984), p 299).

[301] *Davies v Williams* (1851) 16 QB 546.

[302] *Hall v Swift* (1838) 4 Bing NC 381.

made.[303] Thus the claimant can still establish his right by prescription despite an interruption if he can show that he has not submitted to or acquiesced in that interruption for a period of one year, by, eg, making protests to the interrupter or, if necessary, commencing an action against him.[304]

Furthermore, the one year period does not begin to run until the claimant has notice of both the fact that interruption is taking place and the identity of the person making it.[305] This means that a claimant should succeed in establishing his easement under the Act after 19 years and one day, provided he is quick off the mark. It must be remembered that the Act benefits the litigant only, who in this case must show 20 years uninterrupted user. He must, therefore, issue his summons or writ on the first day of the twenty-first year of his user, for from that day only can he successfully argue that the interruption has not run for one complete year. If he is one day late, the interruption will have run for the full year and he will have lost his claim in respect of the previous twenty years.[306] If he is one day early, he will also fail because he cannot show the full 20 years user required by the Act.[307] And, of course, this means that the servient owner can still defeat the claim by bringing an action against the dominant owner at any time up to the first day of the twenty-first year of user.[308] Such an action would seem to amount to more than a mere interruption of the claimant's user or enjoyment[309] and, apart from that, clearly prevents any subsequent claim by him "as of right".[310]

(e) Deductions

[6.095] Even though on the face of it a claimant can show user or enjoyment of the right in question for the statutory period, he may still fail because of other special provisions in the Act requiring deductions to be made from the period of user shown. Section 7

---

[303] Section 4.

[304] *Claxton v Claxton* (1873) IR CL 23. Presumably protests and, *ex hypothesi*, an action are significant only after the requisite period under the Act has run. Prior to that the claimant has no right to protect and the servient owner is at liberty to interrupt as he pleases and, if necessary, can take action against the claimant. In other words, the references in s 4 of the Act to submission to or acquiescence in the interruption relate only to the intermediate period between the time *after* the requisite statutory period of user has run and *before* an action is brought to establish the claim. This is simply another illustration of the basic principle that the Act aids a litigant only (para **[6.090]** *ante*) and it reiterates the point that, when the action is finally brought, considerably more time may have elapsed than is required by the Act. Yet the crucial period remains that immediately preceding the action and the claimant will fail if interruption has occurred in that period, even though a full uninterrupted period can be established earlier than that, para **[6.090]** *ante*. See also *Glover v Coleman* (1874) LR 10 CP 108.

[305] *Seddon v Bank of Bolton* (1882) 19 Ch D 462.

[306] *Flight v Thomas* (1840) 11 Ad & E 668 at 771.

[307] *Lord Battersea v Commrs of Sewers for the City of London* [1895] 2 Ch 708; *Barff v Mann, Crossman & Paulin Ltd* (1905) 49 Sol Jo 794. Note also s 6 of the Act, para **[6.089]** *ante*.

[308] *Reilly v Orange* [1955] 1 WLR 616.

[309] Section 4 refers to an "act or other matter" in relation to interruption. See Hugessen, 'Interruption by Institution of Action' (1954) 32 CBR 582.

[310] Para **[6.091]** *ante*.

provides that, in the case of the shorter periods (20 and 30 years) only, there has to be deducted from the period of user any period during which the servient owner was under a disability, such as being an infant, a lunatic or a tenant for life.[311] The same automatic deduction has to be made under s 7 in respect of any period during which an action was pending and actively prosecuted. Section 8 then provides that, where the servient tenement has been held for a "term of life, or any term of years exceeding three years from the granting thereof", that term is to be deducted when computing the longer period (40 years) in the case of a "way or other convenient[312] watercourse or use of water",[313] provided the claim is resisted by the reversioner within three years of determination of the term.[314] In other words, under s 8 the deduction is not made automatically and depends upon action being taken by the reversioner. This was explained by May CJ in *Beggan v MacDonald*:

> "Assuming that the right has in fact been exercised as of right for forty years, it would become absolute; but if, during the whole or part of this period of forty years, the servient lands were in the occupation of tenants, the period of such tenancies may be excluded, but only subject to the condition that the reversioner shall resist the claim within a certain time. If that condition has not been complied with, the tenancy cannot be excluded from the computation. The right will have been enjoyed for the full period, and becomes *prima facie* absolute, subject to this qualification, that in case the tenancy be not determined, and the reversioner should hereafter upon its determination resist the right, as against him the period of such tenancy cannot be included in computing the term of forty years, and therefore against him the statute will not operate. In the case before the Court, the enjoyment of the right of way took place entirely during the subsistence of a lease demising the servient tenement, and which lease at the time of action brought had not determined. *Non constat* that the landlord ever would or will resist the right; but in the meantime, and before he has done so, what authority can there be for excluding the term from the computation of the period of forty years? And if it be not excluded, then it seems to me that the statute operated to establish a right in favour of the dominant tenement, capable of being challenged and defeated by the reversioner in the case supposed, but otherwise absolute and indefeasible. This result appears to me plainly to follow from a fair construction of the several clauses of the Act."[315]

[6.096] To summarise, then, the effect of the two sections, s 7 provides for automatic deduction in the appropriate cases whenever a claim is based on the shorter periods of

---

[311] The section also referred to a *feme covert*, but married women are no longer under any disability in law in either part of Ireland, see Ch 25 *post*.

[312] It has been suggested that the word "convenient" here is a misprint for "easement", so that s 8 should be regarded as applying to all easements; *cf*, the wording of s 2 of the Act ("way or other *easement*, or of any watercourse ..."). (Italics added). See *Laird v Briggs* (1880) 50 LJ Ch 260 at 261 (*per* Fry J); *cf* the report in 16 Ch D 440 at 447 and, on appeal (1881) 19 Ch D 22 at 33, 36 and 37.

[313] Section 8 does not apply to profits at all, whereas s 7 does.

[314] See the discussion of s 8 in *Wilson v Stanley* (1861) 12 ICLR 345 and *Beggan v McDonald* (1877) 2 LR Ir 560.

[315] *Op cit*, pp 570-1. Note that s 8 is expressly confined to a "reversion" and does not seem to cover a "remainderman" taking after a life owner under a settlement, *Symons v Leaker* (1885) 15 QBD 629; *cf Holman v Exton* (1692) Carth 246.

user. Thus if X uses a right of way for 15 years against the fee simple owner of the servient land, followed by 10 years' user against a tenant for life, followed by 5 years' user against the fee simple owner, making 30 years' user in all before an action is brought by him, he succeeds in his claim. The 10 years' user against the tenant for life is deducted, leaving 20 years' user, made up from two periods, as required by the Act.[316] If, instead, the 10 years' user in the example just given had been against a tenant for years. X could have brought his action to establish his right of way after only 5 of those years of user. He would in that case be claiming his right on 20 years' user (15 against the fee simple owner plus 5 against the tenant for years) and s 7 does not allow deductions in the case of terms of years. On the other hand, s 8, which does, does not apply to cases where the claim is based on the shorter period of user. Thus it is preferable from the claimant's point of view to base a case involving leases on the shorter period, if possible, rather than the longer period which may result, as May CJ indicated, in the claimant establishing a right subject to a condition whereby it may subsequently be defeated.[317] On the other hand, s 8 does not apply to cases of infancy or insanity, so that it is preferable to base a claim in such cases on the longer statutory period of user, if possible, so as to avoid any deduction.

(f) Easements of Light

[6.097] The 1832 Act contains special provisions relating to easements of light, perhaps for the reason that such easements were the most difficult to establish at common law.[318] Section 3 of the Act provides that, when "the access and use of light to and for any dwelling house, workshop or other building[319] shall have been actually enjoyed for 20 years without interruption"[320] the right thereto is to be deemed "absolute and indefeasible, any local usage or custom to the contrary notwithstanding, unless it shall appear that the same was enjoyed by some consent or agreement expressly made or given for that purpose by deed or writing". In other words, contrary to the common law position, acquisition of an easement of light under the Prescription Act is easier than for any other kind of easement. This is the case because of the general provision, just quoted, that 20 years' user of an easement of light is equivalent to 40 years' user of other easements, ie, the easement is then deemed "absolute and indefeasible".[321] However, there are other important differences in the case of acquisition of easements of light under the Act.

---

[316] Sections 4 and 7.

[317] Note, however, that s 8 also applies to life tenancies, so that deductions in such cases may have to be made whichever period of user is the basis of the claim.

[318] Ie, it can usually be shown that the building to which the light comes has not been standing since 1189, para **[6.082]** *ante*.

[319] Held to include a church, *Ecclesiastical Commrs for England v Kino* (1880) 14 Ch D 213, a greenhouse, *Clifford v Holt* [1899] 1 Ch 698, and a cowshed, *Hyman v Van den Bergh* [1908] 1 Ch 167. *Cf Harris v Pinna* (1886) 33 Ch D 238 (structure for storing timber).

[320] See the discussion in *Tisdall v McArthur & Co (Steel and Metal) Ltd* [1951] IR 228 (see *A Casebook on Irish Land Law* (1984), p 357).

[321] Para **[6.088]** *ante*.

[6.098] First, s 3 does not, unlike s 2 of the Act which covers other easements, refer to a person "claiming right" to the easement and so it has been held that it does not require user "as of right".[322] For this reason even the English courts have been prepared to permit a tenant to acquire an easement of light against his own landlord[323] or against another tenant of the same landlord.[324] The only aspect of the common law's requirement of enjoyment *nec vi*, *nec clam* and *nec precario* surviving in the case of an easement of light is that s 3 does state that user by consent in writing or by deed defeats a claim.[325]

Secondly, there can be no deduction under ss 7 and 8 in the case of easements of light on the ground of user during periods when some disability affected the servient owner. Section 7 excepts cases where the easement is declared to be "absolute and indefeasible" and s 8 is confined to claims based on 40 years' user.

Thirdly, unlike ss 1 and 2 of the Act, which expressly refer to the Crown, s 3 does not and so it is not possible to acquire easements of light over Crown, or, in the Republic of Ireland, State land.[326]

[6.099] Fourthly it seems clear that s 3 of the Act negatives any presumption of a grant in the case of an easement of light, at least to the extent that it does not require user as of right,[327] and so it has been held that such an easement may be acquired against a corporation with no power to grant such a right.[328] Indeed, it has even been suggested by some of the English authorities that the Act has by implication abolished the applicability of the doctrine of lost modern grant to easements of light.[329] This view, however, was doubted in *Tisdall v McArthur & Co (Steel and Metal) Ltd*,[330] where the contrary view was expressed that "since *Hanna v Pollock*[331] it has always been considered to be settled law in Ireland that any easement can be properly claimed on the basis of a lost modern grant."[332]

---

[322] *Frewen v Phillips* (1861) 11 CB (ns) 449, approved by Lawson J in *Fahey v Dwyer* (1879) 4 LR Ir 271 (which, in fact, involved an easement of way). *Cf Timmons v Hewitt* (1887) 22 LR Ir 627. Note, however, that s 5, which governs pleadings in all cases within the Act, does refer to allegations of enjoyment "as of right", a point which the courts hitherto do not seem to have taken.

[323] *Foster v Lyons & Co Ltd* [1927] 1 Ch 219 at 227. See also *Frewen v Phillips* (1861) 11 CB (ns) 449.

[324] *Morgan v Fear* [1907] AC 425. See para **[6.078]** *ante*.

[325] It seems that a reservation in a lease of the right to rebuild adjoining property may amount to such consent, see *Willoughby v Eckstein* [1937] Ch 167; *Blake & Lyons Ltd v Lewis Berger & Sons Ltd* [1951] 2 TLR 605.

[326] *Wheaton v Maple & Co* [1893] 3 Ch 48. Stroud, 'Rights of Light over Crown Land' (1942) 58 LQR 495.

[327] *Tappling v Jones* (1865) 11 HLC 290 at 304 and 318. See also Delaney 'Leases and Doctrine of Lost Grant' (1958) 74 LQR 82 at 86-7.

[328] *Jordeson v Sutton, Southcoates & Drypool Gas Co* [1898] 2 Ch 614 at 626, aff'd [1899] 2 Ch 217.

[329] *Tappling v Jones* (1865) 11 HLC 290.

[330] [1951] IR 228 espec at 235-8 (see *A Casebook on Irish Land Law* (1984), p 357).

[331] [1900] 2 IR 664 (see *ibid*, p 329). See para **[6.079]** *ante*.

[332] [1951] IR 228 at 241 (*per* Kingsmill Moore J), aff'd on appeal by the Supreme Court, which expressly left the point open, *ibid*, pp 246 (Maguire CJ), 247 (Murnaghan J) and 248 (Black J).

[6.100] Apart from these special provisions in the 1832 Act, which apply to both parts of Ireland, the Rights of Light Act (NI) 1961[333] has to be considered with respect to easements of light in Northern Ireland. This Act, like its English equivalent, was passed to protect owners of land destroyed or badly damaged by bombs or landmines dropped during the Second World War. Several parts of Belfast were severely damaged during the War and this resulted in numerous derelict sites which remained in existence for many years thereafter. As the years went by, rebuilding on many of these sites might have been hampered if neighbouring owners claimed rights of light over the derelict sites and so the 1961 Act introduced first a temporary protection. This took the form of extending the statutory period for prescription under the Prescription Act 1832, from 20 to 27 years in respect of actions begun before January 1963.[334] This in effect prevented claims based on user since the War air raids being established and gave the site owners time to invoke the permanent provisions of the 1961 Act, which remain in force and have taken on a new significance with the bombing campaigns in the North of recent years. After the Second World War, some derelict site owners attempted to interrupt acquisition of rights of light by erection of screens and hoardings. These were inconvenient, unsightly and scarcely consistent with modern town planning and environmental concepts. The permanent provisions of the 1961 Act enable a site owner to achieve the same result, ie, interruption of the passage of light, by a much more satisfactory method.

[6.101] The 1961 Act enables a servient owner to prevent acquisition of an easement of light by registering in the Statutory Charges Registry[335] of a light obstruction notice which is equivalent to erection of "an opaque structure of unlimited height".[336] This notice must identify the servient land and the dominant building and the servient owner must satisfy the Registrar of Titles[337] that he has given adequate notice of the proposed registration to all concerned and has advertised the same in a newspaper circulating in the district.[338] Registration is effective for one year,[339] unless cancelled before then, and so amounts to an effective interruption under s 4 of the Prescription Act 1832.[340] However, the dominant owner may bring an action to challenge the registered notice when his right of light has accrued while the notice remains effective[341] and the court is empowered to order cancellation or variation of the registration as may be appropriate.[342] The Act applies to Crown land to the extent of enabling private subjects

---

[333] Modelled on the English Rights of Light Act 1959, which was in turn based on the recommendations contained in the *Report of the Committee on Rights of Light* (1958: Cmnd 473). See Obayan, 'The Rights of Light Act (NI) 1961' (1964) 15 NILQ 248.

[334] Section 3.

[335] Under the Statutory Charges Register Act (NI) 1951. See Ch 21 *post.*

[336] Section 1(3)(*f*).

[337] Who is responsible for the Statutory Charges Register as well as the Land Registry, Ch 21 *post.*

[338] Section 2(1).

[339] Section 3.

[340] Para **[6.094]** *ante.*

[341] Section 2(3) and (4).

[342] Section 2(5).

to resist claims by the Crown, but otherwise preserves the immunity of the Crown from prescriptive claims under the Prescription Act.[343]

C. Extinguishment

There are three main ways in which an easement or profit can be extinguished or destroyed, ie, by statute, by release of the right by the owner and by union of ownership and possession of the dominant and servient tenements.[344]

1. Statute

[6.102] A statute may extinguish an easement or profit expressly or by implication, such as the statutes relating to compulsory acquisition of land in Ireland.[345] In both parts of Ireland, rights which were formally regarded as belonging to the owner of the land because he was owner have been declared to be the property of the State. In the Republic, Article 11 of the 1922 Constitution declared that all the natural resources (including the air and all forms of potential energy) belonged to the State, "subject to any valid private interest therein". Article 10 of the 1937 Constitution makes a similar declaration "subject to all estates and interests therein for the time being lawfully vested in any person or body".[346] Legislation has been passed in both parts of Ireland dealing with mining[347] and petroleum and other minerals.[348] These are not easements or profits in the strict sense, but are rights which formerly were incidents of ownership of the land itself.

[6.103] There is no modern legislation in either part of Ireland dealing with extinguishment of common rights of pasturage by approvement and inclosure such as exists in England.[349] At common law, the lord of a manor had a common law right to "approve" the waste land on the manor over which his tenants had rights of pasture, ie, the lord could take part of that land for his own use. No doubt this law applied equally in the manors in Ireland governed by the feudal system introduced by the Normans in the twelfth century. Indeed, the early English legislation confirming this right of

---

[343] Section 4. See para **[6.098]** *ante*.

[344] See also Abbott, 'Extinguishment of Easements by Impossibility of User' (1913) 13 Col L Rev 409.

[345] Eg, Lands Clauses Consolidation Act 1845, and the Railways (Ir) Acts 1851, 1860 and 1864. See generally Suffern, *Law Relating to Compulsory Purchase and Sale of Lands in Ireland* (1882). Also the Republic's Local Government (Planning and Development) Act 1963, Pt 7; Local Government Act (NI) 1972, Sch 6; Planning (NI) Order 1991, Article 87. *Comyn v Att-Gen* [1950] IR 142. See also Housing Act 1966, s 83 (RI); Housing (NI) Order 1981, Articles 47-51. See McDermott and Woulfe, *Compulsory Purchase and Compensation in Ireland: Law and Practice* (1992); Trimble, 'The Procedure Governing Compulsory Acquisition of Land in Northern Ireland' (1973) 24 NILQ 466; Hadden and Trimble, *Northern Ireland Housing Law* (1986), Ch 7.

[346] See the discussion in Hogan & Whyte, *Kelly: The Irish Constitution* (3rd ed, 1994), pp 71-75.

[347] See Minerals Exploration and Development Company Act 1941 (RI); Mineral Development Act (NI) 1969; *Cf Comyn v Att-Gen (No 2)* [1951] 85 ILTR 67; *Tara Prospecting Ltd v Minister for Energy* [1993] ILRM 771.

[348] Minerals Development Acts 1940 and 1979 and Petroleum and other Minerals Development Act 1960 (RI); Petroleum (Production) Act (NI) 1964.

[349] See *Governors of St Patrick's Hospital v Dowling* (1826) Batty 296.

approvement in the lord of a manor was applied to Ireland.[350] Furthermore, even as late as the beginning of the nineteenth century *private* Acts of Parliament were being passed relating to inclosure of land in Ireland.[351] However, later English legislation, especially that of the second half of the nineteenth century,[352] did not apply to Ireland, presumably because by then the land purchase scheme was sweeping away the remnants of the manorial or copyhold system which had survived the upheavals in land ownership of the previous centuries.[353] Nor did the English Inclosure Acts,[354] which facilitated the discharge of manorial waste land from all rights of common, apply to Ireland and there is no equivalent in either part of Ireland of the English Commons Registration Act 1965, which requires the registration of rights of common with local authorities.[355] The point is that in Ireland rights of common in agricultural land were or, in the Western parts of the Republic, will be dealt with under the Land Purchase Acts.[356]

2. Release

[6.104] The owner of an easement or profit may release it expressly or impliedly. So far as express release is concerned, at common law this has to be executed by deed.[357] However, equity may give effect to an informal release where it can be established that the dominant owner has by his words or conduct led the servient owner into acting on the belief that a release has been made, so that it would be inequitable for the dominant owner to rely on the informality.[358] It is crucial to emphasise that we are considering here the release of private rights in the nature of easements and profits. If the rights are public rights, such as a public right of way, there can be no question of any release by a deed, especially one executed by an individual member of the public.[359] A right like a

---

[350] Statute of Merton 1235, c 4; Statute of Westminster II 1285, c 46. See para **[1.24]** *ante*.

[351] Eg, 55 Geo 3, c 35 (1814) and 56 Geo 3, c 25 (1816). See *Governors of St Patrick's Hospital v Dowling* (1826) Batty 296; *Jones d Byrne v Humphreys* (1827) 1 Hud & Br 26; *Jones d Burrowes v Lynam* (1841) Jebb & Sym 590.

[352] Eg, Commons Act 1876 and Law of Commons Amendment Act 1893. Note, however, that legislation was still being passed in Ireland dealing with commons in the last years of the Irish Parliament before the Act of Union 1800. See the Commons Act (Ir) 1789 and the Commons Act (Ir) 1791, which are still in force in the Republic of Ireland. *Cf* Criminal Justice (Miscellaneous Provisions) Act (NI) 1968, s 16 and Sched 4.

[353] Paras **[1.27]** *et seq, ante*.

[354] Eg, Inclosure (Consolidation) Act 1801; Inclosure Act 1842; Commons Act 1876; Note, however, the very early legislation in Ireland dealing with inclosure, eg, 36 Hen 6, c 2 (Ir) 1458 (inclosure of towns and villages).

[355] See the *Report of the Royal Commission on Common Land* (1958; Cmnd 462). Also Gadsden, *The Law of Commons* (1988).

[356] Para **[6.113]** *post*. See also Irish Land Commissioners' *Annual Report 1971-72*, pp 6-9.

[357] *Coke on Littleton* (19th ed, 1832), 264b. *Burke v Blake* (1861) 13 ICLR 390.

[358] See *Moore v Rawson* (1824) 3 B & C 32; *Davies v Marshall* (1861) 10 CBNS 697; *Cook v Mayor and Corporation of Bath* (1868) LR 6 Eq 177. *Cf* the converse case of an implied grant in equity, *Annally Hotel Ltd v Bergin* (1970) 104 ILTR 65.

[359] Indeed, the general rule is "once a highway always a highway', so that even the public in general cannot abandon or release a public right of way by non-user: *Dawes v Hawkins* (1860) 8 CBNS 848; *Turner v Ringwood Highway Board* (1870) LR 8 Eq 418. See also *Carroll v Sheridan* [1984] ILRM 451.

public right of way, generally, can only be determined by invoking special statutory procedures such as those provided by the highways legislation.[360]

[6.105] An implied release may arise where it is established that there was an intention on the part of the owner of the easement or profit to abandon it.[361] Such an intention may be presumed from non-user by the dominant owner for a long period, eg, 20 years,[362] but the courts are generally reluctant to presume abandonment from mere non-user and look for circumstances to explain the non-user and to justify raising the presumption.[363] The abandonment may also be presumed where an alternative right is granted, eg, another right of way is substituted for the existing one,[364] or where a substantial alteration is made to either the dominant or servient tenement, so as to make the use or enjoyment of the right impossible or no longer necessary.[365] Once again, it is emphasised that special rules apply to public rights, where generally statutory procedures must be invoked.[366]

3. Unity of Ownership and Possession

[6.106] If the dominant and servient tenements come into the ownership and the possession of the same person, any easement or profit annexed to those lands is extinguished.[367] Unity of one without the other is not enough. Thus if one person becomes owner of the fee simple in both tenements, but one or other of the tenements is leased, the right may still be exercised by or against the tenant.[368] Similarly. if one person takes a lease of both tenements from their separate fee simple owners any easements or profits are at most suspended until the leases determine.[369]

---

[360] See Roads Act 1993, s 73 (RI); Roads (NI) Order 1993, Article 68. It would appear that a public right of way will be extinguished by natural destruction of the road or pathway itself, eg, where it is washed away by the sea: see *R v Bamber* (1843) 5 QB 279; *cf R v Greenham* (1876) 1 QBD 703 (landslide).

[361] *Chambers v Betty* (1815) Beat 488; *Stevenson v Parke* [1932] LJ Ir 228; *Re Bohan* [1957] IR 49; *Carroll v Sheridan* [1984] ILRM 451.

[362] *Moore v Rawson* (1824) 3 B & C 32. See also *Swan v Sinclair* [1925] AC 227.

[363] See the discussion by O'Hanlon J in *Carroll v Sheridan* [1984] ILRM 451 and Davies, 'Abandonment of an Easement' [1995] Conv 291.

[364] *Mulville v Fallon* (1872) IR 6 Eq 458; *Smith v Wilson* [1903] 2 IR 45. *Cf Benn v Hardinge* (1992) P & CR 246.

[365] See *RCB v Barry* [1918] 1 IR 402. See also *National Guaranteed Manure Co Ltd v Donald* (1859) 4 H & N 8; *Ecclesiastical Commrs for England v Kino* (1880) 14 Ch D 213. *Cf* the effect on a right to ancient lights of putting modern windows in an old building, see *Scott v Goulding Properties Ltd* [1972] IR 200 (see *A Casebook on Irish Land Law* (1984), p 299). Abbott, 'Extinguishment of Easements by Impossibility of User' (1913) 13 Col L Rev 409.

[366] See fns 451 and 452 *supra*.

[367] See discussion in *Wilson v Stanley* (1861) 12 ICLR 345; *Pullan v Roughfort Bleaching and Dying Co Ltd* (1888) 21 LR Ir 73. Also *Re Flanagan and McGarvey and Thompson's Contract* [1945] NI 32 (see *A Casebook on Irish Land Law* (1984), p 317). See also Brooke-Taylor 'Perdurable Estates' (1977) 41 Conv 107.

[368] *Richardson v Graham* [1908] 1 KB 39.

[369] *Canham v Fisk* (1831) 2 Cr & J 126. Suspension operates only as regards pre-existing easements, *B & W Investments Ltd v Ulster Scottish Friendly Society* (1969) 20 NILQ 325.

D. Examples of Easements and Profits

It may be useful at this point to describe in more detail some of the more common types of easement and profit claimed in Ireland. It must be emphasised that the following list should not be taken to be exhaustive.

1. Easements

(i) Rights of Way

[6.107] Rights of way are, perhaps. the most common type of easement claimed in Ireland today.[370] Such a right may be either general, in the sense that it can be used at any time in any way by the dominant owner, or limited, in the sense that some restriction binds the dominant owner, eg, as to the time or mode of user.[371] As a general rule, any works in the nature of construction or repairs to the way have to be executed by the dominant owner, ie, the grantee, but this is subject to any agreement made by the original parties.[372] It was held in *Gaw v CIE*[373] that the benefit of a covenant by the grantors of a right of way ran with the easement so as to enable a successor in title of the grantee to obtain a mandatory injunction against statutory successors of the grantors. requiring them to execute repairs to the footpath relating to the right of way.

(ii) Rights of Light

[6.108] Rights of light are also common though they can be acquired only in respect of a building, indeed only in respect of a window or other aperture in a building.[374] Long established rights of light are frequently referred to in the courts as "ancient lights".[375] It is now firmly settled that the amount of light to which a dominant owner is entitled in the form of an easement is limited. The quantum of light to which he can successfully lay claim is the amount, according to ordinary user, necessary for the use of the particular building for its particular purpose, ie, as a dwelling or as business premises or whatever is its purpose.[376] The dominant owner can complain only if the quantum left falls below this amount and a substantial diminution in the amount will not be actionable if that still leaves enough for ordinary user of the premises for their general

---

[370] *McCullagh v Wilson* (1838) 1 Jebb & Sym 120; *Burke v Blake* (1861) 13 ICLR 390; *Kavanagh v Coal Mining Co of Ireland* (1861) 14 ICLR 82; *Austin v Scottish Widows' Fund Mutual Life Assurance Society* (1881) 8 LR Ir 385; *Head v Meara* [1912] 1 IR 262; *Flynn v Harte* [1913] 2 IR 322; *Molphy v Coyne* (1919) 53 ILTR 177; *Cleary v Bowen* [1931] LR Ir 148; *Tallon v Ennis* [1937] IR 549; *McCaw v Rynne* [1941] Ir Jur Rep 12; *Dunne v Rattigan* [1981] ILRM 365; *Flannigan v Mulhall* [1985] ILRM 134. On ways of necessity, see para **[6.070]** *ante*.

[371] *Tubridy v Walsh* (1901) 35 ILT 321 (obligation to close gates). *Geoghegan v Henry* [1922] 2 IR 1; *Griffin v Keane* (1927) 61 ILTR 177; *Daly v Cullen* (1958) 92 ILTR 127. See also *St Edmundsbury and Ipswich Diocesan Board of Finance v Clark (No 2)* [1975] 1 WLR 468.

[372] *Gaw v CIE* [1953] IR 232 (see *A Casebook on Irish Land Law* (1984), p 622).

[373] *Ibid.*

[374] *Mackey v Scottish Widows' Fund Life Assurance Society* (1877) IR 11 Eq 541. *Cf Judge v Lowe* (1873) IR 7 CL 291.

[375] *Tisdall v McArthur & Co (Steel and Metal) Ltd* [1951] IR 228 (see *A Casebook on Irish Land Law* (1984), p 357); *Scott v Goulding Properties Ltd* [1972] IR 200 (*ibid*, p 299). See also *O'Connor v Corr* (1826) Batty 421; Hudson 'Ancient Lights for an Office' (1960) 24 Conv 424.

[376] *Maguire v Grattan* (1868) IR 2 Eq 246; *Smyth v Dublin Theatre Co* [1936] IR 692. *Cf Annally Hotel Ltd v Bergin* (1970) 104 ILTR 65. (contd.../)

purpose.[377] It would appear that a case must be decided according to this objective test of the quantum allowable and it is irrelevant that the dominant owner has in fact enjoyed more or less than that quantum.[378] There is no set standard of light which must be applied in all cases, eg, the so-called 45 degrees rule[379] or according to the "grumble point" limit.[380] To some extent the practice and standard of the particular locality must be taken into account in setting the standard applicable and measuring the quantum allowable.[381]

[6.109] If the dominant owner alters the user of his premises or changes his windows, eg, replacing old ones by more modern ones, he generally cannot object if the nature of the alternation results in less light coming in.[382] Indeed, in *Scott v Goulding Properties Ltd*,[383] where the dominant owner claimed damages as compensation for the diminution of light and resultant loss of amenity and reduction in value of the property caused by an obstruction of ancient lights, the Republic's Supreme Court held that the amount of compensation should not contain an element for the reduction of light to modern windows put in the building. An interesting point about this case, however, was that it seemed to be accepted by all the judges that, if the plaintiff had obtained an injunction,

---

[376] (\...contd) In *Allen v Greenwood* [1980] Ch 119, the English Court of Appeal held that the plaintiff had acquired by prescription rights to the higher degree of light required in the normal use of a greenhouse and the benefits of the rays of sun required to grow plants, and not just the amount of light required for illumination. It was also held that a right to an exceptional or extraordinary amount of light for a particular purpose may be acquired by prescription, but it was expressly left open for decision when a case arises whether, in the case of solar heating, it may be possible and right to separate heat or some other property of the sun from its light (*ibid*, p 134, *per* Goff and Orr LJJ).

[377] Cf *Manning v Gresham Hotel Co* (1867) IR 1 CL 115. See also *Gresham Hotel Co v Manning* (1867) IR 1 CL 125; *O'Connor v Walsh* (1908) 42 ILTR 20; *Smyth v Dublin Theatre Co* [1936] IR 692; *Gannon v Hughes* [1937] IR 284; *McGrath v Munster and Leinster Bank Ltd* [1959] IR 313. Bodkin, 'Acquisition of Rights of Light for Badly-Lighted Premises' (1974) 38 Conv 4.

[378] Cf *Mercer Rice and Co v Ritchie Hart & Co* (1903) 3 NIJR 123 (special quantity). See also *Mackey v Scottish Widows' Fund Life Assurance Society* (1877) IR 11 Eq 541.

[379] Ie, interference by an obstruction rising about an imaginary line drawn at an angle of 45 degrees upwards and outwards from the centre of the window in question. See the discussion in the leading English case on the subject, *Colls v Home and Colonial Stores Ltd* [1904] AC 179, followed by *Smyth v Dublin Theatre Co* [1936] IR 692 and *McGrath v Munster and Leinster Bank Ltd* [1959] IR 313. Note, 'Local Standard of Light' (1926) 42 LQR 443; Merritt, 'Rights of Light and Air' (1972) 36 Conv 15.

[380] Ie, how much of the light, which would reach the outside sill of the window from an unobstructed horizon, reaches parts of the room inside, eg, taken at a height of three feet above the floor. See *Charles Semon & Co Ltd v Bradford Corp* [1922] 2 Ch 737 at 747-8; *Fishenden v Higgs & Hill Ltd* (1935) LT 128 at 130. Swarbrick *Easements of Light* (1933).

[381] *Mercer Rice and Co v Ritchie Hart & Co* (1903) 3 NIJR 123.

[382] *Scott v Goulding Properties Ltd* [1972] IR 200 (see *A Casebook on Irish Land Law* (1984), p 299). See the discussion of the *Scott* case in Hudson, 'Parasitic Damages for Loss of Light' (1975) 39 Conv 116.

[383] *Ibid*. (Walsh J, *Dissentiente*).

this would have prevented the infringement of the ancient lights and would, of course, have had the incidental effect of protecting the light to the modern windows.[384]

The dominant owner may still claim a right of light even though the light coming to the windows of his building has first to pass through windows or other parts, eg, a glass roof, of the servient owner's building.[385] However, in assessing whether an actionable diminution of light has occurred, the court will take into account other sources of light to which the dominant owner is entitled, eg, through a skylight in his own building.[386]

(iii) Rights of Water

[6.110] There are many kinds of rights concerning water which have been recognised as easements. In some cases they have been akin to natural riparian rights,[387] eg, a right to a flow of water from the servient owner's land,[388] or a right to draw water from a well.[389] In other cases, the easement has consisted of a right to the flow of water from or to discharge water through an artificial watercourse,[390] such as a conduit,[391] gullet[392] or drain.[393] In such cases, the dominant owner may be entitled, if necessary, to enter the servient owner's land to remove any obstruction or to clean out a blocked pipe or drain, though he will not usually be entitled to a mandatory injunction[394] to compel the servient owner to clean out a pipe or drain which has become silted up.[395] Other water rights recognised as easements include rights such as a right to water cattle in a stream.[396]

(iv) Rights of Support

[6.111] Since natural rights of support exist only in respect of the land itself,[397] support for buildings on the land must be acquired as an easement.[398] Mutual rights of support

---

[384] Walsh J based his dissent from the Supreme Court's decision in the *Scott* case on the principle that the plaintiff should not have been worse off because she had sought damages instead of an injunction.

[385] *Tisdall v McArthur & Co (Steel and Metal) Ltd* [1951] IR 228 (see *ibid*, p 357).

[386] *Smith v Evangelization Society (Incorporated) Trust* [1933] Ch 515. See also *Sheffield Masonic Hall Co Ltd v Sheffield Corp* [1932] 2 Ch 18.

[387] Para **[6.040]** *ante*.

[388] *Deeble v Linehan* (1860) 12 ICLR 1; *Wilson v Stanley* (1861) 12 ICLR 345. *Cf McCartney v Londonderry & Lough Swilly Rly* [1904] AC 301; *Thompson v Horner* [1927] NI 191. See also *Craig v McCance* (1910) 44 ILTR 90.

[389] *Macnaghten v Baird* [1903] 2 IR 731. See also *Whelan v Leonard* [1917] 2 IR 323.

[390] *Hamilton v Fawcett* (1859) 9 Ir Ch R 397; *Powell v Butler* (1871) Ir 5 CL 309; *Pullan v Roughfort Bleaching and Dying Co Ltd* (1888) 21 LR Ir 73; *McEvoy v GNR Co* [1900] 2 IR 325.

[391] *Hanna v Pollock* [1900] 2 IR 664 (see *A Casebook on Irish Land Law* (1984), p 329).

[392] *Callaghan v Callaghan* (1897) 31 ILT 418.

[393] *Kelly v Dea* (1966) 100 ILTR 1.

[394] Para **[3.130]** *ante*.

[395] *Kelly v Dea* (1966) 100 ILTR 1. *Cf Larkin v Smith* (1939) 73 ILTR 234.

[396] *Re Harding's Estate* (1874) IR 8 Eq 620. Water, when taken, is incapable of ownership and so, unlike other things, such as soil, found naturally on land, cannot form the subject matter of a profit *à prendre*, para **[6.034]** *ante*.

[397] Para **[6.039]** *ante*.

[398] See discussion in *Carroll v Kildare CC* [1950] IR 258; Also *Green v Belfast Tramways Co* (1886) 20 LR IR 35; *Gateley v Martin* [1900] 2 IR 269; *Nugent v Keady UDC* (1912) 46 ILTR 221.

almost invariably exist where buildings keep each other standing and this usually makes demolition work in towns and cities an exercise requiring careful planning.[399] Where an easement of support does exist, it seems that the servient owner is under no duty to keep the supporting building repaired, as opposed actively to removing or damaging it by his own acts, but in such cases it seems that the dominant owner may protect himself by entering and executing the necessary repairs.[400]

(v) Miscellaneous Easements

[6.112] From time to time rights which do not seem to come within one of the well-known categories of easements are claimed and often recognised by the courts. Thus in *Middleton v Clarence*[401] a right to throw quarry refuse on another person's land was recognised as an easement. In *Henry Ltd v McGlade*,[402] the right to have a man stand at the entrance of an arcade, with a pole advertising licensed premises situated in the arcade, was recognised as an easement, or at least a similar right capable of passing on a grant of the dominant land under s 6 of the Conveyancing Act 1881.[403] The right to use a blacksmith's "shoeing stone" was recognised as an easement in *Calder v Murtagh*.[404] On the other hand, the court in *Cochrane v Verner*[405] refused to recognise a right to "shade and shelter" from a hedge as an easement.

2. Profits à Prendre

The following are the most common profits *à prendre*:

(i) Pasturage

[6.113] This is the right to graze animals, such as horses, oxen, cows and sheep, on someone else's land. The "taking and carrying away" arises from the cattle's eating of the grass and other vegetation growing naturally on the pasturage land.[406] Frequently these rights in the past have been held in common with other farmers in the neighbourhood[407] and several rights in common survived in the West of Ireland[408] where all, or some, of the landowners could apply to the Irish Land Commission for

---

[399] *Latimer v Official Co-Operative Society* (1885) 16 LR Ir 305 (see *A Casebook on Irish Land Law* (1984), p 293). See also *Hanly v Shannon* (1833) Hay & Jon 645; *O'Neill v Grier* (1846) Bl D & O 72; *Toole v Macken* (1855) 7 Ir Jur (os) 385.

[400] See the discussion in the English cases of *Jones v Pritchard* [1908] 1 Ch 630 at 637-8 and *Bond v Nottingham Corp* [1940] Ch 429 at 438-9. *Cf* as regards a right to water flowing through a drain, *Kelly v Dea* (1966) 100 ILTR 1.

[401] (1877) IR 11 CL 499.

[402] [1926] NI 144 (see *A Casebook on Irish Land Law* (1984), p 324).

[403] Para **[6.066]** *ante*.

[404] [1939] IR Jur Rep 19.

[405] (1895) 29 ILT 571.

[406] Preston, *Treatise on Estates* (2nd ed, 1827) Vol 1, p 15. See the discussion in *Anderson v Bostock* [1976] Ch 312 (para **[6.036]**, fn 138 *ante*).

[407] Para **[6.103]** *ante*.

[408] See, eg, *Waterpark v Fennell* (1855) 5 ICLR 120 (commonage of mountain). *Cf* "souming" in parts of NI like Co Tyrone: see Land Law Working Group's *Final Report* (HMSO, 1990) Vol 1, para 2.2.3-5.

compulsory partition of the land.[409] Also common in Ireland is a system of granting grazing rights known as agistment.[410] An agistment contract in general[411] confers on the grantee rights of grazing only[412] and not possession of the grazing land itself.[413] Though sometimes referred to as a "letting" of the grazing land, it has long been settled in Ireland that an agistment contract does not create the relationship of landlord and tenant nor is the consideration paid by the grantee to be regarded as rent.[414] Thus an agistment arrangement seems to fulfil the essentials for a profit *à prendre*, with one important exception. That is that the arrangement is regarded as a "contract" and so does not have to comply with the general requirement that easements and profits have to be created by deed.[415] In this respect, an agistment contract is more like a licence and it is, perhaps, significant that the Irish courts have often used terminology relating to licences when referring to agistment and to the other very common agricultural system in Ireland - conacre,[416] ie, the right to till land, sow and harvest crops on it and to enter the land whenever necessary for these purposes.[417] This subject is taken up again in the later chapter dealing with licences.[418]

(ii) Turbary

[6.114] Another common profit in Ireland is a right of turbary, ie, the right to go onto another person's land and to dig and take away turf for use as fuel.[419] In general this right is limited to cutting turf for personal use as fuel,[420] but there is nothing to prevent a grant of the right for commercial purposes, ie, cutting turf for sale.[421] In the absence of

---

[409] See Land Act 1939 (RI), s 24; *Re Commonage at Glennamaddoo* [1992] 1 IR 297.

[410] Ch 20 *post*.

[411] To some extent the terms of agistment contracts vary according to the custom and practice of different parts of the country, see *O'Connor v Faul* (1957) 91 ILTR 7. Also *Fletcher v Hackett* (1906) 40 ILTR 37.

[412] *Mulligan v Adams* (1846) 8 Ir LR 132; *Hickey v Cosgrave* (1860) 6 Ir Jur (ns) 251; *Thornton v Connolly* (1898) 32 ILT 216; *Re Moore's Estates* [1944] IR 295. See also *O'Flaherty v Kelly* [1909] 1 IR 223; *Boothman v Kane* (1923) 57 ILTR 36.

[413] *Dalton v O'Sullivan* [1947] Ir Jur Rep 25; *Carson v Jeffers* [1961] IR 44.

[414] *Allingham v Atkinson* [1898] 1 IR 239; *Cf Crane v Naughten* [1912] 2 IR 318. Also *Plunkett v Smith* [1904] 4 NIJR 136. See also *Collins v O'Brien* [1981] ILRM 328 (see *A Casebook on Irish Land Law* (1984), p 679).

[415] Para **[6.054]** *ante*.

[416] See especially the discussion in *Dease v O'Reilly* (1845) 8 Ir LR 52 and *Booth v McManus* (1861) 12 ICLR 418. Also *Westmeath v Hogg* (1841) 3 IR LR 27; *Carson v Jeffers* [1961] IR 44. And see *Maurice E Taylor (Merchants) Ltd v Commissioners of Valuation* [1981] NI 236 (see *A Casebook on Irish Land Law* (1984), p 680).

[417] *McKeowne v Bradford* (1861) 7 Ir Jur (ns) 169; *Evans v Monagher* (1872) IR 6 CL 526; *Irish Land Commission v Andrews* [1941] IR 79.

[418] Ch 20 *post*.

[419] *Dobbyn v Somers* (1860) 13 ICLR 293; *Beere v Fleming* (1862) 13 ICLR 506; *Cochrane v McCleary* (1869) IR 4 CL 165; *Lowry v Crothers* (1871) IR 5 CL 98; *Dawson v McGroggan* [1903] 1 IR 92; *Convey v Regan* [1952] IR 56; *Re Bohan* [1957] IR 49.

[420] See, eg, Landlord and Tenant Law Amendment Act, Ireland 1860, s 29. *Lifford v Kearney* (1883) 17 ILTR 30; *Douglas v McLaughlin* (1883) 17 ILTR 84. See also Renewable Leasehold Conversion Act 1849, s 4; Land Law (Ir) Act 1881, s 17. *R (Keenan) v Tyrone County Court Judge* [1940] NI 108.

[421] *Coppinger v Gubbins* (1846) 9 Ir Eq R 304; *Stevenson v Moore* (1858) 7 Ir Ch R 462; *Cf Fowler v Blakely* (1862) 13 Ir Ch R 58.

any agreement to the contrary, it seems that a right of turbary includes the right to use bog material for any reasonable purpose other than fuel, eg, as manure.[422] However, it seems to be settled that the soil left over after turf has been cut away is not part of the turbary and must be left.[423] Similarly it has been held that a right of turbary does not include a right to take away "scraws", ie, strips of surface turf.[424] On the other hand, where a right of turbary over a bog generally has been conferred, the grantee has the right to exercise it anywhere in the bog and is not confined to a particular part.[425] In the Republic of Ireland, much land has now been acquired by a statutory body, Bord na Mona, for development of the turf industry,[426] which plays a significant role in the country's economic life.[427]

(iii) Mines and Quarries

[6.115] Mining and quarrying rights, whether relating to existing mines or quarries or for opening new mines or quarries, are another common form of profit *à prendre*.[428] Such rights are commonly excepted or reserved to the grantor when he makes a grant of part of his land or even the whole of the land where the mine or quarry is situated.[429] However, many minerals are extremely valuable and the pattern of recent decades has been for the State to exercise increasing control over minerals and their exploitation.[430] We have already mentioned that, in the Republic, all natural resources (including the air and all forms of potential energy) are under the Constitution vested in the State, so that it is in the position to control all exploration and development.[431] In Northern Ireland, the

---

[422] *Hutchinson v Drain* (1899) 33 ILTR 147. See also *Dawson v Baldwin* (1832) Hay & Jon 24; *Fitzpatrick v Vershoyle* [1913] 1 IR 8.

[423] *Beere v Fleming* (1862) 13 ICLR 506; *Oates v Stoney* (1882) 16 ILTR 30.

[424] *Jameson v Fahey* [1907] 1 IR 411.

[425] *Hargrove v Lord Congleton* (1861) 12 ICLR 362. *Cf Waterpark v Fennell* (1855) 5 ICLR 120 (common turbary rights on mountain); also *Knox v Earl of Mayo* (1858) 9 Ir Ch R 192.

[426] Turf Development Acts 1946, 1950, 1953, 1957, 1958, 1959, 1961, 1965 an 1968. See *O'Brien v Bord na Móna* [1983] ILRM 314. Note also turbary regulations made under the Land Purchase Acts in both parts of Ireland, *Re Drummond's Estate* [1933] IR 166; *Re Higginbotham's Estate* [1946] NI 208.

[427] Eg, turf-burning power stations for generation of electricity have been established in various parts of the Republic, see Electricity (Supply) (Amendment) Act 1941, s 3.

[428] *Comyn v Att-Gen* [1950] IR 142. See also *Mansfield v Crawford* (1846) 9 Ir Eq R 271; *Brown v Chadwick* (1857) 7 ICLR 101; *Listowel v Gibbings* (1858) 9 ICLR 223. *Cf Atkinson v King* (1877) IR 11 CL 536; *Stanley v Riky* (1893) 31 LR Ir 196.

[429] *McDonnell v Kenneth* (1850) 1 ICLR 113; *Fishbourne v Hamilton* (1890) 25 LR Ir 483; *Earl of Antrim v Dobbs* (1891) 30 LR Ir 424; *Staples v Young* [1908] 1 IR 135. See also Landlord and Tenant Law Amendment Act, Ireland 1860, ss 25-8, Ch 17 *post*.

[430] See the Republic's Minerals Development Acts 1940 and 1979, Minerals Exploration and Development Company Act 1941, and Minerals Company Acts 1945, 1947 and 1950; Petroleum and other Minerals Development Act 1960 (RI); *Comyn v Att-Gen* [1950] IR 142; *Tara Prospecting Ltd v Minister for Energy* [1993] ILRM 771. Note also the control of management and regulation of safety, health and welfare under the Mines and Quarries Act 1965. *Cf*, Mines Act (NI) 1969. *Hamilton v Niblock* [1956] NI 109; *Gallagher v Mogul of Ireland* [1975] IR 204.

[431] See para **[6.102]** *ante*.

Mineral Development Act (NI) 1969,[432] vests, subject to a few exceptions,[433] most mines and minerals existing in a natural condition in land in the Province, and all mines for their working, in the Ministry of Commerce,[434] which is given wide powers for securing future prospecting and working or disposal of the mines and minerals. The result of this legislation in both parts of Ireland has been to curtail to a considerable extent private rights to mines and minerals.

(iv) Fisheries

[6.116] Perhaps one of the most litigated subjects in Ireland has been fishing rights. At common law, the right to fish in the sea and all tidal waters belonged to the Crown.[435] The Crown did often grant fishing rights in specified parts of the sea or tidal waters to private individuals, usually in the form of a franchise known as a free or several fishery.[436] However, it has been accepted in Ireland that this practice was prohibited by Magna Carta 1215, so far as the common law had jurisdiction over the several parts of the island,[437] so that the general public may now in the name of the State or, in Northern Ireland, the Crown, fish freely in the sea and tidal waters,[438] unless some ancient grant survives to restrict that right.[439] The general public has no such rights in respect of non-tidal waters, even if navigable.[440] Much litigation has also arisen in Ireland in the same connection relating to rights to the seashore or foreshore, in particular the right to take seaweed from the shore.[441] At common law, the foreshore was vested in the Crown and this remains the case in Northern Ireland.[442] In the Republic of Ireland it is vested in the

---

[432] See also Petroleum (Production) Act (NI) 1964.

[433] 1969 Act, ss 2-7 and Sched 1.

[434] Section 1 (now Department of the Environment).

[435] *Allen v Donnelly* (1856) 5 Ir Ch R 452; *Murphy v Ryan* (1868) Ir 2 CL 143; *Whelan v Hewson* (1872) Ir 6 CL 283.

[436] *Gabbett v Clancy* (1845) 8 Ir LR 299; *Ashworth v Browne* (1860) 10 Ir Ch R 421; *Bristow v Cormican* (1875) 3 App Cas 641; *Miller v Little* (1879) 4 LR Ir 302; *Power v Heffernan* (1881) 8 LR Ir 130.

[437] *Malcolmson v O'Dea* (1863) 10 HLC 593; *R (Moore) v O'Hanrahan* [1927] IR 406; *Moore v Att-Gen* [1934] IR 44 (see *A Casebook on Irish Land Law* (1984), p 5); *Cooper v Att-Gen* [1935] IR 425; *Little v Cooper* [1937] IR 1; *Foyle and Bann Fisheries Ltd v Att-Gen* (1949) 83 ILTR 29.

[438] *Duke of Devonshire v Hodnett* (1827) 1 Hud & Br 322; *Malcolmson v O'Dea* (1863) 10 HLC 593.

[439] *Ashworth v Browne* (1855) 7 Ir Jur (os) 315; *Little v Wingfield* (1858) 11 ICLR 63; *Neil v Duke of Devonshire* (1882) 8 App Cas 135; *Att-Gen v Cooper* [1956] IR 1; *Toome Eel Fishery (Northern Ireland) Ltd v Cardwell* [1966] NI 1; *Gannon v Walsh* Unrep (HC, RI) 20 June 1996. Note, however, that the State has in recent decades imposed increasing control and regulation by statute on sea fishing, see the Republic's Whale Fisheries Act 1937; Sea Fisheries Acts 1952, 1955, 1956, 1959 and 1963; Maritime Jurisdiction Act 1959; Fishery Harbour Centres Act 1968. For Northern Ireland, see the UK Sea-Fish Industry Acts 1933, 1938, 1951, 1959, 1962, 1967, 1968, 1970 and 1992; Herring Industry Acts 1935, 1938 and 1944; Fisheries Act 1981; Fishery Limits Act 1964 and 1976.

[440] *Bloomfield v Johnston* (1868) IR 8 CL 68; *Pery v Thornton* (1889) 23 LR Ir 402; *Re De Burgho's Estate* [1896] 1 IR 274; *Johnston v O'Neill* [1911] AC 552.

[441] See Lee, 'The Right to Take Seaweed from the Foreshore' (1967) 18 NILQ 33.

[442] Government of Ireland Act 1920, s 4(1). *Duke of Devonshire v Hodnett* (1827) 1 Hud & Br 322; *Hayes v Hayes* (1897) 31 ILT 392; *Att-Gen v McCarthy* [1911] 2 IR 260.

State.[443] The foreshore lies between the high-water and low-water marks on land left by ordinary tides occurring between spring and neap tides, which land is covered and left dry alternatively by the flux and reflux of the tide.[444] Thus it is settled that the general public has no right to enter on the foreshore to take away seaweed,[445] but seaweed driven above the high-water mark belongs to the owner of the land upon which it is driven, and seaweed floating in the sea may be recovered by the general public in exercise of the public right to fish in the sea.[446] Once again, of course, Crown grants of rights to the foreshore, with the right to take seaweed therefrom, have been made from time to time to individuals.[447]

[6.117] Apart from such public fishing rights, there exists an abundance of private fishing rights relating to inland rivers and lakes and other non-tidal waters.[448] However, even here there has been a development of public ownership in recent decades.[449] Furthermore, even where private rights have been allowed to remain in existence, their exercise has been strictly controlled and regulated for well over a century[450] by a long series of Fishery Acts.[451] These Acts have been the subject of much litigation.[452] In this context it is important to distinguish between fishing

---

[443] Foreshore Act 1933. See also the 1937 Constitution, Art 10. *Linnane v Nestor* [1943] Ir 200; *cf Att-Gen v McIlwaine* [1939] IR 437; *Mahoney v Neenan* [1966] IR 559. See Smyth, *The Seashores of Ireland; Public Rights and Restrictions* (1935).

[444] *Casey v McGuanne* (1840) 1 Leg Rep 311; *Att-Gen v McCarthy* [1911] 1 IR 260.

[445] *Howe v Stawell* (1833) Alc & Nap 348; *Mulholland v Killen* (1874) IR 9 Eq 471; *Mahoney v Neenan* [1966] IR 559.

[446] *Brew v Haren* (1877) IR 11 CL 198 at 201-2 (*per* Lawson J).

[447] *Brew v Haren, ibid; Hamilton v Att-Gen* (1881) 9 LR Ir 271; *Stoney v Keane* (1903) 37 ILTR 212; *Coppinger v Sheehan* [1906] 1 IR 519; *Vandeleur v Glynn* [1907] AC 569; *Holien v Tipping* [1915] 1 IR 210; *Clancy v Whelan* (1958) 92 ILTR 39.

[448] *Case of the Royal Fishery of the Banne* (1610) Dav 149; *Hamilton v Marquis of Donegal* (1795) 3 Ridgw PC 267; *Duke of Devonshire v Hodnett* (1827) 1 Hud & Br 322; *Duke of Devonshire v Smith* (1830) 2 Hud & Br 512; *Frewen v Orr* (1842) Long & Town 601.

[449] See, eg, the Republic's Foyle Fisheries Act 1952, Pt II and Sched 2; Fisheries (Consolidation) Act 1959, ss 184-217; *cf* Foyle Fisheries Act (NI) 1952, s 8 and Sched 2 and Fisheries Act (NI) 1966, ss 1 and 2.

[450] See Connor, *Fisheries (Ireland) Acts* (1908); Finlay, *Laws of Game and Inland Fisheries in Ireland* (1827); Longfield, *Fishery Laws of Ireland* (1863).

[451] See now the Republic's Freshwater Fisheries (Prohibition of Netting) Act 1951; Fisheries (Consolidation) Act 1959; Fisheries (Amendment) Acts 1962 and 1964. Also Shannon Fisheries Acts 1935 and 1938, and the Foyle Fisheries Acts 1952 and 1961. Note also the powers terminating, restricting or otherwise interfering with fishing rights in the Arterial Drainage Acts 1945 and 1995; See *Uyttewaal v Commissioners of Public Works* [1987] IR 439. For NI, see Fisheries Acts (NI) 1966 and 1968; Diseases of Fish Act (NI) 1967; Development Loans (Agriculture and Fisheries) Act (NI) 1968. Also Foyle Fisheries Acts (NI) 1952 and 1962. As regards the Fisheries Act (NI) 1966, see *DPP v McNeill* [1975] NI 177. This decision of the Northern Ireland Court of Appeal raises numerous issues of constitutional and international law which are outside the scope of this book, but see the discussion in Symmons, 'Who Owns the Territorial Waters of Northern Ireland?' (1976) 27 NILQ 48.

[452] *R (Hosford) v County Limerick Justices* (1908) 42 ILTR 105; *King v Russell* [1909] 2 IR 25; *McCormack v Carroll* (1911) 45 ILTR 7; *Irish Society v Fleming* [1912] 1 IR 287; *Society of the New Plantation of Ulster v Harold* (1912) 46 ILTR 273; *Alton v Irvine* [1915] 2 IR 72; *Ireland v Quirke* [1928] IR 231; *Tangney v Kerry District Justices* [1928] IR 358; *Ganley v Minister for Agriculture* [1950] IR 191; *Foyle Fisheries Commission v Gallen* [1960] Ir Jur Rep 35. For earlier cases see books cited in fn 542, *supra*.

rights which are held by the owner of the bed or soil of the river or lake in question (these are attributes of the *corporeal* hereditament of the riparian owner) and fishing rights held by a third party who is not the riparian owner (these are profits *à prendre* belonging to the category of *incorporeal* hereditaments).[453] The owner of such an incorporeal hereditament can protect it from wrongful interference by seeking an injunction or maintaining an action for damages, in form an action for nuisance akin to an action for trespass.[454] Furthermore, the grant of fishing rights as an incorporeal hereditament implies a right of access to the banks of the river or lake over which the rights are exercisable, but such a right of access must be exercised in a manner which is as little detrimental to the riparian owners as is consistent with full beneficial use of the right of fishing.[455]

(v) Other Sporting Rights

[6.118] In addition to fishing rights, it is common to have grants or reservations made of other sporting rights, such as hunting and shooting wild animals and fowl.[456] The exercise of such rights is also controlled by statute, ie, legislation passed for the preservation and protection of game.[457]

(vi) Timber

[6.119] Timber may form the subject-matter of a profit in the shape of a right of estovers, ie, the right to take wood as, in the ancient language of the common law,[458] "house-bote",[459] "plough-bote"[460] and "hay-bote".[461] We saw earlier that a tenant for life can claim such a right,[462] but it is important to note a vital difference in his case. A tenant for life's right of estovers is exercisable in respect of the same land in which he holds his estate whereas, in the present context, we are concerned with a right of

---

[453] See the discussion by Keane J in *Gannon v Walsh* Unrep, (HC, RI), 20 June 1996.

[454] *Ibid.* See also *Tennent v Clancy* [1987] IR 15.

[455] *Ibid.* Note that where sporting rights were reserved on a sale under the Land Purchase Acts there is a statutory right of access: see s 13 of the Irish Land Act 1903; *Boyle v Holcroft* [1905] 1 IR 245; *Caldwell v Kilkelly* [1905] 1 IR 434; *Palmer v Byrne* [1906] 1 IR 373.

[456] *Finlay v Curteis* (1832) Hayes 496; *Foott v Hudson* (1860) 10 ICLR 509; *Radcliff v Hayes* [1907] 1 IR 101.

[457] See the Republic's Game Preservation Act 1930 and Wild Birds Protection Act 1930; *cf* Game Preservation Act (NI) 1928; Wild Birds Protection Acts (NI) 1931, 1950 and 1968; Game Law Amendment Act (NI) 1951; Protection of Animals Acts (NI) 1952 and 1961; Wildlife (NI) Order 1983 and 1995. Note also earlier legislation applying to the whole of Ireland, eg, Game Acts (Ir) 1698 and 1787; Game Act 1831; Game Trespass Act 1864; Ground Game Acts 1880 and 1906. See on this legislation, Connor, *Game Laws of Ireland* (1891); Connor, *Right to Game in Ireland* (1903); Farran, *Game Laws of Ireland* (1907); Finlay, *Laws of Game and Inland Fisheries in Ireland* (1827); Jague, *Irish Game Laws* (1843); Longfield, *Game Laws of Ireland* (1868). *State (Lawlor) v District Justice MacCraith* [1964] IR 364.

[458] *Coke on Littleton* (19th ed, 1832), 41b and 53b.

[459] Ie, for repairing the house occupied by the holder of the right or for burning in it as fuel.

[460] Ie, for making or repairing agricultural equipment.

[461] Ie for repairing fences.

[462] Para **[4.152]** *ante*.

estovers as a profit *à prendre*, ie, held by one person in respect of *another* person's land. A right of estovers is usually restricted to some extent, eg, as to the precise amount of, or, indeed, nature, of the timber which may be cut and taken[463] or limited by reference to the needs of the dominant tenement.[464] Apart from such a right of estovers, a person may acquire much wider timber rights in respect of another's land, in particular the right to cut timber for commercial purposes.[465] Once again there has been the encroachment of statutory regulation, eg, forestry legislation.[466]

---

[463] *Russel and Broker's Case* (1587) 2 Leon 209; *Brown and Tucker's Case* (1610) 4 Leon 241.

[464] *Clayton v Corby* (1843) 5 QB 415 at 419-20 (*per* Lord Denman CJ).

[465] *Re Moore's Estates* (1902) 36 ILTR 14; *Rudd v Rea* [1923] 1 IR 55.

[466] See the Republic's Forestry Acts 1946 and 1956; *cf* Forestry Act (NI) 1953 and note the general provisions of the Amenity Lands Act (NI) 1965, para **[4.152]** *ante*.

Part III

CO-OWNERSHIP

Chapter 7

CO-OWNERSHIP

I. GENERAL

[7.01] In an earlier chapter we were concerned with the law relating to that part of the fragmentation of ownership of real property which concerns ownership *successively*.[1] We shall return to this subject again in a later chapter.[2] For the moment, however, we must consider another aspect of ownership of real property, namely ownership by two or more persons *concurrently*. The law relating to co-ownership is nothing like as difficult as the law relating to future interests but that is not to say that some very complicated problems do not arise in practice.[3] Indeed, these problems led the draftsmen of the English 1925 legislation to revolutionise the law of co-ownership,[4] but as yet no equivalent provisions have been enacted in either part of Ireland.[5]

II. CLASSIFICATION

[7.02] There are four main categories of co-ownership recognised by our law: (1) joint tenancy; (2) tenancy in common; (3) coparcenary; (4) tenancy by the entireties. The use of the word "tenancy" in this context can be misleading. Here the word should be given one of its widest meanings, namely the holding of any estate or interest in land.[6] It is not confined to any particular kind of tenancy, whether freehold or leasehold, legal or equitable, present or future. In all these cases some form of co-ownership may exist, though there may be some problems in particular cases, as we shall see later.[7] We shall

---

[1] Ch 5, *ante*.

[2] Ch 8, *post*.

[3] See para [7.12], *post*.

[4] Megarry and Wade, *The Law of Real Property* (5th ed, 1984), Ch 9; Cheshire and Burn, *Modern Law of Real Property* (15th ed, 1994), Ch 10; Gray, *Elements of Land Law* (2nd ed, 1993), Ch 13; Potter, 'Undivided Shares in Land' (1930) 46 LQR 71. Note, however that the 1925 provisions on co-ownership were one of the less satisfactory features of the scheme, especially the imposition of a trust for sale. Substantial changes were recommended by the Law Commission in its Report *Transfer of Land: Trusts of Land* (Law Com No 181 1989) and these were put into effect in Pt I of the Trusts of Land and Appointment of Trustees Act 1996. These reflect, especially in replacing the dual system of trusts for sale and strict settlements with a single "holding" trust of land, which applies also to co-ownership, recommendations made earlier in NI: see fn 5 *infra*.

[5] See, however, the recommendations in Ch 4 of the *Survey of the Land Law of Northern Ireland* (HMSO, 1971); Land Law Working Group's *Final Report* (HMSO, 1990) Vol 1, Ch 2.2. Note, in particular, the proposals for dealing with the major conveyancing problems which arise where there is a single legal owner who is regarded as holding the legal title on trust for himself and another person, especially where that person is in occupation of the land: see paras 2.2.14-34. This is very common as between spouses in relation to the matrimonial home: see paras [25.15-16] *post*. See also *Irish Conveyancing Law* (2nd ed, 1996), para 16.23.

[6] See para [2.04], *ante*.

[7] See, eg, para [7.18] *post*.

now consider each of the four categories in more detail. The first two, joint tenancy and tenancy in common, bear a close relationship to each other and so will be considered together.

A. Joint Tenancy and Tenancy in Common

[7.03] In the case of both a joint tenancy and a tenancy in common the land held by the persons concerned is held by them concurrently, so that as far as third parties are concerned the co-owners of the land must be treated as a single unit for the purposes of certain transactions in respect of that land. As between themselves, however, the positions of co-owners holding under a joint tenancy and those holding under a tenancy in common are quite different. This difference may be outlined as follows.

1. Elements of a Joint Tenancy

There are two main features which distinguish a joint tenancy from a tenancy in common. These are the so-called *right of survivorship (jus accrescendi)* and the *four unities*.

(i) Right of Survivorship

[7.04] The central principle of a joint tenancy is that, when one joint tenant dies, his undivided share in the land passes to the surviving joint tenants.[8] As the surviving joint tenants die, their respective shares similarly pass to their survivors until ultimately one only of the original joint tenants survives and becomes thereby sole owner of the land and so free to dispose of it accordingly. It is inherent, therefore, in the nature of this right of survivorship that no joint tenant can defeat it by making a will purporting to leave his share in the land to someone other than his co-tenants.[9] We shall see later, however, that a joint tenant can make an *inter vivos* disposition of his interest in the land, though this will have the effect of ending the joint tenancy as between the purchaser and the other joint tenants.[10]

---

[8]   See the discussion in *Cockerill v Gilliland* (1854) 6 Ir Jur (os) 357. Also *Reilly v Walsh* (1848) 11 Ir Eq R 22; *Re Barrett* (1858) 8 Ir Ch R 548; *Jury v Jury* (1882) 9 LR Ir 207.

[9]   Nor can there be any succession on intestacy - the deceased tenant's estate or interest in the land is deemed to cease on his death where he is survived by another joint tenant, see Administration of Estates Act (NI) 1955, s 44(d) and Succession Act 1965, s 4(c) (RI). Thus the interest of an insolvent joint tenant is not available on his death for his creditors. Note that the suggestion in England that an insolvency administration order retrospectively severed the joint tenancy was rejected by the Court of Appeal: see *Re Palmer* [1994] 3 All ER 835. In NI such an order can be made after the death of an insolvent person who had not been declared bankrupt at the date of death: see Insolvent Estates of Deceased Persons Order (NI) 1991, Sch 1 (made under the Insolvency (NI) Order 1989 Act, Article 365). The Court held that the English equivalent enabling provision (Insolvency Act 1986, s 421) applied, like the NI provision, to the insolvent's "estate" on death and so did not allow the general rule that a joint tenant's interest in the property held on the joint tenancy ceases on his death (and passes by the right of survivorship to the surviving joint tenant or tenants) and does not form part of his estate.

[10] Para **[7.28]**, *post*.

[7.05] The right of survivorship sometimes gives rise to problems. For example, the common law found it difficult to deal with the position of a corporation which, according to the common law's own definition, never dies and so would always be the survivor. In medieval times, "corporation" meant any body corporate and so included what we now call companies. For this reason it became the rule at common law that a corporation could not hold land as a joint tenant and any purported conveyance to that effect operated to create a tenancy in common only. This rule, however, was reversed by the Bodies Corporate (Joint Tenancy) Act 1899, which still applies in both parts of Ireland. Under this Act, a corporation may acquire and hold property as if it were an individual. This provision was really passed to facilitate banks and similar corporate bodies acting as trustees of property. As we shall see in a later chapter,[11] it is more convenient for trustees to hold as joint tenants because the right of survivorship ensures the automatic vesting of the trust property in the survivors without the need for any further conveyances.

[7.06] Another problem arises in the case of *commorientes*,[12] ie, where the joint tenants all die together, eg, in a car crash, and it is impossible to determine whether any one survived the others and, if so, which one. The common law's solution to this problem was to hold that there could be no survivorship and so the heirs of the deceased joint tenants succeeded to the property as joint tenants.[13] In England this rule was reversed by the Law of Property Act 1925, which introduced for such cases a presumption that the younger survived the elder.[14] In the Republic of Ireland, however, the Succession Act 1965 preserves the common law rule. Section 5 of that Act provides:

> Where, after the commencement of this Act, two or more persons have died in circumstances rendering it uncertain which of them survived the other or others, then, for the purposes of the distribution of the estate of any of them, they shall all be deemed to have died simultaneously.

In Northern Ireland the Land Law Working Party recommended in 1971 the adoption of the English 1925 provisions,[15] but the later Land Law Working Group concluded that a general presumption of simultaneous deaths should apply for all purposes affecting title to property, but that an exception should apply in the case of joint tenancies. Here the

---

[11]   Ch 10, *post*.

[12]   See para **[14.32]**, *post*.

[13]   *Bradshaw v Toulmin* (1784) Dick 633: "if two persons, being joint tenants, perish by one blow, the estate will remain in joint tenancy, in their respective heirs." *Per* Lord Thurlow LC.

[14]   Section 184. This presumption was, however, made expressly subject to any order of the court, see *Re Lindop* [1942] Ch 377 and *Hickman v Peacey* [1945] AC 304. See also *Re Bate* [1947] 2 All ER 418; *Re Rowland* [1963] Ch 1. The presumption was also modified in the case of a husband and wife, where one spouse dies intestate (the intestate is presumed to die later), Intestates' Estates Act 1952, s 1(4). Finally, the old common law rule of simultaneous deaths was restored in England for the purposes of estate duty by the Finance Act 1958, 29(1), see *Re Scott* [1901] 1 KB 228.

[15]   See the recommendations in the *Survey of the Land Law of Northern Ireland* (HMSO, 1971), paras 406-7.

persons concerned should be deemed to have died in order of age, ie, the elder predeceased the younger.[16] This has yet to be put into effect.[17]

(ii) Four Unities

[7.07] The four unities, all of which must be present for a joint tenancy to exist, are the unities of - (a) possession, (b) interest, (c) title and (d) time.

(a) Possession

It is inherent in the nature of all forms of co-ownership that each co-owner has as much right to possession of the land held under co-ownership as all the other co-owners.[18] This rule, therefore, applies to a joint tenancy and no joint tenant is entitled to exclude his co-tenants from possession of any part of the land, or to prevent them from taking a share in the rents and profits of the land. However, there was one problem about this matter at common law. Normally if a person entitled to possession of land is excluded or deprived of possession, he has an action in trespass[19] and an action for money had and received or an account for loss of rents and profits.[20] The problem for a co-owner, however, was that he could not lay claim to possession of any particular part of the land and so could not bring such an action at common law. This problem was resolved by statute. The Administration of Justice Act (Ireland) 1707[21] conferred on a co-owner the right of action of account against another co-owner who obtains more than his share in a case where the land or its profits has been converted into money.[22] If the land is not so converted, then a joint tenant excluded from possession can compel a partition of the land, a subject we shall discuss later.[23] It has long been established that the courts may,

---

[16]   See the Land Law Working Group's Discussion Document No 4 (*Conveyancing and Miscellaneous Matters*) (1983), Ch 7 and *Final Report* (HMSO, 1990) Vol 1, para 2.14.3-6.

[17]   Note, however, that another exception recommended by the Working Group, *viz*, that effect should be given to a provision in a will designating a substitute executor in the event of the named executor dying before or simultaneously with the testator, was put into effect by Article 30 of the Wills and Administration Proceedings (NI) Order 1994.

[18]   Challis, *The Law of Real Property* (3rd ed), pp 366-67. See also *Reeves v Morris* (1840) 2 Ir LR 309; *Griffith v Leach* (1855) 4 ICLR 621; *W v Somers* [1983] ILRM 122; *Re Hecker's Estate* Unrep (HC, RI), 28 April 1994 (1993/248 Sp).

[19]   See Ch 23 *post*.

[20]   *Montgomery v Swan* (1859) Ir Ch R 131.

[21]   6 Ann, c 10. The English equivalent was the Administration of Justice Act 1705 (4 & 5 Ann, c 3), which was repealed by the Law of Property (Amendment) Act 1924, Sched 10. Under the Law of Property Act 1925, joint tenants hold the legal estate in trust for themselves. This is not changed by the Trusts of Land and Appointment of Trustees Act 1996. That Act changes only the nature of the trust: see para **[7.01]** fn 4 *ante*.

[22]   Section 23. See *Kearney v Kearney* (1861) 13 ICLR 314; *Garnett v Cullen* (1863) 8 Ir Jur (NS) 154; *Montgomery v Swan* (1859) 9 Ir Ch R 131; *Dawson v Baxter* (1886) 19 LR Ir 103.

[23]   Para **[7.35]**, *post*. He may also seek a court order to compel the other tenant or tenants to recognise his equal right to possession and obtain damages if he has been ousted by the other or others: see *Jacobs v Seward* (1872) LR 5 HL 464 at 472-3 (per Lord Hatherley LC). *Cf* in the context of a right of residence, *Johnston v Horace* [1993] ILRM 594; *Re Hecker's Estate* Unrep, (HC, RI) 28 April 1994 (1993/248 Sp): para **[20.13]** *et seq, post*.

in partition actions, engage in equitable accounting, so as to do justice as between the co-owners.[24] Thus one co-owner may be entitled to a contribution from other co-owners for expenditure he has made to improve the value of the property[25] or to receive an occupation rent from a co-owner who has enjoyed possession of the property.[26]

(b) Interest

In law all the joint tenants holding a particular piece of land are regarded as a single unit for the purposes of ownership, so that each and every one of them has to join in any transaction relating to that land if it is to be fully effective.[27] This principle led the courts to hold that each joint tenant must hold the same interest in the land, from the point of view of the nature, extent and duration of the interest.[28] Thus one joint tenant may not hold a leasehold interest if another holds a freehold, nor may one hold a fee simple if another holds a fee tail, nor may one have a present interest if another has a future interest only and so on. However, unity of interest is not affected by the fact that one joint tenant has an additional interest in the property, eg, where all the joint tenants have life estates, but one of them has the fee simple remainder.

(c) Title

It was also a settled rule at common law that all the joint tenants should have acquired their interests in the land by the same title,[29] whether that source of title lay in a particular document of title or the act of another party or, indeed, the joint tenants' own acts of adverse possession.[30]

(d) Time

It was also the rule at common law that the interest of each joint tenant should vest at the same time. The mere fact that there was unity of title was not enough and failure to meet this fourth requirement meant that a tenancy in common was created. However, this fourth unity was not applied to conveyances to uses nor to dispositions by will.[31]

---

[24] See Cooke, 'Equitable Accounting' [1995] Conv. See also *O'Brien & Cronin Ltd v Dillon* Unrep (HC, RI), 2 February 1977 (1974/383 Sp); *H v O* [1978] IR 194.

[25] *Leigh v Dickerson* (1884) 15 QBD 60; *Re Pavlou* [1993] 3 All ER 955; *cf Re Hecker's Estate* Unrep, (HC, RI), 28 April 1994 (1993/248 Sp).

[26] *Turner v Morgan* (1803) 8 Ves 143; *Dennis v McDonald* [1982] 1 All ER 590.

[27] Note, however, the position of proving executors, *vis-à-vis* non-proving executors, of a deceased person's estate under the Succession Act 1965, ss 20 and 50(2) and the Administration of Estates Act (NI) 1955, s 32 (2). See para **[16.23]**, *post*. It appears also that a notice to quit a periodic tenancy does not necessarily have to be served by all the joint landlords or joint tenants, see *Alford v Vickery* (1842) Car & M 280; *Morony v Morony* (1874) IR 8 CL 174; *Hamill v Toomey* (1900) 34 ILTR 163. *Cf* service on one of several joint tenants, *Pollok v Kelly* (1856) 6 ICLR 367; *Biggar v Pyers* (1879)13 ILTR 127. Also paras **[17.078]** and **[17.082]**, *post*.

[28] Challis, *The Law of Real Property* (3rd ed), p 366.

[29] Challis, *loc cit*; *Knox v Earl of Mayo* (1858) 9 Ir Ch R 192.

[30] *Cf* adverse possession as between the joint tenants themselves, para **[23.36]** *post*.

[31] Challis, *op cit*, p. 367. See the Irish cases of *Hickson v Hill* (1857) 3 Ir Jur (ns) 165 and espec the discussion in *O'Hea v Slattery* [1895] 1 IR 7. See also *Kenworthy v Ward* (1853) 11 Hare 196; *Ruck v Barwise* (1865) 2 Dr & Sm 10; *Doe.d Hallen v Ironmonger* (1803) 3 East 533.

2. Elements of a Tenancy in Common

[7.08] The elements of a tenancy in common are best described in contradistinction to those of a joint tenancy. This remark stems from the basic principle of a tenancy in common which is that each tenant in common holds an undivided share in the property.[32] Unlike a joint tenant, a tenant in common from the beginning of his co-ownership has a quite distinct and separate interest or share in the property. He is regarded as a co-owner only because the property has not yet been divided up into the respective shares and, until this is done, it is not possible to say which tenant in common owns which particular part of the property. This principle of undivided shares results in the two basic elements of a tenancy in common.

(i) No Right of Survivorship

[7.09] A tenant in common has a distinct share in the property from the date of the commencement of the tenancy in common, so there can be no question of a right of survivorship existing in the other tenants in common.[33] That is not to say, of course, that a grantor of property may not grant in his disposition rights that are equivalent to rights of survivorship. But these rights arise from the express limitations put in the conveyance, not from the creation of a tenancy in common.[34]

(ii) One Unity

[7.10] It is also settled that one of the four unities required for a joint tenancy only is required for a tenancy in common.[35] The only unity required is unity of possession, though the other three unities may be present in a particular case. However, it is quite permissible for tenants in common to have unequal shares and to hold different estates or interests in the property.[36]

3. Creation of a Joint Tenancy and Tenancy in Common

[7.11] This is a complicated subject, largely owing to the different attitudes taken by the common law, on the one hand, and equity on the other, to these two forms of co-

---

[32] *Cockerill v Gilliland* (1854) 6 Ir Jur (os)357; *Knox v Earl of Mayor* (1858) 9 Ir Ch R 192; *Re Robson* [1940] Ir Jur Rep 7.

[33] *McCarthy v Barry* (1859) 9 Ir Ch R 377.

[34] *Re Barrett* (1858) 8 Ir Ch R 548; *Forrester v Smith* (1852) 2 Ir Ch R 70. For the relevance in this context of the intricate conveyancing device of "cross-remainders" in a family settlement, see Challis, *op cit*, pp 370-3. Also *Sutton v Sutton* (1892) 30 LR Ir 751; *Blake v Blake* [1913] 1 IR 343. See also *Murray v Murray* (1852) 3 Ir Ch R 120; *Fitzgerald v Fitzgerald* (1961) 12 ICLR 551; *Taaffe v Conmee* (1862) 10 HLC 64.

[35] Challis, *op cit*, p 370. See the discussion of the rights to occupation of tenants in common *inter se* by the English Court of Appeal in *Jones v Jones* [1977] 1 WLR 438 and by Lynch J in *Re Hecker's Estate* Unrep (HC, RI), 28 April 1994 (1993/248 Sp).

[36] In *Re Hecker's Estate supra* the testatrix has left, *inter alia* a house to her four children as joint tenants but subject to a right of residence for one of them until she married. They agreed to sever the joint tenancy (see para **[7.22]** *et seq, post*) and an assent was executed vesting it in the four of them as tenants in common, but subject to the right of residence. See further on rights of residence para **[20.13]** *et seq, post*.

ownership. The result is that in considering the effect of a particular disposition one must always distinguish between the legal ownership of the property and the equitable ownership.[37] As we shall see, it will frequently be the case that the co-owners will hold the legal estate or interest in the property as joint tenants, so that the right of survivorship applies, but that that legal estate or interest is held by the joint tenants for themselves in equity as tenants in common. In this case, on the death of one co-owner his legal estate or interest passes to the surviving co-owner, but that survivor must hold the legal estate or interest in trust for the deceased co-owner's estate and his beneficial share under the tenancy in common will pass according to the terms of his will or on intestacy. The legal estate or interest in the property, therefore, remains inviolate, whereas the equitable estate or interest becomes the subject of undivided shares held on trust for different people.

We must consider, therefore, the subject of creation of joint tenancies and tenancies in common both at law and in equity. And in this connection it should be noted that there is a special statutory encouragement to create a joint tenancy in the family home contained in s 14 of the Republic's Family Home Protection Act 1976. This reads:

> No stamp duty, land registration fee, Registry of Deeds fee or court fee shall be payable on any transaction creating a joint tenancy between spouses in respect of a family home where the home was immediately prior to such transaction owned by either spouse or by both spouses otherwise than as joint tenants.

It is not clear from the section whether it is concerned with legal or equitable "ownership" of the family home, or both, but in terms of policy the protection afforded by the right of survivorship is at its most effective if both legal and equitable ownership are held on a joint tenancy by the spouses (a common conveyancing device).

(i) At Common law

[7.12] The common law preferred a joint tenancy and so there arose a presumption at law in favour of such a tenancy whenever a conveyance to two or more persons was being construed.[38] There were several reasons for the common law's attitude.[39] Some lie in history, eg, in feudal times it was more convenient to levy feudal services on a small and decreasing number of tenants of land and this a joint tenancy only would ensure. Others are equally relevant today, eg, joint tenants hold under a single title whereas the title of each tenant in common has to be investigated by conveyancers in a transaction relating to the land held subject to the tenancy in common. With the passage of time, the land held under the tenancy in common may become extremely fragmented as each undivided share is split into more and more parts on the death of each tenant in common and his successors in title. It is quite common today for solicitors to be faced with the

---

[37] See Ch 3 *ante*.

[38] *McDonnell v Jebb* (1865) 16 Ir Ch R 359; *Re Newsom's Trusts* (1878) 1 LR Ir 373; *Jury v Jury* (1882) 9 LR Ir 207; *Re Wallis' Trusts* (1888) 23 LR Ir 460; *Re Hoban* [1896] 1 IR 401; *Welland v Townsend* [1910] 1 IR 177; *Kennedy v Ryan* [1938] IR 620 (see *A Casebook on Irish Land Law* (1984) p 372).

[39] See Megarry and Wade, *The Law of Real Property* (5th ed, 1984), p 424.

daunting task of tracing dozens of shares in what was once a piece of land held by two or three people only as tenants in common.[40] A particular problem in Ireland involves ownership of distributive shares in land when farmers die intestate.[41]

[7.13] This presumption of a joint tenancy at law whenever property is conveyed to two or more people is rebuttable, even at common law. The presumption is rebutted in two main sets of circumstances: (a) lack of one or more of the four unities or (b) use of "words of severance" in the conveyance.

(a) Lack of Unities

[7.14] Since all four unities are essential for a joint tenancy,[42] lack of any one of them will prevent the creation of a joint tenancy. If, however, unity of possession exists then a tenancy in common will be created, whatever the position with respect to the other three unities.[43] If there is no unity of possession, then there can be neither a joint tenancy nor a tenancy in common and separate ownership exists between the grantees in the conveyance.

(b) Words of Severance

[7.15] It became the settled rule, even at common law, that any words used in the conveyance indicating that the grantees were intended to take distinct shares in the property had the effect of creating a tenancy in common instead of a joint tenancy.[44] The following expressions have been held to be words of severance: "in equal shares",[45] "equally";[46] "share and share alike";[47] "to be divided between";[48] "between";[49] "respectively".[50] It must be remembered that this matter is largely one of construction of

---

[40] Hence the radical changes in the law of co ownership introduced in England by the Law of Property Act 1925. See also *Survey of the Land Law in Northern Ireland* (HMSO, 1971), Ch 4 and the Land Law Working Group's *Final Report* (HMSO, 1990) Vol 1, Ch 2.2. These recommendations deal also with the conveyancing problems created by the "hidden" co-beneficial owner situation exemplified by the English decision in *Williams and Glyn's Bank v Boland* [1981] AC 487, ie, where a *single* legal owner is regarded in equity as holding the beneficial interest in trust for himself and another person who has acquired an equitable interest by virtue of, eg, contributing to the purchase or improvement of the property: see para **[25.15-16]** *post*. Under the proposals such an interest would be void as against a purchaser or mortgagee unless protected by prior registration. See also **[21.38]** *post*.

[41] See paras **[23.40-42]**, *post*.

[42] Para **[7.07]**, *ante*.

[43] Para **[7.10]**, *ante*.

[44] *Fleming v Fleming* (1855) 5 Ir Ch R 129, espec at 134-6 (per Brady LC).

[45] *Jury v Jury* (1882) 9 LR Ir 207. Cf *Cockerill v Gilliland* (1854) 6 Ir Jur (os) 357.

[46] *Lambert v Browne* (1871) IR 5 CL 281.

[47] *Clarke v Bodkin* (1851) 13 Ir Eq R 492; *Re Dennehy's Estate* (1865) 17 Ir Ch R 97; *Mill v Mill* (1877) IR 11 Eq 158.

[48] *Crozier v Crozier* (1843) 3 Dr & War 373.

[49] *Crozier v Crozier, ibid*; *Murray v Murray* (1852) 3 Ir Ch R 120.

[50] *Fleming v Fleming* (1855) 5 Ir Ch R 129; *Re Wallis' Trusts* (1888) 23 LR Ir 460.

the particular conveyance, so that absence of such express words of severance does not mean that the court will not find evidence of an intention to create a tenancy in common from other provisions in the conveyance.[51] Thus in one Irish case involving a settlement for infants, which contained a power of advancement conferred on the trustees to benefit any one of the infants, the court held that such a power, which would necessarily have to be exercised by using the "share" of the infant to be advanced,[52] was inconsistent with a joint tenancy and so a tenancy in common was created.[53] FitzGibbon LJ commented:

> "The incompatibility of a discretionary power of advancement with a joint tenancy is absolute, because the exercise of such a power implies the reduction of several parts of the property into possession."[54]

[7.16] On the other hand, it is quite possible that the court may construe the language of a deed or will apparently containing words of severance as nevertheless evincing an intention to create a joint tenancy. And effect to this intention will be given even at law.[55]

[7.17] Finally, it has been held in England that in the case of a gift to a "compound" class of beneficiaries (eg, to the testator's children in equal shares, provided that the children of a deceased child should take his parent's share), compound words of severance should be used, otherwise any substitute children taking a parent's share may take as joint tenants only.[56]

(ii) In Equity

[7.18] Equity took a different approach to co-ownership from that of the common law.[57] In fact, equity adopted a contrary view: "equity leans against joint tenancies" was its maxim,[58] based upon what was considered to be a much fairer division of the ownership of property in many cases. This approach resulted in a presumption arising in certain circumstances that the settlor or testator really intended to create a tenancy in common.

---

51 *Bray v Jennings* (1902) 36 ILTR 6; *Re Gray* (1927) 61 ILTR 65.

52 See further on a power of advancement, para **[10.048]**, *post*.

53 *L'Estrange v L'Estrange* [1902] 1 IR 467 (see *A Casebook on Irish Land Law* (1984), p 375. See also *Taggart v Taggart* (1803) 1 Sch & Lef 84; *Twigg v Twigg* [1935] IR 65.

54 *Ibid*, p 469.

55 Megarry and Wade, *The Law of Real Property* (5th ed, 1984), p 426. See the Irish case of *Cockerill v Gilliland* (1854) 6 Ir Jur (os) 357. Also *Daly v Aldword* (1863) 15 Ir Ch R 69; *Taaffe v Conmee* (1862) 10 HLC 64.

56 *Re Brooke* [1953] 1 WLR 439. *Cf Re Burke* [1945] Ir Jur Rep 12; *Re Froy* [1938] Ch 566. In a case where a vague expression like "relations" is used in a will, the court may resolve the uncertainty by construing this to mean the deceased's statutory intestate successors, Ch 15, *post*. This does not mean, however, that the set successors necessarily take their shares as tenants in common according to the statutory provisions this remains a question of the intention of the testator and, if no express or implied reference to the statutory provisions can be found, the court is likely to find that the successors take as joint tenants. *Re Gansloser's Will Trusts* [1952] Ch 30; *Re Kilvert* [1951] Ch 388. *Cf Re Burke, op cit*.

57 Para **[7.11]**, *ante. Fleming v Fleming* (1855) 5 Ir Ch R 129.

58 See para **[3.059]**, *ante*.

Equity could not, of course, directly overrule the common law,[59] so frequently today a court will accept that the parties take the property as joint tenants at law, but will insist that they hold it on trust[60] for themselves as tenants in common in equity. In this way, co-ownership nowadays often involves a split in ownership of the property, into the legal ownership on the one hand and the equitable or beneficial ownership on the other hand. The following are the main circumstances in which the courts will hold that joint tenants in law hold for themselves as tenants in common in equity.

(a) Purchase Money in Unequal Shares

[7.19] It has been held for many years in both England[61] and Ireland[62] that, if the purchasers of property provide the purchase-money in unequal shares, they will be presumed to take the property in equity as tenants in common. Thus on the death of one co-owner, the survivor takes the whole legal interest in the property himself but he must hold part of the beneficial interest (equivalent to the beneficial share of the deceased co-owner) for the deceased's successors, testate or intestate. On the other hand, if the money was provided in equal shares the presumption lies the other way. However, these are presumptions only and it is always open to the court to find the other way as a matter of construction in the particular case.[63] Furthermore, there are special statutory provisions giving the courts jurisdiction to determine matters relating to property as between a husband and wife, which may add an additional dimension in such cases.[64]

(b) Mortgage Loans

[7.20] In this case equity took the view that lenders of money on mortgage took their legal interest (though equitable mortgages only may also be created) in the property

---

[59] Para **[3.059]** *ante.*

[60] For more on this use of the trust concept see Ch 9, *post.*

[61] *Lake v Gibson* (1729) 1 Eq Ca Abr 290; *Jackson v Jackson* (1804) 9 Ves 591; *Bull v Bull* [1955] 1 QB 234.

[62] *O'Connell v Harrison* [1927] IR 330, espec at 335-36 (*per* Kennedy CJ) (see *A Casebook on Irish Land Law* (1984), p 378.

[63] *Fleming v Fleming* (1855) 5 Ir Ch R 129, espec at 140-1 (*per* Brady LC).

[64] See Married Women's Status Act 1957, s 12 (RI); Married Women's Property Act 1882, s 17 (as explained by s 3(7) of the Law Reform (Husband and Wife) Act (NI), 1964). As regards s 12 of the Republic's Married Women's Status Act 1957, see *C v C* [1976] IR 254; *W v W* [1981] ILRM 202; Duncan and Scully, *Marriage Breakdown in Ireland: Law and Practice* (1990),Ch 10. It should also be noted that in Northern Ireland s 17 of the Married Women's Property Act 1882, and s 3 of the Law Reform (Husband and Wife) Act, (NI) 1964, were extended by Article 55 of the Matrimonial Causes (NI) Order 1978, so as to cover (a) either of the parties to a void marriage, whether or not it has been annulled; (b) either of the parties to a voidable marriage which has been annulled; (c) either of the parties to a marriage which has been dissolved. But an application under s 17 (or as so extended) by a party to a marriage which has been dissolved or annulled cannot be made more than 3 years after the dissolution or annulment, and one by a party to a void marriage, which has not been annulled, cannot be made more than 3 years after the parties have ceased to live with each other in the same household. Para **[25.15]**, *post.*

offered as security for the loan[65] as tenants in common, whether the money was lent in *equal or unequal shares.*[66] The usual form of legal mortgage of land not registered under the registration of title legislation is a conveyance of the legal estate to the mortgagee or the creation of a long term of years which is granted to the mortgagee. The reason for the presumption in this case, and again it is a rebuttable presumption only, seems to be that it is in the nature of a mortgage transaction that each lender intends to get back what he has lent. It is essentially a commercial transaction[67] and, as such, the right of survivorship annexed to a joint tenancy seems to be an inappropriate concept to apply to the parties.[68]

(c) Partnership Property

[7.21] Just as a mortgage transaction was considered in equity to be too much of a commercial transaction for a joint tenancy to be allowed to operate, so equity presumed that land acquired by partners as part of their partnership assets should be presumed to have been acquired on the basis of a tenancy in common.[69] Indeed, It seems that equity nowadays would hold this to be the position in most joint undertakings or enterprises of a largely commercial or business nature whether or not any formal partnership has been entered into by the parties concerned.[70]

(iii) Severance of a Joint Tenancy

[7.22] Even at common law it was appreciated that the right of survivorship annexed to a joint tenancy could operate unfairly in some circumstances. So it was recognised that events could occur which would be regarded as "severing" the joint tenancy in the sense that the right of survivorship would be destroyed and the parties thereupon would cease to hold under a joint tenancy and would, instead, hold under a tenancy in common.[71] Severance, therefore, in this context means the conversion of a joint tenancy into a tenancy in common.[72]

[7.23] As we discussed above,[73] no joint tenant can be regarded as having any distinct share in the property during the continuance of the joint tenancy, but rather a potential

---

65 On the law of mortgages generally, see Ch 12, *post*.

66 *Petty v Syward* (1632)1 Ch Rep 57; *Steeds v Steeds* (1889) 22 QBD 537.

67 See further Ch 12, *post*.

68 Note that a "joint account" clause often inserted in a mortgage deed, which purports to make the lenders joint tenants, is intended to govern some matters only relating to the mortgage, eg, its ultimate discharge, and does not necessarily govern the relations of the mortgagees (lenders) *inter se*, para **[9.050]**, *post*.

69 *Hawkins v Rogers* [1951] IR 48; *O'Dwyer v Cafolla & Co* [1949] IR 210; *Meagher v Meagher* [1961] IR 96.

70 See *McCarthy v Barry* (1859) 9 Ir Ch R 377. *Cf Reilly v Walsh* (1848) 11 Ir Eq R 22.

71 See *Connolly v Connolly* (1866) 17 Ir Ch R 208; *Butterly v McKechnie* (1902) 36 ILTR 77; *Re Armstrong* [1920] 1 IR 239. See also *Williams v Hensman* (1861) 1 J & H 546, at 557-8 (*per* Page-Wood V-C); Garner, 'Severance of a Joint Tenancy' (1976) 40 Conv 77.

72 It should not be confused with "partition", see para **[7.35]**, *post*.

73 Para **[7.03]**, *ante*.

share dependent upon the number of his co-tenants and with prospects of growing larger if he survives them. Thus, on severance of a joint tenancy, the undivided share of each tenant in common, as the surviving joint tenants have become, is an equal share in the property commensurate with the number of co-tenants surviving at the date of severance.

[7.24] A joint tenancy may be severed either at law, so as to create a tenancy in common of the legal title to the property, or in equity, so as to leave the legal title held under a joint tenancy but to have this held on trust as to the beneficial ownership under a tenancy in common. There are two main ways of bringing about a severance either at law or in equity, namely (a) by acquisition of some further interest in the property by one of the joint tenants and (b) alienation of his interest in the property by one of the joint tenants. It is apparent, then, that severance of a joint tenancy involves the destruction of one of the four unities[74] essential for such a form of co-ownership. Unity of time cannot, of course, be destroyed because otherwise no joint tenancy would have come into existence in the first place[75] capable of being severed. Further, as we shall see,[76] destruction of unity of possession has even more drastic effects on a joint tenancy than severance and conversion into a tenancy in common; it involves "partition" of the property so as to destroy co-ownership altogether.

(a) Acquisition of Another Interest

[7.25] The important point to note here is that a severance will be effected by the acquisition of another interest in the property by one of the joint tenants only if that acquisition takes place after the joint tenancy has come into existence.[77] The mere fact that, at the date of the creation of the joint tenancy, one of the joint tenants was given some additional interest in the property does not prevent him holding another interest in the same property under a joint tenancy with other co-owners.[78] At that date the four unities may be present as to that other interest. For example, land may be conveyed to "X and Y for life to hold as joint tenants, remainder to X in fee simple." In this case, X and Y would take their joint life estates despite the fact that X also has a fee simple remainder. If, however, in this example the remainder had been conveyed to Z instead of X, and X subsequently bought Z's estate, this subsequent purchase by X would sever the joint tenancy for life X held with Y. The result would be that Y would hold a half-share in the property for life as tenant in common with X, and X's other half-share for life would merge[79] with his fee simple acquired from Z. In other words, X's subsequent purchase of the fee simple destroys the unity of interest that existed between X and Y

---

[74] Para. **[7.07]**, *ante.*

[75] *Ibid.*

[76] Para **[7.37]**, *post.*

[77] *Connolly v Connolly* (1866) 17 Ir Ch R 208; *Flynn v Flynn* [1930] IR 337.

[78] See *Re Hecker's Estate* Unrep, (HC, RI), 28 April 1994 (1993/248 Sp) (house devised to testatrix's four children subject to a right of residence in favour of one of them).

[79] On the doctrine of merger, see Ch 24, *post.*

with respect to the property.[80] It should be noted, however, that since the doctrine of merger nowadays is based upon the intention of the party in whom the two estates have vested,[81] it is presumably open to that party to argue that no merger was intended and so the joint tenancy and the right of survivorship remain operative.[82]

[7.26] It will have been noticed that, in the above example, X acquired an estate in the land different from the estate he held as joint tenant with Y. There may occur, however, another situation, eg, a conveyance "to X, Y and Z as joint tenants in fee simple" and then a release (in effect an alienation, see below) by X of his estate to Y.[83] The effect of this is that a tenancy in common arises as between the one-third share in the property Y has acquired from X, and which he now holds as tenant in common, and the other two-thirds he still holds with Z. But that other two-thirds of the property remains subject to the joint tenancy and is held by Y and Z as joint tenants.[84]

[7.27] Furthermore, one must, it seems, distinguish between a conveyance and a surrender of an interest in this context. In the case of a conveyance "to X for life, remainder to Y and Z as joint tenants in fee simple," if X conveys or transfers his estate to Y, the joint tenancy between Y and Z will be severed. If, however, X surrenders his interest to Y, this has the effect of extinguishing[85] that interest, so that the fee simple held jointly by Y and Z thereupon takes effect in possession, *but still subject to the joint tenancy.*[86]

(b) Alienation

[7.28] The courts have long-recognised that a joint tenancy will be severed if any one of the joint tenants alienates his interest in the property, or a part of his interest, by an *inter vivos* transaction.[87] The alienation had to be made *inter vivos* for the courts would not allow a will to defeat the right of survivorship.[88]

---

[80] The rule does not apply where statutory provisions suggest otherwise. See *Flynn v Flynn* [1930] IR 337 where it was held that a purchase of the fee simple in a farm by one joint tenant under the Land Purchase Acts and his registration as owner "subject to equities" (see para **[21.07]** *post*) made him a trustee of the estate holding for himself and the other tenant as joint tenants in equity.

[81] See para **[24.12]** *post*.

[82] See *Conolly v Conolly* (1867) IR 1 Eq 376, 383 (*per* Christian LJ). See also the discussion in Dowling, 'Severance of Joint Tenancies by Acquisition of a Further Interest' (1990) 41 NILQ 359.

[83] One joint tenant may subsequently release his interest but one may not disclaim the interest *ab initio* unless the other joint tenants become parties to the disclaimer, *Re Schar* [1951] Ch 280.

[84] Megarry and Wade, *The Law of Real Property* (5th ed, 1984), p 433.

[85] See Ch 24, *post*.

[86] See *Coke upon Littleton* (19th ed, 1832), 183a and 192a. This seems to be another example of the form of a transaction governing substantive rights, see para **[3.060]**, *ante*.

[87] See cases cited in fn 71, para **[7.22]**, *ante*. The statement in the text was adopted by McWilliam J in *Byrne v Byrne* Unrep, (HC, RI), 18 January 1980 (1978/402 Sp) (see *A Casebook on Irish Land Law* (1984), p 376). See also *Williams v Hensman* (1861) 1 J & H 546, at 557-8 (*per* Page-Wood V-C).

[88] Para **[7.04]**, *ante*.

[7.29] No severance occurs if all the joint tenants join together in the alienation,[89] but severance may occur by involuntary alienation, eg, by the vesting of one joint tenant's property in his trustee in bankruptcy or the Official Assignee.[90] A contract by one joint tenant to alienate has the effect of causing a severance in equity[91] until such time as the alienation at law is completed, eg, by execution of a deed of conveyance relating to land.[92]

[7.30] The effect of such an alienation is similar to that of acquisition of another interest. The alienee or purchaser of one joint tenant's interest holds that interest in the property as tenant in common as to that joint tenant's share, the other total share in the property being held in common by the other joint tenants, who still hold it as joint tenants *inter se*.

[7.31] A severance is also effected by a partial alienation, ie, the creation or transfer of a lesser interest in the property. However, it seems that the interest created or transferred must pass such rights in the property as are inconsistent with the right of survivorship. Thus it has been held that the creation of a life estate by a joint tenant will sever the joint tenancy,[93] as will the granting of a mortgage.[94] There has been some dispute amongst the authorities as to the effect of a lease granted by a joint tenant.[95] It seems to be settled now that, if the joint tenant of a lease for a term of years grants a sub-lease for a shorter term, this effects a severance.[96] What is, perhaps, not so clear is the position of a joint tenant in fee simple who grants a lease for a term of years. The majority view seems to be that this too effects a severance.[97] The creation of lesser interests, such as mere incumbrances, will not usually cause a severance, though the registration of a judgment mortgage against the interest of one joint tenant will sever the joint tenancy.[98] Thus it seems to be settled that a rentcharge, which grants no right of occupation of the land itself and which may be satisfied out of one joint tenant's share of the rents and profits issuing out of the land held in joint tenancy,[99] effects no severance.[100] The creation of a

---

[89] *Re Hayes' Estate* [1901] 1 IR 207, espec at 211 (per O'Connor LJ). See also *Byrne v Byrne*, fn 87, *supra*.

[90] *Morgan v Marquis* (1853) 9 Ex Ch 145. The court may sever a joint tenancy in lunacy proceedings, *O'Connell v Harrison* 71 IR 330, espec at 338 (*per* Kennedy CJ) (see *A Casebook on Irish Land Law* (1984), p 378).

[91] *Contra* where the contract is entered into by all the joint tenants, *Re Hayes' Estate* [1920] 1 IR 207; *Byrne v Byrne*, fn 89, *ante*.

[92] In such a case, all the joint tenants hold the whole legal estate in the property on trust as to the share to which one of them becomes entitled as tenant in common in equity, *Brown v Raindle* (1796) 3 Ves 256.

[93] See the discussion in Challis, *The Law of Real Property* (3rd ed), p 367.

[94] *York v Stone* (1709) 1 Salk 158; *Re Pollard's Estate* (1863) 3 De GJ & s 541.

[95] See, eg, Challis, fn 93, *supra*.

[96] *Connolly v Connolly* (1866) 17 Ir Ch R 208, espec at 223 (*per* Walsh MR).

[97] *Re Armstrong* [1920] IR 23. See also *Clerk v Clerk* (1694) 2 Vern 323; *Gould v Kemp* (1834) 2 My & K 304; *Cowper v Fletcher* (1865) 6 B & s 464. *Cf Harbin v Loby* (1629) Noy 157.

[98] *McIlroy v Edgar* (1881) 7 LR Ir 521. See generally, Ch 13, *post*.

[99] Megarry and Wade, *op cit*, p 431.

[100] Paras **[6.131]** *et seq*, *ante*.

charge, as opposed to a mortgage, was held recently in Northern Ireland to effect no severance because it does not confer a legal or equitable estate or interest in the chargee, but merely certain rights over the property charged.[101] This had major implications for the system of charging orders operating under the Judgments Enforcement (NI) Order 1981,[102] because Article 49 of that Order provides that such an order has "the like effect as a charge on that land created by the debtor in favour of the creditor".[103] This has now been modified by Article 50 of the Property (NI) Order 1997, which reads:

> The creation of a charge on the estate or estates of one or more joint tenants (but not all of them) causes (and always has caused) a severance of the joint tenancy.[104]

It should be noted that this provision applies to any charge and not just a charging order made under the 1981 Order. It would appear that doubts remain whether a mere charge will sever a joint tenancy in the Republic.[105]

(c) In Equity

[7.32] It has already been mentioned that a contract to alienate entered into by one of the joint tenants may effect a severance of the joint tenancy in equity.[106] Apart from this, there is no reason why the joint tenants together should not enter into a contract that thenceforward they should hold as tenants in common, and equity will give effect to such a contract.[107] Indeed, the joint tenants may not even formalise their agreement to that extent. There is ample authority in Ireland to the effect that equity will infer such an agreement from the joint tenants' conduct, eg, where they seem to have treated their interests in the property as severed over a substantial period of time.[108]

---

[101] *Northern Bank Ltd v Heggarty* Unrep (HC, RI), 8 February 1995. See para **[12.19]** *post*.

[102] See para **[13.183]** *et seq, post*.

[103] Thus Campbell J held in the *Heggarty* case that the Bank holding the charging order over one joint tenant's interest had no standing to apply for an order of sale under s 4 of the Partition Act 1868: see para **[7.36]** *post*.

[104] Article 48 entitles the owner of any charge on land held in co-ownership to apply for partition or a sale *in lieu* of partition as a "person interested": see para **[7.35]** *post*. Note that Articles 48-50 are among the first to be brought into force (on 1 September 1997): See Property (1997 Order) (Commencement No 1) Order 1997 (SR No 328).

[105] The Australian courts have doubted whether a mere charge effects a severance: see *Lyons v Lyons* [1967] VR 169.

[106] *Frewen v Relfe* (1787) 2 Bro CC 220 at 224 (*per* Lord Thurlow LC); *Gould v Kemp* (1834) 2 My & K 304.

[107] *Williams v Hensman* (1861) 1 J & H 546, at 557-8 (*per* Page-Wood VC).

[108] *Wilson v Bell* (1843) 5 Ir Eq R 501; *Roche v Sheridan* (1857) 2 Ir Jur (NS) 409; *Harris v Harris* (1868) IR 3 CL 294; *Re Wallis' Trusts* (1888) 23 LR Ir 460. See also *Coughlan v Barry* (1842) 2 Leg Rep 195. See also the discussion of how far an intention to sever can be evinced from the conduct of the joint tenants by the English Court of Appeal in *Burgess v Rawnsley* [1975] Ch 429 where Lord Denning MR took the view that a unilateral declaration by one joint tenant communicated to the other or others may be enough. *Cf Neilson-Jones v Fedden* [1975] Ch 222, at 231 (*per* Walton J: course of dealing must provide a basis of implying a mutual agreement). The courts in other jurisdictions have been reluctant to go as far as Lord Denning: see, eg, Australia (*Corin v Patton* (1990) 92 ALR 1) and Canada (*Re Sorensen and Sorenson* (1977) 30 DLR 3d 26).

(iv) Husband and Wife

[7.33] At common law, a husband and wife were treated as one person for many purposes and this gave rise to a number of legal consequences. One was the creation of a separate form of co-ownership known as a tenancy by the entireties, confined to the husband and wife situation.[109] This we shall discuss in detail later in this chapter.[110] For the moment, however, we are concerned with another consequence of the common law concept of a husband and wife constituting a single unit of ownership. This is that there seems to have arisen a rule of construction (and it is no more than that) that in a conveyance of property to a husband and wife and a third party, the husband and wife between them take one share only and the third party takes the other share.[111] This rule seems to apply whether a conveyance to the three parties was to them as joint tenants or tenants in common.[112] Thus a conveyance "to H and W and X in equal shares was held to create a tenancy in common as to one half-share held by H and W and the other half held by X.[113] However, the English courts have gone to great lengths to avoid application of this rule to particular cases and much seems to depend upon the precise wording of the conveyance.[114] In view of the nicety of the distinctions drawn sometimes by the English courts, it is questionable how far the Irish courts would follow their decisions and the matter must remain open in the Republic of Ireland until more authoritative guidance is given by the courts.[115] In Northern Ireland the matter has become academic because the rule of construction discussed here has now been abrogated by Article 13 of the Property (NI) Order 1978 (as recommended in the *Survey of the Land Law of Northern Ireland* (HMSO, 1971), paragraphs 151-52). Article 13 reads:

> A husband and wife shall, for all purposes of acquisition of any interest in property under a disposition made or coming into operation after the commencement of this Article, be treated as two persons.[116]

---

[109] Legislation in the latter half of the nineteenth and this century has gradually whittled away this common law concept, the latest of which is the Married Women's Status Act 1957 (RI), and the Law Reform (Husband and Wife) Act (NI) 1964.

[110] Para **[7.47]**, *post*.

[111] See the discussion of this rule in Megarry and Wade, *The Law of Real Property* (5th ed, 1984) pp 449-50. All the authorities cited there are English and there seems to be a paucity of Irish authority on this rule of construction. However, the English authorities are many and, at the very least, of persuasive authority on this side of the Irish Sea. See the *Survey of the Land Law of Northern Ireland* (HMSO, 1971), paras 151-3.

[112] *Re Wylde's Estate* (1852) 2 De GM & G 724; *Re March* (1884) 27 Ch D 166; *Warrington v Warrington* (1842) 2 Hare 54.

[113] *Re Wylde's Estate, op cit.*

[114] Especially the placing of the copulative word "and." See the examples given in Megarry and Wade, *op cit*, p 450.

[115] See *O'Hea v Slattery* [1895] 1 IR 7.

[116] As regards the Republic of Ireland, note should again be taken of the statutory encouragement of creation of a joint tenancy as between spouses in the family home contained in section 14 of the Family Home Protection Act 1976 (see para **[7.11]**, *ante*).

4. Determination of Joint Tenancies and Tenancies in Common

[7.34] Apart from determination of a joint tenancy by severance, which has the effect of converting it into a tenancy in common, a joint tenancy and a tenancy in common may be determined in other ways. These, unlike severance, involve the determination of the co-ownership of the property altogether. There are two main methods of determination: (i) partition and (ii) union in a sole tenant.

(i) Partition

[7.35] First, all the co-owners may voluntarily agree to put an end to their co-ownership and to partition the property in the manner they agree.[117] By statute, such a voluntary partition by joint tenants or tenants in common must be by deed.[118] If, however, the joint tenants or tenants in common could not agree on such a partition, there was no right at common law in any one of them to force a partition on the others.[119] Such a right was first introduced by a statute passed by the Irish Parliament in 1542,[120] which enabled a joint tenant or tenant in common to force a partition of the property on the other co-owners, whether or not it was sensible or convenient to have such a partition.[121] This position was improved considerably by the passing of the Partition Acts, 1868 and 1876, both of which applied to Ireland.

[7.36] These Acts gave the court power to order a sale of the property instead of physical partition, and to divide the proceeds amongst the co-owners in accordance with their shares.[122] The obvious situation where this power would be invoked would be

---

[117] *Clarke v Bodkin* (1851) 13 Ir Eq R 492.

[118] Real Property Act 1845, s 3. The repeal of this section so far as it related to the relation of landlord and tenant in Ireland, by Sched (B) of Deasy's Act 1860, expressly excluded from the repeal "partitions".

[119] *Cf* the position at common law of a coparcener, para **[7.45]**, *post*.

[120] 33 Hen 8, c 10 (Ir). The English equivalent legislation were the statutes 31 Hen 8, c 1 (1539) and 32 Hen 8, c 32 (1540). See also the amending 1697 statutes in Ireland (9 Will 3, c 12) and England (8 & 9 Will 3, c 31). The Irish statutes have since been repealed as obsolete, see the Statute Law Revision (Ireland) Act 1878, Statute Law Revision (Pre-Union Irish Statutes) Act 1962 (RI), and Statute Law Revision Act 1950. In *O'D v O'D* Unrep, (HC, RI), 18 November 1983 (1983/20 Cir App) (see *A Casebook on Irish Land Law* (1984), p 386). Murphy J expressed puzzlement at the repeal of the statute establishing the jurisdiction to force partition on the other co-owner. However, he proceeded to decide that case on the assumption that an inherent equitable jurisdiction to partition existed. In *F v F* [1987] ILRM 1 Barr J held that the right to partition was an "existing principle or rule of law or equity" preserved by s 2(1) of the Republic's 1962 Act, and a similar provision is to be found in s 1 of the 1950 Act which applies to NI. The Law Reform Commission recommended resolution of remaining doubt by restoration of the statutory power: see *Report on Land Law and Conveyancing Law: (1) General Proposals* (LRC 30-1989), paras 16-17. Note that power to make an order under the Partition Acts is conferred on the Republic's courts when granting decrees of judicial separation: see Family Law Act 1995, s 10(1)(e) (replacing s 16(f) of the Judicial Separation and Family Law Reform Act 1989: see Duncan and Scully, *Marriage Breakdown in Ireland: Law and Practice* (1990), pp 312-15. See also *CH v DGO'P* (1978) 109 ILTR 9.

[121] *Foster v Higgins* (1851) 6 Ir Jur (os) 409; *Tottenham v Molony* (1856) 2 Ir Jur (os) 88. See also *O'Sullivan v McSweeny* (1813) Dru *temp* Sug 213; *O'Hara v Strange* (1847) 11 Ir Eq R 262; *Herbert v Hedges* (1844) Ir Eq R 479; *St Leger v Ferguson* (1860) 10 Ir Ch R 488; *Re Foley's Estate* (1862) 7 Ir Jur (ns) 402.

[122] *Re Hawkesworth's Estate* (1878)1 LR Ir 179; *Re Martin's Estate* (1879) 3 LR Ir 255; *Re Balfour's Estate* (1887) 19 LR Ir 487; *Gingles v Magill* [1926] NI 234. See also *H v O* [1978] IR 194.

where the co-owners had held a single item of property, such as a house or other building, which could not be easily partitioned so as to give each co-owner a viable part. Several points should be noted about the jurisdiction conferred by the Partition Acts. First, a distinction is drawn between cases where the interest of the applicant for partition or sale,[123] or of the applicants collectively, comprises at least half the value of the property co-owned[124] and cases where it does not. In the case of the former the applicant is entitled to a direction for a sale unless the Court "sees good reason to the contrary".[125] In the other cases the applicant must establish circumstances justifying a sale *in lieu* of partition such as the nature of the property[126] or the number of interested parties, and convince the court that a sale "would be more beneficial for the parties interested" for it to exercise its discretion to order a sale.[127] In the Republic of Ireland the courts have been at pains to stress that where the property in question is a "family home" within the meaning of the Family Home Protection Act 1976, a court cannot exercise the jurisdiction so as to overreach any spouse's consent required under that Act.[128] Furthermore, even where such consent is not required, because the other spouse is a co-owner, the fact that the property is a family home is, nevertheless, an important factor to be taken into account by the court in exercising its discretion.[129] Secondly, it is not entirely clear what the parameters of the jurisdiction under the two provisions is, a matter which has come under consideration by the Irish courts recently in cases where one co-owner's interest has been mortgaged or charged and the mortgagee or chargee has invoked the jurisdiction to enforce its security against the other co-owner. For example, the suggestion that a court must order either partition or, if that is inappropriate or impracticable,[130] a sale[131] has been rejected on the basis that the jurisdiction confers a

---

[123] Note that, although the jurisdiction arises only in cases where previously a decree for partition might have been made, an application may be made for a sale without claiming partition: see 1876 Act, s 7.

[124] A somewhat odd interpretation was made by the Master in the NI case *Northern Bank Ltd v Adams* Unrep, 1 February 1996, where he held that a mortgage of a husband's half share in a house did not come within this provision because the value of the loan was well short of a half (loan of £10,000 secured on property worth £80,000). A mortgagee's interest attaches to the entirety of the estate or interest mortgaged: see the NI *Third Annual Survey of Property Law* (1996), pp 20-25.

[125] 1868 Act, s 4. The mere fact the property has fallen in value may not be a good reason: *Re Whitwell's Estate* (1887) 19 LR Ir 45, at 47-48 (*per* Monroe J); on the other hand, if partition is as easy as a sale and the application for the latter is "vindictive", this may be a good reason: *Re Langdale's Estate* (1871) IR 5 Eq 572, at 575-76 (*per* Lynch J). See also the discussion by Denham J where a family house within the Republic's Family Home Protection Act 1976 is involved: *First National Building Society v Ring* [1992] 1 IR 375. *Cf H v O* [1978] IR 194.

[126] *Turner v Morgan* (1803) 8 Ves 143, 11 Ves 157n.

[127] 1868 Act, s 3.

[128] *O'D v O'D* Unrep, (HC, RI), 18 November 1983 (1983/20 Cir App) (*Casebook on Irish Land Law* p 386); *L v L* Unrep, (HC, RI), 27 February 1984 (Cir App). See Pearce, 'The Right to Partition and Sale Between Co-Owners' (1987) 5 ILT 36; Mee, 'Partition and Sale of the Family Home' (1993) 15 DULJ 78.

[129] *First National Building Society v Ring* [1992] 1 IR 375.

[130] It will usually be so where a mortgagee is seeking to enforce security against a co-owner whose interest is not mortgaged: see *Tubman v Johnston* [1981] NI 53; *Northern Bank Ltd v Beattie* [1982] 18 NIJB; *Ulster Bank Ltd v Shanks* [1982] NI 143. *Cf H v O* [1978] IR 194.

[131] See Murray J in *Northern Bank Ltd v Beattie, supra* and Wallace 'Mortgagees and Possession' (1986) 37 NILQ 336, at 353-6.

wider discretion, including the power to refuse both applications.[132] Furthermore, the view has been taken that the court has a discretion, in cases where it is minded to order a sale, to postpone making an order pending enquiries about the feasibility of a sale[133] or to make the order but to postpone the date of its becoming effective.[134] Thirdly, the jurisdiction can be invoked only by a party or parties "interested" in the co-owned property. This clearly includes a mortgagee of a co-owner's interest,[135] including a judgment-mortgagee.[136] However, we saw earlier that doubts were expressed recently in Northern Ireland[137] as to whether it applied to a mere chargee, ie, a party who has only rights against the property as opposed to an estate or interest such as is conferred by a mortgage.[138] These doubts still remain in the Republic, but they have been resolved in Northern Ireland.[139] Article 48 of the Property (NI) Order 1997 provides that the owner of a charge[140] on land in co-ownership can apply for partition or a sale *in lieu* of partition under the Partition Acts and accordingly is to be treated as a "party interested". Lastly, in making an order for partition or a sale the court is to give "all necessary or proper consequential directions". It has long been settled that the courts will employ the principles of "equitable accounting" and make appropriate adjustments to ensure each co-owner is treated fairly.[141] Costs of a sale are usually borne out of the proceeds, but special costs incurred in respect of a particular co-owner may be ordered to be borne by his share.[142]

(ii) Union in a Sole Tenant

[7.37] It is axiomatic that co-ownership will determine once the property the subject of the co-ownership becomes vested in one only of the joint tenants or tenants in common. This may occur eventually in the case of a joint tenancy through the operation of the right of survivorship.[143] It will also occur if one of the joint tenants or tenants in common buys out the interests of the other co-owners. The method of transfer required in such a case varies according to whether the co-owners hold under a joint tenancy or tenancy in common.

---

[132] *O'D v O'D* Unrep (HC, RI), 18 November 1983 (1983/30 Cir App); *First National Building Society v Ring* [1992] 1 IR 375; *Northern Bank v Adams* (fn 124 *supra*).

[133] *First National Building Society* case *supra*.

[134] *Northern Bank v Adams supra*. This jurisdiction to impose a stay or supervision has been confirmed in NI by Article 49 of the Property (NI) Order 1997.

[135] *Ibid*.

[136] *Farrell v Donnelly* [1913] 1 IR 50; *First National Building Society* case *supra*.

[137] *Northern Bank Ltd v Heggarty* Unrep, (HC, RI) 8 February 1995.

[138] See para **[12.19]** *post*.

[139] They also applied to a charging order under the Judgments Enforcement legislation: see para **[7.31]** *ante*.

[140] Including a charging order under the Judgments Enforcement (NI) Order 1981. Note that Article 48 comes into force on 1 September 1997: see Property (1997 Order) (Commencement No 1) Order (NI) 1997 (SR No 328).

[141] See para **[7.07]** (a) *ante*. See also the order made by Denham J in the *First National Building Society* case, *supra*.

[142] *Re Mahoney's Estate* [1909] 1 IR 132. See also *H v O* [1978] IR 194.

[143] Para **[7.04]**, *ante*.

[7.38] A joint tenant's method of transfer is by way of release of his interest in the property[144] and any other purported transfer will be construed as a release.[145] This is significant for at least two reasons. First, a release, technically speaking, operates to extinguish an interest rather than to convey it, so words of limitation are not required.[146] Secondly, unlike a surrender,[147] it benefits only the party to whom it is made, so that in the case of three or more joint tenants, a release by one (A) to another (B) of his interest gives that one-third interest only to that other joint tenant (B). He (B) will remain joint tenant with the other joint tenants (C, D, etc.) in respect of the rest of the property (ie, excluding A's released share).[148] In England, a joint tenant was given the retrospective right to convey his interest to another joint tenant by an ordinary grant in 1925,[149] but there is no equivalent provision in the Republic of Ireland.[150]

[7.39] A tenant in common, however, cannot release his interest in the land to his co-tenants, though he may sell or transfer it. As one learned writer put it:

> "A tenancy in common, though it is an ownership only of an undivided share, is, for all practical purposes, a sole and several tenancy or ownership; and each tenant in common stands, towards his own undivided share, in the same relation that, if he were sole owner of the whole, he would bear towards the whole. And accordingly, one tenant in common must convey his share to another, by some assurance which is proper to convey an undivided hereditament; and he cannot convey by release."[151]

---

[144] See Challis, *The Law of Real Property* (3rd ed), pp 368-69.

[145] *Eustace v Scawen* (1624) Cro Jac 696; *Chetser v Willan* (1670) 2 Wms Saund 96. As to a disclaimer, see *Re Schar* [1951] Ch 280.

[146] *Coke upon Littleton* 193b.

[147] Para **[7.27]**, *ante*.

[148] *Coke upon Littleton* 193a.

[149] Law of Property Act 1925, s 72(4). The power of release was also preserved in the 1925 Act, see s 36(2).

[150] One was recommended for Northern Ireland by the *Survey of the Land Law of Northern Ireland* (HMSO 1971), Appendix B, Property Bill (NI), cl 93(3) and this recommendation was given effect to by Article 10(3) of the Property (NI) Order 1978 (see para **[3.020]**, fn 64, *ante*).

[151] Challis, *op cit*, pp 368-69. *Cf Beauman v Kinsella* (1859) 11 ICLR 249.

Part V

MORTGAGES

Chapter 12

MORTGAGES

I. NATURE

[12.01] The essential feature of a mortgage is the concept of *security*.[1] If a lender of money makes a loan without security he runs the risk of the borrower becoming insolvent and unable to repay anything more than a small fraction of what is owed. The lender's only remedy is to sue for his debt and, if the borrower has become bankrupt, to claim in the bankruptcy proceedings as an unsecured creditor over whom secured creditors will have priority.[2] This is obviously not a very satisfactory position to be in and so many lenders of money make it a practice to insist upon the borrower giving security for the loan. The giving of security usually involves the conferment on the lender of some claim against or interest in an item of property, so that, in the event of the borrower failing to, or becoming unable to, repay the loan, the lender may claim against that property in priority to other creditors.[3] The property may be land which is the traditional subject of a mortgage, or personal property, as it is common to use things like life insurance policies or shares in a company as security. Usually the security is a claim against some specific item of property, but this is not always the case, eg, it is possible to have a "floating charge" over company assets.[4] Since this book is concerned primarily with land law, the ensuing discussion will concentrate on mortgages of land.

---

1. See, generally on the law of mortgages, Kiely, *Principles of Equity as Applied in Ireland* (1936), Chs XVI and XVII. Also Coote, *Treatise on the Law of Mortgages* (9th ed, by Ramsbotham 1927), Fairest, *Mortgages* (1975); Fisher and Lightwood, *Law of Mortgages* (10th ed, by Tyler 1988): Waldock, *Law of Mortgages* (2nd ed, 1950). See also Jackson, 'The Need to Reform the English Law of Mortgages,' (1978) 94 LQR 571 and the English Law Commission's Report, *Transfer of Land - Land Mortgages* (Law Com No 204, 1991).
2. The subject of priorities is discussed in detail in para **[13.127]** *post*.
3. See Sheridan, *Rights in Security* (1974).
4. See *Industrial Development Authority v Moran* [1978] IR 159; *Kelly v McMahon Ltd* [1980] IR 347; *Crowley v Northern Bank Finance Corporation Ltd* [1981] IR 353; *Re Armagh Shoes Ltd* [1982] NI 59; *Re Keenan Brothers Ltd* [1985] ILRM 254; *Re Masser Ltd* [1986] IR 455. See also *Kreglinger v New Patagonia Meat and Cold Storage Co Ltd* [1914] AC 25; Courtney, *The Law of Private Companies* (1994), paras 3.074-75 and 14.040-65. Farrer, 'Floating Charges and Priorities' (1974) 38 Conv 315 and 'The Crystallisation of a Floating Charge' (1976) 40 Conv 397; Pennington, 'The Genesis of the Floating Charge' (1960) 23 MLR 630.

A. Historical Background

1. Common Law

[12.02] The earliest forms of mortgage recognised at common law seem to have been of two main kinds.[5] One form was for the borrower of money (mortgagor) to lease his land to the lender (mortgagee), who went into possession.[6] This lease was subject to a condition subsequent[7] to the effect that, if the mortgagor had not repaid the loan by the time the lease expired, the mortgagee's lease was enlarged into a fee simple.[8] If the income from the land was used to discharge the debt, the mortgage was called a *vivum vadium*, ie, a "live" pledge; if not, the mortgage was called a *mortuum vadium*, a "dead" pledge.[9] The other early form of mortgage was a conveyance of the fee simple in land by the mortgagor to the mortgagee, subject to a condition that the mortgagor could re-enter and determine the mortgagee's estate, provided the loan was repaid on the named date. Again the mortgagee entered into possession of the land. The crucial factor, however, was that such a condition was construed strictly at common law. If the mortgagor did not repay the loan by the set date, the mortgagee's estate in the land became absolute and the mortgagor found himself in the unfortunate position of being deprived of his land for ever, yet still liable for the debt. As we shall see, it was equity's great contribution to the law of mortgages to change this position.

[12.03] These early common law forms of mortgage remain the basis of the forms used for unregistered land in Ireland today.[10] The major difference that has developed over the centuries is that nowadays a mortgage by conveyance of the fee simple or assignment of a lease is subject to a proviso for redemption in favour of the mortgagor, whereby the mortgagee covenants to reconvey or reassign the property to the mortgagor on repayment of the loan. Similarly, a mortgage by demise is subject to a proviso for cesser of the lease or sub-lease on redemption by the mortgagor.

2. Equity

[12.04] The starting point of equity's approach to a mortgage transaction was to regard it as being in substance a secured loan only. To the extent that the mortgagee obtained an interest in property it should be a device to provide him with security and nothing more.

---

[5] See Holdsworth, *History of English Law*, Vol 3, espec pp 128-130. Also Barton, 'The Common Law Mortgage' (1967) 83 LQR 229; Chaplin, 'The Story of Mortgage Law' (1890) 4 HLR 1; Hazeltine, 'The Gage of Land in Medieval England,' (1904) 17 HLR 549 and (1905) 18 HLR 26. See also the fourteenth-century example digested at (1967) 18 NILQ 348.

[6] This does not conform with the modern form of mortgage and resembles a pledge, see para **[12.18]** *post*.

[7] See para **[4.048]** *ante*.

[8] There were doubts about the validity of such conditions, see Holdsworth, *op cit*, pp 129-30. See further on enlargement of leases, Chs 17 and 18 *post*.

[9] The early writers on the common law regarded this as the derivation of the word mortgage ie, mort (dead) and gage (pledge). see Glanville's *Tractatus de Legibus*, bk x 6 and 8; *Coke upon Littleton* (19th ed, 1832) Vol 2, 205a.

[10] See further para **[12.30]** *post*.

This approach led to the establishment of several principles which remain to this day cornerstones of the law of mortgages.

[12.05] Equity regarded it as inconsistent with the concept of security that the mortgagor should lose his property merely because he was late in repaying the loan. Once it was determined that the transaction was a mortgage, and in this equity looked to the intent and not the form,[11] equity would allow the mortgagor to redeem his mortgage, by repayment of the loan and any interest charged thereon, long after the date fixed for redemption. Equity's maxim was "once a mortgage, always a mortgage", and this would be enforced against any attempts to hinder the mortgagor in exercising his right to redeem, ie, by "clogs" on the equity of redemption.[12] This resulted in the following features of a modern form of mortgage becoming recognised. First, there is what is known as the *legal date for redemption.* This is the date, usually fixed as three or six months from the date of the mortgage, specified in the mortgage instrument for the repayment of the loan. At common law this date was crucial, but because of the attitude of equity it does not mean what it appears to say.[13] No one expects the mortgagor to repay the loan by that date and it is probably in neither party's interest that he should.[14] As we shall see, the main significance of this date today is that it governs the availability of certain of the mortgagee's remedies for realisation of his security in the event of something going wrong with the transaction.[15] Apart from that, both parties usually expect that the loan and any interest charged on it will be repaid over a substantial period of time, frequently running into decades. The second major feature of a mortgage is, therefore, the *equitable right to redeem,* which is exercisable by the mortgagor at any time after the legal date for redemption, though this exercise is always subject to general principles of equity, eg, "he who comes into equity, must come with clean hands".[16] This second feature of a mortgage is connected with, but must be distinguished from, a third, known as the mortgagor's *equity of redemption.* This is a larger concept than the particular right to redeem and consists of the sum total of the mortgagor's interest in the property which is the security for the loan.[17] It can best be described as ownership[18] of

---

[11] See *Goodman v Grierson* (1813) 2 Ba & B 274; *Balfe v Lord* (1842) 4 Ir Eq R 648. Also *Hughes v Glenny* (1841) Arm Mac & Og 387. Para **[3.060]**, *ante.*

[12] See, further, para **[13.088]** *et seq, post.*

[13] Maitland thus remarked: "That is the worst of our mortgage deed - owing to the action of equity, it is one long *suppressio veri* and *suggestio falsi." Equity* (rev ed, by Brunyate 1936), p 182. See also Lord Macnaghten in *Samuel v Jarrah Timber and Wood Paving Co Ltd* [1904] AC 323 at 326.

[14] See paras **[12.07]-[12.09]**, *post.*

[15] Paras **[13.026]** and **[13.050]**, *post.*

[16] Para **[3.058]**, *ante.* See the application of this maxim in the doctrine of consolidation of mortgages, para **[13.069]** *post.*

[17] In this context, the distinction between an equitable interest and a mere equity may again be applicable, though rarely, if ever, of practical significance since the equitable right to redeem is part of the equity of redemption and so at any point in time a mortgagor will not be forced to rely solely on the lesser of the two concepts.

[18] Commensurate, of course. with the interest in the property mortgaged, ie, freehold, leasehold, etc. See *Wrixon v Vize* (1842) 4 Ir Eq R 463.

the property subject only to the rights of the mortgagee.[19] While at common law the mortgagee was regarded as owner of the property, in equity the mortgagor is regarded as owner and the mortgagee as an incumbrancer only. This equity of redemption, sometimes rather loosely referred to as the mortgagor's "equity" in the property,[20] is a valuable interest in property which can be sold, demised or mortgaged, like any other item of property.[21] Furthermore, it is usually quite easy to put a monetary value upon it, especially in days of rising property values in Dublin. For example, if in 1990 X bought a house[22] for IR£100,000 and borrowed IR£80,000 from a bank or building society to help pay for it, he immediately had an equity in the house of about IR£20,000 in value. By 1995 the market value of the house might have risen to IR£150,000, so that by then X had an asset worth IR£150,000 in respect of which the liabilities amounted to rather less than IR£80,000 (assuming he had been repaying capital as well as interest charged on the original loan[23]). Thus his equity in the house had increased in value from IR£20,000 to well over IR£70,000 (ie the 1995 market value of IR£150,000 less the outstanding debt of something less than the IR£80,000 originally borrowed) and, if he had sold his house, he could have expected to make a profit of roughly this amount. Instead of selling his house, he might have preferred to make improvements to it and to pay for these by borrowing more money through a second mortgage on the house. Assuming market prices at the very least hold steady, the house will be adequate security for further loans up to the value of the difference between the market value of the house and the amounts of capital outstanding on existing secured loans. At this point it may be useful to give a few illustrations of the operation of a modern mortgage.

B. Modern Illustrations

[12.06] From the outset it should be emphasised that there are two main aspects to be considered with respect to a mortgage. One may be described as the financial aspect and the other as the conveyancing aspect. By tradition it is the latter which is of primary concern to the lawyer, yet in recent years it has become more common for solicitors to widen their sphere of operation and to be prepared to give their clients what is essentially advice on financial matters. The technical conveyancing aspect of a mortgage transaction is also the aspect with which this book is primarily concerned, but it is useful in considering this to keep in mind the financial aspect which will, after all, be of more concern to the client. This should become clear if we take first what is, perhaps, the most common example of a mortgage, namely the purchase of a house as the private residence of the mortgagor.

---

[19] See *Blake v Foster* (1813) 2 Ba & B 387; *Burrowes v Molloy* (1845) 2 Jo & Lat 521.

[20] See fn 17, *supra*.

[21] See *Maxwell v Tipping* [1903] 1 IR 498. Note also that the value of the "equity" will fluctuate for a variety of reasons, as repayments and future borrowings secured by the same mortgage may be made: see the remarks of Barron J and, on appeal, Walsh J in *Bank of Ireland v Purcell* [1989] IR 327, at 330-31 and 334 quoted in para **[12.45]** *post*.

[22] The Republic has not suffered the property slump which afflicted UK in 1990s.

[23] Some mortgage loan arrangements postpone repayment of the capital, as opposed to the interest charged on the loan, until the end of the mortgage term, say, 25 years: see para **[12.09]** *post*.

1. House Purchase

[12.07] Let us consider again the example given earlier of X who in 1990 bought a house, the purchase price of which then was IR£100,000, but which is now worth, say, IR£150,000 and which X is negotiating to sell to Y at that price. Assuming that Y does not have the cash to pay the full purchase price, which is usually the case, he will need to borrow money from an institution willing to lend it.[24] In view of the substantial amount of money Y is likely to want to borrow, the repayment of the loan will have to be spread over a substantial period of years.[25] The period for repayment of a house-purchase mortgage can be anything from 15-30 years (and sometimes even longer in special cases), and this generally rules out borrowing from institutions which specialise in short-term lending, eg, until recent times, when they had a change of policy, banks.[26] Fortunately, there are institutions which specialise in such long-term lending, particularly when it relates to house purchase, eg, building societies.[27] Y will probably find that he is required by X's solicitor or estate agent to pay a deposit on the house, usually 10 per cent of the purchase price (ie, IR£15,000). Apart from that, it is comparatively rare for institutions such as banks and building societies to be willing to lend the full 100 per cent of the purchase price. A common practice is to adopt a rough rule-of-thumb such as one to the effect that normally 80 per cent of the price[28] only can

---

[24] Of course, if, as is often the case, Y is not a "first-time" buyer and is selling his existing house at the same time, he may make a profit from that (ie he is realising an "equity" in it, see para **[12.05]** *ante*) because the selling price exceeds any outstanding loans secured on it and other incidental costs and expenses of the sale. The profit, or a proportion of it, can be put towards the purchase of X's house and thereby reduce the amount to be borrowed for that purchase.

[25] See further on "instalment" mortgages, *Re Nepean's Settled Estate* [1900] 1 IR 298; *Re Strabane RDC* [1910] 1 IR 135; *Re Gore Booth's Estate* [1910] 1 IR 139: *Carlow CC v O'Connor* [1952] Ir Jur Rep 5.

[26] That does not mean that Y's bank may not have another, but related, part to play in the transaction. If Y is also, as is common, selling his present residence, he may be dependent upon the profit he makes on that sale to meet the deposit required for the purchase of X's house or the difference between the price of X's house and the loan he is seeking for its purchase, which sums incidentally may not be the same. But he may not have that profit or surplus in his hands at the date he is required to pay the deposit on X's house or, indeed, even when he is required to complete the purchase of X's house, in which case he will need a "bridging" loan, ie a loan to bridge the gap between the date for payment of the deposit or completion and the date when the sale of his present house is completed and he receives the surplus from that sale (ie, after redemption of his mortgage, if any, on that house, etc). Bridging loans, which are usually comparatively short-term loans, are exactly the sort of loans banks were traditionally expert in arranging.

[27] Whose activities are largely regulated by statute: for the Republic of Ireland, see Building Societies Acts 1874, 1877, 1884, 1894 and Building Societies Act 1942, which were consolidated in the Building Societies Act 1976: see *Rafferty v Crowley* [1984] ILRM 350 (see now Building Societies (Amendment) Act 1983, s 1); the 1976 Act, as amended, has since been replaced by the Building Societies Act 1989. Also *Provincial Building Society v Brown* [1950] NI 163; *Martin v Irish Industrial Benefit Building Society* [1960] Ir Jur Rep 42.

[28] To be strictly accurate, a lending institution usually bases its calculations not on the price the purchaser/borrower is paying but on the valuation of the property made by its surveyor or valuer: see Wylie, *Irish Conveyancing Law* (2nd ed, 1996), para 4.23. Note that in the Republic the applicant for a housing loan is entitled to a copy of the valuation report and no valuation charge is payable if the loan is refused: Consumer Credit Act 1995, s 123.

be borrowed and, if more than that is to be lent to bring, say, the amount borrowed up to 90 or 95 per cent, the society may require the borrower to take out a "mortgage indemnity" insurance policy to cover the excess amount lent.[29] Alternatively, if the bank or building society refuses to advance more than, say, 80 per cent of the purchase price, Y may be able to obtain a further "topping-up" loan which may be secured on the same house by a second mortgage. Such a loan is sometimes advanced by employers under a special scheme providing "fringe-benefits" for employees, though some of the larger employers even have full-blown mortgage schemes, under which they are willing not only to advance anything up to 100 per cent of the purchase price, but to do so at very favourable rates of interest. Finally, there is one further consideration to be borne in mind by Y and that is that the lending institution will obviously take into account Y's ability to keep up regular repayments over a substantial period of time in calculating exactly how much money it is prepared to lend him.[30] Here again many institutions adopt a rule-of-thumb whereby they are willing to lend a total amount of only so many times the borrower's gross annual earnings, eg, two-and-a-half or three times his earnings.[31] Thus, if Y were currently earning a gross income of IR£30,000 per annum, he might find it difficult to persuade many institutions to lend him more than a total of IR£75,000 and, depending upon a variety of circumstances, in particular the general state of the loan market at the time, might well find it impossible to persuade any institution to lend even up to that amount.

[12.08] Assuming that Y succeeds in arranging a mortgage loan of the amount he needs to complete the purchase of X's house, let us say, IR£75,000 from a bank or building society, he, then, has to agree with the bank or society how this is to be repaid. Normally, lending institutions charge interest on the capital sum lent, which interest is charged by a rate calculated on an annual basis. Owing to difficulties facing most economies and world markets in modern times, which has resulted in fluctuating interest rates in the money markets of most developed countries, it is rare nowadays for the rate of interest to be fixed for the duration of the mortgage period, say, 25 years in the case of

---

[29] Ie, this provides the society with an indemnity against loss should it later have to realise its security, perhaps by selling the house, and find that the house's value has by then dropped below the amount borrowed and still outstanding, because this was in excess of the 80% normally lent. An indemnity policy should not be confused with a "mortgage protection" insurance policy, which is a life insurance policy providing the borrower with cover for the amount borrowed, so that, in the event of the borrower dying before the mortgage is paid off, the insurance company will thereupon pay off the balance outstanding and leave the house discharged from the mortgage. Such a life policy will usually provide cover for the fixed term of the mortgage only and so is relatively cheap, and will be assigned to the lending institution until the mortgage is paid off: see Trainor, 'Assignability of Life Policies as Security for Bankers' Advances - A Security More Apparent than Real?' (1994) CLP 127. Note also the statutory duty imposed on the lending institutions by s 126 of the Republic's Consumer Credit Act 1995 to arrange such insurance in respect of properties intended for use as the principal residence of the borrower or his dependants.

[30] Other matters which may be taken into consideration are such things as the age, state of repair and title (eg, freehold or leasehold and, if the latter, the term of years remaining on the lease) of the property which is going to be the lender's security.

[31] Apart from this, as mentioned earlier, a lending institution's offer of a loan will usually be based on its valuation of the property and not the purchase price.

Y.[32] The result is that over the period of the mortgage Y may find that the rate of interest charged on his loan varies from year to year. The standard repayment mortgage will require Y to make regular payments, usually monthly, to the bank or building society over the 25-year term of the mortgage. Each payment is usually a composite amount representing, partly, repayment of some of the capital originally borrowed and, partly, payment of some of the interest charged on that capital.[33] The result will be, of course, that if Y's mortgage runs for its full term of 25 years, he will have paid to the building society considerably more than IR£75,000, but he will at least have some consolation that with modern inflation and the steady fall in the value of money, the real cost of his mortgage will decrease as the years go by, while the value of the house may increase very substantially, depending upon the performance of the property market.[34]

[12.09] A standard repayment mortgage (involving payments of both capital borrowed and interest charged on the loan) is not the only kind of mortgage available for someone in Y's position. For example, Y could instead arrange what is usually called an "endowment" mortgage. This is a mortgage linked to a life-endowment insurance policy.[35] The usual procedure is for Y to borrow the capital sum, IR£75,000 in our example, from a bank or building society and, in addition, to take out a life-endowment insurance policy with an insurance company. This insurance policy, as the name implies, combines the elements of life insurance, ie, payment of a guaranteed sum on the insured's death, and of endowment, ie, payment of a guaranteed sum on a specified future date. In Y's case the sum in question would be IR£75,000, so that the insurance company would undertake to pay IR£75,000 in 25 years' time (ie, at the end of the mortgage term) or on Y's death, if this occurs before the 25 years are up (thereby introducing mortgage protection of Y's successors). Because the building society is thereby guaranteed payment of its capital, it will require Y to pay during the mortgage term only the interest charged on the capital, so that, in this sort of mortgage, Y pays interest (again usually by monthly instalments) to the bank or building society, in respect of which he may obtain tax relief, and premiums to the insurance company. However, even allowing for any tax relief, it is questionable whether such a mortgage

---

[32] Fixed rates, usually slightly higher than the going rate, are sometimes available for relatively short periods, but rarely for more than five years at a time. In the Republic no redemption fee is payable on early discharge of a housing loan, but an exception to this rule is made for certain fixed interest loans: see Consumer Credit Act 1995, s 121 and paras **[13.088]** and **[13.125]** *post*.

[33] In fact, often due to the way some institutions do their accounting, in the early years of a standard repayment mortgage the payments represent largely payments of interest and this may be significant where the borrower is entitled to income tax relief on the interest charged on the mortgage loan. It will have the effect of reducing the real cost of the mortgage in the early years, which may be a vital factor for a young married couple struggling to make ends meet at the start of the marriage.

[34] Though in a sense it can be argued that there is no real increase in that, if Y decides to realise his "profit", which is due to the rise in property values, by selling his house, he will find that any new house he buys will have similarly risen in value because of factors which affect the property market generally.

[35] It should not be confused with a mortgage protection insurance policy, see fn 29, para **[12.07]**, *ante*. See Goodbody, 'The Right Type of Mortgage', Law Society *Gazette* (RI), March 1993, p 55.

scheme will work out any cheaper than a standard repayment mortgage and, for this reason, such schemes are usually adopted only where the endowment insurance policy is a "with-profits" one. Under such a policy, higher premiums will be charged than in the case of a "without-profits" policy, but, in return for these, the policy-holder is allowed to participate in the profits made by the insurance company on its investments and these profits are accumulated and added to the guaranteed endowment sum payable at the end of the policy. Thus, in Y's case, provided his insurance company has a successful investment record over the 25 years of his mortgage term,[36] not only will he have the IR£75,000 capital owed to the building society paid off at the end of the 25 years, he will also receive an additional lump sum representing his share of the accumulated profits of the company over that 25 years, and sometimes a terminal bonus which represents his share of the increase in capital value of the company's investments. His share of the accumulated profits could be very large indeed and the principal attraction is that it is a saving built up from payments in respect of which the saver may have received substantial tax relief. However, there is no doubt that such a mortgage involves a higher cost than a standard repayment mortgage and the borrower will need to seek expert advice on which scheme is more suitable for him. It will often require careful calculation in particular cases whether it is more beneficial to choose the cheaper scheme with minimum future benefits or the expensive scheme with maximum future benefits.[37]

2. Consumer Credit

[12.10] The history of inflation during this century has indicated that land and buildings are one of the very few investments likely to keep pace with, and sometimes outstrip, the general rise in the cost of living. The result has been that there has been every encouragement for those fortunate enough to have made such an investment, even if it is the family residence only, to maximise its financial potential, especially in terms of security for credit or borrowing transactions. As we pointed out earlier in this chapter, many a house "owner" has been pleasantly surprised by the growth of his "equity" in his house and has found sometimes that its value has even risen well above the existing debt outstanding on the property under its current first mortgage. The temptation has thus arisen to use this equity for further borrowing, which has not always been confined to what are sometimes referred to as house improvements, eg, building extensions to the house or installation of major capital items like central heating, to cover the cost of which many building societies are willing to lend additional money, since they increase

---

[36] There is always an element of risk involved here and this indicates the sort of financial advice that Y may need and which more and more solicitors are becoming skilled in giving. Note the warning which must be given to borrowers taking out an endowment housing loan set out in s 133 of the Republic's Consumer Credit Act 1995.

[37] See again Goodbody, fn 35 *supra*. There are also available variations on the "endowment" scheme, such as "unit-linked" and "pension-linked" schemes, where again the essential feature is that there is an expectation that a lump sum will become payable at a future date sufficient to pay off the capital borrowed.

the value of the security for both the original loan and the additional loan. Sometimes, however, owners of houses subject to a mortgage have in the past been tempted to use the equity as security for borrowing as an alternative to consumer credit arranged through transactions like hire-purchase, and the object has been to raise money for consumer goods like new cars or yachts. This has, on occasion, resulted in an increase in second mortgage borrowing and in England there was much controversy over the activities of several second-mortgage companies,[38] some of whom charged exorbitant rates of interest and, then, ran into considerable liquidity problems. Fortunately, there has been little evidence of similar controversy in Ireland and it is to be hoped that any similar development will be strictly controlled.[39] The dangers of unrestricted and uncontrolled second mortgage schemes have become so apparent now as a result of the English experience that serious consideration, and, above all, expert advice, ought to be taken before a commitment to a second mortgage is entered into.

3. Property Development

[12.11] Use of mortgage facilities plays a vital role in property investment and development. Few developers nowadays can afford to pay cash for development sites or properties lest their future development or expansion will be hampered by a lack of capital. Most developers prefer to utilise the mortgage potential of their properties and to get capital loans for development of existing properties, or even for more speculative ventures, by putting down deposits on other properties. The interest charged on such mortgage loans can generally be set against profits and so a policy of "high gearing" is pursued, ie, as properties increase in value, further loans on their security are taken out to buy more properties, and so on. Sometimes the practice is adopted, eg, in respect of blocks of office premises, of revaluing the property, raising a new loan on the new value, paying off the old loan and using the difference as fresh capital.[40]

---

[38] Sometimes referred to as "secondary" banks (ie, operating outside the sphere of the central clearing banks), these companies attempted to avoid regulation by the Moneylenders Acts (see the Republic's 1933 Act and the NI Acts of 1933 and 1969). See the discussion in the English Crowther Committee *Report on Consumer Credit* (1971, Cmnd. 4596). See also *Premor Ltd v Shaw Bros* [1964] 1 WLR 978; *UDT Ltd v Kirkwood* [1966] 2 QB 431. And now for NI, the Consumer Credit Act 1974 (UK). See also Adams, 'Mortgages and the Consumer Credit Act 1974' (1975) 39 Conv 94 and Bright and Bright, 'Unfair Terms in Land Contracts' (1995) 111 LQR 655. *Cf* the Republic's Consumer Credit Act 1995; Elliot, 'Housing Loans under the Consumer Credit Act 1995' (1996) CLP 195.

[39] In NI the UK Consumer Credit Act 1974 introduced some limited controls over mortgages (see paras **[13.021]** and **[13.094]** *post*), but the Republic's Consumer Credit Act 1995 has a wider application to "housing loans" (in this respect it goes further then the EC Consumer Credit Directives 1986 (87/102/EEC) and 1990 (90/88/EEC). See the articles cited in fn 38 *supra*.

[40] *Cf* "sale and lease-back" operations, whereby the property owner sells the property for a capital sum but on the condition that the purchaser grants a lease-back to the vendor, which provides the vendor with fresh capital, but leaves him with an interest in the property. See the discussion in (1971) 68 L Soc Gaz 346: (1971); 115 Sol Jo 87; (1972) 122 New LJ 429.

4. Companies

[12.12] Companies frequently borrow money for their activities, usually under express powers of borrowing in the memorandum and articles of association.[41] This is usually done by issuing debentures, which may or may not be charged on the company's assets and which are a form of investment like shares.[42] Debentures may be secured by a fixed charge on some specified company property or by a general charge on all or some of the company's lands, present and future.[43] Alternatively, what is known as a "floating" charge on some or all of the company's assets may be created. This form of security, as the name suggests, floats over all the company's assets, but does not attach to any of them until it "crystallises". The advantage of such a charge is that the company is free to use its assets in the ordinary course of business so long as the charge remains floating. The charge will not crystallise until some default is made by the company on the charge or steps are taken to enforce the security.[44]

5. Informal

[12.13] Perhaps one of the most common forms of mortgage in Ireland is the informal mortgage created by deposit of title documents.[45] The Irish banks have long facilitated this method of providing security for an overdraft or other type of bank loan. All the bank customer has to do is to lodge with his bank manager the title documents relating to some item of property, eg, the title deeds or land certificate[46] relating to land or an insurance policy.[47] There need be no written agreement or any other formality other than

---

[41] See, generally, Keane, *Company Law in the Republic of Ireland* (2nd ed, 1991); Courtney, *The Law of Private Companies* (1994).

[42] And are maintained on a company register and transferable like shares. See *Alexander Hull & Co Ltd v O'Carroll Kent & Co Ltd* (1955) 89 ILTR 70; *Re O'Carroll Kent Ltd* (1955) 89 ILTR 72; *Re White & Shannon Ltd* [1965] NI 15; *United Bars Ltd v Revenue Commissioners* [1991] I IR 396; *Jackson v Lombard and Ulster Banking Ltd* [1992] 1 IR 94; *Re Wogan's (Drogheda) Ltd* [1993] 1 IR 157. See generally, Keane, *Company Law in the Republic of Ireland* (2nd ed, 1991), Ch 21; Courtney, *The Law of Private Companies* (1994), Ch 14. For an early example, see *Norman v Reid* (1846) 10 Ir LR 207.

[43] Frequently such a general charge is created as additional security to a fixed charge on a particular asset.

[44] See *Halpin v Cremin* [1954] IR 19; *Re Daniel Murphy Ltd* [1964] IR 1; *Lynch v Ardmore Studios (Ireland) Ltd* [1963] IR 133; *Re Interview Ltd* [1975] IR 382; *Murphy v Revenue Commissioners* [1976] IR 101; *Industrial Development Authority v Moran* [1978] IR 159; *Kelly v McMahon Ltd* [1980] IR 347; *Crowley v Northern Bank Finance Corporation Ltd* [1981] IR 353; *Re Armagh Shoes Ltd* [1982] NI 59; *Re Keenan Brothers Ltd* [1985] ILRM 254; *Re Tullow Engineering (Holdings) Ltd* [1990] 1 IR 452; *Smurfit Paribas Bank Ltd v AAB Export Finance Ltd (No 2)* [1992] 2 IR 19; *Re Holidair Ltd* [1994] 1 IR 416; *Re Manning Furniture Ltd* [1996] 1 ILRM 13. See also *Kreglinger v New Patagonia Meat and Cold Storage Co Ltd* [1914] AC 25.

[45] See further, para **[12.43]** *post*.

[46] Depending upon whether or not the title to the land is registered, see Ch 21, *post*. In the case of registered land, where there is a first registered charge on the property, a second, informal mortgage can be created by deposit of the charge certificate, see para **[12.29]**, *post*.

[47] Or share certificates, see *Dunster v Lord Glengall* (1853) 3 Ir Ch R 47; *Dunne v Hibernian Bank* (1868) IR 2 Eq 82; *Connolly v Munster Bank* (1887) 19 LR Ir 119.

the deposit of the documents and it is the attractions of speed, efficiency, informality and secrecy (except in the case of companies) which seem to have led to the popularity of such arrangements with the Irish people.[48]

C. Similar Concepts

[12.14] Before considering in detail the technical law of mortgages, it may be useful also to compare briefly with mortgages similar, and, in some cases, related, concepts. Only some of these concepts will be discussed in more detail later in this and the next chapter. Furthermore, it must be emphasised that it is a matter of construction in each particular case as to whether or not the transaction in question amounts to a mortgage. On a question of this kind, equity always looks to the intent and not to the form of any instrument executed and what at first sight may appear to be a sale of property, whether conditional or, even, outright, may nevertheless be construed as a mortgage.[49]

1. Lien

[12.15] A lien is a concept which has been recognised at common law and in equity.[50] A common law lien confers on the holder a mere right of retention of another person's property until such time as a debt is paid, eg, the right of a garage proprietor to retain a car repaired by him until its owner pays the repair bill.[51] Such a common law lien gives the holder no right (in the absence of a contractual or statutory provision) to sell the property retained or to deal with it in any other way.[52] In this respect, as we shall see, there is a marked difference between a common law lien and a mortgage.[53] Furthermore,

---

[48] See the Lowry Committee's *Report on Registration of Title to Land in Northern Ireland* (Cmd 512 1967), paras 93-6: Corscadden, 'Deposit of Title Deeds' (1953) 55 JIBI 253; Delany, 'Company Shares as Security for Banker's Advances' (1960) 62 JIBI 263; Greene, 'Law Relating to Leaseholds as security for Bank Advances' (1963) 65 JIBI 123. Also Holden, *Securities for Bankers' Advances* (5th ed 1971).

[49] See the discussion of the principles of construction, including the use of extrinsic evidence to establish the parties' intention. in *Goodman v Grierson* (1813) 2 BA & B 274; *Taylor v Emerson* (1843) 4 Dr & War 117; *Fee v Cobine* (1847) 11 Ir Eq R 406; *Murphy v Taylor* (1850) 1 Ir Ch R 92; *Re De Freyne's Contract* (1871) 5 ILTR 193; *O'Reilly v O'Donoghue* (1875)1 R 10 Eq 73, *Crone v Hegarty* (1879) 3 LR Ir 50.

[50] See Bell, *Modern Law of Personal Property in England and Ireland* (1989), p 138 *et seq*.

[51] See *Green v All Motors Ltd* [1917] 1 KB 625. And see *re* a horse stable-keeper, *Lee v Irwin* (1852) 4 Ir Jur (os) 372 and a shipowner, *Drivar v White* (1820) Rowe 207; *The Princess Royal* (1859) 5 Ir Jur (ns) 74; *Belfast Harbour Commrs v Lawther* (1866) 17 Ir Ch R 54. Also Hall, *Possessory Liens in English Law* (1917); Price, *Law of Maritime Liens* (1940); Sheridan, *Rights in Security* (1974), Chs 10 and 11. *Cf re* a claim by auditors to a lien over company books and documents, *Re JJ Hopkins & Co Ltd* (1959) 93 ILTR 32 and by a forwarding agent over goods for shipping and bills of lading *Essfood Eksportlagtiernes Sallgsforening v Crown Shipping (Ir) Ltd* [1991] ILRM 97. Note that a solicitor has a lien at common law in respect of unpaid fees over his client's documents still in the solicitor's possession: *Re Kavanagh Ltd* [1952] Ir Jur Rep 38; *Ring v Kennedy* Unrep, (HC, RI), 18 July 1997 (1997/71 Sp). This does not apply, however, to title documents held on accountable receipt for the client's lending institution: see *Re Galdan Properties Ltd* [1988] IR 213; Wylie, *Irish Conveyancing Law* (2nd ed, 1996), para 20.50 and para 12.17 *infra*.

[52] *Mulliner v Florence* (1878) 3 QBD 484.

[53] Ch 13 *post*.

if the holder of the lien parts with possession of the property to the debtor or his agent, or to anyone other than his own agent, it is lost.[54] In short, the "security" for the debt is dependent entirely upon the creditor's possession of the property and this too is a point of difference from a modern mortgage.

[12.16] In equity a lien arises by operation of law in the sense that, in certain circumstances, general principles of equity require the enforcement of a lien in the form of a charge against property. Because it arises by operation of law such a lien differs from a mortgage which arises by agreement between the mortgagor and the mortgagee.[55] An example of an equitable lien is a vendor's lien for unpaid purchase money, ie, a vendor who conveys land before he has been paid the full purchase price has a lien on the land for the unpaid balance.[56] Such a lien does not entitle the vendor to claim possession of the land,[57] but it does allow him to apply to the court for a declaration of a charge[58] and, enforcement of this by an order for sale[59] of the property, so that he can be recouped out of the proceeds of sale.[60]

[12.17] Finally it should be noted that certain bodies and persons have liens on property created by statute, in which case, of course, the liens are governed by the precise terms of the statute in question. Thus a solicitor has a common law lien over his client's

---

[54] *Pennington v Reliance Motor Works Ltd* [1923] I KB 127. See also the *Essfood* case fn 51 *supra*.

[55] Paras **[12.24]** *et seq*, *post*. See further Durfee, 'Lien or Equitable Theory of Mortgage: Some Generalisations' (1912) 10 Mich L Rev 587; 'Lien Theory of Mortgage; Two Crucial Problems' (1913) 11 Mich L Rev 495. *Cf*, however, the lien which is sometimes said to arise where an equitable mortgage is created by deposit of title documents: see para **[12.45]** *post*.

[56] *Richardson v McCausland* (1817) Beat 457; *Stuart v Ferguson* (1832) Hayes 452; *Munster and Leinster Bank Ltd v McGlasham* [1937] IR 525; *Mackreth v Symmons* (1808) 15 Ves 329. See also *Eyre v Sadlier* (1863) 14 Ir Ch R 119; (1863) 15 Ir Ch R 1. In effect this reverses the normal position of the vendor being construed in equity as constructive trustee of the land (subject to a contract for sale) for the purchaser; here the purchaser is treated as trustee for the vendor for the amount of unpaid purchase money. See para **[9.061]**, *ante*. It also seems that, where a purchaser pays the purchase money before the vendor conveys the land to him, the purchaser has a similar lien on the land for the return of his purchase money, see *Rose v Watson* (1864) 10 HLC 672. Also *Woods v Martin* (1860) 11 Ir Ch R 148. *Cf* in respect of a pre-contract deposit *Re Barratt Apartments Ltd* [1985] IR 350. See, generally, Wylie, *Irish Conveyancing Law* (2nd ed, 1996), paras 12.15-17 and 12.44.

[57] *Cf* a mortgagee's right to possession, para **[13.042]**, *post*. However, it seems that the vendor's lien for unpaid purchase money arises as soon as the contract for sale of the land is entered into, so that his lien does entitle him to retain possession in the same way that a creditor can at common law, see *Shaw v Foster* (1872) LR 5 HL 321; *Re Birmingham* [1959] Ch 523. Note that the lien may be regarded as relinquished if, eg, some other security for the unpaid purchase price is put in place: see *Re Aluminium Shop Fronts Ltd* [1987] IR 419.

[58] See further on charges, para **[12.47]**, *post*. Also *Croly v O'Callaghan* (1842) 5 Ir Eq R 25.

[59] *Cf* a mortgagee's power of sale, para **[13.022]** *post*.

[60] The purchaser's lender may have a lien by way of subrogation in respect of money advanced for the purchase: see *Bank of Ireland Finance Ltd v Daly* [1978] IR 79; *cf Re Farm Fresh Frozen Foods Ltd* [1980] IR 131 and *Highland Finance Ireland Ltd v Sacred Heart College of Agriculture Ltd* [1997] 2 ILRM 87.

documents for his costs,[61] but has a statutory right to apply to the court for a charging order on property recovered or preserved in litigation.[62] It was emphasised by the Republic's Supreme Court in *Re Galdan Properties Ltd*[63] that the solicitor's lien is confined to his client's documents and does not extend, eg, to the title deeds relating to his property which had been lodged with a lending institution as part of the security for their mortgage loan[64] and which were released to the solicitor on the usual accountable receipt to enable the solicitor to carry out a sale of the property.[65] In such circumstances the solicitor holds[66] the deeds not as agent for his client but rather as a trustee for the lending institution.[67]

2. Pledge

[12.18] A pledge is a transaction whereby chattels are given in possession as security for a loan, eg, by way of pawn to a pawnbroker. Pawnbrokers' activities are now controlled and regulated in the Republic of Ireland by the Pawnbrokers Act 1964, as amended by the Consumer Credit Act 1995, and in Northern Ireland by the UK Consumer Credit Act 1974.[68] Apart from the fact that a pledge is confined to chattels,[69] another difference from a mortgage is that the pledgee (lender) obtains no ownership of the chattel pledged.[70] He does obtain possession whereas under a mortgage the borrower usually retains possession until the lender decides to exercise his right to possession.

---

[61] *Blunden v Desart* (1842) 5 Ir Eq R 221, *Molesworth v Robbins* (1845) 8 Ir Eq R 223; *Re Bayly's Estate* (1861) 12 Ir Ch R 315. The client is entitled to return of his documents once he has paid the solicitor: see *Ring v Kennedy* Unrep, (HC, RI), 18 July 1997 (1997/71 Sp).

[62] See s 3 of the Legal Practitioners (Ir) Act 1876 and *Re Legal Practitioners (Ir) Act 1876* [1951] Ir Jur Rep 1; *Temple Press Ltd v Blogh* [1955-56] Ir Jur Rep 53; *Fitzpatrick v DAF Sales Ltd* [1988] IR 464. *Cf Re Kavanagh Ltd* [1952] Ir Jur Rep 38. See also *Finegan v McGarrell* (1909) 43 ILTR 184. In NI, s 3 of the 1876 has been replaced by Article 71 of the Solicitors (NI) Order 1976. *Cf* a factor's lien against his principal's goods: see Factors Act 1889, s 7. See *Stevens v Biller* (1883) 25 Ch D 31; Sheridan, *Rights in Security* (1974), pp 216-18.

[63] [1988] IR 213.

[64] See para **[13.03]**, *post*.

[65] See Wylie, *Irish Conveyancing Law* (2nd ed, 1996), para 2.43.

[66] Usually under a personal undertaking given to the lending institution: see *ibid*, para 20.17.

[67] *Per* McCarthy J, *op cit*, p 216.

[68] See also the former Moneylenders Act 1933 (RI), and Moneylenders Acts (NI) 1933 and 1969; Attenborough, *Law of Pawnbroking* (3rd ed, 1925). See also *Cripps Warbury Ltd v Cologne Investment Ltd* [1980] IR 321. See Bell, *Modern Law of Personal Property in England and Ireland* (1989), Ch 6.

[69] Chattels, as well as land, may be mortgaged by means of a bill of sale. See the Bills of Sale (Ir) Act 1879 and the Bills of Sale (Ir) Act 1879, Amendment Act 1883, which still apply to both parts of Ireland; also *Harries v Handy* (1851) 3 Ir Jur (os) 290 (ship); *Dobbyn v Comerford* (1860) 10 Ir Ch R 327 (ship); *Board of Harbour Commrs v Lawther* (1865) 17 Ir Ch R 54 (ship). *Bell, op cit*, pp 189-90. Folsom, 'Chattel Mortgage Substitutes Therefor in Latin America' (1954) 3 AJCL 477. Furthermore, a deposit of the deeds relating to land (see paras **[12.13]**, *supra*, and **[12.43]**, *post*) could be regarded as a pledge at common law, but since it has long been regarded as a mortgage in equity the point has little practical significance. See also *Re Morrissey* [1961] IR 442 (deposit of share certificates by way of pledge); *cf Re McClement* [1960] IR 141.

[70] *Re Morritt* (1886) 18 QBD 222.

Furthermore, a pledgee, like a mortgagee, does have various powers to realise the security initially conferred upon him by having possession of the chattel, eg, a power to sell the chattel in the event of the loan not being repaid.[71]

3. Charge

[12.19] The first point to note is that the word "charge" can have several meanings and in many cases it can be regarded as a form of mortgage.[72] The distinction usually drawn between the two concepts is that a mortgage, by tradition, involves the conveyance of some rights of ownership to the lender whereas a charge involves no transfer of ownership or, indeed, possession, but merely the conferment of rights over the property as security,[73] though, when these are exercised, there may be little practical difference between the position of a mortgagee and chargee. This point has been underlined in Ireland with respect to registered land which can be mortgaged by the registered owner only by means of a registered charge.[74] Apart from that, an equitable charge on property may be created by an express agreement for such a charge and an attempt to create a legal mortgage which fails for want of some formality may nevertheless be upheld as an equitable charge.[75]

[12.20] Not to be confused with these forms of charge are other forms like rentcharges, which are annual sums charged on land by way of security and form a branch of the law of incorporeal hereditaments.[76] Such rentcharges or annuities are commonly created under family settlements of land.[77] Also in Ireland there are land purchase annuities charged on agricultural land, the freehold of which has been bought out by tenant-farmers under the Land Purchase Acts scheme.[78]

---

[71] *Frances v Clark* (1883) 22 Ch D 830; *Jones v Marshall* (1889) 23 QBD 269.

[72] *Cf* Walker C in *Shea v Moore* [1894] 1 IR 158, at 168: "... every charge is not an equitable mortgage though every equitable mortgage is a charge". See also *Antrim County Land, Building, and Investment Co Ltd v Stewart* [1904] 2 IR 357, at 369 (*per* FitzGibbon LJ) (see *A Casebook on Irish Land Law* (1984), p 426); *Bank of Ireland v Feeny* [1930] IR 457 at 469 (*per* Kennedy CJ).

[73] See *Northern Banking Co Ltd v Devlin* [1924] 1 IR 90. Also *National Bank Ltd v Hegarty* (1910) 1 NIJR 13. *Northern Bank Ltd v Hegarty* Unrep (HC, NI), 8 February 1995 (as to which see now Articles 48-50 of the Property (NI) Order 1997): see paras **[7.31]** *ante* and **[13.183]** *et seq post.*

[74] Registration of Title Act 1964. s 62 (RI); Land Registration Act (NI) 1970. s 41. See further para **[12.24]** *post.* Note also orders charging land made under the Judgments (Enforcement) Act (NI) 1969 (now consolidated in the Judgments Enforcement (NI) Order 1981). See para **[13.183]** *et seq, post.* It is arguable that the concept of charge is a more accurate reflection of the parties intentions with respect to. and of equity's view of, the effect of a mortgage. See para **[12.04]** *supra,* and Ch 13, *post.*

[75] See, further, para **[12.41]** *post.* Also Rowley, 'Conveyancing and Equitable Charges' (1962) 26 Conv 445.

[76] See para **[6.131]** *ante.*

[77] See para **[6.131]** *et seq ante.* See also as regards quit rents and Crown rents. *Massy v O'Dell* (1858) 9 Ir Ch R 441 and see para **[6.008]** *ante.*

[78] Paras **[6.017]** *ante* and **[18.02]** *post.*

4. Judgment Mortgage

[12.21] Under a special statutory scheme introduced in Ireland[79] in the nineteenth century, a judgment creditor became entitled to register[80] his judgment as a mortgage against the land of the judgment debtor. This nineteenth-century legislation remains in force in the Republic of Ireland but was replaced in Northern Ireland as part of the scheme for establishment there of a central Enforcement of Judgments Office.[81] However, under the new scheme the Office has power to make an order charging the land of the debtor which has much the same effect as a judgment mortgage under the old scheme, except that, as is common practice nowadays when legislatures intervene, a charge only is created and not a mortgage.[82]

In view of the importance of this topic in Ireland, it will be discussed in a separate section in the next chapter.[83]

5. Welsh Mortgage

[12.22] A "Welsh" mortgage is a special kind of mortgage which in the past has been used quite commonly in Ireland.[84] The following definition has been given:

> "[A] Welsh mortgage [is] a kind of security which has fallen into disuse, by which, on the one side, the land is assured to the lender as his security -his possession of the land and enjoyment of the profits being in lieu of interest-while, on the other side, the borrower is under no personal obligation to pay the principal money, but yet is entitled to redeem at any time upon its payment."[85]

This differs from an ordinary mortgage in that here the very essence of the transaction is that the lender takes possession of the land. Furthermore, the lender is entitled to receive the rents and profits of the land which are to be applied by him in lieu of interest charged on the capital sum borrowed or, even, sometimes, in lieu of both capital and interest. Because of this, unlike an ordinary mortgage,[86] a Welsh mortgagee is not liable to account for the rents and profits received by him.[87] On the other hand, since there is no personal obligation to repay imposed on the borrower[88] and he may redeem at any time, the lender has no right to compel redemption by the borrower or other methods of

---

79 See the Judgment Mortgage (Ir) Acts 1850 and 1858. Also the Judgments (Ir) Acts 1844 and 1849 and the Judgments Registry (Ir) Acts 1850 and 1871. Para **[13.163]** *et seq, post.*

80 In the Registry of Deeds if the title to the land was unregistered and, later, in the Land Registry if the title became registered, see Chs 21 and 22 *post.*

81 Under the Judgments (Enforcement) Act (NI) 1969; See Trimble (1970) 21 NILQ 359. The 1969 Act has now been consolidated in the Judgments Enforcement (NI) Order. 1981.

82 Para **[12.19]** *supra.*

83 Para **[13.163]** *et seq, post.*

84 See Coote, *Law of Mortgages* (9th ed 1927), Ch III.

85 *Cassidy v Cassidy* (1889) 24 LR Ir 577, at 578-79 (*per* Johnson J). See also *Montgomery v Rogers* (1903) 37 ILTR 93.

86 Para **[13.047]** *post.*

87 See *Johnston v Moore* (1904) 4 NIJR 218. *Cf Henderson v Burns* (1920) 54 ILTR 149.

88 *Cf* an ordinary mortgagor, paras **[13.011]** and **[13.088]** *post.*

enforcement of security, such as sale.[89] However, once the debt has been repaid, whether out of the rents and profits or otherwise, the borrower may lose his right of redemption by adverse possession,[90] ie, it may be barred under the statute of limitations where the lender holds over for the statutory period after such repayment.[91]

[12.23] Whether or not a particular arrangement constitutes a Welsh mortgage is a matter of construction. The courts usually approach this matter from the standpoint that, if the transaction was intended to create security for a loan, it should be construed as creating an ordinary mortgage, with the usual incidents, unless the terms of the arrangement expressly or impliedly exclude such a presumption.[92] Thus the inclusion of an express power of sale in favour of the mortgagee will negative creation of a Welsh mortgage.[93] On the other hand, it seems that inclusion or exclusion of a proviso for redemption will not necessarily determine the issue one way or the other.[94]

II. Creation

In considering the creation of mortgages a distinction has to be drawn between registered land and unregistered land.

A. Registered Land

[12.24] Registration of title to land in Ireland[95] is now governed in the Republic of Ireland by the Registration of Title Act 1964 and in Northern Ireland by the Land Registration Act (NI) 1970.[96] These Acts govern the method of creation of mortgages of land the title to which is registered, but they do not prevent the creation of equitable mortgages which do not appear on the registers in the respective Land Registries. Thus, although the distinction between legal and equitable mortgages, which is so vital in the case of unregistered land, is not strictly applicable to registered land, it will be adopted for convenience sake in the following discussion. A legal mortgage of registered land in Ireland is a charge registered in one of the Land Registries.

1. Legal

[12.25] In both parts of Ireland the standard way in which the registered owner of land can create a legal mortgage of the land is to execute a charge which must be registered

---

[89] *Balfe v Lord* (1842) 2 Dr & War 480 at 486 (per Sugden LC). See also *O'Connell v Cummins* (1840) 2 Ir Eq R 251; *Taylor v Gorman* (1844) 7 Ir Eq R 259.

[90] See Ch 23, *post*. Also *Shields v Shields* (1904) 3 ILTR 188; *Johnston v Moore* (1904) 4 NIJR 218; *Fenton v* Walsh (1909) 43 ILTR 54.

[91] *Re Cronin* [1914] 1 IR 23.

[92] *Balfe v Lord* (1842) 2 Dr & War 480.

[93] *Re Cronin* [1914] 1 IR 23.

[94] *Johnston v Moore* (1904) 4 NIJR 218.

[95] Previously governed by the Local Registration of Title (Ir) Act 1891, and before that by the Record of Title (Ir) Act 1865.

[96] The 1970 Act was amended substantially by the Registration (Land and Deeds) (NI) Order 1992. See Ch 21, *post*.

as such.[97] Such a charge may be created by deed or by will, but, in the case of a deed, it should be in the prescribed form or in such other form as is sufficient[98] to charge the land.[99] Under the earlier statutory provisions contained in the Local Registration of Title (Ir) Act 1891,[100] there was some controversy as to the effectiveness of a deed in the form appropriate for a mortgage of unregistered land to create a charge on registered land.[101] Section 62(3) of the Republic's 1964 Act now provides that a mortgage by way of conveyance with a proviso for redemption or by way of demise or subdemise[102] shall not of itself operate to charge registered land or be registerable as a charge on registered land. Taken with the requirement in s 62(2) of the 1964 Act that the instrument used must be in a form which appears "to the Registrar to be sufficient to charge the land, provided that such instrument shall expressly charge or reserve out of the land the payment of the money secured," it would seem that in the Republic a registered owner ought to use express words of charge in his instrument to avoid dispute.[103] In Northern Ireland, paragraph 1 of Part I of Schedule 7 to the 1970 Act expressly excluded from the category of a recognised form, other than the prescribed form of charge, one which was a "purported conveyance or demise (whether or not subject to defeasance)", but as we shall discuss in a moment, this has caused problems in practice.[104] It should also be noted that both the 1964 and 1970 Acts contain saving provisions for charges in the form of mortgages which were in fact registered in the respective Land Registries under the 1891 Act. In the Republic, s 63(1) of the 1964 Act contains a saving for charges registered before the commencement of the 1964 Act to the effect that they are not void or to be deemed ever to have been void either by reason only that they were expressed to have been created by way of mortgage,[105] or by reason only that a requisite consent,

---

[97] 1964 Act, s 62; 1970 Act, s 41. Both sections refer to charging the land "with payment of money either with or without interest and either by way of annuity or otherwise".

[98] The Republic's 1964 Act, s 62(2) uses the formula -"as may appear to the Registrar to be sufficient" - while the NI 1970 Act, Sched 7, Pt I para 1 does not refer to the Registrar but adds the formula - "and as shall not be calculated to mislead". Note, however, the amendment introduced by Article 21 of the Registration (Law and Deeds) (NI) Order 1992: see *infra*.

[99] The Republic's 1964 Act s 62(2) also adds the proviso, in the case of a form other than the prescribed one. that it must "expressly charge or reserve out of the land the payment of the money secured." See *Gale v First National Building Society* [1985] IR 609. *Cf* Sched 7 Pt I, para I of the NI 1970 Act, as amended now by the 1992 Order: see *infra*.

[100] See especially s 40(2).

[101] In *Re Moley* [1957] NI 130, at 132, Curran J expressed doubts on the efficacy of such an instrument and this led to the practice in the NI Land Registry of refusing to accept for registration such a deed, unless it also included express words of charge. See Lowry Committee *Report on Registration of Title to Land in Northern Ireland* (1967, Cmd 512), para 92.

[102] Ie, the usual forms for unregistered land, paras **[12.30]** *et seq, post.*

[103] Ie, adopt the warning of Curran J in *Re Moley,* fn 101, *supra.*

[104] This furthered the Lowry Committee's view that use of the form of charge, as opposed to a form of mortgage, ought to become standard practice for registered land, see Cmd. 512, para 92.

[105] Which includes both a mortgage by demise or sub-demise and a mortgage by conveyance or assignment with a proviso for redemption, see s 63(2) and paras **[12.30]** *et seq, post.*

from, eg, the Land Commission or Commissioners of Public Works,[106] was not obtained to any demise or sub-demise expressed to be created by such mortgages, and the registration of such charges as burdens on registered land is, and is deemed always to have been, valid. In Northern Ireland, a similar saving provision is contained in Part III of Schedule 7 to the 1970 Act, except that its operation is confined to charges registered in the Land Registry at 28 July 1957.[107] As mentioned above the provision in paragraph 1 of Part I of Schedule 7 of the 1970 Act quoted above, caused considerable practical problems because numerous mortgages of registered land continued to be drafted in the traditional form of a mortgage rather than as a charge and, when lodged for registration, had to be rejected by the Land Registry. In order to deal with this Article 21 of the Registration (Land and Deeds) (NI) Order 1992 repeals the wording quoted above[108] and inserts a new sub-paragraph (2) in paragraph 1 as follows:

> A document purporting to transfer or demise (whether or not subject to defeasance) a freehold or leasehold estate in registered land by way of mortgage shall so far only as it relates to such land be deemed to be a deed of charge of, respectively, that estate or the estate out of which the leasehold estate is purported to be demised, and shall not operate to vest any freehold or leasehold estate in the registered land in the person in whose favour the document is executed.[109]

It is important to note that this provision is designed simply to facilitate registration of the mortgage and does not alter the substantive effect of the deed or of its registration. Despite the deed's wording in the traditional form of a mortgage and its registration, it still creates a charge only over the land in question.

[12.26] With respect to wills, in the Republic of Ireland these are expressly excluded from the requirement as to execution of an instrument of charge in the prescribed or other suitable form,[110] but it would seem that nevertheless a will must still avoid the trap of using a form appropriate for unregistered land only.[111] In Northern Ireland, it is provided that, where a charge created by will does not expressly charge any registered land with payment to a specified person of a specified amount, with or without interest,

---

[106] The Land Purchase Acts imposed such restrictions on sub-division and sub-letting by tenant-purchasers in order to protect the security for the land purchase annuity charged on the land bought under the Acts by way of repayment of the loan advanced for the purchase, see eg, the Irish Land Act 1903, s 54, and the Republic's Land Acts 1923, s 65; 1927, ss 3 and 4; 1936, s 44; 1939, s 30; 1946, ss 3 and 6; 1965, ss 12 and 13; *Carew v Jackman* [1966] IR 177. This was the actual ground for decision in *Re Moley* [1957] NI 130, fn 101 *supra,* and resulted in the NI Parliament rushing through the Land Registry Charges Act (NI) 1957, to establish the validity of charges already registered.

[107] The date fixed by the Land Registry Charges Act (NI) 1957.

[108] Articles 21(1) and 52 and Sched 2.

[109] Article 21(2).

[110] 1964 Act, s 62(2).

[111] Ie, wills are not excluded from s 62(3) of the 1964 Act.

or of an annuity, the Registrar is not, unless the court otherwise directs, obliged to register the ownership of that charge in any register.[112]

[12.27] In both parts of Ireland it is provided that any power, howsoever conferred, to borrow or lend money on the security of a mortgage is to be construed as including power to do so on the security of a registered charge.[113] Where a power to charge registered land, or a trust for securing money on registered land, is registered as a burden on the land,[114] it may be exercised or executed by creation of a registered charge and not otherwise.[115] Where a person has a statutory charge on, or a statutory power to charge, registered land, he is to have the same power to create a registered charge on the land as if he were the registered owner of the land.[116]

On registration of the ownership of a charge the owner is entitled to delivery of a certificate of charge in the prescribed form from the Registrar.[117]

2. Equitable

[12.28] One of the guiding principles of a registration of title system is that the registers should "mirror" the current title to the land and that all transactions relating to the land should be presented for registration to the Land Registry, for the appropriate consequent amendments to the registers to be made there.[118] However, it has been recognised from the very beginning of the introduction of a registration system in Ireland that, for convenience and administrative reasons, amongst others, the system cannot and, perhaps, should not seek to conform with this principle absolutely, and the modern Acts in both parts of Ireland still allow several types of transactions to be effective without registration in the Land Registries and to create interests in the registered land which are not noted on the registers. One of these transactions is the method of informal creation of mortgages which, we pointed out above, is so common in Ireland. It has always been considered that the advantages of such a method of creation of mortgages justify a breach of the "mirror" principle of registration.

---

[112] 1970 Act, s 41(3). Note, however, that the new sub-para (2) inserted by Article 21 of the 1992 Order in para 1 of Pt I of Sched 7 of the 1970 Act (see para **[12.25]** *supra*) refers to a "document" and so may cover a will.

[113] 1964 Act, s 62(4); 1970 Act, s 41(4).

[114] See 1964 Act, s 69(1)(d) and (e); 1970 Act, s 39 and Sched 6 Pt 1, paras 3 and 4.

[115] 1964 Act, s 76; 1970 Act, s 42. See also ss 78 and 79 of the 1964 Act and ss 45 and 46 of the 1970 Act, which deal with the cases of terms of years vested in trustees or other persons for the purpose of raising money out of registered land and for the purpose of raising money out of or mortgaging land prior to first registration of the title to that land.

[116] 1964 Act, s 77; 1970 Act, s 44.

[117] 1964 Act, ss 62(5) and 105; 1970 Act, s 79(1). *Cf* custody of the land certificate, see para **[13.004]**, *post*.

[118] See further on this subject, Ch 21 *post*.

[12.29] Both the 1964 and 1970 Acts provide that the deposit[119] of a land certificate[120] or certificate of charge[121] has the same effect as a deposit of the title deeds of unregistered land.[122] As Kenny J put the matter: "The right created by the deposit is not limited to keeping the deeds until the money has been paid but gives an equitable estate in the lands."[123] In other words, such a deposit creates an equitable mortgage on the registered land which need not be registered in the Land Registry as a burden on the land[124] in order to secure priority as against subsequent transactions relating to it.[125] The mortgage is protected because subsequent transactions relating to the registered land generally cannot be completed by registration in the Land Registry without production of the land or charge certificate,[126] which the mortgagee holds. However, if the mortgagee wishes, he may lodge a caution with the Registrar against subsequent registered dealings.[127]

B. Unregistered Land

[12.30] The two main categories of mortgages of unregistered land are those which are legal and those which are equitable. This distinction is of vital importance when a question of priorities as between successive mortgagees of the same land arises.

1. Legal

The methods of creation of legal mortgages of unregistered land in Ireland vary according to whether the land is freehold or leasehold.[128]

---

[119] The Republic's 1964 Act, s 105(5) (as did s 81(5) of the 1891 Act) refers to - "for the purpose of creating a lien on the land or charge to which the certificate relates." See, on liens and charges, para **[12.15]** *et seq, ante.* The NI 1970 Act, s 50 refers simply to "for the purposes of giving security for the payment of any sum of money."

[120] Which the Registrar is obliged to deliver on registration of a person as owner of the land, see 1964 Act, s 28; 1970 Act, s 79.

[121] Issued to the owner of a registered charge on the land, para **[12.27]** *supra.*

[122] 1964 Act, s 105(5) (which adds - "or of a charge thereon"); 1970 Act, s 50. See on the similar s 81(5) of the 1891 Act, Glover, *Registration of Ownership of Land in Ireland* (1933), pp 262-63.

[123] *Allied Irish Banks v Glynn* [1973] IR 188 at 192 (see *A Casebook Book Irish Land Law* (1984), p 85). *Cf Bank of New South Wales v O'Connor* (1889) 14 App Cas 273, at 282 (*per* Lord Macnaghten). See also *Bank of Ireland Finance Ltd v Daly* [1978] IR 79; *Bank of Ireland v Purcell* [1989] IR 327; *Allied Irish Banks plc v O'Neill* [1995] 2 IR 473.

[124] Ie under s 69 of the 1964 Act and s 39 of and Pt I of Sched 6 to the 1970 Act. See *Re Folio 3540 Co Tyrone* [1991] NI and para **[21.36]** *post.*

[125] It is, however, subject to existing "equities" as discussed in *Tench v Molyneux* (1914) 48 ILTR 48. The subject of priorities is discussed in detail in para **[13.137]** *et seq, post.*

[126] See 1964 Act, s 105(1); 1970 Act, s 79(2).

[127] 1964 Act, s 97; 1970 Act, s 66. See further, para **[21.51]** *post.* Note the practice in NI under the 1891 Act of entry in the register of a notice of deposit of the land certificate. See *Re Watters* [1934] NI 188, and now r 13(1) and Form 7 in the Land Registration Rules (NI) 1994. This procedure would seem to provide an alternative form of protection against subsequent dealings: see Wallace, *Land Registry Practice in Northern Ireland* (2nd ed 1987), p 129.

[128] See Sheridan, 'Some Aspects of Legal Mortgages' (1949) 52 JIBI 114.

(i) Freehold

[**12.31**] There are two main ways of mortgaging freehold land, namely (a) by conveyance of the fee simple[129] subject to a proviso for redemption[130] and (b) by demise (ie, grant of a term of years) subject to a proviso for cessor on redemption. If the parties wish, they may adopt the short-form precedent for a mortgage deed provided by s 26 of, and Part I of the Third Schedule to, the Conveyancing Act 1881. This provides a statutory form of mortgage for both freehold and leasehold land, through a deed expressed to be made by way of statutory mortgage, in which various covenants are automatically implied by the 1881 Act. In fact, this statutory form is rarely used in Ireland.

(a) Conveyance of Fee Simple

[**12.32**] As the name indicates, this form of mortgage involves the borrower (mortgagor) in transferring the legal title to his land to the lender (mortgagee) so as to confer the legal ownership on the lender. Such a conveyance is distinguished from a sale by insertion in the conveyance of an express proviso for redemption, usually by a covenant entered into by the mortgagee to reconvey the property to the mortgagor if the money due under the mortgage is paid on a fixed date.[131] We have already discussed the significance of this legal date for redemption and equity's intervention so as to create an equitable right to redeem after this date is passed and despite the wording of the mortgage instrument.[132]

[**12.33**] A mortgage by conveyance is usually executed by deed for the reason that various statutory provisions apply automatically to mortgages by deed.[133] Since a mortgage by conveyance transfers the legal title to the land to the mortgagee, it follows that any subsequent mortgages created out of the same land by the mortgagor are, of necessity, equitable only, ie, they are mortgages of the interest in the land retained by the mortgagor after the first legal mortgage, his equity of redemption.[134]

---

[129] As regards powers of mortgaging of a tenant of a lesser freehold estate, ie a tenant for life under the Settled Land Acts, see para [**8.078**] *ante.*

[130] This is no longer possible in England where the concept of a "charge by way of legal mortgage" was substituted for a conveyance of the fee simple by s 85(1) of the Law of Property Act 1925. Such a charge has an operation in respect to unregistered land in England similar to that of a registered charge in Ireland.

[131] *Gorman v Byrne* (1857) 8 ICLR 394. *Cf* the proviso implied in the statutory form under the Conveyancing Act 1881, s 26(2). See further on redemption of mortgages, para [**13.088**] *et seq, post.*

[132] Para [**12.05**], *ante.*

[133] Eg under the Conveyancing Acts 1881-1911, see paras [**13.007**] (insurance), [**13.024**] (sale by mortgagee) and [**13.050**] (appointment of receiver). Note also the statutory forms provided by Pt V of the 1881 Act.

[134] See para [**12.39**] *post.*

(b) Demise

[12.34] Instead of conveying the fee simple to the mortgagee, the mortgagor may demise the land for a term of years in favour of the mortgagee. Such a mortgage by demise is made expressly subject to a proviso for cesser of the term on redemption, ie, on repayment of all monies due under the mortgage. The vital difference from a mortgage by conveyance is, of course, that the mortgagor retains the freehold of the land and to this extent a mortgage by demise accords more with the notion of a mortgage creating security only. As the mortgagee does not get the freehold, it is usual for the mortgagor to appoint the mortgagee his attorney to convey the freehold reversion, so that the mortgagee can sell the freehold[135] and, unless the mortgagee stipulates that he is to have custody of the deeds, he is not entitled to them because he is not entitled to the freehold.[136] It is, however, sometimes convenient in Ireland to create a mortgage by demise where the fee simple is, eg, held under a fee farm grant.[137] In such a case, it is common practice to mortgage the land by demise for a long term of years, since this avoids imposing on the mortgagee any liability in respect of the fee farm rent and other covenants and conditions attaching to the fee simple estate held by the mortgagor.[138] Furthermore, it is possible to create successive legal mortgages out of the same land by means of successive demises for terms of years, with the term granted to each successive mortgagee being usually for a slightly longer period than the previous mortgage term.

(ii) Leasehold

[12.35] Where the borrower himself holds a leasehold estate only in the land being used as security for the loan, he may again create a mortgage in one of two ways, namely (a) by assignment of his lessee's interest and (b) by sub-demise.

(a) Assignment

[12.36] A mortgage of leasehold land by assignment[139] involves a transfer of the lessee's interest in the lease to the mortgagee, subject to a proviso for redemption under which the mortgagee covenants to reassign the interest under the lease on repayment of the loan and all other monies due under the mortgage. This form of mortgage is rarely used because it has the effect of making the mortgagee liable to all the obligations in respect of rent and repairs imposed by the lease on the lessee.[140] Further, since the mortgagor has parted with his entire legal estate in the land, he retains his equity of redemption

---

[135] See further on the power of sale, para**[13.024]** *post.*

[136] Though he will, of course, have his lease. See further, para **[13.005]** *post.*

[137] See para **[4.057]** *et seq, ante.*

[138] See *Re Sergie* [1954] NI 1 (demise for term of 10,000 years) (see *A Casebook on Irish Land Law* (1984), p 70), para **[3.026]** *et seq, ante.*

[139] See further on assignment of leases, para **[17.027]** *et seq, post.* Mortgages by assignment of leases are also prohibited in England under the Law of Property Act 1925: see para **[12.31]**, fn 130 *ante.*

[140] Ie, privity of estate arises between the lessor and the mortgagee, see para **[19.08]** *et seq post.* See *Sligo CC v Murrow* [1935] IR 771. Also *Re Macartney's Estate* [1933] NI 1.

only and any subsequent mortgages created out of the same land will necessarily be equitable only.[141]

(b) Sub-demise

[12.37] Instead of parting with his entire estate in the land, the mortgagor lessee may simply sub-demise the land in favour of the mortgagee for a term slightly shorter than the term of the lease. This sub-lease is made expressly subject to a proviso for cesser of the sub-term on redemption of the mortgage. Unlike the case of an assignment, the mortgagee-sub-lessee is under no liabilities in respect of the mortgagor's head-lease, since there is neither privity of contract nor privity of estate between him and the head-lessor.[142]

[12.38] Once again, successive legal mortgages may be created by a series of sub-leases, each usually for slightly longer periods than the previous one.[143] For this reason it is wise in the initial sub-lease to leave an adequate gap, say 10 days, between the determination date of the sub-lease and that of the head-lease, ie, subsequent sub-leases can each be for periods longer by one day than the previous sub-leases until the day before the determination date of the head-lease is reached.[144]

2. Equitable

There are several methods of creating an equitable mortgage in Ireland.

(i) Equitable Interest

[12.39] First, it follows necessarily that, if the mortgagor at the time of creating a mortgage holds an equitable interest only in the land, any mortgage he creates on the security of that land must also be equitable only. We have already mentioned that, if a first legal mortgage on the land has been created by conveyance of the legal estate in the land, any subsequent mortgage can by created out of the mortgagor's equity of redemption only[145] and is equitable. Such a mortgage is often referred to as a puisne mortgage.[146] Apart from a mortgage of the equity of redemption, an equitable mortgage can be created out of other equitable interests in land, eg, a beneficiary's interest under a trust.[147]

[12.40] A mortgage of an equitable interest in land is usually created formally, by execution of a deed conveying the equitable interest to the mortgagee subject to a

---

[141] Para **[12.39]** *post.*

[142] See para **[17.028]** *post.*

[143] However, note that in Ireland it is possible to sublet land for the whole term of the head-lease under s 3 of Deasy's Act 1860; *Seymour v Quirke* (1884) 14 LR Ir 455. See para **[17.006]** *post.*

[144] This probably holds good despite s 3 of Deasy's Act, in that it makes clear who the immediate reversioner is in respect of a particular mortgage sub-lease.

[145] Para **[12.33]** *ante.*

[146] *Antrim County Land, Building and Investment Co Ltd v Stewart* [1904] 2 IR 357 (See *A Casebook on Irish Land Law* (1984) p 426).

[147] Ch 9 *ante.*

proviso for redemption. A deed, however, is not essential. The Statute of Frauds (Ireland) 1695 simply requires that an assignment of an equitable interest held under a trust must be in writing signed by the assignor or made by will.[148] Apart from that, there are no requisite formalities and, provided the parties' intentions are clear, equity will give effect to them.[149]

(ii) Agreement for a Legal Mortgage

[12.41] As part of its general policy of giving effect to contracts for the creation of legal estates,[150] equity will enforce a contract[151] to create a legal mortgage by its usual remedy of a decree of specific performance.[152] Because of this special approach equity goes further and says that, until the legal mortgage is actually created by conveyance of the legal estate or demise, as the case may be, the intended mortgagee has an equitable mortgage on the land. Thus in *Eyre v McDowell*,[153] it was held that a covenant by a debtor to the effect that, if the debt was not paid by a certain date, the creditor could, by entry, foreclosure, sale or mortgage, levy the amount from the lands of the debtor, was held to create such an equitable mortgage.

[12.42] Such an agreement must comply with the Statute of Frauds (Ireland) 1695, s 2 of which requires the agreement to be evidenced in writing and signed by the party to be charged or his authorised agent.[154] Alternatively, there may be sufficient acts of part performance or elements of fraud present to take the case out of the statute.[155]

(iii) Deposit of Title Deeds

[12.43] The recognition of a deposit of title deeds as creating an equitable mortgage is often regarded as an extension of the doctrine of part performance.[156] At first sight there appear to be similarities in that it has been settled that a deposit on its own, without any memorandum in writing sufficient to evidence any agreement as required by the Statute

---

[148] Section 6. See para **[9.025]** *ante*.

[149] See the discussion in *William Brandt's Sons and Co v Dunlop Rubber Co Ltd* [1905] AC 454.

[150] See para **[3.144]** *ante*.

[151] Note that there must be a "contract" - an *antecedent* debt, eg, is not consideration for an agreement to mortgage, see *Crofts v Feuge* (1854) 4 Ir Ch R 316. If, however, the loan is advanced on the basis of the agreement, then the lender is entitled to specific performance (provided, of course, the borrower is in a position to transfer the legal title) since damages are an inadequate remedy, being an unsecured debt, and an equitable mortgage arises, which is secured and can be realised in priority to other unsecured claims against the debtor, see *Hunter v Lord Langford* (1828) 2 Mol 272.

[152] Para **[3.142]** *et seq, ante*.

[153] (1861) 9 HLC 619 (on appeal from Ireland). See also *Card v Jaffray* (1805) 2 Sch & Lef 374; *Abbott v Stratten* (1846) 3 Jo & Lat 603; *Re Parkinson's Estate* (1865) 10 Ir Jur (ns) 82: *Re Hurley's Estate* [1894] IR 488.

[154] See para **[9.024]** *ante*. Note that here only evidence of the agreement has to be in writing, whereas under s 6 of the 1695 Statute the assignment itself must be in writing, para **[12.40]** *supra*.

[155] Para **[3.149]** *ante*.

[156] See Corscadden, 'Deposit of Title Deeds', (1953) 55 JIBI 253. See also Coote, *Treatise on the Law of Mortgages* (9th ed, by Ramsbotham 1927), Vol 1, p 86; *Thames Guaranty Ltd v Campbell* [1985] QB 210.

of Frauds, will create an equitable mortgage.[157] This, however, involves extending the doctrine beyond its usual limits, one of which is that only the person who performs can take advantage of the performance, as the other party to the transaction is affected by his own fraud.[158] Yet it is the mortgagee who is interested in enforcing the mortgage created by deposit and it is difficult to see what acts of part performance have been done by him.[159] Giving the loan to the mortgagor involves usually payment of money and the general rule is that mere payment of money is not specifically referable to such an agreement for a mortgage.[160] It is arguable that this sort of equitable mortgage should be regarded as creation of a special equitable charge or lien *sui generis*, rather than a contract to create a legal mortgage or otherwise a "contract-based" mortgage.[161] Whatever the difficulties over the underlying theory of deposit of title deeds, the fact remains that it is a well-established method of creating mortgages in both Ireland and England and, as we have seen, has now been given statutory recognition.[162]

[12.44] It appears that a mere deposit of the title deeds will be regarded as *prima facie* evidence of an equitable mortgage, unless the deposit is otherwise accounted for, eg, deposit with a bank for safe keeping.[163] On the other hand, a mere agreement to deposit is not enough if the deeds are not actually deposited, though that agreement may create another kind of equitable mortgage.[164] It is not necessary to deposit all the title deeds

---

[157] *Bulfin v Dunne* (1861) 12 IR Ch R 67; *Gilligan v National Bank Ltd* [1901] 2 IR 513; *Northern Banking Co Ltd v Carpenter* [1931] IR 268; *National Bank Ltd v McGovern* [1931] IR 368. See also the early English authorities, *Russel v Russel* (1783) 1 Bro CC 269; *Edge v Worthington* (1768) 1 Cox CC 211; *Hankey v Vernon* (1788) 2 Cox CC 12. *Cf* The criticisms of the earlier decisions by Lord Eldon in *Ex parte Whitbread* (1812) 19 Ves 209, at 210; *Ex parte Hooper* (1815) 19 Ves 477, at 478-79.

[158] See para **[3.149]** *ante*.

[159] Ie, the acts of part performance must be done by the plaintiff; *cf* signing of the note or memorandum in writing required by s 2 of the Statue of Frauds (Ir) 1695.

[160] Further, even if the mortgagee gives a receipt for the deeds, this is not to his detriment.

[161] See *Emmet on Title* (19th ed), para 25.116, but note the rejection of this view by Chadwick J in *United Bank of Kuwait plc v Sahib* [1995] 2 All ER 973, at 986-990.

[162] Para **[12.28]** *ante*.

[163] *McKay v McNally* (1879) 4 LR Ir 438; *Gilligan v National Bank Ltd* [1901] 2 IR 513; *cf* where a wife, who is sole owner of the property, deposits her title deeds to secure her husband's debts, especially where she received no independent advice: see *Northern Banking Co Ltd v Carpenter* [1931] IR 268; *National Bank Ltd* [1901] IR 368. The deposit of the title deeds in one branch of a bank may provide security for loans due in respect of accounts in other branches, provided this is made clear, eg, by a reference to "all liabilities" of the depositor. See also *Bank of Ireland v Coen* Unrep (HC, RI) 11 November 1988.

[164] *Simmons v Montague* [1909] 1 IR 87. See para **[12.41]** *supra*. *Cf Ex parte Crossfield* (1840) 3 Ir Eq R 67. *Ex parte Crossfield* and *Simmons v Montague* were followed by Hamilton J in *Bank of Ireland Finance Ltd v Daly* [1978] IR 79, at 82. See also *Highland Finance Ireland Ltd v Sacred Heart College of Agriculture Ltd* [1997] 2 ILRM 87. An equitable mortgage may still be created even though the depositor has no right to the title deeds, provided the mortgagee advances the money *bona fide*, see *Joyce v De Moleyns* (1845) 8 Ir Eq R 215. *Cf Purcell v Buckley* (1849) 12 Ir Eq R 55. The lien is lost if the depositee parts with the deeds. *Re Driscoll's Estate* (1867) IR 1 Eq 285.

relating to the land, provided those in fact deposited are material evidence of title and sufficient to indicate the parties' intention.[165] It has also been held in Ireland that a deposit of title deeds with a creditor's solicitor, for the purpose of preparation of a mortgage to secure an antecedent debt and further advances, in itself creates an equitable mortgage without any further agreement.[166] Furthermore, a verbal agreement, supported by parol evidence, to make future advances on a deposit of title deeds as security for a present loan may be sufficient to create an equitable mortgage as security for any subsequent advances.[167]

[12.45] The equitable mortgage created by deposit of title deeds gives the mortgagee a lien on the land to which the deeds relate,[168] not on the deeds themselves.[169] Thus an equitable mortgagee may be ordered, without prejudice to his rights, to lodge the deeds in court.[170] Unless the parties agree otherwise, it appears that an equitable mortgage by deposit will carry interest at the rate of 4 per cent from the date of the deposit,[171] though, if made to a bank, it will secure interest at the current overdraft rate. It will also often be a matter of construction as to what is the extent of the indebtedness covered by the mortgage created by the deposit.[172] Frequently, such a deposit is used to secure not only existing indebtedness to a bank but also "future advances". The effect of this was explained by Barron J, in giving the first instance decision in *Bank of Ireland v Purcell,*[173] a case involving the issue whether such a deposit constituted a "conveyance" of an "interest" needing a spouse's consent for the purposes of the Family Home Protection Act 1976.[174] He stated:

> "Undoubtedly, the deposit of the land certificate[175] gives to the bank an estate in the lands, but the word 'interest' in the sub-section is defined more widely than a reference to an estate. The conveyance of the estate in lands is the conveyance of an interest for the purposes of the section, but the fact that the estate has already been conveyed need not prevent a subsequent transaction from conveying an 'interest' in the lands. In the case of a mortgage the extent of the estate depends upon the amount which has been

---

[165] *Re Lambert's Estate* (1884) 13 LR Ir 234. See also *CP v DP* [1983] ILRM 381.

[166] *Bulfin v Dunne* (1861) 12 Ir Ch R 67. *Cf Norris v Wilkinson* (1806) 12 Ves 192. Where an equitable mortgage by deposit of title deeds is followed by execution of a legal mortgage of the same lands, the equitable mortgage does not necessarily merge in the legal one. *Re Smallman's Estate* (1867) IR 2 Eq 34. See further on merger, Ch 24 *post.*

[167] *Bulfin v Dunne, op cit.* See also *Ex parte Langston* (1810) 17 Ves 227; *Ex parte Kensington* (1813) 2 V & B 79.

[168] *Simmons v Montague* [1909] 1 IR 87. Note the references to a lien on the land in s 81(5) of the Local Registration of Title (Ir) Act 1891 and now in s 105(5) of the Republic's Registration of Title Act 1964; *cf* s 50 of the Land Registration Act (NI) 1970. Para **[12.29]** *supra.*

[169] *Gilligan v National Bank Ltd* [1901] 2 IR 513.

[170] *Re Girdwood's Estate* (1881) 5 LR Ir 45.

[171] *Carey v Doyne* (1856) 5 Ir Ch R 104.

[172] See *O'Keeffe v Russell* [1994] ILRM 137.

[173] [1989] IR 327.

[174] On this aspect of the case, see Wylie, *Irish Conveyancing Law* (2nd ed, 1996), para 16.62.

[175] Land in the *Purcell* case was registered land: see para **[12.29]** *ante.*

borrowed. Even in a case of a legal mortgage where there is a conveyance of the fee simple the interest of the mortgagor and of the mortgagee in the lands so mortgaged will depend at any given time upon the extent of the monies lent and borrowed. No doubt so long as any monies are charged on the lands the fee simple estate will be in the mortgagee. However, that of itself does not mean that thereafter the mortgagor cannot purport to convey a further interest to the mortgagee, because in that situation the value of the equity of redemption is being altered on the occasion of each further advance. The same situation arises in the present case. Each time there is a further advance the amount which is being charged on the lands is altered and accordingly the interest of the mortgagor in these land is altered."

These views are upheld by the Supreme Court, where Walsh J commented:

"As the learned judge pointed out, each time a further advance is made the interest in the property which is being charged is altered. As deposed to in the affidavit filed on behalf of the plaintiff the deposit of title deeds made on 1st April 1975, without any writing, was intended to secure all liabilities present and future. Thus the transaction contemplated future charging of the interest in the land in question by way of mortgage. If at any time no monies were due on foot of the mortgage then for the purpose of s 3 the property was unencumbered, notwithstanding the deposit of deeds, and the bare equitable interest therein by the deposit of deeds, was not the substantive interest in the property contemplated by s 3. If such monies were due on that date then the family home was encumbered only to that extent." [176]

[12.46] The parties must decide whether to accompany the deposit of the title deeds with any written memorandum. There is no need for any such formality, since the mere deposit is sufficient to create an equitable mortgage and one of the main attractions of such arrangements is their relative informality, which makes them so popular with banks and their customers.[177] On the other hand, if there is no written evidence of the purpose of the deposit there may be disputes later between the parties.[178] Yet if some further document is executed to prevent disputes arising, the parties may find that they are affected by statutory provisions. First, it may be argued that the intention of the parties was not to create a mortgage by deposit but rather to enter into an agreement for a mortgage, in which case the requirements of s 2 of the Statute of Frauds (Ireland) 1695 must be met.[179] Secondly, it has been held that such a written memorandum comes within the Registration of Deeds Act (Ireland) 1707,[180] and so a memorial of it must be

---

[176] *Op cit*, pp 330-31 and 334. Note that it has been held that, even where a mortgage by deposit is void for want of consent under the 1976 Act, it can be "severed", ie, the land affected (eg, a farm) can be split into the "family home" part (the farmhouse and ancillary land) and the rest of the lands in respect of which the mortgage remains valid: see *Bank of Ireland v Slevin* [1995] 2 IR 454; *Allied Irish Banks plc v O'Neill* [1995] 2 IR 473; Wylie, *Irish Conveyancing Law* (2nd ed, 1996), para 16.69.

[177] See Corscadden, 'Deposit of Title Deeds' (1953) 55 JIBI 253.

[178] And see *Hibernian Bank v Gilbert* (1889) 23 LR Ir 321. Note also *Simmons v Montague* [1909] 1 IR 87 (mistake in map lodged with title deeds).

[179] Para **[12.42]** *supra*.

[180] Replaced in Northern Ireland by the Registration of Deeds Act (NI) 1970, as amended by the Registration (Land and Deeds) (NI) Order 1992: see Ch 22 *post*.

registered in a Registry of Deeds to secure priority.[181] This obviously defeats the desire of a bank customer for secrecy and informality in securing a loan or an overdraft. The result is that such a deposit is rarely accompanied by any written memorandum in Ireland.[182]

(iv) Equitable Charge

[12.47] An owner of property may appropriate it as security for a debt so as to give the creditor an equitable charge on the property.[183] We have already explained that such a charge is to be distinguished from a mortgage in that it confers only a lien on the land and no legal or equitable estate in the land nor any right to possession.[184] Such a charge may be created by written agreement[185] or by will.[186] Apart from that, no special words are necessary so long as the intention is clear.[187]

---

[181] *Re Lambert's Estate* (1884) 13 LR Ir 234; *Fullerton v Provincial Bank of Ireland* [1903] AC 309, on appeal from [1902] 1 IR (*sub nom Re Stevenson's Estate* (see *A Casebook on Irish Land Law* (1984), p 432). See, further, on priorities, Ch 13 *post.*

[182] Some banks have in the past tried to get round this problem by having the customer read a memorandum containing the terms of the loan at the time of the deposit and then having this signed in the customer's presence by bank officials only as a record of the transaction. See the remarks in *Bank of Ireland v Macaura* [1934] LJ Ir 89, at 90 (*per* Kennedy CJ). This may avoid later disputes in practice and, because the customer-mortgagor has not signed anything, there is no written memorandum coming within the Statute of Frauds, nor, indeed, any deed or conveyance within the Registry of Deeds legislation.

[183] See further, para **[12.19]** *ante.*

[184] *Antrim County Land Building and Investment Co Ltd v Stewart* [1904] 2 IR 357. espec at 369 (*per* Fitzgibbon LJ) (see *A Casebook on Irish Land Law* (1984), p 426); *Bank of Ireland Ltd v Feeney* [1930] IR 457 espec at 469 (*per* Kennedy CJ).

[185] *Coonan v O'Connor* [1903] 1 IR *449.* Or, at least, evidenced by writing, see *Matthews v Goodday* (1861) 31 LJ Ch 282; *Ex parte Hall* (1878) 10 Ch D 615.

[186] *Re Owen* [1894] 3 Ch 220.

[187] *Coonan v O'Connor* [1903] 1 IR 449. See also *Cradock v Scottish Provident Institution* (1894) 70 LT 718.

Chapter 13

POSITION OF PARTIES UNDER MORTGAGES

[13.001] In this chapter we consider the various rights and duties of the mortgagor and mortgagee once a mortgage has been created, including their transfer to other persons. As we shall see, the mortgagor and mortgagee each have their own rights and duties, but some are common to both parties. The nature and extent of these rights and duties depend partly on the contractual terms of the mortgage agreed between the mortgagor and mortgagee and partly on statute law.

I. MORTGAGEE

[13.002] In most cases, the mortgagee is a financial institution concerned simply that its loan, plus the interest charged on it, should be repaid according to the terms of the agreement. If the loan and interest are not repaid it can always sue the mortgagor as for any other debt.[1] What makes a mortgage special is the existence of further remedies the mortgagee has for enforcement of his security for the contractual debt. In addition to his various remedies for enforcement of the security, there are several other matters to be considered with respect to the position of a mortgagee vis-à-vis the mortgagor and the land which is the security for the debt.

A. Title Documents

[13.003] The general principle is that it is part of a mortgagee's security to have in his possession the title documents relating to the land, because this will protect him against further dealings with the property by the mortgagor without the mortgagee knowing of them, which might affect the priority of his security.[2] There are, however, several situations to be considered.

[13.004] First, so far as registered land is concerned, where the security is created by means of a registered charge, the chargee is entitled in both parts of Ireland to delivery of a charge certificate.[3] He is not generally entitled to the land certificate relating to the registered ownership of the land which remains in the mortgagor,[4] but he is protected by

---

[1] Para **[13.011]**, *infra.*

[2] *Smith v Chichester* (1842) 4 Ir Eq R 580 at 581 (*per* Sugden LC). See further on priorities, especially the relevance of negligence as to custody of title documents, para **[13.133]**, *post.*

[3] Registration of Title Act, 1964, s 62(5); Land Registration Act (NI) 1970, s 79(2)(a).

[4] In the Republic of Ireland there is a specific provision to the effect that the registered owner of a charge is not, merely by reason of his being such owner, entitled to possession of the land certificate relating to the registered land which is subject to the charge and any stipulation to the contrary is void, 1964 Act, s 67 (replacing s 14 of the Registration of Title Act 1942). See *Re Associated Banks* [1944] Ir Jur Rep 29. *Cf* 1970 Act, s 79(2)(a), which merely provides for rules to be made regarding custody of certificates: see now Pt IV of the Land Registration Rules (NI) 1994, which do not deal with the point.

the fact that his charge is registered and will take priority over any subsequent equitable mortgage created by deposit of the land or charge certificate.[5] It is true that the Registrar, on the application of the registered owner of the land or any person appearing to him to be entitled to require it, may order the chargee to produce the certificate to the Registrar for the purpose of a dealing with the land or charge which can be effected without the consent of the person in whose custody it is.[6] This production, however, does not alter the right to custody of the certificate nor any lien created on the land.[7] If an equitable mortgage on the registered land is created by deposit of the land or charge certificate, then, of course, the mortgagee is entitled to custody of the certificate in question since, upon this, his entire position depends.[8]

[13.005] Secondly, so far as unregistered land is concerned, if a legal mortgage is created by conveyance of the fee simple, the mortgagee as owner of the fee simple in the land is automatically entitled to the title deeds. If, however, the mortgage is created by demise, the mortgagee will only be entitled to the lease, unless he contracts expressly for surrender of the deeds relating to the freehold.[9] In the case of a mortgage of leasehold property, if created by assignment the mortgagee is entitled to possession of the lease only. If it is created by sub-demise, he is not automatically entitled even to this, though he will usually stipulate expressly for its surrender.[10]

[13.006] In the case of an equitable mortgage of unregistered land, the mortgagee obviously has custody of the title deeds where the mortgage is created by their deposit. It is, however, important to remember that the mortgage or lien thereby created relates to the land rather than the deeds,[11] so that the mortgagee may be ordered in certain cases, for example, to lodge the deeds in court.[12] In the case of other equitable mortgages, eg, a mortgage of an equitable interest only in the property or an agreement for a legal mortgage, the title deeds will be retained by the legal owner of the property. *A fortiori* an equitable chargee who has no estate at all, legal or equitable, in the land has no right to the title deeds.[13]

---

[5] Para **[13.131]**, *post.*

[6] 1964 Act, s 105(2); 1970 Act, s 79(2)(b).

[7] 1964 Act, s 105(3); 1970 Act, s 72(2)(b).

[8] Para **[12.29]** *ante.* His lien is lost if he parts with the certificate, *Re Driscoll's Estate* (1866) IR 1 Eq 285.

[9] See *Wiseman v Westland* (1826) 1 Y & J 117, espec at 122. *Cf* the English Law of Property Act 1925, s 85(1) (first long lessee-mortgagee or legal chargee given statutory right to possession of the documents of title).

[10] *Cf* Law of Property Act 1925, s 86(1) (first mortgagee of leaseholds same statutory right to possession of documents as if mortgagee by assignment).

[11] *Gilligan v National Bank Ltd.* [1901] 2 IR 513.

[12] *Re Girdwood's Estate* (1881) 5 LR Ir 45.

[13] *National Bank Ltd v Hegarty* (1901) 1 NIJR 13; *Antrim County Land, Building and Investment Co Ltd v Stewart* [1904] 2 IR 357 (see *A Casebook on Irish Land Law* (1984), p 426); *Bank of Ireland Ltd v Feeny* [1930] IR 457.

B. Insurance

[13.007] In both parts of Ireland a mortgagee has a statutory power to insure the mortgaged property conferred by s 19 of the Conveyancing Act 1881. This power is implied automatically in mortgages by deed only,[14] but it is provided in both parts of Ireland that a registered charge confers on the owner of the charge all the rights and powers of a mortgagee under a mortgage by deed within the meaning of the Conveyancing Acts.[15] The power to insure may be exercised at any time after the date of the mortgage deed to cover loss or damage by fire to any building, or any effects or property of an insurable nature forming part of the mortgaged property.[16] The premiums are to be a charge on the mortgaged property, in addition to the mortgage debt, with the same priority and with interest at the same rate as that debt.[17] However, the amount of insurance cover is not to exceed the amount specified in the mortgage deed or, if no amount is specified, two-thirds of the amount required to restore the property in the event of total destruction.[18]

[13.008] A mortgagee cannot exercise his statutory power to insure in three cases: (i) where there is a declaration in the mortgage deed that no insurance is required; (ii) where an insurance is kept up by or on behalf of the mortgagor in accordance with the mortgage deed; (iii) where the mortgage deed contains no stipulation respecting insurance, and an insurance is kept up by or on behalf of the mortgagor, to the amount in which the mortgagee is by the Act authorised to insure.[19]

[13.009] The mortgagee is entitled to require all money received under an insurance effected under the 1881 Act or the mortgage deed to be applied by the mortgagor in making good loss or damage to the mortgaged property,[20] or, subject to any obligation to the contrary imposed by law or a special contract, in discharge of the mortgage debt.[21] It had been held in Ireland that, even though the insurance is effected neither under the 1881 Act nor under the mortgage deed, the mortgagee may still require the insurance money to be applied in discharge of the mortgage debt.[22]

---

[14] 1881 Act, s 19(1).

[15] Registration of Title Act 1964, s 62(6); Land Registration Act (NI) 1970, Sched 7, Pt 1, para 5. See *Re McCairns (PMPA) plc* [1991] 2 IR 465.

[16] 1881 Act, s 19(1)(ii).

[17] *Ibid.*

[18] 1881 Act, s 23(1).

[19] Section 23(2).

[20] Section 23(3).

[21] Section 23(4).

[22] *Re Doherty* [1925] 2 IR 246. *Cf Halifax Building Society v Keighly* [1931] 2 KB 248. And in *Myler v Mr. Pussy's Nite Club Ltd,* unrep (HC, RI) 11 December 1979 (1978 No 1472p) (see A *Casebook on Irish Land Law* (1984), p 445), McWilliam J applied this principle to a mortgage by deposit of title deeds.

C. Fixtures

[13.010] By virtue of the general definitions in the Conveyancing Act 1881 of "land" as including houses and other buildings,[23] of a "conveyance" as including an assignment or lease made by deed on a mortgage of property[24] and of a "mortgage" as including any charge on property for securing money or money's worth,[25] there are included in a mortgage of land in Ireland all buildings and fixtures appertaining to that land.[26] It appears that the well-known exceptions which apply as between landlord and tenant[27] do not apply as between mortgagor and mortgagee.[28] Indeed, the mortgagor may not even be entitled to remove fixtures which he has attached to the property after the date of the mortgage.[29]

D. Action for Debt

[13.011] It must not be forgotten that a mortgagee, like any other lender of money, is owed a contractual debt and is entitled to sue for it if it is not repaid. One limitation on this right is, of course, that he can sue only after the date for repayment is past and not before then.[30] Furthermore, it appears that the right of action for the debt cannot be considered entirely in isolation from the other remedies the mortgagee has against the land. Central to the concept of a mortgage is the principle that the mortgagor is entitled to have his land back freed from the mortgage once he repays the debt, plus interest, in full. So it has been held that a mortgagee who parts with his interest in the land, and who, therefore, cannot hand it back to the mortgagor on redemption, loses his right to sue on the covenant for the debt.[31]

---

[23] Section 2(ii).

[24] Section 2(v).

[25] Section 2(vi), and note that a registered charge operates as a mortgage by deed within the meaning of the Conveyancing Acts, Registration of Title Act 1964, s 62(6); Land Registration Act 1970, Sched 7, Pt I, para 5. See *Re McCairns (PMPA) plc* [1991] 2 IR 465.

[26] 1881 Act, s 6. *Cf Re Dawson* (1868) IR 2 Eq 218 (growing crops). See *Lees (Concrete) Ltd v Lees* [1992] 11 NIJB 44; see also the recent discussion by the English Court of Appeal in *TSB Bank plc v Botham* [1996] EGCS 149.

[27] Ie, so-called tenant's fixtures which can be removed by him and do not belong to the landlord, eg, trade or ornamental fixtures, see para **[4.155]** *ante* and Ch 17, *post*. Also *Re Dawson* (1868) IR 2 Eq 218 (looms spiked to tiled floor); *Re Calvert* [1898] 2 IR 501 (trade fixtures in chemist's shop); *Moore v Merrion Pier and Baths Co* (1901) 1 NIJR 184 (gas engine and pump).

[28] *Climie v Wood* (1869) LR 4 Ex 328; *Monti v Barnes* [1901] 1 QB 205; *Lyon & Co v London City & Midland Bank* [1903] 2 KB 135. See Firth, 'Mortgages and Trade Fixtures' (1899) 15 LQR 165.

[29] *Longbottom v Berry* (1869) LR 5 QB 137; *Reynolds v Ashby & Son* [1904] AC 466. *Cf* fixtures annexed by a third party under an agreement with the mortgagor, *Gough v Wood & Co* [1894] 1 QB 713.

[30] *Hinds v Blacker* (1878) 1 LR Ir 233; *Sinton v Dooley* [1910] 2 IR 162 at 165 *(per* Gibson J); *Bradshaw v McMullan* [1915] 2 IR 187. See also *Bolton v Buckenham* [1891] 1 QB 278.

[31] *Schoole v Sall* (1803) 1 Sch & Lef 176. See also *Palmer v Hendrie* (1859) 27 Beav 349; *cf Willes v Levett* (1847) 1 De G & Sm 392. The same applies where the mortgagee's title is extinguished by adverse possession, see *Beamish v Whitney* [1909] 1 IR 360.

[13.012] The essence of a mortgage, however, is, as we have mentioned several times already, that the mortgagee does not have to rely on such a remedy, which is always subject to the risk that the mortgagor will turn out to be insolvent. If necessary, the mortgagee can seek instead to realise his security and move against the land which forms the subject-matter of the mortgage. It is to the remedies for enforcement of his security that we now turn.

E. Enforcement of Security

[13.013] The mortgagee's methods of enforcing his security against the land have evolved since mortgages were recognised by the Court of Chancery. The remedies were not created by statute but by the courts and, accordingly, they are the result of constantly changing economic and social factors. Equity, common law, conveyancers, and, subsequently, statute law, have contributed to the present position. We wish to emphasise that in this field there is a significant difference between the practice in Ireland and in England: in England one of the main remedies, when the money due on a mortgage has not been paid, is foreclosure while this has not been used in Ireland in modern times. In Ireland the remedies available to a mortgagee when the principal or, in some cases, the interest on the principal, has not been paid are:[32] (1) a court order for possession of the mortgaged property, followed by a sale of that property by the mortgagee out of court; (2) a sale of the mortgaged property without the intervention of the court; (3) a court order for the sale of the mortgaged property; (4) the mortgagee going into possession of the mortgaged property and taking the rents and profits of it; (5) the appointment of a receiver, and (6) foreclosure, in theory, though as we stated above, it is never granted in practice.

[13.014] Four of these (a court order for possession followed by a sale out of court, sale of the mortgaged property without the intervention of the court, a court order for the sale of the mortgaged property and foreclosure) are intended to secure repayment of the capital originally borrowed and so have the result that the mortgagee is paid his capital and interest and the mortgage determines. The mortgagee going into possession of the mortgaged property and taking the rents and profits and the appointment of a receiver are designed primarily to secure the regular payment of the outgoings on the property and the interest due on the mortgage and, though they may be preliminary to a sale, they are essentially different from it. A mortgagee may make use of more than one of these remedies at the same time, provided he does not act inconsistently. Thus, in Ireland, a mortgagee may sue the mortgagor for the debt created by the covenant in the mortgage to repay the principal and interest and may, at the same time, bring proceedings for a court order for the sale of the mortgaged property.[33] This is not the practice in England, but in *Barden v Downes*[34] the Supreme Court in the Republic decided that a mortgagee could bring separate proceedings against the mortgagor to recover judgment for the

---

[32] See Scanlon, *Practice and Procedure in Administration and Mortgage Suits in Ireland* (1963).

[33] *Bradshaw v McMullan* [1915] 2 IR 187.

[34] [1940] IR 131.

amount of the mortgage debt and interest when he had already brought proceedings for a court sale.

[13.015] If there are a number of mortgages affecting the land, each of the mortgagees may pursue different remedies so that, while one may sue for his debt, another may apply for a court order for the sale of the mortgaged property.[35] These remedies are not confined to legal mortgages: some of them may be used by equitable mortgagees and special provision has been made by the Registration of Title Act 1964, in the Republic of Ireland, and by the Land Registration Act (NI) 1970, in Northern Ireland, for a summary remedy by a person who has advanced money on the security of a charge on land which is registered and who seeks to get possession. At one time there existed in Ireland statutory control over the terms on which mortgages could be created through the rent restriction legislation. This control no longer exists in Northern Ireland and was abandoned in the Republic many years ago.[36] We now proceed to discuss each of these remedies.

1. Court Order for Possession and Sale out of Court

[13.016] Until recent times in Ireland, the most commonly used remedy by a mortgagee when the principal was due, or there had been default in the payment of interest and he could not get vacant possession of the property, was an application to the court for a declaration that the amount secured by the mortgage was well charged on the mortgagor's interest and for a sale, if the mortgagor did not pay the sum due within three months after service of the court order on him. These proceedings have a number of disadvantages: there is the delay caused by the mortgagor having three months to pay and the inevitable difficulties about a sale by the court. Moreover, the amount realised by a court sale is usually less than the amount that can be realised on a private sale or on a sale which is not advertised as being a court sale. Order 55, rule 7, of the Rules of the Supreme Court (Ireland) 1905, provided that any mortgagee or mortgagor, whether legal or equitable, or any person entitled to or having property subject to a legal or equitable charge or any person having the right to foreclose or redeem any mortgage could take out an originating summons for sale, delivery of possession by the mortgagor, redemption, reconveyance or delivery of possession by the mortgagee.[37]

[13.017] The earlier authorities on this rule had decided that an order for possession against a mortgagor would be made in special circumstances only, but in *Irish Permanent Building Society v Ryan*[38] the Republic's High Court decided that, in a case where the mortgagee had made default in paying instalments on a building society loan, an order that the mortgagor give up possession to the building society should be made as the property, when sold with vacant possession, would realise more.

---

[35] *Hinds v Blacker* (1877) IR 11 Eq 322; *Sinton v Dooley* [1910] 2 IR 162.

[36] See para **[13.064]**, *post.*

[37] See Wylie, *Judicature Acts (Ireland) and Rules of the Supreme Court (Ireland)* (1906), p 740. See also discussion in *Re O'Neill* [1967] NI 129.

[38] [1950] IR 12 (see *A Casebook on Irish Land Law* (1978), p 447).

[13.018] In *Re O'Neill*,[39] Lowry J (as he then was) held that the court had an inherent jurisdiction to put a legal or equitable mortgagee into possession and that such an order could be made not only in the Chancery Division, but also by a judge exercising bankruptcy jurisdiction in the Queen's Bench Division. In that case, the applicant had already obtained a declaration in bankruptcy proceedings that he was mortgagee of the bankrupt's interest and the court had ordered a sale by public auction, the applicant to have carriage of the sale. The applicant later applied for a further order for delivery of possession by the bankrupt, so that the sale could be made with vacant possession. In granting this further order, Lowry J pointed out for the guidance of the legal profession in Northern Ireland that it will usually be more convenient and less expensive if, in applications for an order for sale of mortgaged premises, the applicant applies for an order for possession at the same time, if such is required.

[13.019] The 1905 rules were replaced in the Republic by the 1962 Rules of the Superior Court[40] and this remedy is now dealt with by Order 54, rule 3 of the Rules of the Superior Courts 1986. The procedure is by special summons. A considerable extension of this useful jurisdiction was made in the Republic by s 13 of the Registration of Title Act 1942 (now s 62(7) of the Registration of Title Act 1964[41]), by which an owner of a registered charge may apply to the court for an order for possession when repayment of the principal money secured by the charge has become due. It had been held by the Court of Appeal in Northern Ireland[42] that an owner of a charge on land registered under the Local Registration of Title (Ireland) Act 1891 had not got an estate or interest which enabled him to recover possession but, as a result of statutory changes, such an owner may now apply for an order that the mortgagor give up possession of the lands to him. In Northern Ireland this power to award possession to the owner of a registered charge is given by para 5(2) of Part I of Schedule 7 to the Land Registration Act (NI) 1970, and may be exercised when, although payment of the principal has not become due, "there are urgent and special reasons for exercising the power."[43]

[13.020] In the Republic, when the rateable valuation of the lands is within the limits of the court's jurisdiction, the application may be made to the Circuit Court of the area in which the lands are situate for, although there is nothing in the Circuit Court's rules corresponding to Order 54, rule 3, of the 1962 Rules of the Superior Court, the mortgagee has a right to possession because either the legal estate has been conveyed to him or he is the owner of a term of years created by sub-demise.[44] Most building society

---

[39] [1967] NI 129. It will rarely be appropriate to grant an order for possession against one only of the joint mortgagors: see *Albany Home Loans Ltd v Massey* [1997] 2 All ER 609. As regards power to stay or suspend execution of the order for possession see para **[13.021]** *post*.

[40] SI 72/1962. *Cf* Rules of the Supreme Court (NI) 1936, as amended, espec Orders 47 and 51 and now Supreme Court (NI) Rules 1980, O 31 and 88.

[41] See *First Southern Bank Ltd v Maher* [1990] 2 IR 477.

[42] *Northern Banking Co Ltd v Devlin* [1924] 1 IR 90.

[43] Para 5(3)(b).

[44] In NI the county courts have the like powers of the High Court within the limits of their jurisdiction; see County Courts (NI) Order 1980, Article 34(1).

mortgages provide that the sum advanced is to become due within three or six months after the advance, but that the society will not exercise the power of sale or of entering into possession unless there has been a default by the mortgagor in the payment of instalments. The mortgagor usually acknowledges that he is in possession as a tenant of the building society. The result is that proceedings by ejectment may be brought by the building society in the Circuit Court when there has been default in the payment of the principal moneys or interest secured by the mortgage or, in the case of a mortgage repayable by instalments, when there has been default in the payment of the instalments for the period specified in the mortgage deed. In the case of advances made under the Small Dwellings Acquisition Act 1899, a special provision is made for recovery of possession in the event of default in the payments secured by the deed of mortgage.[45] The order made on an application such as these is that the mortgagor do forthwith upon the service of the court order on him give up possession of the property to the mortgagee. If he fails to do this, an order of *habere* by which the County Registrar is ordered to put the mortgagee into possession may be obtained in the court offices. When a mortgagee obtains possession, he may sell the property and the principles which we describe in the next part in relation to sale of mortgaged property without the intervention of the court apply. The mortgagee is entitled to pay his costs of the proceedings out of the money realised on the sale and he holds any surplus remaining after payment of the principal and interest and costs as a trustee for any subsequent mortgagees or, if there are none, in trust for the mortgagor.

[13.021] It has been a matter of considerable controversy how far the court has jurisdiction to postpone granting the mortgagee an immediate order for possession, eg, by staying the action or granting the order but suspending its execution to give the mortgagor time to retrieve the situation.[46] The traditional view at common law was that there was no general equitable jurisdiction to interfere with the mortgagee's right to possession,[47] but in recent decades this was queried by some English judges.[48] However, more recently the English judges have reiterated the basic common law rule,[49] subject to a very limited jurisdiction to defer execution of the order for possession which should be used sparingly.[50] This probably remains the position in the Republic, except where a family home is the mortgaged property. Under s 7 of the Family Home Protection Act 1976 the court has power to adjourn proceedings by a mortgagee for possession or sale of a family home on the ground of non-payment of sums due under the mortgage by one

---

[45] 1899 Act, ss 5(5) and 14(2). *Cf* Magistrates' Courts Act (NI) 1964, ss 76-81.

[46] See Wallace, 'Mortgagees and Possession' (1986) 37 NILQ 336. Also Smith, 'The Mortgagee's Right to Possession - The Modern Law' [1979] Conv 266.

[47] *Marquis of Cholmondeley v Clinton* (1817) 2 Mer 171; *Four Maids Ltd v Dudley Marshall (Properties) Ltd* [1957] Ch 317; *Birmingham Citizens Permanent Building Society v Caunt* [1962] 1 All ER 163.

[48] Especially by Lord Denning MR: see, eg, *Quennell v Maltby* [1979] 1 All ER 568 at 571.

[49] *Midland Bank plc v McGrath* [1996] EGCS 61.

[50] Eg, where the mortgagor has entered into or is about to enter into a contract to sell the property at a price which will realise a sum sufficient to discharge the mortgage debt still outstanding: see *Cheltenham & Gloucester plc v Booker* [1997] 19 EG 155.

spouse. The court may do so where it appears that the other spouse is desirous and capable of paying the arrears within a reasonable time and future periodical payments falling due under the mortgage, and it would be just and equitable to do so in all the circumstances, having regard to the terms of the mortgage and the interests of the mortgagee and spouses. The adjournment may be for such period and on such terms as appear to the court to be just and equitable, having regard in particular to whether the spouse of the mortgagor has been informed, by or on behalf of the mortgagee or otherwise, of the non-payment of the sums in question or any of them.[51]

In Northern Ireland, however, the common law position has been changed substantially by various statutory provisions.[52] First, if the mortgage comes within the UK Consumer Credit Act 1974,[53] the mortgagee is required to seek possession through a court order,[54] and, when faced with an application for such an order, the court has power to make a "time order" as it "considers just". This may require payment of instalments over a period of time, having regard to the mortgagor's means, or call for remedy of the breach of the mortgage within a specified time.[55] Secondly, where the mortgaged property is a "dwelling-house", the UK Administration of Justice Acts 1970[56] and 1973[57] empowers the court, where it appears that "the mortgagor is likely to be able within a reasonable period to pay any sums due under the mortgage or to remedy a default consisting of a breach of any other obligation arising under or by virtue of the mortgage",[58] to adjourn the proceedings or, on giving an order for possession, to stay or suspend execution or postpone the date for delivery of possession. It was long thought that the reference to "within a reasonable period" meant that adjournments, suspensions or deferrals under these Acts should be of limited duration,[59] but the English Court of Appeal has recently

---

[51] See Duncan and Scully, *Marriage Breakdown in Ireland: Law and Practice* (1990), p 310.

[52] The common law, whatever is the correct interpretation, was preserved in NI by s 86(3) of the Judicature (NI) Act 1978, but it probably has no greater effect, despite its wide wording: see the comments of Lord Lowry LCJ on its forerunner, s 27(5) of the Judicature (NI) Act 1877, in *NIHE v Macauley* [1974] NI 233 at 235.

[53] Ie, created by a private individual to secure a loan not exceeding £15,000 from a non-exempt lender (lenders like building societies and insurance companies are exempted): 1974 Act, ss 8 and 16; Consumer Credit (Increase of Monetary Limits) Order 1983 (SI No 1878) and Consumer Credit (Exempt Agreements) Orders 1985 (SI Nos 620, 757, 1736 and 1918).

[54] Section 126.

[55] Section 129(2). See *Southern & District Finance plc v Barnes* [1995] NPC 52.

[56] Section 36.

[57] Section 8. This was enacted to deal with difficulties in applying the 1970 Act to the common situation where the mortgage debt is repayable by instalments; see *Halifax Building Society v Clark* [1973] 2 All ER 33; *cf First Middlesborough Trading and Mortgage Co Ltd v Cunningham* (1974) 28 P & CR 69. It seems that the jurisdiction applies to endowment mortgages (where no capital payments are made until the end of the mortgage term: see para **[12.09]** *ante*); see *Bank of Scotland v Grimes* [1985] 2 All ER 254; *cf Habib Bank Ltd v Tailor* [1982] 3 All ER 561. See also *Centrax Trustees Ltd v Ross* [1979] 2 All ER 952.

[58] Section 36(1). See on the operation of this jurisdiction *Royal Trust Co of Canada v Markham* [1975] 3 All ER 433; *Target Homes Loans Ltd v Clothier* [1994] 1 All ER 439.

[59] Murray LJ subscribed to this view in *Allied Irish Banks Ltd v McAllister* [1993] 5 NIJB 82; see *infra*.

held that the "logic and spirit" of the legislation requires the court to take as its "starting point" the "full term" of the mortgage and to "pose at the outset the question would it be possible for the mortgagor to maintain payment-off of the arrears by instalments over that period".[60] This suggests that the English courts may be prepared now to use the jurisdiction to reschedule the mortgage debt in respect of a dwelling-house in the same way that commercial lenders are used to doing in respect of substantial business ventures.[61] However, it would appear that there must be some evidence of ability to pay on the part of the mortgagor and the courts will not stand in the way of a sale of the property,[62] if this is the only realistic way of the mortgagee recouping its debt, especially if the market is falling. These provisions, as was stated earlier, apply only where the mortgaged property is a dwelling-house, but it was recently pointed out by Murray LJ in *Allied Irish Banks Ltd v McAllister*[63] that Article 13 of the Judgments Enforcement (NI) Order 1981 empowers the Enforcement of Judgments Office[64] to "stay enforcement of any judgment ... either absolutely or on such terms and conditions as it may consider proper". He concluded that, since this power was subject to "any other statutory provisions", it does not apply to cases involving dwelling-houses covered by the Administration of Justice Acts. However, where it does apply, the interesting point is that the power in Article 13 does not seem to be circumscribed in any way, a point which concerned Murray LJ. In his view, it should be exercised "in a way which does not undermine the whole basis of the mortgage transaction" for:

> "If the protection for a lender under a secured loan is in effect taken away by a too liberal use of the discretion to delay enforcement, the banks and other lending institutions in this country may become quite unwilling to lend this money in situations where up to now they have been willing to do so ..."[65]

For this reason, he concluded that it should be exercised in a way analogous to the jurisdiction under the Administration of Justice Acts, but the worry is, of course, that the English Court of Appeal has since interpreted that jurisdiction in a way which has caused considerable alarm among lending institutions.[66] It remains to be seen how far the Northern judges will push the jurisdiction conferred by Article 13.

---

[60] *Gloucester Building Society plc v Norgan* [1996] 1 All ER 449 at 458 (*per* Waite LJ). Indeed, Evans LJ suggested that in certain cases an extension of the term may be appropriate: *ibid*, pp 461-2. For earlier suggestions of such "rescheduling" of the debt see *Western Bank Ltd v Schindler* [1976] 2 All ER 393.

[61] The classic illustration of this is, of course, the Channel Tunnel enterprise. See the statement of relevant considerations by Waite LJ at p 463. See also Wilkinson, 'Mortgage Repayments - In Your Own Time' (1996) 146 NLJ 252.

[62] The order for possession is frequently a preliminary to such a sale, para **[13.016]**, *ante*.

[63] [1993] 5 NIJB 82.

[64] See para **[13.183]** *post*.

[65] *Op cit*, pp 105-6.

[66] Fn 60, *supra*.

2. Sale

[13.022] The second remedy which a mortgagee has is power to sell the mortgaged property without the intervention of the court but, if the mortgagee is unable to obtain vacant possession of the property, he will find considerable difficulty in selling it, for no purchaser will buy property in the possession of a mortgagor. If, however, the property mortgaged consists of the right to receive rents, this power of sale without the intervention of the court may be used.

[13.023] In the early days, selling the property was not an effective way of realising the mortgagee's security because neither the common law nor equity recognised any right in the mortgagee to sell the property free from the mortgagor's equity of redemption. The most that the mortgagee was entitled to do was to transfer only the interest he had in the property, ie, ownership subject to the mortgagor's equity of redemption,[67] and few purchasers could be found who regarded this as a commercial interest in land. The result was that the practice developed of inserting in mortgage deeds an express power of sale enabling the mortgagee to sell the property without the need for any application to the court and free from the mortgagor's equity of redemption. So long as such an express power limited the mortgagee to retaining out of the proceeds of sale only what was due to him in terms of the mortgage debt and the costs and expenses of the sale, equity would not intervene. Then in 1860 Lord Cranworth's Act conferred a limited statutory power of sale on mortgagees (*inter alia*)[68] and this was replaced by a wider and more satisfactory power conferred by s 19 of the Conveyancing Act 1881.[69] The following are the main points to be borne in mind with respect to the statutory power of sale.

(i) Mortgagees Entitled

[13.024] Section 19(1) of the 1881 Act confers the power of sale under the Act on all mortgagees, provided the mortgage was made by deed after 1881. This covers most, if not all, in practice, legal mortgages[70] but not some equitable mortgages, eg, an informal mortgage by deposit of title deeds not accompanied by a memorandum under seal[71] or a contract for a legal mortgage not executed by deed.[72] The most that equitable mortgagees in such cases can do, in the absence of express powers, is to apply to the court for an order declaring the sum due on the mortgage well charged on the land and directing a sale of the land if it is not paid within a specified time (three months).[73]

---

[67] See further on transfer of the mortgagee's interest, para **[13.122]**, *post*.

[68] Sections 11-15.

[69] As extended by s 4 of the Conveyancing Act 1911. See also ss 20-22 of the 1881 Act.

[70] Including registered charges in respect of registered land, see Registration of Title Act 1965, s 62(6); Land Registration Act (NI) 1970, Sched 7 Pt I, para 5. *Kidd v O'Neill* [1931] IR 664; *Re Neely* [1936] IR 381; *Re McCairns (PMPA) plc* [1991] 2 IR 465.

[71] Para **[12.46]**, *ante*.

[72] Para **[12.41]**, *ante*.

[73] *Shea v Moore* [1894] 1 IR158, espec at 178-9; (*per* Palles CB); *Antrim County Land, Building and Investment Co Ltd v* Stewart [1904] 2 LR 357 at 369 (see *A Casebook on Irish Land Law* (1984), p 426): see para **[13.016]** *ante*. See also *Going v Farrell* (1814) Beat 472; *Ex parte Domvile* (1862) 14 Ir Ch R 19; *Munster and Leinster Bank v Jervis* (1902) 36 ILTR 113. Note also the court powers with respect to discharge of incumbrances conferred by s 5 of the Conveyancing Act 1881, as amended by s 1 of the Conveyancing Act 1911. See para **[6.145]**, *ante*.

Furthermore, in other cases where a deed is often used, eg, a mortgage of an equitable interest,[74] there may be difficulties on the ground that the "mortgaged property" within the meaning of s 19(1) of the 1881 Act,[75] which the mortgagee can sell, is an equitable interest only.[76] To get round this problem the mortgage deed may contain either a power of attorney empowering the mortgagee or his assigns to convey the legal estate[77] or a declaration by the mortgagor that he holds the legal estate on trust for the mortgagee and empowering the mortgagee to convey it.[78]

[13.025] So far as an equitable chargee is concerned, if the charge is created by deed, he is in the same position as an equitable mortgagee since the definition of a mortgage in the Conveyancing Act 1881 includes "any charge on any property for securing money or money's worth."[79] Otherwise, an equitable chargee must apply to the court for an order for sale of the property charged.[80] It should also be borne in mind that, once an application is made to the court for a sale and the court orders a sale, the mortgagee's extra-judicial power under the Conveyancing Acts can no longer be exercised since the judicial sale is intended to benefit all encumbrancers and not just the mortgagee who applied for it and then wishes to exercise his statutory power.[81]

(ii) Power Arises

[13.026] Section 19(1)(i) of the 1881 Act provides that the statutory power of sale does not arise until the "mortgage money has become due". In the case of most mortgages this means when the legal date for redemption[82] has passed; in the case of a mortgage "by instalments" it has been held that the power of sale arises as soon as any instalment is in arrear.[83] As we shall discuss in a moment, it is vital for a purchaser from the mortgagee to determine whether or not the power of sale has arisen. It is not so important, indeed it is immaterial to him, whether the power is also exercisable, as laid down by the 1881 Act.

---

74 Para **[12.39]**, *ante*.

75 *Cf* the wording of s 21(1) "the property ... [which] is the subject of the mortgage".

76 See the discussion in *Re Hodson & Howe's Contract* (1887) 35 Ch D 668 and *Re White Rose Cottage* [1965] Ch 940, espec at 951 *(per* Lord Denning MR). *Cf* under Lord Cranworth's Act 1860, *Re Solomon & Meagher's Contract* (1889) 40 Ch D 508; *Re Boucherett* [1908] 1 Ch 180.

77 See *Re White Rose Cottage* [1965] Ch 940. Also on powers of attorney, *Industrial Development Authority v Moran* [1978] IR 159 (see *A Casebook on Irish Land Law* (1984), p 419) and generally, Ch 11, *ante*.

78 *Re Sergie* [1954] NI 1.

79 Section 2(vi).

80 *Antrim Land, Building, and Investment Co Ltd v Stewart* [1904] 2 IR 357 (see *A Casebook on Irish Land Law* (1984), p 426); *Bank of Ireland Ltd v Feeney* [1930] IR 457. See also *Bolton v Fairtlough* (1864) 15 Ir Ch R 229.

81 *Re Beauclerk s Estate* [1907] 1 IR 76. See also *Re Prendergast* (1850) 2 Ir Jur (os) 145: *Royal Bank of Ireland Ltd v Sproule* [1940] Ir Jur Rep 33; *Bagots, Hutton & Kinahan Ltd v Talbot* (1952) 86 ILTR 186.

82 Para. **[12.05]**, *ante*. See, however, *Re Lowe* (1850) 2 Ir Jur (os) 131.

83 *Payne v Cardiff RDC* [1932] 1 KB 241. *Cf Twentieth Century Banking Corporation Ltd v Wilkinson* [1977] Ch 99.

(iii) Power Exercisable

[13.027] Section 20 of the 1881 Act provides that the power of sale cannot be exercised by the mortgagee unless and until one of three conditions is satisfied, namely:

(1) Notice requiring payment of the mortgage money has been served on the mortgagor or one of several mortgagors, and default has been made in payment of the mortgage money, or of part thereof, for three months after such service;[84] or

(2) Some interest under the mortgage is in arrear and unpaid for two months after becoming due; or

(3) There has been a breach of some provision contained in the mortgage deed[85] or in this Act,[86] and on the part of the mortgagor, or of some person concurring in and making the mortgage, to be observed or performed, other than and besides a covenant for payment of the mortgage money or interest thereon.

(iv) Protection of Purchaser

[13.028] The distinction drawn in the 1881 Act between when the mortgagee's power of sale *arises* and when it becomes *exercisable* is crucial from the point of view of a purchaser of the mortgaged land. The significance of the distinction is this. If the power of sale has not arisen, the mortgagee has no statutory power at all and, unless he has an express power of sale under the mortgage instrument, he can only transfer his interest under the mortgage, still subject to the mortgagor's equity of redemption. On the other hand, if the power has arisen and the mortgagee purports to exercise it, even though it is not yet exercisable, the purchaser nevertheless obtains a good title because, as s 21(2) of the 1881 Act provides:

Where a conveyance is made in professed[87] exercise of the power of sale conferred by this Act, the title of the purchaser shall not be impeachable on the ground that no case had arisen to authorise the sale, or that due notice was not given, or that the power was otherwise improperly or irregularly exercised; but any person damnified[88] by an unauthorised, or improper, or irregular exercise of the power shall have his remedy in damages against the person exercising the power.

To this s 5(1) of the Conveyancing Act 1911 adds:

Upon any sale made in professed exercise of the power conferred on mortgagees by the Act of 1881, a purchaser is not, and never has been, either before or on conveyance concerned to see or inquire whether a case has arisen to authorise the sale, or due notice has been given, or the power is otherwise properly and regularly exercised.[89]

---

[84] It has been held that the mortgagee may instead serve a notice demanding payment in three months' time and, if payment is not made by then, may sell at once. *Baker v Illingworth* [1908] 2 Ch 20.

[85] Eg, in respect of repairs to or insurance of the mortgaged property.

[86] Eg, in respect of leases granted under the powers conferred by s 18 of the 1881 Act, *Public Trustee v Lawrence* [1912] 1 Ch 789. See further para **[13.111]**, *post*.

[87] It is no longer necessary in England to state that the sale is made in exercise of the statutory power; this is presumed under s 104(2) of the Law of Property Act 1925.

[88] Eg, the mortgagor.

[89] See discussion in *Re Irish Civil Service Building Society and O'Keeffe* (1880) 7 LR Ir 136.

[13.029] These provisions are designed to simplify conveyancing by reducing the enquiries which the purchaser is expected to make. He is only obliged to satisfy himself that the power of sale has arisen, ie, that the legal date for redemption is passed, and in most cases this can be done very easily by reading the terms of the mortgage deed. He is not obliged to make enquiries, which could become extremely complex, into the detailed relations between the mortgagor and the mortgagee during the currency of the mortgage. In particular, he does not have to look at the accounts, if any, kept by the mortgagor and mortgagee as to payments made and received in respect of the mortgage. However, as is their practice with such a statutory provision,[90] the courts will not allow it to be used as an instrument of fraud and it has been stated that a purchaser with *knowledge* of any impropriety or irregularity about the exercise of the power will not obtain a good title.[91] This does not require of a purchaser from a mortgagee the standard of care in conveyancing matters imposed by the doctrine of notice, but it has been said that he must not shut his eyes to suspicious circumstances.[92]

[13.030] Further protection is afforded a purchaser by s 22(1) of the 1881 Act which provides that a receipt in writing of the mortgagee is a sufficient discharge for any money arising under the statutory power of sale and "a person paying or transferring the same to the mortgagee shall not be concerned to inquire whether any money remains due under the mortgage."

(v) Mode of Sale

[13.031] The great advantage the statutory power of sale has over a judicial sale in Ireland[93] is that it can be exercised by the mortgagee without the need to apply to the court for any order. Section 19(1)(i) of the Conveyancing Act 1881 confers a wide discretion on the mortgagee as to how he sells the mortgaged property or any part of it, namely:

> either subject to prior charges, or not, and either together or in lots, by public auction or by private contract, subject to such conditions respecting title, or evidence of title, or other matter, as he (the mortgagee) thinks fit, with power to vary any contract for sale, and to buy in at an auction, or to rescind any contract for sale, and to re-sell, without being answerable for any loss occasioned thereby.

Furthermore, s 4 of the Conveyancing Act 1911 empowers the mortgagee to impose or reserve covenants and conditions[94] on such a sale and to sell the land or any mines and

---

[90] See para **[3.048]**, *ante.*

[91] See, eg, *Lord Waring v London and Manchester Assurance Co Ltd* [1935] Ch 310 at 318 (*per* Crossman J); *Bailey v Barnes* [1894] 1 Ch 25 at 30 (*per* Stirling J). The same principle seems to apply in the case of exercise of an express power of sale, see *Jenkins v Jones* (1860) 2 Giff 99; *Selwyn v Garfit* (1888) 38 Ch D 273.

[92] *Bailey v Barnes, op cit*, p 34.

[93] Section 21(5) provides that the statutory power of sale does not affect the right of foreclosure, though it has been held that an order for foreclosure *nisi* renders the statutory power temporarily not exercisable without leave of court, *Stevens v Theatres Ltd* [1903] 1 Ch 857. However, foreclosure is never granted in Ireland, para **[13.059]**, *post.*

[94] Eg, restrictive covenants as to building on or other uses of the land, s 4(1)(i).

minerals apart from the surface, with the grant or reservation of rights of way, water and other easements and privileges[95] or the exception or reservation of mines and minerals.[96]

[13.032] Section 21(1) provides that the statutory power may be exercised[97] by deed "to convey the property sold, for such estate and interest therein as is the subject of the mortgage, freed from all estates, interests, and rights to which the mortgage has priority, but subject to all estates, interests, and rights which have priority to the mortgage." Once the power becomes exercisable, the mortgagee can demand and recover from any person, other than a person having priority to the mortgage, all the deeds and documents relating to the mortgaged property and its title which a purchaser is entitled to demand and recover from a mortgagee exercising the power of sale.[98]

[13.033] It has been held that the statutory power is exercised once the mortgagee enters into a contract to sell the property. Once the contract comes into existence, the mortgagor loses his right to redeem the mortgage and cannot prevent the sale going through by tendering the money due under the mortgage.[99]

(vi) Duty of Care

[13.034] The important point to be considered here is the duty of care imposed on the mortgagee when he exercises his power of sale, a matter upon which there has been considerable controversy over the years. In particular, there has been much discussion over how far the mortgagee, in agreeing to sell the mortgaged land for a certain price, can simply have regard to his own interests, by ensuring that this price at least covers what he is owed, and can disregard the interests of others, eg, subsequent mortgagees also dependent upon that land for their security. It must always be remembered that the question of a sale usually arises because the mortgagor has defaulted and so is probably not worth suing on his personal covenant for repayment of the debt. The selling mortgagee and any other interested mortgagees are almost certainly dependent entirely on their security in the mortgaged land for repayment of their respective debts. Each of them, therefore, has the most vital of interests in how the mortgagee who does exercise the power of sale in fact carries out the sale. Apart from that, the mortgagor, however precarious his moral position in view of his default which has led to the sale, also has a very clear financial interest in how much money the selling mortgagee raises on the sale, because the mortgagor, as we shall see, is entitled to what is left over from the proceeds of sale after payment off of all the mortgages.

[13.035] The only guidance on this matter which the Conveyancing Acts give is contained in s 21(6) of the 1881 Act, as amended by s 5(2) of the 1911 Act:

---

95 Section 4(1)(ii)(a).

96 Section 4(1)(ii)(b). See also s 4(1)(ii)(c) which permits inclusion of covenants by the purchaser to expend money on the land sold.

97 By any person for the time being entitled to receive and give a discharge for the mortgage money, see s 21(4) of the 1881 Act.

98 1881 Act, s 21(7).

99 *Lord Waring v London & Manchester Assurance Co Ltd* [1935] Ch 310; *Property & Bloodstock Ltd v Emerton* [1968] Ch 94.

The mortgagee, his executors, administrators, or assigns, shall not be answerable for any involuntary loss happening in or about the exercise or execution of the power of sale conferred by this Act or of any trust connected therewith [or of any power or provision contained in the mortgage deed[100]].

[13.036] The result of the courts' interpretation of this rather vague provision may be summarised as follows. First, it seems to be accepted that a mortgagee is not a "trustee" for the mortgagor, or any other interested persons, of his power of sale.[101] The power is conferred on the mortgagee primarily to realise his own security and the question of trusteeship does not arise except in respect of the proceeds of sale which come into his hands after the sale has been completed.[102] Secondly, and following on from this, the mortgagee in general cannot be attacked because of his motives in selling, eg, out of spite for the mortgagor.[103] Thirdly, the mortgagee must, however, act in good faith and this principle was considered by the Supreme Court of the Republic of Ireland in *Holohan v Friends Provident and Century Life Office*.[104] In that case the mortgagor was granted an injunction restraining the mortgagees from exercising an express power of sale. The mortgagees had entered into a contract to sell the mortgaged premises, subject to existing tenancies, as an investment and refused to consider the alternative of selling them with vacant possession, which, it was suggested, would secure a much higher price. O'Dalaigh CJ took the view that the good faith principle really involved a test of what a reasonable man would do in the mortgagee's position.[105] In this respect, good faith is not enough, for there should be no reason to doubt the good faith of the reasonable man. What is required is that the mortgagee should bear in mind the interests of the mortgagor and other subsequent mortgagees interested in the property and should take reasonable precautions or care to see that the fair market price for the property is obtained. Indeed, O'Dalaigh CJ took the view that the reasonable man would strive to

---

[100] Added by s 5(2) of the 1911 Act.

[101] *Kennedy v De Trafford* [1897] AC 180 *Haddington Island Quarry Co Ltd v Huson* [1911] AC 722; *Wright v New Zealand Co-Operative Association of Canterbury Ltd* [1939] AC 439. *Cf* the position under a judicial sale. *Re Beauclerk's Estate* [1907] 1 IR 76.

[102] Para **[13.038]**, *infra*.

[103] *Nash v Eads* (1880) 25 Sol Jo 95.

[104] [1966] IR 1 (see *A Casebook on Irish Land Law* (1984) p 447). *Cf* as regards a judicial sale *Bank of Ireland v Smith* [1966] IR 646. In *Van Hool McArdle v Rohan Industrial Estates Ltd* [1980] IR 237 it was held that when an official liquidator sells "subject to the approval of the High Court" and a higher offer is received before that approval is obtained the court is not obliged to approve the first sale even though the liquidator acted with all necessary diligence and in good faith. *Cf re* a sale by a receiver *McCarter & Co Ltd v Roughan* [1986] ILRM 447.

[105] *Ibid*, p 21. Lavery and Walsh JJ concurred with O'Dalaigh CJ. *Cf* the similar reasoning applied in England by the Court of Appeal in *Cuckmere Brick Co Ltd v Mutual Finance Ltd* [1971] Ch 949. See also *Standard Chartered Bank Ltd v* Walker [1982] 1 WLR 1410, where the mortgagee's duty was extended for the benefit of the mortgagor's guarantors. However, note that the application of the concept of negligence to such cases has since been doubted, ie, there is no general duty of care owed by a mortgagee, so that, eg, the mortgagor's other creditors may have no cause of action. See *Parker-Tweedale v Dunbar Bank plc* [1991] Ch 12; *Downsview Nominees Ltd v First City Corporation Ltd* [1993] AC 295; *cf Routstone Ltd v Minories Finance Ltd* [1997] 21 EG 148. Devonshire, 'The Mortgagee's Power of Sale: A Case for the Equitable Standard of Good Faith' (1995) 46 NILQ 182.

get the best price available in the circumstances. While this seems to accord with the views expressed in some of the earlier authorities,[106] it does seem to impose a somewhat stricter duty on mortgagees than seems to have been suggested in some of the other earlier authorities. In particular, it seems to impose a much more positive duty to consider the interests of others and to get a fair price for the property than was implied in judicial statements to the effect that the mortgagee need not delay the sale to obtain a better price[107] or advertise the property or attempt a sale by auction before agreeing to sell by private treaty,[108] or that the court will not interfere with a sale at an apparently low or unusual[109] price unless there is evidence of fraud.[110] In passing it should be noted that in both parts of Ireland this matter has been put beyond doubt by statute so far as building societies acting as mortgagees are concerned. By s 36 of the Building Societies Act (NI) 1967,[111] they are under a duty "to take reasonable care to ensure that the price at which the estate is sold is the best price which can reasonably be obtained ...".[112] By s 26(1) of the Republic's Building Societies Act 1989, they are obliged to ensure "as far as is reasonably practicable that the property is sold at the best price reasonably obtainable".[113]

[13.037] Finally, it must be remembered that the mortgagee must carry out a "sale." In particular, he must not try to achieve some other purpose by means of a sale, eg, acquire the land for himself.[114] Just as the mortgagee cannot sell to himself directly,[115] he cannot

---

[106] See, eg, the House of Lords in *Kennedy v De Trafford* [1897] AC 180 and the Court of Appeal in *Tomlin v Luce* (1889) 43 Ch D 191. *Cf* Lord de Villiers in *Haddington Island Quarry Co Ltd v Huson* [1911] AC 722 at 727 (there must be "no reckless disregard of the interests of the mortgagors").

[107] *Davey v Durant* (1857) 1 De G & J 535 at 533. *Cf, Farrar v Farrar Ltd* (1888) 40 Ch D 395 at 398 (entitled to proceed to a forced sale); *Jones v Matthie* (1847) 11 Jur 504 at 506 (court not concerned to see if mortgagee "acted with kindness and charity"); *Routstone Ltd v Minories Finance Ltd* [1997] 21 EG 148 (no duty to "work" the property by, eg, refurbishing it or dealing with rent reviews under the lease). In *Casey v Irish Intercontinental Bank Ltd* [1979] IR 364 the Republic's Supreme Court held that where mortgagees exercising their power of sale of the mortgaged property accepted an offer to purchase at a price (£111,000) which they considered was the best price available they could not subsequently rescind the contract upon receiving a higher offer (£190,000). Kenny J said:

> "The subsequent offer of £190,000 did not in any way invalidate that contract which in my opinion Intercontinental were bound to carry out. A mortgagee who enters into a contract for sale at a price which all the circumstances and valuations show is at the date of the contract the best price available is not discharged if a higher price is offered after the contract is made."

[108] *Davey v Durrant, op cit* p 560. *Cf* the *Cuckmere* case fn 105 *supra*.

[109] Eg, exactly the right amount needed to cover the debt and costs of mortgagee selling, see *Kennedy v De Trafford* [1897] AC 180.

[110] *Adams v Scott* (1859) 7 WR 213; *Warner v Jacob* (1882) 20 Ch D 220 at 224; *Wright v New Zealand Farmers Co-Operative Association of Canterbury Ltd* [1939] AC 439.

[111] The same is the position in England, see now s 36 of the Building Societies Act 1962 and *Reliance Permanent Building Society v Harwood-Stamper* [1944] Ch 362.

[112] See *Survey of the Land Law of Northern Ireland* (1971) para 228.

[113] Replacing s 82(1)(*a*) of the Building Societies Act 1976.

[114] *Farrar v Farrars Ltd* (1888) 40 Ch D 395 at 409.

[115] *Henderson v Astwood* [1894] AC 150.

acquire the property indirectly through an agent or nominee.[116] Nor may servants of mortgagee institutions purchase mortgaged property in a sale by their employers.[117] However, a second mortgagee of the same land may purchase from the first mortgagee.[118]

(vii) Proceeds of Sale

[13.038] While the mortgagee is not a trustee of his power of sale, it is expressly provided by s 21(3) of the Conveyancing Act 1881, that he is trustee of the proceeds of sale arising from his exercise of the power of sale.[119] Under this trust it is provided that the mortgagee must apply the proceeds in the following order:[120]

(1) in discharge of prior encumbrances to which the sale is not made subject;

(2) in payment of all costs, charges, and expenses, properly incurred by him, as incident to the sale or any attempted sale, or otherwise;

(3) in discharge of the mortgage money, interest, and costs, and other money, if any, due under the mortgage;

(4) by paying the residue to the person entitled to the mortgaged property,[121] or authorised to give receipts for the proceeds of the sale thereof, ie, the next mortgagee or, if none, the mortgagor.[122]

Thus the mortgagee is liable to account to subsequent mortgagees[123] and interest may become payable if the money is not paid to those entitled.[124] In *Murphy v Allied Irish Banks Ltd*[125] Murphy J held that it was not enough for the mortgagee-bank to pay the money into an account in the mortgagor's name. As he put it:

> "Placing the balance in any account in the name of the deceased [mortgagor] did not constitute payment, it was simply a procedure by which payment could be made conveniently when sought by the personal representative of the deceased."[126]

---

[116] *Downers v Grazebrook* (1817) 3 Mer 200; *Robertson v Norris* (1854) 4 Jur (ns) 443; *Nutt v Easton* [1899] 1 Ch 873.

[117] *Martinson v Clowes* (1885) 52 LT 706; *Hodson v Deans* [1903] 2 Ch 647. *Cf* the case of the mortgagee employing his own firm of auctioneers to conduct the sale, *Matthison v Clarke* (1854) 3 Drew 3 (firm disallowed their commission).

[118] *Shaw v Bunny* (1865) 2 De GJ & s 468; *Kirkwood v Thompson* (1865) 2 De GJ & s 613.

[119] See *Thorne v Heard* [1895] AC 495; *Re Counter's Charge* [1960] Ch 491.

[120] *Re Thompson's Mortgage Trusts* [1920] 1 Ch 508.

[121] At first sight this appears to refer to the purchaser from the selling mortgagee but it obviously must be taken to mean the person who was entitled to the mortgaged property immediately prior to the sale.

[122] *West London Commercial Bank v Reliance Permanent Building* (1885) 29 Ch D 954.

[123] *Davey v Durrant* (1857) 1 De G & J 535; *Bettyes v Maynard* (1883) 31 WR 461; *Belton v Bass, Ratcliffe and Gretton Ltd* [1922] 2 Ch 449.

[124] *Charles v Jones* (1887) 35 Ch D 544.

[125] [1994] 2 ILRM 220.

[126] *Ibid*, p 224.

He then went on to hold that the bank was liable to pay interest on the amount not paid over, chargeable either by reference to the court rate,[127] or the yield on a deposit account payable on demand by a licensed bank.

However, if the rights of subsequent mortgagees and the mortgagor have been barred by lapse of time,[128] it appears that the selling mortgagee may keep the entire proceeds of sale for himself.[129] This would seem to be the only circumstance when the mortgagee may keep the proceeds. It was held in England recently that, even where the mortgagor had procured a 100% mortgage loan by fraud, the mortgagee could not keep the surplus on the basis that the mortgagor was liable to account for profits made as a result of the fraud,[130] whether on restitutionary principles or as a constructive trustee.[131]

(viii) Effect of Sale

[13.039] Section 21(1) of the Conveyancing Act 1881 provides that a sale of the mortgaged property under the Act passes to the purchaser "such estate and interest therein as is the subject of the mortgage, freed from all estates, interests, and rights to which the mortgage has priority, but subject to all estates, interests, and rights which have priority to the mortgage". Thus, in the case of a legal mortgage created by conveyance of the fee simple, the fee simple passes. In the case of a mortgage by demise or sub-demise, the term of years or sub-term in question only passes.[132] In the case of a registered charge on registered land, the power of sale includes power to sell the estate or interest which is subject to the charge.[133] In the case of an equitable mortgage, the equitable interest mortgaged only will pass unless some conveyancing device such as a power of attorney or declaration of trust has been used to enable the legal estate in the land to be transferred.[134] Apart from that, an application may be made to the court for a

---

[127] He agreed with Kenny J's criticism of the 4% court rate as inappropriate in the 1960s (see *Law v Roberts & Co (Ir) Ltd* [1964] IR 306) and even more inappropriate in later decades, settling on 8% in the *Murphy* case.

[128] See, further, Ch 23 *post*.

[129] *Young v Clarey* [1948] Ch 191. See also *Murphy v Allied Irish Banks Ltd* [1994] 2 ILRM 220. Alternatively, as a "trustee" of the proceeds the mortgagee pays them into court under the statutory power conferred on trustees in Ireland by s 42 of the Trustee Act 1893 and s 63 of the Trustee Act (NI) 1958. See as regards mortgagees, *Banner v Berridge* (1881) 18 Ch D 254 (surplus proceeds); *Re Walkhampton Estate* (1884) 26 Ch D 391 and *Charles v Jones* (1887) 35 Ch D 544 (doubt as to proper recipients of proceeds).

[130] *Halifax Building Society v Thomas* [1995] 4 All ER 673.

[131] See para **[9.059]**, *ante*. In fact the mortgagor had been prosecuted for fraud and his profits were made the subject of a confiscation order under Pt VI of the English Criminal Justice Act 1988.

[132] In the case of a sub-demise the mortgagor may make a declaration of trust as to the whole term so as to enable the mortgagee to sell this, see *London & County Banking Co v Goddard* [1897] 1 Ch 642.

[133] Registration of Title Act 1964 s 62(6) (RI); Land Registration Act (NI) 1970 Sched 7, Pt 1, para 5(1). See *Re Neely* [1936] IR 381; *Re McCairns (PMPA) plc* [1991] 2 IR 465.

[134] See para **[13.024]**, *ante*.

sale of the property[135] and the court has a general discretion to make any order for conveyance, or vesting order, to give effect to the sale.[136]

3. Court Order for Sale

[13.040] If the mortgagee cannot or does not wish to bring proceedings for possession and if he cannot sell the property without the intervention of the court, he may bring proceedings to have the property sold by the court and the proceeds applied in discharge of the principal and interest secured by his mortgage.[137] The summons claims a declaration that the sum secured by the mortgage is well charged on the defendant's interest in the lands and a sale. The court order gives the declaration, directs an inquiry as to the amount due on the mortgage for principal and interest, and directs a sale of the property if the amount found due is not paid within 3 months from the date of service of the examiner's certificate finding the amount due on the defendant. The sale is carried out under the control of the court which engages an auctioneer and fixes a reserve price, and the money realised on the sale is paid into court.[138] Although it is a court sale, the vendor is the mortgagee who procures the order for sale and if the mortgagor remains in possession after the property has been sold with vacant possession, it is the duty of the mortgagee to apply to the court for an order that the purchaser be put into possession.[139]

[13.041] The order made by the court directing a sale also directs an inquiry as to other mortgages and their priorities and, when the funds in court are being allocated, if there is sufficient to pay the first mortgagee's principal, interests and costs, the balance remaining will be applied in discharge of the amount due to the second mortgagee for principal and interest, and any sum remaining after payment of all the sums due on the mortgages will be paid to the mortgagor.[140] When there is no dispute about the amount due on the mortgage for principal and interest, the court finds the amount due in its original order and does not direct an inquiry as to the amount due. When this is done, the order, and not the examiner's certificate, has to be served on the mortgagor, and the three months run from the date of this service.

---

[135] See s 5 of the Conveyancing Act 1881, as amended by s 1 of the Conveyancing Act 1911, relating to discharge of incumbrances on land.

[136] 1881 Act, s 5(2).

[137] This seems to be inherent jurisdiction lying in the court; see *Bank of Ireland v Waldron* [1944] IR 303. See also the Republic's Rules of the Superior Courts 1986, O 51 and O 54, r 3; Rules of the Supreme Court (NI) 1980, O 31 and O 88. *Cf* the statutory jurisdiction in England conferred by s 91 of the Law of Property Act 1925. This is based on the earlier provision in s 25 of the Conveyancing Act 1881, but this did not apply to Ireland; see sub-s (7) and para **[13.057]**, *post*. See *Arab Bank plc v Mercantile Holdings Ltd* [1994] 2 All ER 74. In *Palk v Mortgage Services Funding plc* [1993] 2 All ER 481 it was held that a mortgagor, faced with "negative" equity, could obtain an order under s 91 so as to reduce accumulating interest. It is doubtful whether the inherent jurisdiction to order a sale in Ireland stretches that far; see para **[13.107]**, *post*.

[138] See *Bank of Ireland v Smith* [1966] IR 646.

[139] *Bank of Ireland v Waldron* [1944] IR 303; *Re O'Neill* [1967] NI 129 at 132-5 (*per* Lowry J). See generally on court sales, Wylie, *Irish Conveyancing Law* (2nd ed, 1996), paras 11.02-7.

[140] See *Re Sherry-Brennan* [1979] ILRM 113.

4. Taking Possession

[13.042] This is the fourth main remedy available to a mortgagee and the main distinction from the first three is that taking possession does not of itself put an end to the mortgage and secure repayment of the capital debt.[141] It may, of course, be invoked as a preliminary to exercising another remedy, eg, the power of sale,[142] but for the most part a mortgagee is not interested in taking possession and is happy to allow the mortgagor to keep it.[143] If the mortgagee does take possession it is often to secure regular payment of the interest charged on the capital sum lent, by interception of the rents and profits issuing out of the land.[144]

(i) Mortgagees Entitled

[13.043] Where a legal mortgage is created by conveyance, assignment, demise or sub-demise of a freehold or leasehold estate in the land, it is inherent in the nature of the transaction that the mortgagee is entitled to claim possession of the property as holder of the estate in question as soon as the mortgage is created.[145] He can either claim physical possession or, if this is in the hands of some person with a prior claim to it, eg, an existing tenant, he can direct that person to pay to him any rents which might otherwise be paid to the mortgagor. So far as a registered chargee on registered land is concerned, since he has no estate in the land it would seem that he has no right initially to take possession of the land.[146] It would seem that the only way to gain possession, if he wants it, is to seek the permission of the chargor or, if that is refused, an order of the court.[147] As we mentioned earlier, in the Republic of Ireland, the registered owner of the charge

---

[141] See, generally, Rudden, 'Mortgagee's Right to Possession' (1961) 25 Conv 278; Smith, 'The Mortgagee's Right to Possession: The Modern View' [1979] Conv 266.

[142] *Bank of Ireland Ltd v Slattery* [1911] 1 IR 33; *Royal Bank of Ireland v O' Shea* (1943) 77 ILTR 4; *Ulster Bank Ltd v Conlon* (1957) 91 ILTR 193. *Cf Doran v Hannin* (1906) 40 ILTR 186 (to prevent forfeiture of licence of licensed premises).

[143] Para **[12.15]**, *ante*.

[144] *Horlock v Smith* (1842) 6 Jur 478; *Heales v McMurray* (1856) 23 Beav 401; *Mexborough UDC v Harrison* [1964] 1 WLR 733. And see Bodkin, 'Tenants and Mortgagees" (1952) 16 Conv 285.

[145] *Green v Burns* (1879) 6 LR Ir 173. See also *Four-Maids Ltd v Dudley Marshall (Properties) Ltd* [1957] Ch 317; *Birmingham Citizens Permanent Building Society v Caunt* [1962] Ch 883. If the mortgagee allows the mortgagor to remain in possession, then, subject to the terms of the mortgage, the mortgagor is a tenant at sufferance, but he is entitled to receive and keep all the rents and profits from the land, without accounting for them to the mortgagee. *Ex parte Calwell* (1828) 1 Mol 259; *Patterson v Reilly* (1882) 10 LR Ir 304; *Campion v Palmer* [1896] 2 IR 445.

[146] *Northern Banking Co Ltd v Devlin* [1924] 1 IR 90. The reference in s 62(6) of the Registration of Title Act 1964 (RI) to a registered chargee having "all the rights and powers of a mortgagee under a mortgage by deed" seems to refer back to the earlier reference to "a mortgage by deed within the meaning of the Conveyancing Acts," ie, it is confined to matters within s 19 of the 1881 Act - sale, appointment of a receiver, insurance etc. *Cf.* the wording of para 5(1) of Pt I of Sched 7 to the Land Registration Act (NI) 1970, which seems to make this point clearer.

[147] *Bank of Ireland Ltd v Feeney* [1930] IR 457 espec at 469 (*per* Kennedy CJ). Alternatively there may be an express provision in the charge permitting the chargee to take possession on, eg, specified defaults by the chargor: see *Gale v First National Building Society* [1985] IR 609.

or his personal representative may apply to the court in a summary manner, under s 62(7) of the Registration of Title Act 1964, for possession of the land and, if the court thinks it proper to order possession and the applicant obtains it, he is deemed to be a mortgagee in possession.[148] This power in the Republic is confined to when the principal money secured by the mortgage has become due, but, in Northern Ireland, the power of the court to award possession to the registered owner of a charge under para 5(2) of Part I of Schedule 7 to the Land Registration Act (NI) 1970, though generally similarly confined, may be exercised, under para 5(3)(b) of the same Part and Schedule, where the court is satisfied that, although payment of the principal sum has not become due, "there are urgent and special reasons for exercising the power."[149]

[13.044] So far as an equitable mortgagee is concerned, there has been much controversy as to his right to claim possession.[150] It is clear that he has no right to possession at law since he has no legal estate in the land, unless, of course, the mortgage agreement confers such a right on him.[151] On the other hand, it is arguable that, in equity at least, he ought to be put in the same position as if he had the legal title to the property and there is some authority in Ireland for saying that he is entitled to possession in his own right, especially as against the mortgagor.[152] Whatever an equitable mortgagee's position in theory,[153] it is settled that he can apply to the court for an order for possession[154] and the only restriction is the principle that all equitable remedies are

---

[148] See *First Southern Bank Ltd v Maher* [1990] 2 IR 477. See also *Re McCairns (PMPA) plc* [1991] 2 IR 465.

[149] See *Re Jacks* [1952] IR 159.

[150] See Wade, 'Equitable Mortgagee's Right to Possession' (1955) 71 LQR 205; Willoughby, 'Rights of Second Mortgagees Regarding Possession' (1908) 24 LQR 297. See also Coote, *Law of Mortgages* (9th ed, 1927), p 823; Waldock, *Mortgages* (2nd ed, 1950), p 235.

[151] Or the mortgagor, or first legal mortgagee, subsequently agrees to this. See *Northern Banking Co Ltd v Devlin* [1924] 1 IR 90 at 92 (*per* Andrews LJ). *Cf Ocean Accident & Guarantee Co Ltd v Ilford Gas Co* [1905] 2 KB 493.

[152] See especially the judgment of Palles CB in *Antrim County Land Building and Investment Co Ltd v Stewart* [1904] 2 IR 357 (see *A Casebook on Irish Land Law* (1984), p 426). Also *National Bank Ltd v Hegarty* (1901) 1 NIJR 13; *Re O'Neill* [1967] NI 129. *Cf Re Gordon* (1889) 61 LT 299; *Spencer v Mason* (1931) 75 Sol Jo 295; *Barclays Bank Ltd v Bird* [1954] Ch 274. See also *Malone v Geraghty* (1852) 1 HLC 89.

[153] It seems that he cannot intercept the rents and profits from the land, since the right to these belongs to the legal reversioner and there is no legal relationship of landlord and tenant between an equitable mortgagee and a tenant in possession of the mortgaged land. See *Finck v Tranter* [1905] 1 KB 427; *Vacuum Oil Co Ltd v Ellis* [1914] 1 KB 693.

[154] See Lowry J in *Re O'Neill* [1967] NI 129 at 135: "... the Supreme Court has an inherent jurisdiction to make an order putting a legal or equitable mortgagee into possession and ... such an order may be made not only in the Chancery Division, but also by a judge exercising bankruptcy jurisdiction in the Queen's Bench Division." Para **[13.018]**, *ante*.

discretionary.[155] A mere equitable chargee has no right to possession since he has neither a legal nor an equitable estate or interest in the property mortgaged.[156]

(ii) Procedure

[13.045] Should the mortgagor refuse to allow a mortgagee to exercise his right to take possession of the mortgaged land, the mortgagee may initiate an action for ejectment or, if he prefers nowadays, simply make a summary application for an order of possession.[157] This summary procedure, which we mentioned earlier,[158] has removed one of the main reasons for frequent insertion of a particular clause in mortgage deeds, namely, an attornment clause.[159] Through such a clause, the mortgagor usually attorns, ie, acknowledges, himself to be the tenant of the mortgagee, thereby creating the relationship of landlord and tenant between himself and the mortgagee, so far as this is consistent with the mortgage transaction.[160] The clause may still be relevant today because, eg, it may provide that the mortgagor's tenancy cannot be determined except by the mortgagee giving a certain period of notice. The necessity for such a notice would obviously restrict the mortgagee in claiming possession of the land.[161] The existence of a relationship of landlord and tenant under an attornment clause may also facilitate the running more widely of the burden of covenants entered into between the mortgagor and mortgagee.[162]

---

[155] Para **[3.050]**, *ante*. The court has, by tradition, no discretion to refuse an order to a legal mortgagee but may grant a short adjournment if there is a reasonable prospect that the mortgagor may redeem the mortgage. See *Birmingham Citizens Permanent Building Society v Caunt* [1962] Ch 883; *London Permanent Benefit Building Society v De Baer* [1969] 1 Ch 321. Also Megarry, (1957) 73 LQR 300. But see the discussion in para **[13.021]**, *ante*.

[156] *National Bank Ltd v Hegarty* (1901) 1 NIJR 13: *Bank of Ireland Ltd v Feeney* [1930] IR 457.

[157] See *Doran v. Hannin* (1906) 40 ILTR 186; *Bank of Ireland Ltd v Slattery* [1911] 1 IR 33; *Bunyan v Bunyan* [1916] 1 IR 70; *National Bank v Shanahan* (1932) 66 ILTR 120; *Irish Permanent Building Society v Ryan* [1950] IR 12; *Ulster Bank Ltd v Conlon* (1957) 91 ILTR 193; *Irish Civil Service (Permanent) Building Society v Ingram's Representatives* [1959] IR 181. Also *Re Jacks* [1952] IR 159 (registered chargee). See further paras **[13.016]-[13.021]**, *ante*.

[158] Paras **[13.019]-[13.020]**, *ante*.

[159] Gray, 'The Attornment Clause' (1948) 13 Conv 31; Keeton and Sheridan, *Equity* (1969), pp 232-5. Note also the Form of Attornment (No 6) by under-tenants or occupiers of land in Sched A to Deasy's Act 1860, para **[17.020]**, *post*.

[160] See the discussion in the English cases where it has been held that the mortgagor-tenant cannot claim statutory protection under legislation like the Rent Acts or Agricultural Holdings Acts, *Portman Building Society v Young* [1951] 1 All ER 191: *Steyning and Littlehampton Building Society v Wilson* [1951] 1 Ch 1018; *Alliance Building Society v Pinwill* [1958] Ch 788; *Jessamine Investment Co v Schwartz* [1977] 2 WLR 145. And see Megarry, (1958) 74 LQR 348; Baker, (1965) 81 LQR 341; (1966) 82 LQR 21. *Cf* summary recovery of possession of "cottier"' tenements under ss 81-9 of Deasy's Act 1860, para **[17.102]**, *post*. *Cf* the English Small Tenements Recovery Act 1838. See *Dudley and District Benefit Society v Gordon* [1929] 2 KB 105.

[161] *Hinckley and Country Building Society v Henry* [1953] 1 WLR 352. *Cf Alliance Building Society v Pinwill* [1958] Ch 788.

[162] *Regent Oil Co Ltd v JA Gregory (Hatch End) Ltd* [1966] Ch 402. See further on the running of the benefit and burden of covenants, ch 19, *post*.

(iii) Liability to Account Strictly

[13.046] In exercising his right to take possession of the mortgaged land the mortgagee is entitled to safeguard the payments of interest due to him and may, though he is not obliged to do this, devote any surplus rents and profits towards repayment of the capital remaining owing to him.[163] He is also entitled to allowances where he expends money in repairs to the property or in meeting other outgoings, such as head-rents.[164] Section 19(1)(iv) of the Conveyancing Act 1881 permits a mortgagee by deed in possession to cut and sell timber and other trees ripe for cutting and not planted or left standing for shelter or ornament. This section also permits the mortgagee in possession to enter into a contract for any such cutting and sale, provided it is to be completed within twelve months from the making of the contract. While the mortgagee is not generally liable for waste, he is not allowed to cut timber other than as allowed under the 1881 Act or to open new mines as opposed to working existing ones.[165] However, in equity he will be allowed to do such things if the land is otherwise insufficient security for the debt, with the qualification that he must not commit "equitable" waste or wanton destruction.[166]

[13.047] Apart from this, a mortgagee in possession is liable to account strictly, ie, on the footing of wilful default, to the mortgagor.[167] He must account not only for the rents and profits which he actually receives but also for those which he would have received, but for his default or mismanagement.[168] If a mortgagee fails to render accounts, he may find himself charged with interest[169] and subsequently deprived of his costs in a redemption suit, even though the entire debt has not been paid.[170] It is part of the same principle of accounting that a mortgagee in possession must try to keep the charges involved as low as possible and so, in general, is not entitled to charge remuneration for any work he does, eg, in keeping a business going on the mortgaged premises. Indeed,

---

[163] *Nelson v Booth* (1858) 3 De G & J 119; *Wrigley v Gill* [1905] 1 Ch 241.

[164] *Burrowes v Molloy* (1845) 8 Ir Eq R 482. He may also be entitled to make reasonable improvements to the property, chargeable to the mortgagor, so long as these do not hinder the power of redemption, *Shepard v Jones* (1882) 21 Ch D 469 at 479.

[165] See *Miller v Davey* (1836) 31 Beav 470; *Elias v Snowdon Slate Quarries Co* (1879) 4 App Cas 454.

[166] *Sandon v Hooper* (1844) 14 LJ Ch 120; *Millett v Davey* (1863) 31 Beav 470 at 476 (*per* Romilly MR). See further, on equitable waste, para **[4.154]**, *ante*.

[167] *Lord Trimleston v Hamill* (1810) 1 Ba & B 377; *Sloane v Mahon* (1838) 1 Dr & Wal 189. See also *Unthank v Gabbett* (1830) Beat 453. And see Markson, 'Liability of Lenders in Possession' (1979) 129 New LJ 334. A first mortgagee in possession may also have to account to subsequent mortgagees, *Ocean Accident and Guarantee Co Ltd v Collum* [1913] 1 IR 328.

[168] *Metcalf v Campion* (1828) 1 Mol 238; *O'Connell v O'Callaghan* (1863) 15 Ir Ch R 31. See also *Burke v O'Connor* (1853) 4 Ir Ch R 418. *Cf Hughes v Williams* (1806) 12 Ves 493; *Marshall v Cave* (1824) LJ (OS) Ch 57; *White v City of London Brewery Co* (1889) 42 Ch D 237.

[169] Where courts have made orders directing accounts against mortgagees in Ireland the practice seems to have been to make half-yearly rests and not to charge interest on payments received by the mortgagee during intermediate periods, which exceed the interest due, see *Graham v Walker* (1847) 11 Ir Eq R 415.

[170] *Cassidy v Sullivan* (1878) 1 LR Ir 313. See also *Burke v O'Connor* (1853) 4 Ir Ch R 418.

in *Comyns v Comyns*[171] Sullivan MR even held void an express stipulation in the mortgage deed that the mortgagee could have £100 a year for his trouble in managing the mortgaged land.[172] Sometimes, this principle is put another way, that, having taken possession himself instead of appointing a receiver,[173] the mortgagee cannot turn round and charge a receiver's commission.[174] Finally, it may be noted that the mortgagee may acquire the full title to the land by adverse possession, ie, his possession may extinguish the mortgagor's right to redeem under the Statute of Limitations.[175]

5. Appointment of a Receiver

[13.048] As we have just discussed, there are many drawbacks about the mortgagee himself taking possession of the mortgaged property and from the earliest stages of development of the law of mortgages it became the practice to achieve the same result, ie, more efficient management of the property to safeguard the mortgagee's interest payments, by a slightly different means.[176] This was the appointment of a receiver who would be given extensive powers to manage the mortgaged property, a procedure which can most usually be adopted in cases where that property comprises a business, such as an hotel, restaurant or shop, whose value as security is largely dependent upon the efficient running of the business.[177]

[13.049] In the early days, it seems that receivers were often appointed by the mortgagor at the request of the mortgagee. Then the practice developed of insertion in the mortgage deed of a clause reserving to the mortgagee the right to appoint a receiver.[178] However, this clause would usually state expressly that such a receiver would be deemed to be nevertheless agent of the mortgagor, a theory which, as we shall see, holds good today and avoids many of the difficulties involved in the mortgagee himself taking possession.[179] Then Lord Cranworth's Act 1860[180] conferred a limited statutory power to

---

[171] (1871) IR 5 Eq 583.

[172] The learned judge took the view that this amounted to a clog on the equity of redemption, see para **[13.090]**, *post*.

[173] See para **[13.048]**, *infra*.

[174] *Carew v Johnston* (1805) 2 Sch & Lef 280 at 301 (*per* Lord Redesdale) See also *Kavanagh v Workingman's Benefit Building Society* [1896] 1 IR 56 (agent appointed to collect rents by mortgagees in possession not allowed commission).

[175] See para **[23.33]**, *post*.

[176] One point of distinction from the mortgagee himself taking possession is that the doctrine of adverse possession cannot work in favour of a mortgagee who has appointed a receiver. See para **[23.33]**, *post*.

[177] See Lyle, *Handbook for Receivers* (1878); Picarda, *The Law relating to Receivers, Managers and Administrators* (2nd ed); also *Alven v Bond* (1841) 3 Ir Eq R 365; *Ardmore Studios (Ireland) Ltd v Lynch* [1965] IR 1; *Kernohan Estates Ltd v Boyd* [1967] NI 27 (see *A Casebook on Equity and Trusts in Ireland* (1985) p 306).

[178] See, generally, Kerr, *Law and Practice as to Receivers* (14th ed, by Walton 1972). Also Molesworth, *Receivers in Chancery in Ireland* (1838). See also *Industrial Development Authority v Moran* [1978] IR. 159 (para **[11.33]**, *ante*).

[179] Para **[13.054]**, *post*.

[180] Sections 17-23.

appoint receivers on mortgagees and this was replaced by s 19(1) of the Conveyancing Act 1881, which still governs the matter in both parts of Ireland.

(i) Mortgagees Entitled

[13.050] As in the case of the power of sale also conferred by s 19(1) of the 1881 Act, the power to appoint a receiver[181] is conferred on mortgagees whose mortgages are created by deed and this covers most legal mortgagees and registered chargees.[182] It also applies to an equitable mortgagee or chargee if the mortgage or charge is created by deed.[183] If the mortgage or charge is not created by deed, the equitable mortgagee or chargee will have to apply, as can any mortgagee or chargee, to the court for the appointment of a receiver. Prior to the Judicature (Ireland) Act 1877, the courts of equity claimed jurisdiction to appoint a receiver, who, incidentally, in such a case is not an agent for either party but an officer of the court.[184] Normally relief would be given to equitable mortgagees only, on the ground that a legal mortgagee could help himself by invoking his right to take possession. Now s 28(8) of the 1877 Act confers jurisdiction on the court to make appointments on such terms as it thinks fit in all cases, including legal mortgages, where it appears to be just or convenient to do so.[185]

(ii) Power Arises

The power to appoint a receiver out of court arises when the mortgage money is due,[186] as in the case of the power of sale out of court.[187]

(iii) Power Exercisable

The power does not become exercisable until one of the three events specified in the 1881 Act[188] for exercise of the power of sale occurs.[189]

(iv) Procedure

[13.051] The mortgagee must appoint in writing the person he thinks fit to act as receiver.[190] The mortgagee may also remove the receiver and appoint a new one, again

---

[181] See s 19(1)(iii).

[182] Para **[13.024]**, *ante*. A mortgagee in possession may still appoint a receiver who will take over possession, see *Refuge Assurance Co Ltd v Pearlberg* [1938] Ch 687.

[183] Para **[13.075]**, *ante*.

[184] See *Marchioness of Downshire v Tyrrell* (1831) Hayes 354: *Weldon v O'Reilly* (1841) Fl & K 320: *Geale v Nugent* (1849) 1 Ir Jur (os) 341; *Barber v Roe* (1842) Long & Town 655; Reilly, *Practice of High Court of Chancery in Ireland* (1855).

[185] In NI s 28(8) of the 1877 Act has been replaced by s 91 of the Judicature (Northern Ireland) Act 1978 (UK). See *Commissioners of Church Temporalities of Ireland v Harrington* (1833) 11 LR Ir 127; *Kennedy v O'Keeffe* (1900) 34 ILTR 75; *McCausland v O'Callaghan* (1903) 3 NIJR 144; *Langdale Chemical Manure Co Ginty* (1907) 41 ILTR 40; *Butler v Butler* [1925] 1 IR 185; *National Bank Ltd v Barry* (1966) 100 ILTR 185.

[186] 1881 Act, s 19(1).

[187] Para **[13.026]**, *ante*.

[188] Section 20, see para **[13.027]**, *ante*.

[189] 1881 Act, s 24(1).

[190] *Ibid.*

provided he does so in writing.[191] The receiver may be directed in writing by the mortgagee to insure and keep insured against loss or damage by fire, out of money received, any building, effects or property comprised in the mortgage, whether affixed to the freehold or not, being of an insurable nature.[192]

(v) Functions

[13.052] The main function of a receiver is to manage the mortgaged property[193] and to intercept the rents and profits to ensure that they do not go directly to the mortgagor and that they are first used, *inter alia*, to pay interest due on the loan to the mortgagee.[194] To enable him to carry out these functions, s 24(3) of the Conveyancing Act 1881 provides:

> The receiver shall have power to demand and recover all the income of the property of which he is appointed receiver, by action, distress,[195] or otherwise, in the name either of the mortgagor or of the mortgagee, to the full extent of the estate or interest which the mortgagor could dispose of, and to give effectual receipts, accordingly, for the same.[196]

The receiver is entitled to keep out of any money received by him, as remuneration and in satisfaction of all costs, charges and expenses incurred by him as receiver, commission at the rate specified in his appointment, provided this does not exceed 5 per cent on the gross amount of all money received.[197] If no rate is specified, the rate of commission is to be 5 per cent or such higher rate as the court thinks fit to allow, on an application made by the receiver for that purpose.[198] It would seem that a receiver is expected to carry out his functions in good faith[199] and in this respect owes a duty to the mortgagor similar to that of the mortgagee in exercising its power of sale.[200]

(vi) Application of Receipts

[13.053] Section 24(8) of the Conveyancing Act 1881 provides that all money received by a receiver must be applied by him in the following order:

(1) In discharge of all rents, taxes, and outgoings whatever affecting the mortgaged property; and

---

[191] 1881 Act, s 24(5).

[192] *Ibid*, s 24(7).

[193] But not property which is outside the scope of the mortgage or charge: see *Donohoe v Agricultural Credit Corporation* [1986] IR 165 (dairy herd on the mortgaged land).

[194] *Callaghan v Reardon* (1837) s & Sc 682; *Walsh v Walsh* (1839) 1 Ir Eq R 209; *Alven v Bond* (1841) 3 Ir Eq R 365; *Balfe v Blake* (1850) 1 Ir Ch R 365; *Re Annaly* (1891) 27 LR Ir 523 (see *A Casebook on Equity and Trusts in Ireland* (1985), p 300).

[195] Abolished in Northern Ireland under s 122 of the Judgments (Enforcement) Act (NI) 1969. See para **[17.066]**, *post*.

[196] See *Fairholme and Palliser v Kennedy* (1889) 24 LR Ir 498.

[197] 1881 Act, s 24(6).

[198] *Ibid*. Note that a mortgagee in possession may not, in general, charge commission; *Carew v Johnson* (1805) 2 Sch & Lef 280 at 301 (*per* Lord Redesdale). See para **[13.047]**, *ante*.

[199] *Downsview Nominees Ltd v First City Corporation Ltd* [1993] AC 295. See Healy, 'Receivers' Duties: A Return to Othodoxy' (1994) 45 NILQ 61.

[200] See para **[13.036]**, *ante*.

(2) In keeping down all annual sums or other payments, and the interest on all principal sums, having priority to the mortgage in right whereof he is receiver; and

(3) In payment of his commission, and of the premiums on fire, life or other insurances, if any, properly payable under the mortgage deed or under the 1881 Act, and the cost of executing necessary or proper repairs directed in writing by the mortgagee[201]; and

(4) In payment of the interest accruing due[202] in respect of any principal money due under the mortgage; and

(5) In payment of the residue of the money received by him to the person who, but for the possession of the receiver, would have been entitled to receive the income of the mortgaged property, or who is otherwise entitled to that property.[203]

The sub-section is cast in imperative terms, which suggests that the receiver must follow the order laid down. An argument that the sub-section does not "in terms" provide for the order of payments and leaves this to the discretion of the receiver to choose was advanced in *Donohoe v Agricultural Credit Corporation*[204] but Keane J concluded that it was unnecessary to express an opinion on the point. He did, however, comment that it was sufficient to say that a leading commentary[205] on the equivalent English provision[206] appeared to assume that it "does in fact prescribe an order of payments".[207]

(vii) Agent of Mortgagor

[13.054] Section 24(2) of the 1881 Act now provides expressly on this matter:

The receiver shall be deemed to be the agent of the mortgagor; and the mortgagor shall be solely responsible for the receiver's acts or defaults, unless the mortgage deed otherwise provides.[208]

---

[201] See *White v Metcalf* [1903] 2 Ch 567.

[202] Whether before or after the appointment of the receiver, *National Bank Ltd v Kenney* [1898] 1 IR 197. However, the receiver must not pay statute-barred arrears of interest. *Hibernian Bank v Yourell (No 2)* [1919] 1 IR 310. It also seems that the mortgagee is entitled to an account from the receiver in respect of such payments, see *Leicester Permanent Building Society v Butt* [1943] Ch 308. In England, s 109(8) of the Law of Property Act, 1925 added, after no (4), in or towards discharge of the principal money if so directed in writing by the mortgagee.

[203] Ie, normally the mortgagor. A prior mortgagee is normally entitled in priority to a puisne mortgagee, *Lord Lismore v Chamley* (1831) Hayes 329.

[204] [1986] IR 165.

[205] Picarda, *Law Relating to Receivers, Managers and Administrators* (2nd ed), p 204.

[206] Section 109(8) of the Law of Property Act 1925.

[207] *Op cit*, p 170.

[208] See *Irish Intercontinental Bank Ltd v Brady* unrep (SC, RI), 1 June 1995. See also *Chinnery v Evans* (1864) 11 HLC 115.

The result, therefore, is that by appointing a receiver the mortgagee cannot be regarded as taking possession and so is not liable to account strictly to the mortgagor.[209]

(viii) Protection of Third Parties

[13.055] Just as purchasers dealing with a mortgagee exercising his statutory power of sale are given statutory protection,[210] so too are persons paying money to a receiver. Section 24(4) of the Conveyancing Act 1881 provides that such persons are not to be concerned to inquire whether any case has happened to authorise the receiver to act. In other words, they are not concerned with whether the mortgagee's power of appointment was exercisable as opposed to whether it had arisen.

6. Foreclosure

[13.056] Foreclosure is a judicial proceeding by which the mortgagee seeks to have the mortgagor's equitable right to redeem the property declared to be extinguished so that the mortgagee becomes full owner of the property. When the principal secured by the mortgage has become due, the mortgagee may bring these proceedings. The initial order is a decree *nisi*, which directs that accounts be taken to establish the amount due and whether other encumbrances affect the land and which provides that unless (*nisi*) the mortgagor redeems the mortgage by a date fixed by the court (usually either 3 or 6 months from the day when the decree *nisi* is made), the order will become absolute and the mortgagor is then foreclosed. Foreclosure means that the mortgagor's equity of redemption is extinguished. It is thus possible that the mortgagee would become owner of a property which was worth considerably more than the amount due to him. It also has the result that mortgagees whose charges are subsequent to that of the first mortgagee are not paid anything unless they redeem the first mortgage, because the first mortgagee, when the order *nisi* becomes absolute, takes the property free of all subsequent mortgages.

[13.057] After 1881, the courts in England were given a statutory power to order a sale of the property in a foreclosure action by s 25 of the Conveyancing Act 1881, but this did not apply to Ireland.[211] This provided that any person entitled to redeem mortgaged property could have a judgment for sale instead of for redemption and that in any action, whether for foreclosure or redemption or sale or for the raising and payment of monies due on the mortgage, the court, on the request of the mortgagee or of any person

---

[209] See *Re Marchesa Della Rocella's Estate* (1899) 29 LR Ir 464 (see *A Casebook on Equity and Trusts in Ireland* (1985), p 305). Also *Lever Finance Ltd v Needleman's Estate* [1956] Ch 375. *Cf* where the powers of leasing and of accepting surrenders of leases conferred by s 18 of the Conveyancing Act 1881, and s 3 of the Conveyancing Act 1911, are exercised after a receiver is appointed, see s 3(1) of the 1911 Act. Also para **[13.111]**, *post*.

[210] Para **[13.028]**, *ante*.

[211] Section 25(7). Nor did the earlier provision to be found in s 48 of the Chancery Amendment Act 1852.

interested either in the mortgage money or in the right of redemption, might, if it thought fit, direct a sale of the mortgaged property.[212]

[13.058] The basis of foreclosure was explained by Palles CB in this way:

> "The essence of a charge by way of mortgage was that a period should be named at which, in the event of non-payment, there should be forfeiture of the estate at law. The contract was to pay at a definite time, but equity, not deeming the time material, gave a further reasonable time for payment; but as it insisted upon the mortgagor losing the estate in case he did not then pay within the further time given, the necessary result was that the estate should be subject to foreclosure as well as redemption."[213]

[13.059] Foreclosure as a remedy for a mortgagee has been unknown in Ireland for centuries, though the courts have been careful to state that there is jurisdiction to order foreclosure but that this power will be exercised in exceptional circumstances only. In *Bruce v Brophy*,[214] Walker LC remarked: "I do not say that under special circumstances, and where a special case is made for foreclosure, the court has not power to grant a decree for foreclosure and not a sale."[215] But in the same case he referred to the "settled practice for centuries of decreeing a sale and not foreclosure". Considerable confusion has been caused by the fact that the decree made in Ireland in a mortgage suit was usually called "a decree for foreclosure and sale"[216] although the order made in a mortgage suit has not been given this name during the past 40 years. *Re Power and Carton's Contract*[217] has sometimes been cited as an example of an Irish court ordering foreclosure, but there the original order for foreclosure was made in England and not in Ireland.

[13.060] The reasons why foreclosure was never a remedy in Ireland, and why the relief given to a mortgagee was a sale, arise not from any statutory provision or decision but from the growth of a settled practice which generations of judges have followed. In one case, Fitzgibbon LJ said that in Ireland foreclosure fell into disuse because there was a special procedure for realising mortgages by court receivers and by sales in the Landed Estates Court.[218] He went on to add, however, that puisne mortgagees had the same right

---

[212] See now for England, Law of Property Act 1925 s 91(2). See also Markson, 'Foreclosure for Closure?' (1979) 129 New LJ 33. Note the recent use made of s 91 in cases like *Palk v Mortgage Funding Services plc* [1993] 2 All ER 481 and *Arab Bank plc v Mercantile Holdings Ltd* [1994] 2 All ER 74; see para **[13.040]**, fn 137, *ante*.

[213] *Shea v Moore* [1894] 1 IR 158 at 178. *Cf* Jessel MR in *Carter v Wake* (1877) 4 Ch D 605 at 606 "the court simply removes the stop it has itself put on". See also Lord Selborne LC in *Heath v Pugh* (1881) 6 QBD 345 at 359-61.

[214] [1906] 1 IR 611 at 616 (see *A Casebook on Irish Land Laws in Ireland* (1984), p 456). The learned judge did not elaborate on what he regarded as special circumstances or a special case.

[215] See also McMahon MR in *McMahon v Shewbridge* (1814) 2 Ba & B 555 at 563 and Holmes LJ in *Waters v Lloyd* [1911] 1 IR 153 at 161-3.

[216] See *Bruce v Brophy, op cit (per* Barton J).

[217] (1890) 25 LR Ir 459.

[218] *Antrim County Land, Building, and Investment Co Ltd v Stewart* [1904] 2 IR 357 at 369 "In Ireland, foreclosure fell into disuse because there was here a special procedure for realising mortgages by court receivers and by sales in the Landed Estates Court; ..." (contd.../)

of foreclosure in Ireland as they had in England, but the accuracy of this statement is extremely doubtful. The view that foreclosure fell into disuse because there was a method of getting a sale in the Landed Estates Court does not explain why the relief granted to a mortgagee in Ireland is invariably a sale, because the practice of ordering a sale had become settled long before the Landed Estates Court was established.[219] The more likely explanation is that second and third mortgages were far more common in Ireland than in England and that, as foreclosure as a remedy would have the result that they would get nothing in respect of their principal unless they redeemed the first mortgage, a sale of the property was the only way in which their interests could be safeguarded.

[13.061] Although foreclosure as a remedy is unknown in Ireland, the court undoubtedly has jurisdiction to make an order of foreclosure and so we propose to outline the main features of it. Those who want a more detailed account of it should refer to some of the standard English text books on the subject.[220]

(i) Parties Entitled

[13.062] An equitable mortgagee may get a foreclosure order and, if he does, it takes the form of a direction to the mortgagor, as holder of the legal title in the land, to convey that title to the mortgagee freed any right of redemption.[221] The right to bring foreclosure proceedings does not arise until repayment of the mortgage becomes due at law, ie, the legal date for redemption has passed.[222] Foreclosure proceedings are brought against those interested in the equity of redemption relating to the mortgage in question, and so the mortgagor and any subsequent mortgagees must be made defendants.[223] A mortgagee whose encumbrance is prior in point of time to the mortgagee seeking redemption need not be made a party because he will not be affected by the foreclosure

---

[218] (\...contd) (see *A Casebook on Irish Land Law* (1984) p 426). See further on sales in the Landed Estates Court, para **[1.42]**, *ante. Cf* Coffin. 'Foreclosure and Sale in Nova Scotia' (1954) 32 CBR 217.

[219] *Hulton v Mayne* (1846) 9 Ir Eq R 343. *Cf Loughran v Loughran* (1885) 15 LR Ir 71, *Re Lloyd* [1911] 1 IR 153. See also *Greene v Stoney* (1851) 13 Ir Eq R 301; *Burrowes v Molloy* (1845) 8 Ir Eq R 482.

[220] Note that in England it is now rarely sought: see *Palk v Mortgage Services Funding plc* [1993] 2 All ER 481 at 485 (*per* Nicholls VC) ("foreclosure actions are almost unheard of today and have been so for many years").

[221] *Shea v Moore* [1894] 1 IR 158 at 178; *Antrim County Land, Building and Investment Co Ltd v Stewart* [1904] 2 LR 357 at 369 (see *A Casebook on Irish Land Law* (1984) p 426). This includes the case of an equitable mortgagee by deposit, see *Parker v Housefield* (1834) 2 My & K 419 (title deeds); *Backhouse v Charlton* (1878) 8 Ch D 444 (title deeds); *Harrold v Plenty* [1901] 2 Ch 314.

[222] Para **[12.05]**, *ante*. See the recent discussion on this point in *Twentieth Century Banking Corp Ltd v Wilkinson* [1976] 3 WLR 489 wherein Templeman J relied heavily on the judgment of Sugden LC in the Irish case of *Burrowes v Molloy* (1845) 2 Jo & Lat 521.

[223] See *Munster Bank Ltd v Jervis* (1902) 36 ILTR 113. Also *Rolleston v Morton* (1842) 4 Ir Eq R 149; *Davis v Rowan* (1843) 3 Dr & War 478. *Cf Going v Farrell* (1814) Beat 472. Also *Bishop of Winchester v Paine* (1805) 11 Ves 194.

order,[224] but if the second mortgagee wishes to get a foreclosure order against the mortgagor and to redeem the first mortgagee, he must join him as a party.

(ii) Effect

[13.063] The normal effect of the foreclosure becoming absolute is that the mortgagee becomes the owner of the land or, as it was put in one Irish case, "a foreclosure decree is an absolute conveyance",[225] but the court has jurisdiction to reopen the foreclosure.[226] This will be done in exceptional circumstances only. The reopening of the foreclosure is entirely a matter for the discretion of the court, but the factors which can lead to a decision to reopen the foreclosure and allow the mortgagor to redeem are that the mortgagor was prevented by some misfortune from redeeming between the date of the foreclosure decree *nisi* and when it became absolute, or that there was a considerable difference between the value of the property and the debt owed to the mortgagee.[227] It is, however, settled that, if a mortgagee who has obtained a foreclosure order *nisi*, which has become absolute, sues on the personal covenant of the mortgagor contained in the mortgage deed to pay the debt, this has the effect of reopening the foreclosure and when such an action is brought the mortgagor becomes entitled to redeem.[228]

---

[224] *Richards v Cooper* (1842) 5 Beav 304; *cf Perrott v O'Halloran* (1840) 2 Ir Eq R 428. However, in Ireland, where an order for a sale is invariably given, a puisne mortgagee must obtain the consent of a prior incumbrancer to the carriage of sale being given to the puisne mortgagee, if he is to be allowed the full costs of the sale, see *Wills v Clifford* (1888) 22 ILTR 51; *Hilliard v Moriarty* [1894] 1 IR 316, but the auctioneer's fees will always be given priority over the claim of the prior incumbrancer. *Cf* the case of a sale of mortgaged property in an administration suit, *Leonard v Kellett* (1891) 27 LR Ir 418; *McAloon v McAloon* [1901] 1 IR 470; *Cusack v Cusack* (1903) 37 ILTR 152; *McSpadden v Patterson* (1905) 5 NIJR 151. See Bodkin, 'Mortgagee's costs' (1954) 18 Conv 130.

[225] *Re Power and Carton's Contract* (1890) 25 LR Ir 459. See also *Platt v Mendel* (1884) 27 Ch D 246; *Smithett v Hesketh* (1890) 44 Ch D 161.

[226] The leading statement on this subject was given by Jessel MR in *Campbell v Holyland* (1887) 7 Ch D 166 at 169 and 172-5.

[227] See the series of eighteenth century English House of Lords decisions in *Wichalse v Short* (1713) 3 Bro PC 558; *Lant v Crispe* (1719) 5 Bro PC 200; *Burgh v Langton* (1724) 5 Bro PC 213; *Jones v Kendrick* (1727) 5 Bro PC 244.

[228] *Dashwood v Blythway* (1729) 1 Eq Cas Abr 317, pl 3. *Cf* if the mortgagee sold the land after foreclosure, *Perry v Barker* (1803) 8 Ves 527 and (1806) 13 Ves 198; *Lockhart v Hardy* (1846) 9 Beav 349. It seems that the foreclosure is not reopened by a suit on the covenant by an incumbrancer, eg a subsequent mortgagee also foreclosed, other than the foreclosing mortgagee, see *Worthington & Co Ltd v Abbott* [1910] 1 Ch 588. See also *re* an action on the covenant after an application for a sale. *Bradshaw v McMullan* [1915] 2 IR 187.

Part VIII

COVENANTS, LICENCES AND SIMILAR INTERESTS

Chapter 19

RESTRICTIVE COVENANTS

II. FREEHOLD

[19.12] We now turn to the question of enforceability of covenants relating to freehold land.[1] It must be reiterated that such covenants have been comparatively rare in Ireland because most land was leasehold. However, this is no longer the case with agricultural land owing to the operation of the Land Purchase Acts,[2] and the recent enfranchisement legislation[3] in both parts of Ireland relating to urban land will also cause the question to be raised more often than in the past.

[19.13] In considering the enforceability of freehold covenants, a distinction has to be drawn between the respective approaches of the common law and equity.

A. At Common Law

[19.14] At common law there were considerable difficulties about the enforceability of covenants affecting freehold land, at least as regards the passing of the burden to successors in title. These difficulties were recently reaffirmed by the House of Lords in England, where the invitation to change the law was declined in deference to appropriate action by the legislature.[4] It is also vital to note that the law in Northern Ireland will be altered dramatically by Article 34 of the Property (NI) Order 1997. When this provision comes into force it will replace the rules of common law and equity which we are about to discuss.[5] However, the new statutory rules will not apply to any covenant contained in a deed made before the appointed day[6] nor to a covenant in a deed made on or after that day in pursuance of an obligation assumed before that day.[7] The rules of common law and equity set out in the ensuing paragraphs will, therefore, remain relevant in Northern Ireland for many years to come. The new statutory rules to come into force in the near future are discussed later in the chapter.[8]

---

[1]   To be strictly accurate, the rules discussed in the rest of this chapter may also be invoked in leasehold situations, eg, where the occupier of the land is not an assignee of the lease and so there is no "privity of estate" between him and the head-lessor or his assignee. Thus a sub-tenant may nevertheless be liable on a restrictive covenant in the head-lease under the rule in *Tulk v Moxhay* (para **[19.25]**, *post*), see *Craig v Greer* [1899] 1 IR 258 (see *A Casebook on Irish Land Law* (1984), p 616).

[2]   Ch 18, *ante*.

[3]   *Ibid*.

[4]   See *Rhone v Stephens* [1994] 2 AC 310.

[5]   Article 34(1).

[6]   Article 34(2)(a).

[7]   Article 34(2)(b).

[8]   Para **[19.48]**, *post*.

1. Original Parties

[19.15] The original covenantee can usually enforce the covenant against the original covenantor, unless the covenantee has assigned the benefit of the covenant to someone else.[9] However, if the benefit of the covenant relates to a particular piece of land owned by the covenantee at the time of entering into the covenant, and he has since conveyed that land to someone else, his action for breach of covenant will secure for him at most nominal damages only.

[19.16] Usually the covenantee is one of the parties to the deed containing the covenant, though the covenantor may be expressed to covenant with other persons not parties to the deed. At common law this caused problems because it was a strict rule for a deed made *inter partes* that only a party to it could sue on it.[10] This rule, however, was modified by s 5 of the Real Property Act 1845,[11] which provided:

> Under an indenture executed after the first day of October one thousand eight hundred and forty-five an immediate estate or interest in any tenements or hereditaments. and the benefit of a condition or covenant respecting any tenements or hereditaments, may be taken, although the taker thereof be not named a party to the same indenture ...

It seems to be fairly clear that this was designed to get over the difficulties of the *inter partes* rule and for nothing else.[12] For example, if the purchaser of a piece of land covenants with the vendor "and also the owners for the time being" of certain specified adjacent plots, those owners can also enforce the covenant *as original covenantees*, despite not being executing parties to the deed.[13] Whether their successors in title can enforce the covenant is an entirely different matter, as we shall see.[14]

[19.17] Section 5 of the 1845 Act was replaced in England by the somewhat wider wording of s 56(1) of the Law of Property Act 1925, and the English judges have been arguing about its effect ever since.[15] Mercifully the legislators have so far spared the Irish judges a similar problem of interpretation.[16]

---

[9] Para **[19.28]**, *post*.

[10] *Lord Southampton v Brown* (1827) 6 B & C 718. This was the rule for a deed poll, ie, executed by one party only as a unilateral act, *Chelsea & Waltham Green Building Soc v Armstrong* [1951] Ch 853.

[11] Replacing s 11 of Transfer of Property Act 1844.

[12] See the discussion in *Beswick v Beswick* [1968] AC 58 at 104-5 (*per* Lord Upjohn). Some Irish authorities suggest that it is confined to covenants "touching and concerning" the land, see *Lloyd v Byrne* (1888) 22 LR Ir 269; *Monroe v Plunket* (1889) 23 ILTR 76, *cf Forster v Elvet Colliery Co Ltd* [1908] 1 KB 629, [1909] AC 98; *Grant v Edmondson* [1931] 1 Ch 1.

[13] See *Kelsey v Dodd* (1881) 52 LJ Ch 34; *White v Bijou Mansions Ltd* [1937] Ch 610; *Re Ecclesiastical Commrs' Conveyance* [1936] Ch 430. Wylie, 'Contracts and Third Parties' (1966) 17 NILQ 351 at 403-5.

[14] Paras **[19.18]**, *et seq*, *infra*.

[15] See, eg, *Smith v River Douglas Catchment Board* [1949] 2 KB 500; *Stromdale & Ball Ltd v Burden* [1952] Ch 223; *Drive Yourself Hire Co (London) Ltd v Strutt* [1954] 1 QB 250; *Beswick v Beswick* [1968] AC 58; *Lyus v Prowsa Developments Ltd* [1982] 1 WLR 1044. (contd.../)

2. *Successors in Title*

[19.18] Here two questions must be considered, namely, to what extent at common law the benefit of a covenant affecting freehold land can pass to a successor in title of the covenantee and to what extent the burden can pass to a successor in title of the covenantor.

(i) Benefit

[19.19] Three conditions must be met for the benefit of a covenant to pass to the covenantee's successor in title. From the outset it should be noted that these conditions do *not* include two which are vital in equity, namely that the covenant should be *restrictive* or *negative* only[17] and that it should touch and concern the land of the *covenantor.*[18]

(a) Touch and Concern Covenantee's Land

While the covenant need not concern any land owned by the covenantor, it must touch and concern land of the covenantee which is to be benefited thereby.[19] It appears that "land" in this context includes an incorporeal hereditament, like an easement. In *Gaw v CIE*,[20] Dixon J held that a covenant to repair a footpath ran with a right of way over the path and could be enforced by a successor in title to the original covenantee. It seems, however, that the benefit of a covenant to pay a rentcharge will not run with the rentcharge.[21]

(b) Legal Estate

[19.20] The common law recognised legal estates only and so the successor of the covenantee must show that he holds a legal estate in the land benefited by the covenant.[22]

---

[15] (\...contd) Andrews, 'Section 56 Revisited' (1959) 23 Conv 179; Ellinger, 'Privity of Contract under Section 56(1) of the Law of Property Act 1925' (1963) 2 MLR 396; Elliott, 'The Effect of Section 56(1) of the Law of Property Act 1925' (1956) 20 Conv 43 an 114; Furmston, 'Return to *Dunlop v Selfridge*' (1960) 23 MLR 373; Wylie, *op cit*, pp 404-10.

[16] Note the recommendation in the *1971 Survey (NI)*, para 170. See also the Land Law Working Group's *Final Report* (HMSO, 1990) Vol 2, Property Bill, Article 88.

[17] *Sharp v Waterhouse* (1857) 7 E & B 816. See also *Gaw v CIE* [1953] IR 232 (covenant to repair). Blease, 'Positive Covenants and Third Parties' (1955) 19 Conv 261; Pritchard, 'Making Positive Covenants Run' (1973) 37 Conv 194; Scamell, 'Positive Covenants in Conveyances of the Fee Simple' (1954) 18 Conv 546.

[18] *Smith v River Douglas Catchment Board* [1949] 2 KB 500.

[19] *Rogers v Hosegood* [1900] 2 Ch 388; *Formby v Barker* [1903] 2 Ch 539; *Dyson v Foster* [1909] AC 98.

[20] [1953] IR 232 (see *A Casebook on Irish Land Law* (1984), p 622). Harrison, 'Running of Covenants with Easements and Other Incorporeal Hereditaments' (1957) UQLJ 165.

[21] *Kennedy v Stewart* (1836) 4 L Rec (ns) 160; *Grant v Edmondson* [1931] 1 Ch 1. Strachan, 'Covenants to Pay Rentcharges' (1931) 47 LQR 380.

[22] *Webb v Russell* (1789) 3 TR 393.

241

(c) Same Title

The successor must, in addition, show that he has succeeded to the same legal estate in the land as was held by the original covenantee.[23] Thus, if the original covenantee held the fee simple in the land benefited by the covenant, a tenant of his cannot enforce the covenant. This remains the position under s 58(1) of the Conveyancing Act 1881, which deems covenants "to be made with the covenantee, *his heirs and assigns*",[24] so that they "shall have effect as if heirs and assigns were expressed". The traditional view was that this provision was a mere "word-saving" provision and was not intended to alter the common law rule.[25] "Heirs and assigns" were the appropriate words to use in 1881[26] to indicate that the benefit was intended to pass to successors in title. However, in England s 58 of the 1881 Act has been replaced by s 78 of the Law of Property Act 1925, which uses the apparently wider phrase "successors in title *and the persons deriving title under him or them*".[27] It has been suggested that this enables persons not succeeding to the same estate to enforce covenants.[28]

(ii) Burden

[19.21] The general rule is that the burden of a freehold covenant does not run with the land at common law.[29] There are, however, ways round this rule, albeit somewhat indirect.

(a) Indemnity Agreements

[19.22] If the original covenantor sells the land to which the covenant attaches, he remains liable on it by virtue of privity of contract with the covenantee, so he invariably insists on his purchaser undertaking to indemnify him against future breaches.[30] If the original covenantor is sued, he in turn may sue his purchaser on the indemnity agreement, or bring him into the action as a third party, and, in this way, the covenant is enforced indirectly against the current holder of the land.[31] When that purchaser sells to another one, he too may insist upon an indemnity and so on indefinitely. The danger is, of course, that at some point the chain of indemnities may be broken by failure of one successor in title to insist upon an indemnity being entered into by his successor. Or one

---

[23] *Gaw v CIE* [1953] IR 232 (see *A Casebook on Irish Land Law* (1984), p 622).

[24] Italics added.

[25] *Westhoughton UDC v Wigan Coal & Iron Co Ltd* [1919] 1 Ch 159.

[26] "Heirs", of course, is now misleading to the extent that the law of inheritance has been abolished in Ireland, Ch 15, *ante*.

[27] Italics added. In *Federated Homes Ltd v Mill Lodge Properties Ltd* [1980] 1 All ER 371, the English Court Appeal held that s 78 of the Law of Property Act 1925 was not a mere word-saving provision, but had the effect of annexing the benefit of a restrictive covenant to the covenantee's land, so as to make it run with the land (see para **[19.33]**, *post*). See also s 79, which replaces s 59 of the 1881 Act.

[28] *Smith v River Douglas Catchment Board* [1949] 2 KB 500. See Scamell, 'Positive Covenants in Conveyances of the Fee Simple' (1954) 18 Conv 546 at 553; *1971 Survey (NI)*, para 180.

[29] *Austerberry v Oldham Corp* (1885) 29 Ch D 750; *Smith v Colbourne* [1914] 2 Ch 533; *Rhone v Stephens* [1994] 2 AC 310. See Pritchard 'Making Positive Covenants Run' (1973) 37 Conv 194.

[30] See *De Vesci v O'Connell* [1908] AC 298 (cross-indemnities in respect of fee farm rents).

[31] See the discussion as to the appropriate wording for indemnity covenants in *TRW Steering Systems Ltd v North Cape Properties Ltd* (1995) 69 P & CR 265.

of the successors may disappear or die and thus prevent a chain reaction right down to the current holder of the land.

(b) Reciprocity Covenants

[19.23] It seems to be settled now, at least in England, that a landowner may have the burden of covenants enforced against him because this is reasonable in view of the fact that he has a reciprocal right to enforce the benefit of related covenants.[32] For example, residents on a housing estate may have the right to use common facilities, eg, roads and playgrounds, provided they contribute towards the cost of repair and upkeep. It is reasonable that the benefit of the right of use should be matched by the burden of the liability to make such contribution so far as successors in title to the original residents are concerned. Such reciprocity may also be established by way of analogy with the doctrine of estoppel[33] and, as we shall see, may be achieved in housing estates through an estate scheme.[34]

(c) Enlarged or Converted Leases

[19.24] It would seem that covenants normally enforceable in leases may continue to be enforceable to the same extent where a lease is converted into a fee farm grant, eg, under the Renewable Leasehold Conversion Act 1849,[35] or enlarged into a fee simple, eg, under the Conveyancing Act 1881.[36] The Conveyancing Act provisions have been replaced in Northern Ireland by Article 35 of the Property (NI) Order 1997, under which the position as regards covenants and other matters affecting the lease before enlargement, such as easements and mortgages, is made clear.[37] In essence Article 35 incorporates the provisions applicable where a ground rent is redeemed under Part II of the Order.[38]

---

[32] Sometimes referred to as the rule in *Halsall v Brizell* [1957] Ch 169. Megarry, (1957) 73 LQR 154; Wade, (1957) 73 LQR 154; Wade, (1957) CLJ 35. See also the discussion by Megarry V-C in *Tito v Wade (No 2)* [1977] Ch 106; Aughterson, 'Enforcement of Positive Burdens - A New Viability' [1985] Conv 12. In *Rhone v Stephens* [1994] 2 AC 310, the House of Lords insisted that there must be a close link between the benefit and the burden, such that the performance of the "burden" covenant is a condition of the exercise of the "benefit" rights. *Cf* Laffoy, *Irish Conveyancing Precedents*, Precedent E.8.1.

[33] See the discussion in *ER Investment Ltd v High* [1967] 2 QB 379.

[34] Para **[19.34]**, *post*.

[35] Sections 1, 7 and 10. See the discussion in *Re McNaul's Estate* [1902] 1 IR 114 (see *A Casebook on Irish Land Law* (1984) p 41) and Ch 4 *ante*.

[36] Section 65 and see Conveyancing Act 1882, s 11. Taylor, 'Enlargement of Leasehold to Freehold' (1958) 22 Conv 101. Para **[17.108]**, *ante*. Note also the preservation of certain covenants under recent leasehold enfranchisement legislation, see Landlord and Tenant (Ground Rents) (No 2) Act 1978, s 28 (RI) and Leasehold (Enlargement and Extension) Act (NI) 1971, s 28; Property (NI) Order 1997, Article 26. See paras **[18.28]**, and **[18.47]**, *ante*.

[37] See para **[17.108]**, *ante*.

[38] See para **[18.47]**, *ante*.

B. In Equity

[19.25] Equity provided two major contributions to the law relating to enforceability of covenants. First, equity could provide what was in many cases a more effective remedy for breach of covenant, ie, an injunction to prevent further breaches as opposed to damages.[39] Secondly, it developed special rules relating to *restrictive* covenants, whereby the *burden* of such covenants could be enforced against successors in title.[40] This second contribution was largely a development of the nineteenth century and is usually referred to, after a leading case, as the rule in *Tulk v Moxhay.*[41] In this case Lord Cottenham LC laid down the general principle of equity that the burden of a restrictive covenant will run with the land to which it relates so as to bind all successors in title of the original covenantor, except a *bona fide* purchaser of the land without notice of the covenant.

Before examining this equitable principle further, we must also consider the approach of equity to the question of the running of the benefit of such a covenant.

1. Benefit

[19.26] Since the benefit of a covenant, positive or restrictive, was generally enforceable at common law both by the original covenantee and his successors in title, equity largely followed the law and adopted the same principles,[42] though, of course, it provided its own special remedy, the injunction. Thus, equity adopted the principle that the covenant should touch and concern the covenantee's land.[43] However, when the law relating to the running of the burden of restrictive covenants developed, equity became even more precise in its requirements. The rule developed that a plaintiff seeking the aid of equity in enforcement of a restrictive covenant must establish that he is the current holder of the land to which the benefit relates and also that the benefit has passed to him. Thus in equity even the original covenantee would lose the benefit of such a covenant if he parts with the land benefited by it.[44]

[19.27] The difficult matter, however, in many cases is to establish that the benefit has passed to a successor in title. The point is that the motive of a restrictive covenant, eg, prohibiting certain user of land, is often not an intention to benefit a piece of land, but to serve the interest or convenience of the covenantee personally, while a positive

---

[39] Ch 3, *ante.* See Tettenborn, 'Damages for Breach of Positive Covenants' (1978) Conv 366.

[40] Garner, 'Restrictive Covenants Restated' (1962) 26 Conv 298; Hayton, 'Restrictive Covenants as Property Interests' (1971) 87 LQR 539; Randall, 'Covenants Running with Land' (1909) 25 LQR 380; Robinson, 'Restrictive Covenants' (1974) 38 Conv 90; Strachan, 'Restrictive Covenants Affecting Land' (1930) 46 LQR 159; English Law Reform Committee *Report of the Committee on Positive Obligations Relating to Land* (1965), CMD 2719); *1971 Survey (NI)*, Ch 16.

[41] (1848) 2 Ph 774. For earlier decisions, see *Whatman v Gibson* (1838) 9 Sim 196; *Mann v Stephens* (1846) 15 Sim 377. *Cf Keppell v Bailey* (1834) 2 My & K 517. Also *Tulk v Metropolitan Board of Works* (1868) 16 WR 212.

[42] Paras **[3.047]**, *ante* and **[19.19]**, *supra.*

[43] *Rogers v Hosegood* [1900] 2 Ch 388; Bailey, 'The Benefit of a Restrictive Covenant' (1938) CLJ 339.

[44] *Chambers v Randall* [1923] Ch 280.

covenant, eg, to repair fences, usually is clearly for the benefit of the land. It seems that a plaintiff can establish that the benefit of a restrictive covenant has passed to him in equity in one of two main ways.[45]

(i) Express Assignment

[19.28] The plaintiff can show that he owns some interest in the land benefited by the covenant and that the benefit has been expressly assigned to him, or at least that when he acquired the land it was agreed between him and the assignor that he was to have the benefit of the covenant.[46] There must be something to indicate that the benefit has passed.

[19.29] It seems that the position of an assignee may vary according to whether he is suing the original covenantor or an assignee from him. In the former case, it appears to be sufficient to prove that the benefit has been assigned like a chose in action, which need not occur as part of the same transaction as the transfer of the land benefited by the covenant. If, however, the original covenantee has parted with the land benefited, or even a part of it, the benefit of the covenant must be assigned along with it for the assignee to be able to sue successors of the covenantor in equity.[47] This rule seems to be based on the view that, as we shall see, equity enforces restrictive covenants on the ground that they are concerned with preserving the value of the neighbouring land, and so the benefit must go along with that land in cases where the aid of equity is required, as it is where a claim is made that the burden runs with the covenantor's land to bind his successors.[48]

[19.30] It is also a moot point as to whether, once the benefit has been assigned along with the covenantee's land, it becomes "annexed" to the land, so as to run automatically with the land without express assignment thereafter. It is arguable that such an assignment is a clear indication of intention that the benefit should run and there seems to be no reason why the benefit cannot be annexed to the land subsequent to the covenant being entered into.[49]

(ii) Annexation

[19.31] The other way in which the plaintiff can establish his right to sue on the covenant in equity is to show that the benefit was "annexed" to the land and he has acquired that land. Once the benefit has been annexed to the land in question, it runs with it regardless of whether the subsequent owners have notice of it.[50] Conversely once

---

[45]   These are, perhaps, not the only ways, see *Re Dolphin's Conveyance* [1970] Ch 654; *cf Re Pinewood Estate Ltd* [1958] Ch 280.

[46]   *Renals v Cowlishaw* (1879) 11 Ch D 866; *Formby v Barker* [1903] 2 Ch 539.

[47]   *Re Union of London & Smith's Bank Ltd's Conv* [1933] Ch 611 at 632 (per Romer LJ).

[48]   Para **[19.38]**, *post*.

[49]   See *Rogers v Hosegood* [1900] 2 Ch 388 at 408; *Reid v Bickerstaff* [1909] 2 Ch 305 at 320. *Cf Re Pinewood Estate* [1958] Ch 280. Wade, (1957) CLJ 146. It is, however, doubtful whether s 6 of the Conveyancing act 1881 (see para **[6.066]**, *et seq, ante*) can be invoked to establish an implied assignment: see on the English equivalent (s 62 of the Law of Property Act 1925) *Roake v Chadha* [1984] 1 WLR 40; *Kumar v Dunning* [1989] QB 193.

[50]   *Rogers v Hosegood* [1900] 2 Ch 388.

the original covenantee has parted with all the land, he is no longer entitled to enforce it in equity.[51] Annexation may be established in one of three ways.

(a) Expressly

[19.32] Express annexation may be indicated by the wording of the deed of covenant itself. It must, however, specify the land to be benefited and state that the benefit relates to it or that it is entered into with the covenantee as owner of that land.[52] It is *not* enough simply for the covenant to be made with the covenantee "his heirs and assigns",[53] since this does not necessarily relate to a particular piece of land.[54] To avoid difficulties over whether the covenant can reasonably benefit a very large piece of land, it is wise to annex it to the land "or any part" of it.[55]

(b) Impliedly

[19.33] It seems to be settled now, at least in England, that annexation of the benefit to the land may be implied from the surrounding circumstances of the case, if they indicate with reasonable certainty that the covenant was taken for the benefit of that land.[56] It is not clear whether implied annexation may be imported into the conveyance by s 58 of the Conveyancing Act 1881. In *Federated Homes Ltd v Mill Lodge Properties Ltd*,[57] the English Court of Appeal held that this was the effect of the English replacement of s 58, s 78 of the Law of Property Act 1925 (thus following the view taken in *Smith v River Douglas Catchment Board*[58]). However, the English Court did emphasise that the wording of s 78 is "significantly different" from the wording of s 58. Brightman LJ stated:

> "The distinction is underlined by sub-s (2) of s 78, which applies sub-s (1) only to covenants made after the commencement of the Act. Section 58(1) of the earlier Act did not include the covenantee's successors in title or persons deriving title under him or them, nor the owners or occupiers for the time being of the land of the covenantee intended to be benefited. The section was confined, in relation to realty, to the covenantee, his heirs and assigns, words which suggest a more limited scope of operation than is found in s 78.

---

[51] *Chambers v Randall* [1923] 1 Ch 149 at 157-8.

[52] *Rogers v Hosegood*, *op cit*; *Osbourne v Bradley* [1903] 2 Ch 446.

[53] Which is implied anyway under s 58 of the Conveyancing Act 1881, see para **[19.20]**, *ante*; but *cf* the views of Brightman LJ in *Federated Homes* case, para **[19.33]**, *infra*.

[54] *Renals v Cowlishaw* (1879) 11 Ch D 866.

[55] *Cf Re Ballard's Conveyance* [1937] Ch 473 and *Marquess of Zetland v Driver* [1939] Ch 1. See also *Stilwell v Blackman* [1968] Ch 508. Again *cf* the views of Brightman LJ in the *Federated Homes* case, para **[19.33]**, *infra*.

[56] *Marten v Flight Refuelling Ltd* [1962] Ch 115. *Cf* English *Report of the Committee on Positive Covenants Affecting Land* (1965, Cmnd 2719), para 17. See *also Newton Abbott Co-operative Society v Williamson and Treadgold Ltd* [1952] Ch 286. Ryder, 'Restrictive Covenants: The Problem of Implied Annexation' (1972) 36 Conv 20.

[57] [1980] 1 All ER 371.

[58] [1949] 2 All ER 179.

If, as the language of s 78 implies, a covenant relating to land which is restrictive of the user thereof is enforceable at the suit of (1) a successor in title of the covenantee, (2) a person deriving title under the covenantee or under his successors in title, and (3) the owner or occupier of the land intended to be benefited by the covenant, it must, in my view, follow that the covenant runs with the land, because *ex hypothesi* every successor in title to the land, every derivative proprietor of the land and every other owner and occupier has a right by statute to the covenant. In other words, if the condition precedent of s 78 is satisfied, that is to say, there exists a covenant which touches and concerns the land of the covenantee, that covenant runs with the land for the benefit of his successors in title, persons deriving title under him or them and other owners and occupiers."[59]

Later, Brightman LJ stated that "if the benefit of a covenant is, on a proper construction of a document, annexed to the land, *prima facie* it is annexed to every part thereof, unless the contrary clearly appears."[60] Browne and Megaw LJJ agreed with Brightman LJ's judgment. It remains to be seen what the Irish courts' reaction to this case will be in relation to s 58 of the 1881 Act.[61]

(c) Estate Schemes

[19.34] One of the common situations for imposition of restrictive covenants is a housing estate consisting of many plots, where the value of each individual house and plot depends to some extent on the covenants restricting the use of their land by each of the other owners on the estate. To ensure enforceability all round of the mutual covenants, the building developer would, under the normal rules,[62] have to ensure, as he sells off each plot, that the purchaser covenants expressly with owners of lots previously sold,[63] as well as with the developer, and that the benefit is annexed to the land and any part of it retained by the developer, or that he expressly assigns it with each plot subsequently sold.[64]

---

[59] *Op cit*, p 379. *Cf* where the covenant itself requires the benefit to be assigned expressly, see *Roake v Chadha* [1984] 1 WLR 40.

[60] *Op cit*, p 381.

[61] For the view that s 58 is even more likely to have been intended to assist annexation (by counteracting cases like *Renals v Cowlishaw* (1878) 9 Ch D 125, (1879)11 Ch D 866), see Megarry and Wade, *The Law of Real Property* (5th ed, 1984), p 786, fn 6. *Cf* Preston and Newsom, *Restrictive Covenants Affecting Freehold Land* (7th ed, 1982), p 789; Newsom 'Universal Annexation (1981) 97 LQR 32; Todd, 'Annexation after Federated Homes [1985] Conv 177. Note that the House of Lords has reiterated both *ante* and *post Federated Homes* that the sister provision of s 78, s 79 of the Law of the Property Act 1925 (replacing s 59 of the Conveyancing Act 1881) should *not* be given a similar wide interpretation: see *Tophams Ltd v Sefton* [1967] 1 AC 50; *Rhone v Stephens* [1994] 2 AC 310.

[62] Ie, relating to *freehold* land. Of course, these difficulties have been avoided in the past in Ireland by developers insisting on granting or assigning leasehold interests only to purchasers of plots from them. That option, however, was foreclosed in the Republic by s 2 of the Landlord and Tenant (Ground Rents) Act 1978 (see paras **[1.75]** and **[4.092]** *ante*) and will be in NI when Articles 28 and 30 of the Property (NI) Order 1997 come into force (see paras **[1.76]**, **[4.092]** and **[18.43]**, *ante*.

[63] Ie, to ensure that they can enforce the covenant, since the developer no longer retains their land for it to be benefited.

[64] Ie, to ensure that subsequent purchasers of plots can enforce the covenant.

[19.35] Fortunately, these complexities can be avoided in the case of freehold land if the developer establishes a building or estate scheme, the rules as to which were enunciated in *Elliston v Reacher.*[65] The underlying philosophy was stated in an earlier case by Lord MacNaghten: "Community of interest necessarily ... requires and imports reciprocity of obligation."[66] Since each purchaser buys his plot on the same basis as all the other purchasers of plots on the same estate, each purchaser and his successors in title can sue and be sued by all or any of the other purchasers and their successors. If the requisites for an estate scheme are present, the courts will recognise this form of "local law" in the estate.[67] Thus the covenants entered into by one resident on the estate with his vendor are enforceable by any other resident on the same estate.[68]

[19.36] The requisites for an estate scheme are: (1) the plaintiff and defendant in question must have derived title from a common vendor, eg, the building developer; (2) the common vendor must have originally laid out the estate in plots subject to common restrictions, either consistent only with some general scheme of development or intended to be enforceable under such a scheme;[69] (3) the common vendor must have intended the restrictions to be for the benefit of all plots sold; (4) the plaintiff and defendant must have purchased their plots on the basis that the restrictions would benefit the other plots; (5) the area covered by the scheme must be clearly defined.[70]

[19.37] In more recent times the English courts have been prepared to relax the above requirements especially where the evidence establishes a clear common intention that the covenants should be enforceable by those party to or buying into the scheme.[71] Without such a clear intention it is difficult to see how the vital element of reciprocity of

---

[65] [1908] 2 Ch 374 at 384 (*per* Parker J *aff'd* at 665). For earlier recognition of this principle, see *Western v MacDermott* (1866) LR 1 Eq 499; *Renals v Cowlishaw* (1878) 9 Ch D 125, 11 Ch D 866; *Spicer v Martin* (1888) 14 App Cas 12. It was applied in Ireland in *Fitzpatrick v Clancy* (1964) Unrep (HC, RI) (1964/1879 P) (see *A Casebook on Irish Land Law* (1984), p 642) and recognised in *Belmont Securities Ltd v Crean* Unrep (HC, RI), 17 June 1988 (1988/4005 P): see (1989) 7 ILT 22. The same principle may be applied in analogous situations, eg, a block of residential flats, *Hudson v Cripps* [1896] 1 Ch 265; *Gedge v Bartlett* (1900) 17 TLR 43. *Cf Kelly v Battershell* [1949] 2 All ER 830.

[66] *Spicer v Martin, op cit*, p 25. *Cf* the principle at common law, para **[19.23]**, *ante*.

[67] *Reid v Bickerstaff* [1909] 2 Ch 305 at 319, (*per* Cozens-Hardy MR), adopted as a correct statement of the legal principles applicable by O'Hanlon J in *Belmont Securities Ltd v Crean* Unrep (HC, RI), 17 June 1988 (1988/4005P), Transcript, pp 3-4. See also the discussion in *Brunner v Greenslade* [1971 Ch 993 and *Texaco Antilles Ltd v Kernochan* [1973] AC 609, both of which deal with application of the principle to sub-schemes.

[68] See Laffoy, *Irish Conveyancing Precedents,* Precedent E.8.1.

[69] See *Baxter v Four Oaks Properties Ltd* [1965] Ch 8-16.

[70] *Reid v Bickerstaff, op cit.*

[71] *Baxter v Four Oaks Properties Ltd, op cit* (absence of laying out in lots); *Re Dolphin's Conveyance* [1970] Ch 654 (no common vendor owing to death of original before scheme completed). See also *Jamaica Mutual Life Assurance Society v Hillsborough Ltd* [1989] 1 WLR 1101. *Cf Land v Taylor* (1975) 31 P & CR 167.

obligation can be found as the basis for the "local" law.[72] It avoids difficulties if the developer initially draws up a plan of the estate, with the restrictions endorsed on it, and negotiates sales of each plot by express reference to this. This makes it clear on all sides that a general scheme of development is in force. However, it is probably not necessary that the restrictions should be identical throughout the estate[73] and the common vendor may reserve a power to release all or part of the land from them.[74]

2. Burden

[19.38] The particular contribution of equity to the law of freehold covenants has been the enforcement of the burden of certain covenants against successors in title of the original covenantor. The basis of the rule in *Tulk v Moxhay* is the fact that the covenant in question concerns the preservation of the value of the covenantee's land[75] rather than, as was once thought,[76] the fact that the present owner of the covenantor's land acquired it with notice of the covenant. In this respect the law relating to restrictive covenants has similarities with the law of easements, ie, there must be a *dominant* and *servient* tenement, and this has led some to describe the law as an extension in equity of the doctrine of negative easements.[77] This must not be allowed, however, to obscure the fact that the law relating to restrictive covenants was really a new development in the nineteenth century, so that it is fair to say that equity created then a new interest in land. We must consider now the conditions which must be satisfied if a successor in title of the original covenantor is to be bound by a covenant affecting freehold land in equity.

(i) Restrictive Covenant

[19.39] It is settled that equity will enforce a covenant only if it is restrictive, ie negative, in nature.[78] The reason for this was that equity's contribution to the law of

---

[72] See *Kingsbury v Anderson Ltd* (1979) P & CR 136 at 143 (*per* Browne-Wilkinson J). See also the Privy Council advice given (by now Lord Browne-Wilkinson) in *Emile Elias & Co Ltd v Pine Groves* [1993] 1 WLR 305.

[73] *Collins v Castle* (1887) 36 Ch D 243 at 253-4. *Cf* where there are substantial variations: see *Emile Elias & Co Ltd v Pine Groves Ltd* [1993] 1 WLR 305.

[74] *Newman v Real Estate Debenture Corp Ltd* [1940] 1 All ER 131.

[75] *L & SW Rly v Gomm* (1882) 20 Ch D 562 at 583 (*per* Jessel MR); *Formby v Barker* [1903] 2 Ch 539.

[76] *Catt v Tourle* (1869) 4 Ch App 654; *Luker v Dennis* (1877) 7 Ch D 227. But see the recent academic controversy over the rule between Bell, 'Tulk v Moxhay Revisited' [1981] Conv 55 and Griffith 'Tulk v Moxhay Reclarified' [1983] Conv 29.

[77] Eg Jessel MR in the *Gomm* case, *op cit*, p 583. In *Re Tiltwood* [1978] Ch 269, Foster J adopted the analogy with easements in holding that unity of seisin of the two pieces of land to which a restrictive covenant relates (the "dominant and servient tenements") extinguishes the covenant unless it is expressly revived in a subsequent sale by the common owner.

[78] *Haywood v Brunswick Permanent Benefit Building Soc* (1881) 8 QBD 403. There were earlier doubts on this, *Morland v Cook* (1868) LR 6 Eq 252; *Cooke v Chilcott* (1876) 3 Ch D 694. *Cf* the English recommendations in the *Report of the Committee on Positive Covenants Affecting Land* (1965, Cmnd 2719) and Law Com No 127, *Transfer of Land: The Law of Positive and Restrictive Covenants* (1984); and see *1971 Survey (NI)*, Ch 16 and now Article 34 of the Property (NI) Order 1997: see para **[19.48]**, *post*.

covenants stemmed from the availability of its special remedy, the injunction.[79] This is a remedy which is more often used to restrain the commission or continuance of acts, which presents no particular difficulties of enforcement, than to require the doing of something positive, which may necessitate supervision. It is true that equity can grant mandatory injunctions and also decrees of specific performance, but we saw in an earlier chapter that these are not given as freely as a prohibitory injunction.[80]

[19.40] Whether a covenant is negative or not is a matter of substance and cannot be disguised by the form of words used in the deed or covenant, eg, a covenant to refrain from building on Leicester Square Garden can be put in the form of a covenant to maintain it "in an open state, uncovered with any buildings."[81] The test usually adopted is whether compliance with the covenant requires expenditure of money. If it does, it is not negative in nature, eg, a covenant "not to let the premises fall into disrepair." If it does not, the covenant is more likely to be negative in nature,[82] but not necessarily so.

[19.41] It has been held by the House of Lords that a covenant in the form that the covenantor is not to "cause or permit" certain types of user of land is *not* broken if the covenantor agrees to sell the land to a person who intends, with the full knowledge of the covenantor, to use it for such prohibited purposes.[83]

(ii) Benefit of Covenantee's Land

[19.42] As mentioned above,[84] the basis of the rule in *Tulk v Moxhay* is that the covenant is concerned with preserving the value of the land retained by the covenantee, ie, it is taken for its benefit. The general rule is, therefore, that the plaintiff must be the owner for the time being of the neighbouring land benefited by the covenant.[85] Thus the original covenantee cannot enforce the covenant in equity against a successor of the original covenantor if he has parted with all the "dominant" land.[86] There are, however, some exceptions to this general rule. Thus it has been held that a head-landlord, owning no neighbouring land, can sue under the doctrine of *Tulk v Moxhay* a sublessee with whom he has neither privity of estate nor privity of contract.[87] We saw earlier that an estate scheme may avoid the difficulties of proving retention of neighbouring land.[88]

---

[79] As to assessment of damages for breach of covenant, see the discussion by the English Court of Appeal in *Surrey County Council v Bredero Homes Ltd* [1993] 3 All ER 705 and *Jaggard v Sawyer* [1995] 2 All ER 189.

[80] Paras **[3.130]** and **[3.143]**, *ante*.

[81] *Tulk v Moxhay* (1848) 2 Ph 774.

[82] Eg, to use the premises for private residential purposes only, *German v Chapman* (1877) 7 Ch D 271.

[83] *Tophams Ltd v Sefton* [1967] AC 50. *Cf Leicester v Wells UDC* [1972] 3 All ER 77.

[84] Para **[19.38]**, *supra*.

[85] See *Kelly v Barrett* [1924] 2 Ch 379. It may be a matter of construction of the deed creating the covenant exacting what is the land to be benefited: see *St Luke's and St Anne's Hospital Board v Mahon* Unrep (HC, RI), 18 June 1993 (1992/895 Sp).

[86] *LCC v Allen* [1943] 3 KB 642.

[87] *Craig v Greer* [1899] 1 IR 258 (see *A Casebook on Irish Land Law* (1984) p 616). See also *Regent Oil Co Ltd v JA Gregory (Hatch End) Ltd* [1965] WLR 1206.

[88] Para **[19.34]**, *ante*.

(iii) Intention to Run

[19.43] There must be a clear indication that the burden of the covenant is intended to run with the covenantor's "servient" land.[89] If it is made by the covenantor on behalf of himself and his heirs and assigns, or his successors in title, *prima facie* the burden is intended to run.[90]

(iv) Equitable Interest

[19.44] Since the enforceability of the burden against successors in title of the covenantor depends upon equity, the interest created by the covenant is equitable only. There are two important aspects of this principle. First, the remedy available to the plaintiff is an equitable one, the injunction since it is a negative covenant, and like all equitable remedies it is discretionary.[91] The court may in its discretion refuse to grant an injunction, eg, where the plaintiff has been guilty of *laches*.[92] If the character of the neighbourhood has changed since the covenant was first created, the covenant may have become almost worthless as a means of preserving the value of the dominant land and so the court may take the view that it is unreasonable to grant an injunction.[93] This may be a particularly significant factor where the covenant was imposed many years ago in relation to land on the outskirts of a town or city but now caught up in the middle of the urban "sprawl" so common in recent decades.

[19.45] The second point about a restrictive covenant creating an equitable interest only is, of course, that it may lose priority if the servient land is transferred to a *bona fide* purchaser for value of the *legal* estate without notice of the covenant.[94] To this extent the question of notice is important in relation to the rule in *Tulk v Moxhay*.[95] However, it is questionable whether this often happens in Ireland, because the existence of the Registry of Deeds system normally ensures that a purchaser discovers the existence of the deed containing the covenant, if not the covenant itself.[96] Registration of the deed is necessary to secure priority for the covenantee against subsequent purchasers of the covenantor's land and a failure to register may result in the covenant becoming unenforceable against such a purchaser.[97] If the title to the land is registered, the

---

[89] See *Power Supermarkets Ltd v Crumlin Investments Ltd* Unrep (HC, RI) 22 June 1981 (1978 No 4539P) (see *A Casebook on Irish Land Law* (1984), p 652). See also *Re Fawcett and Holmes' Contract* (1889) 42 Ch 150.

[90] *Cf* annexation of the benefit of a restrictive covenant, para **[19.32]**, *ante*.

[91] Para **[3.050]**, *ante*.

[92] Para **[3.066]**, *ante*.

[93] *Chatsworth Estates Co v Fewell* [1931] 1 Ch 224.

[94] Para **[3.074]**, *ante*. A restrictive covenant is enforceable against a squatter without notice, because he is not a "purchaser," *Re Nisbet and Potts' Contract* [1906] 1 Ch 386.

[95] Para **[19.38]**, *ante*.

[96] In England, since 1926 a restrictive covenant must be registered as a land charge under the Land Charges Act 1925 (now replaced by the Land Charges Act 1972). Rowley, 'Registration of Restrictive Covenants' (1956) 20 Conv 370.

[97] See paras **[3.086-9]**, *ante*.

restrictive covenant must also be registered as a burden on the land so as to bind subsequent purchasers.[98]

C. Discharge and Modification

[19.46] One of the major problems of the present law in the Republic of Ireland relating to restrictive covenants is that there is no really effective method of dealing with freehold covenants which have become obsolete because of the change in the character of the neighbourhood since their original creation. At best, such covenants have a nuisance value as a flaw on the title to the property; at worst, they can impede development of property, including development for which public planning permission may be obtainable, and sometimes they are used to extract exorbitant sums for their release.[99] It is true that this was not as great a problem in Ireland as in England because there was little freehold land available for development, though more has been coming on the market as a result of leasehold enfranchisement.[100] The prohibition of the creation of new ground rents in respect of dwellings by the Landlord and Tenant (Ground Rents) Act 1978, with the resultant switch to freehold conveyancing, has, of course, given impetus to this development. The time may be ripe for the legislators to consider introducing special legislation enabling the discharge or modification of restrictive covenants, which have become obsolete or are impeding reasonable development of land.[101] As we mentioned earlier, the Republic has already taken some steps in this direction in relation to leasehold covenants affecting unregistered land.[102] In Northern Ireland, Part II of the Property (NI) Order 1978[103] now contains comprehensive provisions dealing with identification and modification or extinguishment of certain "impediments" to the enjoyment of land, ie, restrictions arising under covenants, conditions or agreements or a statutory provision of a local or personal character, obligations to execute works on land or pay or contribute to their costs, easements and profits.[104] The Lands Tribunal is given the power, on application by any person interested, to make orders declaring whether or not the land is or would be affected by an impediment, its nature and extent and whether it is enforceable and, if so, by

---

[98] Registration of Title Act 1964, s 69(1)(k) (RI); Land Registration Act (NI), 1970, s 39 and Sched 6, Pt I, para 12. Para **[21.36]**, *post.*

[99] See *1971 Survey (NI)*, paras 392-5.

[100] And note the provisions in this legislation for preserving covenants enhancing amenities, etc, para **[18.28]**, *ante.*

[101] Note, however, Housing (Ir) Act 1919, s 22 (conversion of single house into several tenements). *Cf* the English provisions in the Law of Property Act 1925, s 84, as amended by the Law of Property Act 1969, s 28. Newsom, *Discharge and Modifications of Restrictive Covenants* (1957); Bodkin, 'Discharge and Modification of Restrictive Covenants' (1942) 7 Conv 17.

[102] Para **[17.047]**, *ante.*

[103] Based on the recommendations in the *1971 Survey (NI)*, paras 392-5. For a fuller discussion of these provisions in the Order, see Dawson, 'Modification and Extinguishment of Land Obligations under the Property (NI) Order 1978' (1978) 29 NILQ 223. See also Shaw, 'Modification of Restrictive Covenants under Statute' (1981) 32 NILQ 289. The suggestion that these provisions were a violation of Article 1 of the First Protocol of the European Convention for the Protection of Human Rights and Freedoms (see para **[18.40]**, fn 269, *ante*) was rejected by the European Court of Human Rights in 1984, see *Scott v United Kingdom* (Applic No 10741/84), see Decision and Reports, Vol 41, p 226.

[104] Article 3(1).

whom.[105] It is also given power to modify or extinguish impediments on being satisfied that they "unreasonably" impede the enjoyment of the land or, if not modified or extinguished, would do so.[106] In determining whether to exercise this power, it is to take into account a number of listed matters, eg, any change in the character of the neighbourhood, any public interest (particularly as exemplified by any development plan adopted for the area) and any trend shown by planning permissions granted in the vicinity. But no application may be made (except with the permission of the Tribunal) in respect of an impediment arising under a lease until 21 years from the beginning of the term have elapsed. The Tribunal may require the payment of compensation in certain circumstances. The High Court or county court may refer such questions to the Lands Tribunal, where they arise in proceedings before them, or may exercise similar jurisdiction in certain cases.[107] Orders made under Articles 4 and 5 bind all persons interested in the impediment in question[108] and must be registered in the Land Registry or Registry of Deeds, according to whether the title to the land affected is registered or unregistered.[109]

[19.47] So far as registered land is concerned, since 1892 the court has had power to modify or discharge a restrictive covenant registered on the folio on three grounds: (1) it does not run with the land; (2) it is incapable of being enforced against the land; (3) its modification or discharge will be "beneficial" to the persons "principally-interested" in its enforcement.[110] There seems to be no reported case of this power being invoked, presumably owing, in part, to the rarity of covenants affecting freehold land. In the new registration legislation in both parts of Ireland, the Registrar can modify or discharge a restrictive covenant with the consent of all persons interested in its enforcement.[111] It is questionable whether the third ground mentioned above resolves the problem arising where the dominant owner uses his right to enforce the covenant to impede development or to force the developer to buy him out. In such cases, modification or discharge would be "beneficial" to one side only! It must also be remembered that the legislation applies only to covenants registered on the folio and this is a considerable restriction on the power to modify or discharge covenants in the Republic of Ireland, especially since the problems arise mainly in respect of urban land which is not generally registered land.

D. Property (NI) Order 1997

[19.48] As mentioned earlier, Article 34 of the 1997 Order replaces the rules of common law and equity relating the enforceability of *freehold* covenants.[112] The new statutory

---

[105] Article 4.

[106] Article 5.

[107] Article 6.

[108] Article 7.

[109] Article 8.

[110] Local Registration of Title (Ir) Act 1891, s 45(3).

[111] Registration of Title Act 1964, s 69(3) (RI); Land Registration Act (NI), 1970, s 48(1)(a). Section 48(1) of the Land Registration Act (NI) 1970 was amended by Sched 1 to the Property (NI) Order 1978, to confine the power to modify or discharge with consent to the Registrar and the court's powers to discharging on satisfaction that the covenant does not run with the land or is incapable of being enforced against the owner of the land.

[112] Article 34(1). It does not affect leasehold covenants: see para **[19.03]**, *ante*.

rules are based on recommendations made by the Land Law Working Group[113] and have very few precedents elsewhere.[114] The new statutory rules, when they come into force on an appointed day, will not apply to any covenant in a deed made before that day[115] or in a deed made on or after that day in pursuance of an obligation assumed before that day.[116] Nor will they apply to covenants for title,[117] covenants expressed to bind only the covenantor[118] or covenants affecting the land after redemption of ground rents under Part II of the Order.[119] The new rules are also concerned only with enforceability of freehold covenants as between successors in title to the original parties.[120] The freehold covenants to which the rules apply are listed in the Order[121] and range from covenants to maintain, repair or renew party walls or fences or to preserve boundaries and to do, or to pay for or contribute to the cost of, works to covenants for the protection of amenities or services, such as covenants restricting the use of land. Thus the distinction between positive and negative covenants ceases to be of significance, nor is there any requirement of registration to preserve enforceability.[122]

[19.49] The essence of the new statutory rules is that freehold covenants included within Article 34 are enforceable (as appropriate to the nature of the covenant and the circumstances of the breach or the anticipated or threatened breach) by the owner for the time being of the land benefited by the covenant against the owner for the time being of the land burdened by it.[123] Thus the covenant can no longer be enforced by a person when he ceases to be the owner of the land benefited[124] and it cannot be enforced against the owner of the burdened land after he has ceased to be the owner of it,[125] except in

---

[113] See *Final Report* (HMSO, 1991) Vol 1, Chs 2.7-2.9, which contained much more wide-reaching provisions yet to be put into effect.

[114] A forerunner is, however, to be found in s 118 of the Trinidad and Tobago Land Law Conveyancing Act 1981, part of a package of legislation enacted in that year and drafted by the author: see Wylie, *The Land Laws of Trinidad and Tobago* (Port-of-Spain, 1986); also Bell, 'Enforcement of Positive Covenants in Trinidad and Tobago' [1983] Conv 211.

[115] Article 34(2)(a).

[116] Article 34(2)(b).

[117] Such as those operating under s 7 of the Conveyancing Act 1881: Wylie, *Irish Conveyancing Law* (2nd ed, 1996), para 21.05 *et seq*; Article 34(2)(c).

[118] Article 34(2)(d).

[119] Article 34(2)(e). Article 25 deals with enforceability of such covenants and this applies also where a lease is enlarged under Article 35: see paras **[17.108]**, and **[18.47]**, *ante*.

[120] Article 34(3).

[121] Article 34(4).

[122] See Land Law Working Group's *Final Report* (HMSO, 1990) Vol 1, para 2.7.59.

[123] *Ibid*. For these purposes "owner" means the fee simple owner or limited owner within the Settled Land Acts, but not a squatter unless he has acquired title by adverse possession (see Ch 23, *post*) or the covenant sought to be enforced against him is restrictive in substance or relates to permission: Article 34(9).

[124] Article 34(i). This is also the rule under the general law: see paras **[19.26]** and **[19.31]**, *ante*.

[125] This does not apply to transfer of membership of a body corporate formed for the management of land : see Article 34(4)(f) and (ii).

respect of breaches occurring while he was still the owner.[126] For these purposes it is conclusively presumed that the benefit and burden of the covenant in question attaches permanently to the whole and every part of the covenantor's and convenantee's lands respectively.[127] In the case of a development, where land is divided into two or more freehold parcels with the intention[128] of creating "reciprocity of covenants" as between the various parcel owners,[129] the covenants are enforceable as between the owners for the time being of the parcels.[130]

---

[126] Article 34(4)(iii).

[127] Article 34(5); this does not, however, prejudice release of a covenant by a deed executed by the relevant owners; Article 34(8). *Cf* para [19.32], *ante.*

[128] Shown expressly in conveyances to the parcel owners or by implication from the parcels and covenants and the proximity of the relationship between the parcel owners: Article 34(7)(c).

[129] Article 34(7)(a) and (b).

[130] Article 34(6) and note the definition of "parcel owner" in Article 34(9). *Cf* the estate scheme rules which operate in respect of the benefit of covenants only, not the burden: para [19.34], *et seq, ante.*

Chapter 20

LICENCES AND SIMILAR INTERESTS

[20.01] In this chapter we consider some other concepts which seem to involve recognition of interests in land which do not fall neatly into the well established categories discussed in previous chapters. The first concept we discuss is that of a licence, a subject which has aroused much controversy in England in recent decades.[1] The paucity of authority in Ireland makes it difficult to estimate to what extent similar developments will occur here. However, apart from the subject of licences, we also discuss similar concepts which have been recognised for many years in Ireland.

I. LICENCES

[20.02] So far as land is concerned, a licence is permission to do something in relation to the land which would otherwise be a trespass.[2] At common law, it seems to have been regarded as nothing more than that and certainly was not regarded as capable of creating an interest in land affecting third parties.[3] Usually it does not confer on the licensee any exclusive right to possession of land, as a lease or tenancy agreement does,[4] though there may be a limited right of occupation necessary to the enjoyment of the licence.[5] Thus rights to hire rooms for a whist drive and dance[6] and to moor and anchor eel tanks to an island[7] have been held to be mere licences. However, there is a danger of

---

[1] See the first comprehensive textbook on the subject, Dawson and Pearce, *Licences Relating to the Occupation or Use of Land* (1979). See also Bandali, 'Licence as an Interest in Land' (1973) 37 Conv 402; Briggs, 'Licences: Back to Basics' [1981] Conv 212 and 'Contractual Licences: A Reply' [1983] Conv 185; Crane, 'Licensees and Successors in Title of Licensor' (1952) 16 Conv 323; Hanbury, 'Licences, A Jonah's Gourd' (1954) CLJ 201 and (1955) CLJ 47; Hargreaves, 'Licenced Possessors' (1953) 69 LQR 466; Marshall and Scamell, 'Digesting the Licence' (1953) 31 CBR 847; Mitchell, 'Learner's Licence' (1954) 17 MLR 211; Moriarty, 'Licences and Land Law: Legal Principles and Public Bodies' (1984) 100 LQR 376; Robson and Watchman, 'The Hidden Wealth of Licences' [1980] Conv 27 Sheridan, 'Licences to Live in Houses' (1953) 17 Conv 440; Stoljar, 'Licence, Interest and Contract' (1955 33 CBR 562; Sparkes, 'Certainty of Leasehold Terms' (1993) 109 LQR 93; Todd 'Estoppel Licences and Third Parties [1981] Conv 347; Wade, Licences and Third Parties (1952) 68 LQR 337.

[2] See *Kelly v Woolworth & Co Ltd* [1922] 2 IR 5; *MacGinley v National Aid Committee* [1952] Ir Jur Rep 43.

[3] *King v David Allen and Sons Ltd* [1916] 2 IR 448, on appeal [1916] 2 AC 54. Note the English Court of Appeal's return to this fundamental principle in *Ashburn Anstadlt v Arnold* [1989] Ch 1: see para **[20.05]**, *post.*

[4] See further, Chs 4 and 17, *ante.*

[5] See *Trappe v Halpin* (1928) 62 ILTR 15; *Whyte v Sheehan* [1943] Ir Jur Rep 38.

[6] *Kelly v Woolworth & Co Ltd* [1922] 2 IR 5.

[7] *Whipp v Mackey* [1927] IR 372. See further on the distinction between a lease and a licence Wylie, *Irish Landlord and Tenant Law*, Ch 3, which also discusses the position of persons holding land under arrangements similar to a licence, eg, a caretaker, lodger, hotel guest and franchisee.

generalising in this area of law, because there are several different kinds of licences which may be created and they may have quite different characteristics.

A. Bare Licences

[20.03] A bare licence is mere permission to do something, ie, not involving any contractual arrangement.[8] At common law such a licence is revocable at any time by the licensor and thereupon the licensee becomes a trespasser, provided he is given reasonable notice to leave. If he is not given such notice, it is now settled that he is entitled to a "packing-up" period, ie, he does not become a trespasser until a reasonable time for him to leave with his goods and belongings has elapsed.[9] It is questionable whether equity would restrain the licensor from revoking the licence too early, by granting the licensee an injunction, since the licensee is a volunteer. Apart from that, this would be limited protection only and, in itself, does not justify classification of such a licence as an interest in land. However, the. presence of additional circumstances, such as factors giving rise to an estoppel, may change that.[10]

B. Licences Coupled with an Interest

[20.04] Often a licence is included in a grant of a proprietary interest in land and, in this sense, it may acquire the characteristics of an interest in land.[11] Thus such a licence is irrevocable by the licensor so long as the proprietary interest lasts[12] and may be assigned to a third party along with the interest in land. A common example of such a case is where a profit *à prendre* is granted, eg, shooting or fishing rights.[13] Such rights in respect of the land cannot be enjoyed unless accompanied by a licence to go on to the land to exercise them. The profit can be passed as an interest in land to successors in title of the grantee and it binds successors in title of the grantor, as does the licence

---

[8] See *Isitt v Monaghan CC* (1905) 5 NIJR 118. See also *NI Housing Executive v Duffin* [1985] NI 210.

[9] *Winter Garden Theatre (London) Ltd v Millennium Productions Ltd* [1948] AC 173. The *Winter Garden* case was applied by McWilliam J in *Law v Murphy* Unrep (HC, RI) 12 April 1978 (1976 No 4328P). And see *Devlin v NI Housing Executive* [1982] NI 377; *NI Housing Executive v Duffin* [1985] NI 210. See also *Verrall v Great Yarmouth Borough Council* [1980] QB 202; *Robson v Hallett* [1967] 2 QB 939.

[10] See para **[20.07]**, *infra*.

[11] *Wood v Manley* (1839) 112 A & E 34; *Wood v Leadbitter* (1845) 13 M & W 838. *Cf Smith v Hogg* [1953-54] Ir Jur Rep 58.

[12] The extension of this principle to the holder of a ticket to watch a film in a cinema in *Hurst v Picture Theatres Ltd* [1915] 1 KB 1 by a majority of the Court of Appeal is highly questionable: note the dissenting judgment given by Phillimore LJ and the subsequent criticism of the majority decision in *Winter Garden Theatre Ltd v Millennium Productions Ltd* [1946] 1 All ER 678 (Lord Greene MR) and (on appeal) [1948] AC 173 (Lord Uthwatt); *Hounslow London BC v Twickenham Garden Developments Ltd* [1971] Ch 233. Note also the refusal to follow *Hurst* majority reasoning in Australasia: see *Cowell v Rosehill Racecourse Co Ltd* (1937) 56 CLR 650; *Mayfield Holdings Ltd v Moana Reef* [1973] 1 NZLR 309.

[13] Ch 6, *ante*.

necessarily attached to the profit.[14] As we shall see later in this chapter,[15] similar rights are frequently created in Ireland under conacre and agistment "lettings".

C. Contractual Licences

[20.05] There is much more doubt as to the position of a contractual licence, ie, one where the licensor's power of revocation is governed by a contract, but the licence is not coupled with a proprietary interest in land. So far as the common law was concerned, it seems that the licensor still had *power* to revoke the licence, even if his *right* to do so was restricted by contract. [16] If the revocation was contrary to the agreement, the licensee's remedy, if any, was for damages only. However, it seems that equity might intervene in certain circumstances by granting an injunction to restrain revocation contrary to agreement.[17]

[20.06] The alleged extension of the law relating to contractual licences by the English Court of Appeal in *Errington v Errington*,[18] in which the court decided that such licences may in equity bind successors in title of the licensor with notice, was long regarded as doubtful for several reasons. First, there was little authority to support the view that a contractual licence could create by itself an interest in land[19] and much authority against it.[20] Secondly, much of the reasoning in the case was adopted around the same time in relation to the so-called "deserted wife's equity", which was later rejected by the House of Lords in *National Provincial Bank Ltd v Ainsworth*.[21] Thirdly,

---

[14] Note that, in Ireland, such profits often form the subject-matter of a lease or tenancy agreement, *Bayley v Conyngham* (1863) 15 ICLR 406 (see *A Casebook on Irish Land Law* (1984), p 311).

[15] Para **[20.25]**, *infra*.

[16] See discussion in *Wood v Leadbitter* (1845) 13 M & W 838; *Hurst v Picture Theatres Ltd* [1915] 1 KB 1; *Thompson v Park* [1944] KB 408; *Winter Garden Theatre Ltd v Millennium Productions Ltd* [1948] AC 173; *Hounslow London BC v Twickenham Garden Developments Ltd* [1971] Ch 233. Also *King v David Allen and Sons Ltd* [1916] 2 AC 54.

[17] *Cf Cullen v Cullen* [1962] IR 268 (injunction not appropriate to govern relations between fathers and sons) (see *A Casebook on Irish Land Law* (1984), p 657). For a broad approach to equitable jurisdiction in such cases, see *Taylors Fashions Ltd v Liverpool Victoria Trustees Co Ltd* [1982] QB 133. See also *Tanner v Tanner* [1975] 1 WLR 1346 (damages awarded since no longer practicable to enforce licence); *Horrocks v Forray* [1976] 1 WLR 230 (no contract); *Hardwick v Johnson* [1978] 1 WLR 683 (contractual licence irrevocable); *Chandler v Kerley* [1978] 1 WLR 693 (contractual licence held to be terminable on reasonable notice); *Verrall v Great Yarmouth Borough Council* [1980] QB 202 (specific performance of contractual licence). *Cf McGill v S* [1979] IR 283 where Gannon J held that the relationship between the parties did not give rise to a contractual licence (see also para **[25.15]**, *post*).

[18] [1952] 1 KB 290.

[19] Denning LJ's historical analysis of the cases is unconvincing, see Wylie, 'Contracts and Third Parties' (1966) 17 NILQ 351 at 364-5. But see the support in *Re Sharpe* [1980] 1 WLR 219, where Browne-Wilkinson J invoked the notion of a constructive trust in support, see para **[20.08]**, *post*. And see *Woods v Donnelly* [1982] NI 257. See also *DHN Food Distributors Ltd v Tower Hamlets LBC* [1976] 1 WLR 852.

[20] Eg, *King v David Allen and Sons Ltd* [1915] 2 IR 448, on appeal [1916] 2 AC 54; *Clore v Theatrical Properties Ltd* [1936] 3 All ER 483.

[21] [1965] AC 1175. See Wylie, (1965) 16 NILQ 521 and (1966) 17 NILQ 351 at 365-7. But see the English Matrimonial Homes Act 1967.

it was probable that the case could be explained on grounds more consistent with the authorities. One possibility was that the successor in title in *Errington* was also personal representative of the deceased licensor and might have been bound by the deceased's contract on that basis, rather than as his devisee. Others argued that the contract in the case was a specifically enforceable contract to convey land and, as such, would have bound any successor to the land with notice.[22] Finally, it was probable that, in the light of developments since the case was decided, it would be decided nowadays on the basis of estoppel.[23] The English Court of Appeal revisited the matter in *Ashburn Anstalt v Arnold*,[24] where Fox LJ, giving the judgment of the Court, emphatically rejected the principle that a contractual licence can bind a successor in title to the licensee.[25] There has been no sign of the Irish courts following the *Errington* reasoning and, instead, as in England much more weight has been put on doctrines like the doctrine of estoppel, a subject to which we now turn.

D. Estoppel Licences

[20.07] There is judicial authority in both Ireland[26] and England[27] that the licensor and his successors in title may in certain circumstances be estopped from revoking a licence relating to land, unless the successor is a *bona fide* purchaser of the legal estate without notice. The principle involved seems to be that, if the licensor induces the licensee into acting in relation to the land, eg, by building on it, on the basis that the licence will not be revoked, the licensor is estopped in equity from revoking it in a manner inconsistent with the understanding between the parties.[28] The rights of the licensee thus depend

---

[22] See Megarry and Wade, *Law of Real Property* (5th ed, 1984), p 807.

[23] And see *Dodsworth v Dodsworth* (1973) 228 Est Gaz 1115. But *cf* Briggs, 'Licences: Back to Basics' [1981] Conv 212 and 'Contractual Licences: A Reply' [1983] Conv 285; Thompson, 'Licences: Questioning the Basics' [1983] Conv 50.

[24] [1989] 1 Ch 1; Hill (1988) 51 MLR 226.

[25] He pointed out that the authorities did not support the principle and that it was a unnecessary for the Court to invoke it in *Errington*.

[26] *Cullen v Cullen* [1962] IR 268 (see *A Casebook on Irish Land Law* (1984), p 657). *Cf Morrow v Carty* [1957] NI 174. See Brady, 'An English and Irish View of Proprietary Estoppel' (1970) Ir Jur (ns) 239. See also *Brownlee v Duggan* (1976) 27 NILQ 291.

[27] *Dillwyn v Llewellyn* (1862) 4 De GF & J 517; *Ramsden v Dyson* (1865) LR 1 HL 129; *Plimmer v Wellington Corp* (1884) 9 App Cas 699; *Foster v Robinson* [1951] 1 KB 149; *Inwards v Baker* [1965] 2 QB 29; *Ward v Kirkland* [1967] Ch 194; *ER Ives Investment Ltd v High* [1967] 2 QB 279. *Cf* the use of the concept of a "constructive trust" (para **[20.23]**, *post*) in *Binions v Evans* [1972] Ch 359; *Haughan v Rutledge* [1988] IR 295; *Department of the Environment v Leeburn* [1990] NI 135. See Oughten, 'Proprietary Estoppel: A Principled Remedy' (1979) 129 New LJ 1193; People, 'Promissory Estoppel in a New Context' (1980) 130 New LJ 373; Smith 'Licences and Constructive Trusts' (1973) CLJ 123. See also *Dodsworth v Dodsworth* (1973) 228 Est Gaz 1115.

[28] Thus to some extent the principle appears to be an application of the doctrine of promissory or equitable estoppel developed by Denning J (as he then was) in *Central London Property Trusts Ltd v High Trees House Ltd* [1947] KB 130; see also *Combe v Combe* [1951] 2 KB 215; *Tool Metal Manufacturing Co. Ltd v Tungsten Electric Co Ltd* [1955] 1 WLR 761; *D & C Builders Ltd v Rees* [1966] 2 WLR 288. For recognition of the principle in Ireland, see *Revenue Commrs v Moroney* [1972] IR 372 (Kenny J); *cf* at 382 (Sup Ct). See also *Woods v Donnelly* [1982] NI 257; *Devlin v NI Housing Executive* [1982] NI 377; *Smith v Ireland* [1983] ILRM 300 (see *A Casebook on Equity and Trusts in Ireland* (1985), p 80).

partly on the precise terms of his understanding or agreement with the licensor and partly on his being able to establish that it would be inequitable to allow the licensor to exercise his strict legal right to revoke the licence, because, eg, the licensee, to the knowledge of the licensor, has acted to his detriment in reliance upon the understanding or agreement,[29] or a legitimate expectation on the part of the licensee has arisen.[30] And since the rights are dependent upon equitable principles, they will bind successors in title of the licensor only if such persons are not *bona fide* purchasers for value without notice of the licence.[31] In this respect, licences are like restrictive covenants.[32]

[20.08] Sometimes the remedy sought by the licensee is an injunction to restrain the licensor or a person succeeding to his title to the land from revoking the licence. In other words, the doctrine of estoppel normally acts as a "shield" only and not as a "sword", but in recent times the courts have emphasised that the equity which arises in the licensee is a very flexible one.[33] The courts take the view nowadays that they have a wide discretion to choose the remedy which is most appropriate to satisfy this equity so that, in some cases, the licensee may be entitled to a lien on the land for the amount of any money he may have expended on it,[34] or to a declaration that he is entitled to the land[35] or that the licensor holds the land for him as constructive trustee.[36] What is not very clear is how far the licensee's rights extend, if this is not made clear in his

---

29. See *Dunne v Molloy* [1976-7] ILRM 266; *McGucken v McGucken* [1990] NI 1; *Department of the Environment v Leeburn* [1990] NI 1. *Cf Re JR* [1993] ILRM 657. See also *William A Lees (Concrete) Ltd v Lees* [1992] 11 NIJB 44.

30. See *Kenny v Kelly* [1988] IR 457; *cf Pesca Valentia Ltd v Minister for Fisheries (No 2)* [1990] 2 IR 205.

31. Ch 3, *ante*. As to the importance of the licensee's conduct in deciding whether to give him equitable relief, see *Williams v Staite* [1978] 2 WLR 82-5; *Re Sharpe* [1980] 1 WLR 219. Since such licences are frequently informal arrangements it is unlikely that they will be contained in any document registered in the Registry of Deeds or that they will be noted on the register in the Land Registry, in the case of registered land, Chs 21 and 22, *post*. See *William A Lees (Concrete) Ltd v Lees* [1992] 11 NIJB 44; para **[20.12]**, *post*.

32. Ch 19, *ante*. There are differences, however, see para **[20.11]**, *infra*.

33. See Evans, 'Choosing the right Estoppel' [1988] Conv 346; Battersby, 'Contractual and Estoppel Licences as Proprietary Interests in Land' [1991] Conv 36. See also Davis, 'Proprietary Estoppel: Future Interests and Future Property' [1996] Conv 193.

34. *Unity Joint Stock Mutual Banking Assoc v King* (1858) 25 Beav 72; *Plimmer v Wellington Corp* (1884) 9 App Cas 699 (quoted with approval by Murphy J, giving the judgment of the Supreme Court in *McCarron v McCarron* Unrep, 13 February 1997 (181/95). *Cf Cullen v Cullen* [1962] IR 268 at 282 (see *A Casebook on Irish Land Law* (1984), p 657).

35. *Dillwyn v Llewellyn* (1862) 4 De GF & J 517, followed in *Pascoe v Turner* [1979] 1 WLR 431 and by Geoghegan J in *Smyth v Halpin* [1997] 2 ILRM 38; *Cf McCarron v McCarron* Unrep, 13 February 1997 (181/95). *Cf Cullen v Cullen*, *op cit*, pp 281-2.

36. *Binions v Evans* [1972] Ch 359. *Cf Lyus v Prowsa Development Ltd* [1982] 1 WLR 1044. See also *Crabb v Arun District Council* [1975] 3 WLR 847. *Cf Pascoe v Turner* [1979] 1 WLR 431. See also *Re Sharpe* [1980] 1 WLR 219, where Browne-Wilkinson J held that an irrevocable licence arose under a constructive trust so as to confer an equitable interest on the licensee taking priority over the trustee in bankruptcy of the licensor.

arrangements with the licensor, eg, is it an indefinite right[37] of a right to remain on the land for the licensor's lifetime only?[38] Furthermore, can the licensor revoke the licence to remain on the condition that he pays compensation for its value to the licensee?[39] And lastly, there is the thorny question of whether the licensee can assign the benefit of his licence to a third party. The general view seems to be that he cannot and this is consistent with the approach of equity to questions of estoppel, ie, the equity raised is personal to the licensee and aims to protect or "shield" him from unfairness rather than to confer interests in property which he can sell or pass to others.[40]

[20.09] Some of these difficulties may be illustrated by the Irish case of *Cullen v Cullen*,[41] which involved a family business at Adamstown owned by the father, who gradually became mentally ill, until eventually paranoia was diagnosed. Previously his three sons had helped at various times to run the business, but there were several family quarrels owing to the father's erratic behaviour. The father resisted attempts to remove him to a mental hospital by "escaping" to another part of the country, from where he sent word to his wife informing her that, in return for transferring the business to her, which she was to carry on in her own name, he required a signed statement from his wife and sons that he was sane and withdrawal of any order for his committal to a mental hospital. His wife had won a portable house in a competition and had given this to one of her sons, M, who had offered it to his father, but the latter had refused it. When the father "escaped", the mother thought that M should erect the portable house on the land connected with the family business rather than on his own land. She sought her husband's permission and he sent another message that, as he was making the property at Adamstown over to her, she could erect what she liked. M then went ahead and erected the house on that land. Later the father sent letters to M and P, one of his other sons, requiring them to leave the house and to give up any connection with the business. The father then brought an action claiming (1) an injunction to restrain the defendants (his two sons) from interfering with the business and trespassing on the land (2) accounts and (3) damages for trespass. M counterclaimed that he was entitled to the house and its site. Kenny J dismissed the claim for accounts and refused to grant the injunction for a variety of reasons, eg, such a remedy should not govern relations between fathers and sons and would make reconciliation between the various members

[37] *Plimmer v Wellington Corp* (1884) 9 App Cas 699; *Ward v Kirkland* [1967] Ch 194.

[38] See *Re JR* [1993] ILRM 657. See also *Inwards v Baker* [1965] 2 QB 29; *Binions v Evans* [1972] Ch 359. See also *Jones v Jones* [1977] 1 WLR 438; *Pascoe v Turner* [1979] 1 WLR 431.

[39] *Beaufort v Patrick* (1853) 17 Beav 60. This raises the further question of how the compensation is to be calculated, eg, the licensee's outlay, or the current market value of his addition to the land or the cost of establishing him in the same position on other land? See *Dodsworth v Dodsworth* (1973) 228 Est Gaz 1115. For discussion of the principle that there must be proportionality between the remedy and the detriment which it is designed to avoid, see *Sledmore v Dalby* [1996] NPC 16, citing the Australian decision in *Commonwealth of Australia v Verwayen* (1990) 95 ALR 321.

[40] See *Cullen v Cullen* [1962] IR 268 (see *A Casebook on Irish Land Law* (1984) p 657). Cf *Hopwood v Brown* [1955] 1 WLR 213; *ER Ives Investment Trust Ltd v High* [1967] 2 QB 379.

[41] [1962] IR 268. See also *McMahon v Kerry County Council* [1981] ILRM 419, discussed by Pearce, 'The Mistaken Improver of Land' (1985) 79 Gaz ILSI 179. Cf *Thomas v Thomas* [1956] NZLR 785.

of the family impossible.[42] Anyway, the defendants had never attempted to exclude their father from control of his business and had stated in court that they did not intend to prevent him returning to or interfering in the business. If he did return, his wife might need somebody else in the house to protect her from her husband's hostility. Kenny J did, however, award the father £50 damages against his two sons and, then, considered the position of the mother in relation to ownership of the business and M in relation to the house erected on the land by him. He took the view that M could not require his father to execute a conveyance of the site of the house,[43] but the father was estopped by his conduct from asserting his title to it. The sons made the case that their mother was the owner of the business and that she wished them to stay. Kenny J explained the operation of the principles in relation to the mother's claim to the business, upon which the sons relied, in this way.

> "The equity ... is a discretionary one and when I consider the circumstances in which the plaintiff made the statement that he was about to transfer the property at Adamstown to his wife and that he made it because he believed that it was the only way by which he could remain free, I have no doubt whatever that it would be grossly inequitable to regard Mrs Cullen as being entitled to a transfer of the property at Adamstown or as having acquired any proprietary interest, legal or equitable, in the property as a result of what was said. The use by Mrs Cullen of her own monies for the running of the business, particularly when she could have repaid this advance at any time, does not, in my opinion, create any claim in conscience or in equity which the court should enforce or give any ground for disregarding the general principle that equity will not aid an imperfect gift. As Mrs Cullen has no proprietary interest in the property the defendants cannot shelter behind her permission to them or her employment of them in the business."[44]

[20.10] Kenny J felt that, to the extent that the principles involved were an application of the doctrine discussed in the *High Trees* case, the son who had built the house could invoke them only as a defence to his father's action, at least so far as existing authority stood at the time.[45] He was not entirely happy with the conclusion and ventured the suggestion, *obiter*, that, if the son remained in possession for the 12 year period of limitation, he could have his possessory title registered in the Land Registry.[46] However,

---

[42] *Cf* the approach of Lavan J in *Johnston v Horace* [1993] ILRM 594 (enforcing a right of residence): see para **[20.21]**, *post*.

[43] The question of the son having a lien was mentioned in the counterclaim, but not argued and so not dealt with. On these aspects of the case, *cf Smyth v Halpin* [1997] 2 ILRM 38. See also *McCarron v McCarron* Unrep, 13 February 1997 (181/95).

[44] *Op cit*, p 282. See Allen, 'An Equity to Perfect a Gift' (1963) 79 LQR 238. Kenny J remarked that he was satisfied that M would have erected the house even if not given permission.

[45] *Op cit*, pp 291-2. It is arguable that Kenny J would have taken a different view in the light of later authorities on both sides of the Irish Sea which have emphasised the flexibility of the court's approach to finding the most appropriate remedy to satisfy the equity perceived to exist in the licensee: see para **[20.08]**, *ante*.

[46] Since the title was registered. A similar view was expressed by Finlay P in *McMahon v Kerry County Council* [1981] ILRM 419 See Brady and Kerr, *The Limitation of Actions* (2nd ed, 1994), pp 179-88; Welstead, 'Proprietary Estoppel and the Acquisition of Possessory Title' [1991] Conv 280. See generally Chs 21 and 23 *post*.

there are difficulties about this, which simply illustrate further the uncertainties of this whole subject. Normally, possession for the period of limitation does not result in acquisition of title to land unless it is "adverse" possession, ie, actionable by the owner as a trespass, whereas protection of a licensee on the ground of estoppel is usually based on possession with permission, ie, normally negativing any adverse possession.[47] On the other hand, once the licensor seeks to revoke the licence, it is arguable that the possession then becomes adverse and the licensee is trespasser. Thus Kenny J awarded damages for trespass in the *Cullen* case. The question is whether the limited protection by equity of this technical "trespasser" stops the limitation period running in his favour. If it does not, as Kenny J seems to suggest, many of the difficulties of licence cases may be resolved by the course of time. However this does put the licensor in a very peculiar position. He has a trespasser on his land acquiring title under the Statute of Limitations and, yet, there appears to be nothing effective he can do to prevent this. Equity denies him the remedy necessary to remove the trespasser from possession of his land and thereby to prevent time running against him.

[20.11] It is apparent, then, that the current of authority on both sides of the Irish Sea is running in favour of licences acquiring some proprietary characteristics. It seems to be accepted that, apart from the special case of licences coupled with an interest, these proprietary aspects are recognised in equity only. In that sense there is some similarity with the development in the nineteenth century of equitable rules as to the running of the burden of restrictive covenants.[48] This comparison must not, however, be taken too far. Even at common law, the benefit of a restrictive covenant could pass to a successor in title of the covenantee, yet the general view is that the benefit of a licence relating to land cannot be passed. Thus to the extent that such a licence does create an interest in land, it is an anomalous one, at least according to traditional concepts, ie, the burden runs, but the benefit does not. One further anomaly exists. The main basis of equity's enforcement of restrictive covenants is their *commercial* characteristics, ie, they relate to preservation of land values and do not depend on personal considerations of the particular landowners. Yet so many of the licence cases have involved *family* arrangements, which would not have been made were it not for the personal relationships involved. It is upon this basis that several judges have taken the view that the benefit of the licence must remain a personal privilege of the licensee only. So there appears to be something of a paradox here that licences involving such personal considerations should come to have commercial attributes.[49]

[20.12] Finally, it must be emphasised that, perhaps, the most unsatisfactory feature of the present state of the law of licences relating to land is the difficulty it creates for

---

[47] See *Murphy v Murphy* [1980] IR 183 (see *A Casebook on Irish Land Law* (1984), p 696); *Bellew v Bellew* [1982] IR 447, para **[23.05]**, *post*.

[48] Ch 19, *ante*. *Cf* Cheshire, 'A New Equitable Interest in Land' (1953) 16 MLR 1.

[49] Note that many of the earlier authorities confining licences to personal contractual, as opposed to proprietary, arrangements involved apparently "commercial" arrangements, eg, *King v David Allen and Sons Ltd* [1916] 2 AC 54; *Clore v Theatrical Properties Ltd* [1936] 3 All ER 483. *Cf*, however, *ER Ives Investment Ltd v High* [1967] 2 QB 379.

conveyancers. Since so many of the arrangements in question are of an informal kind, it is unlikely that they will be revealed in a traditional investigation of title. Frequently no documentary evidence will exist and even if it does, it will probably not be registered in the Registry of Deeds, if the land is unregistered. If the land is registered, interests under licences are not registerable[50] and are burdens affecting land without registration.[51] Since, however, the licensee is often in possession of the land, a subsequent purchaser may nevertheless be fixed with constructive notice.[52] If the licensee is not in exclusive possession, it may be difficult to discover his existence and this makes his equitable interest an almost unavoidable trap for the conveyancer. Even a meticulous inspection of the land may not be a foolproof safeguard.[53]

II. RIGHTS OF RESIDENCE

[20.13] It is extremely common in Ireland for wills and family settlements to confer rights of residence on, and to make provision for the maintenance and support of, members of the family.[54] Perhaps the most common example is that of a home-made farmer's will taking the form of a gift of the farm to his son "subject to the right of residence on the farm of my wife for her lifetime and subject to her being maintained in the manner in which she has been accustomed".[55]

---

[50] Ie, they are not listed in the Republic's Registration of Title Act 1964, s 69, nor in the Land Registration Act (NI) 1970, Sched 6, Pt I. Ch 21, *post.*

[51] They presumably come within the category of "rights of every person in actual occupation of the land," see 1964 Act, s 72(1)(j) (RI); 1970 Act (NI) Sched 5, Pt I, para 15. See *William A Lees (Concrete) Ltd v Lees* [1992] 11 NIJB 44.. *Re* England, see *National Provincial Bank Ltd v Ainsworth* [1965] AC 1175; *ER Ives Investment Ltd v High, op cit.*

[52] *Hunt v Luck* [1902] 1 Ch 428. See Wylie, *Irish Conveyancing Law* (2nd ed, 1996), para 16.23.

[53] See Crane, (1967) 31 Conv 341 and (1968) 32 Conv 85.

[54] See Harvey, 'Irish Rights of Residence - The Anatomy of a Hermaphrodite' (1970) 21 NILQ 389; Peel, 'Deserted Wife's Licence and Rights of Residence' (1964) 28 Conv 253. The best judicial discussion is in *National Bank v Keegan* [1931] IR 344 (see *A Casebook on Irish Land Law* (1984), p 673) and *Johnston v Horace* [1993] ILRM 594 (on which see Coughlan, 'Enforcing Rights of Residence' (1993) 11 ILT 168). For earlier examples, see *Richardson v McCausland* (1817) Beat 457; *Ryan v Ryan* (1848) 12 Ir Eq R 226; *Gallagher v Ferris* (1881) 7 LR Ir 489; *Leonard v Leonard* (1910) 44 ILTR 155; *Kelaghan v Daly* [1913] 2 IR 328; *Re Shanahan* [1919] 1 IR 131; *Re Mooney* (1923) 57 ILTR 12; *Re Butler* (1925) 59 ILTR 166.

[55] See the precedent recommended in Harvey, *op cit*, pp 423-4. It is important to note that the right often includes, in addition to a right of residence, provision for support and maintenance, including, eg, a specific bed and bedclothes (*Ryan v Ryan, op cit*), clothing (*Leonard v Leonard, op cit, Re Shanahan, op cit* and *Kelaghan v Daly, op cit*) and fuel (National *Bank v Keegan, op cit*). Note also the creation of a right of residence by exercise of the judicial power to make a property adjustment order on judicial separation in *TF v Ireland* [1995] 2 ILRM 321. See now s 9 of the Republic's Family Law Act 1995 and s 14 of the Family Law (Divorce) Act 1996. *Cf* Article 26 of the Matrimonial Causes (NI) Order 1978 and Article 21 of the Matrimonial and Family Proceedings (NI) Order 1989: see para **[25.15]**, *post.*

[20.14] From the outset it must be emphasised that the law on this subject is far from clear, despite modern legislation in both parts of Ireland.[56] The main reason is that these rights can take several forms and this has hindered the judges in deciding exactly what sort of interest in land, if any, is created. In particular, a distinction has to be drawn between two main categories, as Kennedy CJ pointed out in *National Bank v Keegan*:[57]

> "The residential rights, which are so commonly given in farm holdings in this country, especially by way of testamentary provision for testators' widows, also frequently by the reservations to parents of rights in settlements made on the marriage of sons, are of two types namely, the type which is a general right of residence charged on the holding usually coupled with a charge of maintenance; and the type which is a particular right of residence created by reserving or giving the right to the exclusive use during life of a specified room or rooms in the dwelling-house on the holding. The general right of residence charged on a holding is a right capable of being valued in moneys numbered at an annual sum, and of being represented by an annuity or money charge. It is clear that such is not the type of benefit given by the instrument before us. Here we have the second type of case in which the exclusive use during her life of a specified part of the holding comprising two rooms is given to the beneficiary. If this benefit were given to her by a deed or a will, I think that it is clear that she would hold an estate for life in the property, legal or equitable, according to the terms of the instrument."[58]

Bearing these remarks in mind we must consider the various possibilities as to the nature of such rights of residence.

A. Life Estate

[20.15] There is considerable authority in Ireland for saying that, if the right of residence confers an *exclusive* right in the land or in some specified part of it, this creates a life estate. This was the view of the majority of the Republic's Supreme Court in *National Bank v Keegan*.[59] The creation of a life estate is also often held to occur in English cases dealing with similar situations.[60]

[20.16] The consequences of holding that a life estate is created in such cases are extremely serious. The grantee of the right of residence, eg, the farmer's widow, would have all the powers of a tenant for life under the Settled Land Acts 1882-90.[61] She could, therefore, lease the land, or the part of it in which she has the exclusive right, to

---

[56] *Cf* the Republic's Statute of Limitations 1957, s 40, and Registration of Title Act 1964, ss 69(1)(q) and 81; Limitation (NI) Order 1989, Article 40 (re-enacting Statute of Limitations (NI) 1958, s 42), and Land Registration Act (NI) 1970, s 47 and Sched 6, Pt 1, para 14.

[57] [1931] IR 344 (see *A Casebook on Irish Land Law* (1984), p 673).

[58] *Ibid*, p 354. *Cf* at p 346 (per Johnston J) and at p 356 (per Murnaghan J).

[59] *Ibid. Cf Atkins v Atkins* [1976-7] ILRM 62.

[60] *Re Carne's Settled Estate* [1899] 1 Ch 324; *Re Baroness Llandover's Will Trusts* [1902] 2 Ch 679, *Re Gibbons* [1920] 1 Ch 372; *Bannister v Bannister* [1948] 2 All ER 133; *Binions v Evans* [1972] Ch 359; *Costello v Costello* (1994) 70 P & CR 297. *Cf Dent v Dent* [1996] 1 All ER 659. See Hornby, 'Tenancy for Life or Licence' (1977) 93 LQR 561; Martin, 'Contractual Licensee or Tenant for Life' (1972) 36 Conv 266.

[61] Ch 8, *ante*.

strangers or sell it outright over the heads of the other members of the family. In many cases, especially where the exclusive right relates to a part of the farm or land only, this would probably be quite contrary to the intention of the deceased farmer and so it is not surprising that the legislatures in both parts of Ireland have reconsidered the matter.

[20.17] First, the Statutes of Limitations in both parts of Ireland[62] distinguish between a right in the nature of a lien for money's worth in or over land for a limited period not exceeding life, such as a right of support or a right of residence,[63] and an exclusive right of residence in a *specified part* of the land which they probably thought, in the light of *National Bank v Keegan*, created a life interest like an exclusive right in the whole of the land.

[20.18] The next legislative step was taken in respect of *registered* land. Section 81 of the Republic's Registration of Title Act 1964 now states:

> A right of residence in or on registered land, whether a general right of residence on the land or an exclusive right of residence in or on part of the land, shall be deemed to be personal to the person beneficially entitled thereto and to be a right in the nature of a lien for money's worth in or over the land and shall not operate to create any equitable estate in the land.[64]

This clearly rules out for registered land (and remember that most farm land comes into this category[65]) the possibility of the grantee of the right of residence exercising the statutory powers of a tenant for life and thereby defeating the grantor's intention, except where the right is an exclusive right in respect of the whole land. In *Johnston v Horace*[66] the plaintiff had an unrestricted right of residence in a house which was shared with other members of the family. Lavan J drew attention to s 81 and held that she had a general right of residence in the nature of a lien which was "the right to bind the property for payment of the money's worth of the residential use".[67] There was no question of her having the statutory rights of a tenant for life.[68]

[20.19] In Northern Ireland, s 47 of the Land Registration Act (NI) 1970[69] provides:

> Where—
>
> (a) a right of residence in or on any registered land, whether a general right of residence in or on that land or an exclusive right of residence in or on part of that land; or
>
> (b) a right to use a specified part of that land in conjunction with a right of residence referred to in paragraph (a);

---

62 1957, s 40 (RI); 1958, s 42 (NI) (now in Article 40 of the Limitation (NI) Order 1989).

63 Ie, a *general* right of residence, *Kelaghan v Daly* [1913] 2 IR 328; *Re Shanahan* [1919] IR 131; *National Bank v Keegan* [1931] IR 344 (see *A Casebook on Irish Land Law* (1984), p 673).

64 Such a right is now registerable as a burden on the land under s 69(1)(q).

65 Ch 18, *ante*.

66 [1993] ILRM 594.

67 *Ibid* p 598.

68 *Ibid*.

69 See *Report of the Committee on Registration of Title to Land in Northern Ireland* (1957, Cmd 512), para 97.

is granted by deed or by will, such right shall be deemed to be personal to the person beneficially entitled thereto and the grant made by such deed or will shall not operate to confer any right of ownership in relation to the land upon such person, but registration of any such right as a Schedule 6 burden shall make it binding upon the registered owner of the land and his successors in title.

This achieves the same general result as the Republic's Act, though it should be noted that it does make it clear that, while the right of residence is personal to the grantee, ie, the benefit does not run with the land, it binds successors in title of the owner of the land, ie, the burden does run.[70] This is not made explicit by the Republic's 1964 Act though to the extent that the right creates a lien, this is an "incumbrance" within s 2(vii) of the Conveyancing Act 1881,[71] and presumably runs with the land.[72] Furthermore, rights of residence must be registered as burdens affecting the registered land; they are not burdens affecting such land without registration.[73]

B. Lien

[20.20] *Kelaghan v Daly*[74] is usually taken to have established that a right of residence, unless capable of being constructed as a life estate, is a right "in the nature of a lien for money's worth",[75] which binds successors in title taking with notice of it. The analogy was drawn with a vendor's lien for unpaid purchase money[76] and this view of the nature of the right has been recognised by the legislators in both parts of Ireland.[77] The Republic's Registration of Title Act 1964, as we saw above, continues to use this terminology, whereas the Land Registration Act (NI) 1970 has dropped it.

[20.21] There are, however, difficulties over the use of the concept of a lien. Usually a lien arises under a contract between the parties and is for a specific amount of money,[78] whereas rights of residence arise frequently under wills and are sometimes difficult to quantify in terms of money, especially when accompanied by vague provisions as to

---

[70] *Cf* licences, para **[20.11]**, *ante*.

[71] 1964 Act, s 3(1).

[72] See, however, Harvey, op cit, pp 403-4 and 408-11. The difficulty of the question of running with the land, if, as is usual, it is freehold land, is that while the right of residence is passive and could be construed as negative in substance, any allied right to maintenance or support is positive and normally would not run with unregistered land, if construed as a covenant, Ch 19, *ante*, and see *Kelaghan v Daly* [1913] 2 IR 328 at 330 (*per* Boyd J) and *Colreavy v Colreavy* [1940] IR 71 at 75 (*per* O'Byrne J). Hence the reference to a lien, which usually does run with the land, eg, a vendor's lien for unpaid purchase money.

[73] See the list in the Republic's 1964 Act, s 72; *Cf* 1970 Act (NI), Sched 5, Pt I and note the exclusion in para 15(b).

[74] [1913] 2 IR 328.

[75] *Ibid*, p 330 (*per* Boyd J). See also *Re Shanahan* [1919] 1 IR 131.

[76] See also Glover, *Registration of Ownership of Land in Ireland* (1933), p 188; McAllister, *Registration of Title in Ireland* (1973), p 201.

[77] Statute of Limitations 1957, s 40 (RI), and Limitation (NI) Order 1989, Article 40 (re-enacting Statute of Limitations (NI) 1958, s 42).

[78] *Marckreth v Symmons* (1808) 15 Ves 329 at 343 (*per* Lord Eldon LC).

support or maintenance. Furthermore, it is not clear from the Irish cases how far the analogy with liens, eg, a vendor's lien, can be carried. Thus it is not clear whether, as is usual, the lien can be discharged by payment of money regardless of the wishes of the person entitled to it or, alternatively, whether the person entitled to it can realise it by, eg, requiring the land to be sold to discharge it.[79] Both these courses of action would seem to be inconsistent with the intention of many grantors in Ireland. These were questions which faced Lavan J in *Johnston v Horace*[80] where the holder of a right of residence in a house shared over the years with her parents and other members of the family sought an injunction to restrain her nephew, who had inherited the property from his parents, from preventing her from exercising the right and damages for interference with it. Lavan J found that the nephew had used duress to force the plaintiff out of the property and, having made alterations to the property, had tried to get her to buy the property as he refused to negotiate the question of her right of residence.[81] Lavan J recognised that the plaintiff's unrestricted general right of residence was a lien for money's worth, as specified in s 81 of the Registration of Title Act 1964,[82] but pointed out that neither case law nor statute clarifies whether or not the holder of the right of residence or the owner of the property could insist upon it being converted into money's worth.[83] He concluded that there would be circumstances in which the court makes a valuation of the right, either by agreement of the parties or by compelling a valuation in the general interest of the administration of justice or under the court's equitable jurisdiction.[84] This should be an objective valuation, but the authorities did not indicate how it should be carried out. On the question of a valuation Lavan J drew a number of conclusions:[85]

(1) The valuation should reflect the circumstances of the particular case. Thus in *Johnston v Horace* the right was shared with others, it was of an ongoing nature and the property had been improved by the owner (the nephew). Lavan J concluded that the plaintiff's proportionate share in the use and occupation of the property was one-third, that the right of residence should be valued on the assumption that the property was not improved and that it should be measured by reference to some reasonable periodic period, which could be monthly, quarterly or yearly.

(2) In the absence of a market in rights to residence guidance on valuations would have to be sought in comparables, eg, rental values of similar properties. A less precise guide would be the sum which it would be

---

[79] Para **[20.22]**, *infra*.
[80] [1993] ILRM 594.
[81] Lavan J rejected the argument that the holder of the right had abandoned it and indicated that such an important right to "a roof over one's head" is not abandoned by mere absence and the court would require cogent evidence of an intention to abandon it: *ibid*, pp 597 and 600.
[82] See para **[20.18]**, *ante*.
[83] *Op cit*, p 568.
[84] *Op cit*, p 599.
[85] *Op cit*, pp 599-601.

reasonable to expect a residing relative to contribute to a household in respect of residence, ie, including contributions to household expenses. On the other hand, to value the right in terms of the cost of acquiring alternative accommodation suitable to the individual would be "to stray away from measuring the money's worth of the right of residence and to enter into the area of compensatory assessment".

(3) Given the limited nature and extent of a right in the nature of a lien for money's worth, and the dangers of an "unrealistically high valuation", the valuation "should not unduly force a sale of the property as to destroy the other interests therein. To that extent any valuation needs to be tempered with caution."[86] It should, therefore, be measured as a periodic sum, which should not, in general, be capitalised, because that would give the holder of the right the equivalent of a tenant for life's interest. Capitalisation also assumes the ability of the owner of the property to pay or to raise the sum and might become "punitive" by forcing him to sell the property and, thereby, incur the costs of the sale and of purchasing another property. In Lavan J's view the issue of capitalisation should arise only where the periodic sum is not being paid or where the property is being disposed of and it is a question of securing the periodic sum in some way, which might involve investing a capital sum to cover its future payment.

In the end Lavan J took the view that valuation in the present case was "unreal". It would have to be made:

"on an actuarial basis, having regard to the defendant's conduct and his inability to pay. In addition, I take the view that a secured right of residence would otherwise become an unreserved right with no certainty that periodic payments would or could be made. In my view the defendant has not the means nor the intention to make proper provisions for the plaintiff's right of residence."[87]

He, therefore, granted the injunction to restrain the nephew and awarded £7,500 damages for the past interference with the right, plus costs.[88] Notwithstanding the decision in this case, it seems clear that there may be circumstances where the court will feel justified in valuing the right of residence and requiring the owner of the property to pay a periodic sum in lieu of the right. Where, however, the right of residence is a limited one in the nature of a lien for money's worth, it seems highly unlikely that the court will order a sale of the property to discharge the lien, except possibly as a last resort.

---

[86] *Op cit*, p 600.

[87] *Op cit*, p 601.

[88] This award was not taken as an appropriate measure for other cases of interference which might warrant much more substantial damages, *ibid*. *Cf* the approach to granting an injunction to settle a family dispute over property taken by Kenny J in *Cullen v Cullen* [1962] IR 268: see para **[20.09]**, *ante*.

C. Annuity or Money Charge

[20.22] There is also authority for saying that a right of residence may be an "annuity or money charge". This was the view of Kennedy CJ, and Johnston J at first instance, in *National Bank v Keegan*[89] with respect to a general right of residence. Murnaghan J, who dissented from the Supreme Court decision in that case, regarded the right as "an equitable charge on the premises for residence and support"[90] and a similar view that it may create a charge was expressed in *Re Shanahan*.[91] The trouble about this analysis of the nature of the right is that an annuity charged on land, eg, a rentcharge, is usually for a definite sum of money.[92] Similarly, a charge on land is usually for a fixed capital sum and rights of residence, with allied rights of support or maintenance, are often not easily commutable into fixed sums.[93] Furthermore, the owner of land subject to an incumbrance, like a rentcharge, may sell the land free from the incumbrance, by getting permission from the court to lodge the amount necessary for discharge, plus interest, in court,[94] and a chargee can also have the land sold to pay off the charge.[95] That the farmer's son could do this to displace his mother without her consent would seem to be contrary to the wishes of most farmers who make this sort of family arrangement.

D. Trust

[20.23] Of course a right of residence may be included as part of an express trust arrangement, but there is a suggestion in some of the authorities that such a trust may be implied in favour of the grantee of the right of residence.[96] Thus in *Leonard v Leonard*,[97] where an ante-nuptial settlement contained a covenant by ML to "support, maintain and clothe and keep in a suitable and proper manner in his house on the said farm [TL] and his wife and family they might have," Holmes LJ stated:

> "The only question to be decided is whether or not we can find a trust in favour of the wife in the marriage settlement - that is, a trust attaching to the lands, and not merely a personal covenant to support and maintain her. I am satisfied from the whole document that such a trust exists."[98]

Later judges, however, do not seem to have been convinced by this formulation of the nature of the grantee's right and this is consistent with the courts' reluctance nowadays

---

[89] [1931] IR 344 at 346 and 354 (see *A Casebook on Irish Land Law* (1984), p 673). See also Moynihan (1897) 3 ILTR 604.

[90] *Ibid*, p 356.

[91] [1919] 1 IR 131. *Cf Re McGuinness's Contract* (1901) 35 ILTR 65. *Cf Re Hall* (1919) 53 ILTR 11.

[92] Ch 6, *ante*.

[93] See *Horace v Johnston* [1993] ILRM 594: para **[20.21]**, *supra*. *Cf National Bank v Keegan* [1931] IR 344 (*per* Kennedy CJ).

[94] Conveyancing Act 1881, s 5. *Re McGuinness's Contract* (1901) 35 ILTR 65. Para **[6.145]**, *ante*.

[95] Ch 13, *ante*.

[96] *Cf* Lord Denning MR's finding of a constructive trust in *Binions v Evans* [1972] Ch 359. Smith 'Licences and Constructive Trusts' (1973) CLJ 123. On trusts, generally, see Chs 9 and 10, *ante*.

[97] (1910) 44 ILTR 155. See also *Gallagher v Ferris* (1881) 7 LR Ir 489; *Re Mooney* (1923) 57 ILTR 12; *Re Butler* (1925) 59 ILTR 166.

[98] *Ibid*, p 157. *Cf Ryan v Ryan* (1848)12 Ir Eq R 226 at 227 (*per* Brady LC).

to establish "precatory" trusts.[99] Apart from that, the legislatures in both parts of Ireland have not adopted the concept of a trust with respect to registered land. Indeed, the Republic's Registration of Title Act 1964 specifically states that a general right of residence in or on, or an exclusive right in or on part of, the land does not "operate to create any equitable estate in the land".[100] Similarly, the Land Registration Act (NI) 1970 states that such a right does not confer "any right of ownership in relation to the land" including, presumably, equitable ownership under a trust.[101]

E. Licence

[20.24] It has been suggested that the most satisfactory theory is that a right of residence should be construed as a species of licence,[102] by analogy with recent developments in the law relating to estoppel licences.[103] It must be admitted, however, that there is little support for this view in the Irish authorities,[104] though it does seem to accord more with the real nature of the right intended by most grantors in Ireland.[105] The position adopted by both Irish legislatures with respect to registered land is very similar to that reached by the English and Irish courts with respect to estoppel licences, ie, the licence is personal to the licensee and does not confer an interest in the land capable of being passed to a successor in title, but the burden binds successors in title of the licensor.[106]

III. CONACRE AND AGISTMENT

[20.25] Two other concepts familiar to Irish lawyers which seem to have some of the characteristics of licences are conacre and agistment "lettings" or "contracts".[107] Conacre is the right to till land, sow crops in it and to harvest them in due course,[108] while agistment is the right to graze livestock on land.[109] It is clear from the authorities that such arrangements do not normally create tenancies,[110] for as Crampton J explained in *Dease v O'Reilly*.

---

[99] Para **[9.016]**, *post*.

[100] Section 81.

[101] Section 47.

[102] Harvey, (1970) 21 NILQ 389 at 413-20. *Cf* Peel, 'Deserted Wife's Licence and Rights of Residence' (1964) 28 Conv 253.

[103] Para **[20.07]**, *ante*.

[104] Note the interesting Canadian decision to this effect, *Moore v Royal Trust Co* [1956] 5 DLR 152. *Cf* the Scottish case, *Wallace v Simmers* 1960 SC 255. Note also the approach by Lavan J in *Johnston v Horace* [1993] ILRM 594: para **[20.21]**, *ante*.

[105] *Cf* cases involving conditions attached to gifts, though these usually involve money payments rather than residence provisions, see *Re McMahon* [1901] 1 IR 489; *Duffy v Duffy* [1920] 1 IR 132.

[106] Para **[20.11]**, *ante*.

[107] For more detailed treatment see Wylie, *Irish Landlord and Tenant Law*, para 3.20 *et seq*.

[108] *Dease v O'Reilly* (1845) 8 Ir LR 52; *Booth v McManus* (1861) 12 ICLR 418; *Evans v Monagher* (1872) IR 6 CL 526; *ILC v Lawlor* [1944] Ir Jur Rep 55.

[109] *Mulligan v Adams* (1846) 8 Ir LR 52; *Fletcher v Hackett* (1906) 40 ILTR 37; *Re Moore's Estate* [1944] IR 295; *O'Connor v Faul* (1957) 91 ILTR 7.

[110] Though, of course, the agreement in particular cases may create a tenancy, see *ILC v Andrews* [1941] IR 79. *Cf Crane v Naughten* [1912] 2 IR 318. See also *Collins v O'Brien* [1981] ILRM 679 (see *A Casebook on Irish Land Law* (1984), p 679; *O'Coindealbhain v Price* [1988] IR 14.

"There is not, in fact, any exclusive right to the party in the conacre holding - from the time of the contract until the potato planting begins, the possession remains with the landlord; and from that time, although a special possession for a particular purpose is with the conacre holder, the general possession remains with the landlord. If this be a tenancy, it may be asked, when does it begin, and when does it end? It is said, it begins with the planting, and ends with the digging out of the potatoes. But if so, some part of each man's portion is held for one period, and some for another. For the potatoes are planted from time to time, and they are dug out in like manner and carried away according to the wants or convenience of the owner. It should seem to me that such a contract is not a demise of the land, but a sale of a profit to be derived from the land, a temporary easement, and not an estate in the land ... the grantee has only a particular right in the land ... not a tenancy, but being only a mode of farming the land."[111]

As Crampton J said, this mode of farming, usually arranged on a seasonal basis[112] and often referred to as the "eleven month take", has obvious similarities with profits *á prendre*, eg, pasturage is a common profit.[113] There is one major difference and that is that easements and profits lie in grant, ie, must be created by deed, whereas conacre, and agistment, arrangements are created by "contract" in Ireland and, presumably, may be created orally, though written evidence may be required for enforcement.[114] Since the taker of conacre or agistment has at most only a "special" possession and the "general" possession remains with the owner of the land, such a "letting" does not infringe a covenant or agreement in a lease or tenancy agreement against subletting or otherwise parting with possession.[115]

[20.26] Conacre and agistment arrangements also have similarities with certain licences, eg, licences coupled with a grant,[116] except, of course, that no "grant" in the technical sense is made. In *Booth v McManus*, Pigot CB explained:

"I have been in the habit of considering the dealing of con-acre to be one in which the owner of the land retains the occupation of the premises, the con-acre holder having a licence to till the land, and a right, connected with that licence, of egress and regress, for the purpose of so tilling. It is nothing more than a mode of tilling and farming the land...

---

[111] (1845) 8 Ir LR 52 at 59-60 (see *A Casebook on Irish Land Law* (1984), p 673). *Cf* the views of Gibson LJ in *Maurice E Taylor (Merchants) Ltd v Commr of Valuation* [1981] NI 236 (see *A Casebook on Irish Land Law* (1984), p 680), para **[20.27]**, *infra*. See also *O'Conail v Shakleton & Sons Ltd* [1982] ILRM 451.

[112] It is common, however, for the contract to cover several successive seasons, see *Re Moore's Estate* [1944] IR 295 (40 years' continuous agistment).

[113] Para **[6.113]**, *ante*. *Sed quaere* the analogy with easements, Ch 6, *ante*.

[114] In *Scully v Corboy* [1950] IR 140, Gavan Duffy P held that a "letting" of meadowing not evidenced in writing as required by s 2 of the 1695 Statute of Frauds (Ir) may constitute an enforceable sale of goods under the Sale of Goods Act 1893. *Cf McKenna v Herlihy* (1920) 7 TC 620 (not cited in *Scully*). See also *Collins v O'Brien* [1981] ILRM 679 (see *A Casebook on Irish Land Law* (1984), p 679); Wylie, *Irish Conveyancing Law* (2nd ed, 1996), para 6.09.

[115] *Booth v McManus* (1861) 12 ICLR 418; *McKeowne v Bradford* (1861) 7 Ir Jur (ns) 169; *Evans v Monagher* (1872) IR 6 CL 526; *Allingham v Atkinson* [1898] 1 IR 239. See also Deasy's Act 1860, s 18; Land Law (Ir) Act, 1881, ss 2 and 58.

[116] Para **[20.04]**, *ante*.

The dealing called con-acre in this country is a very peculiar one. The person who takes the con-acre has no absolute right to the crop. He has not a right to take the crop, with merely an obligation to pay for it as a debt. But the person who allows the land to be tilled retains the dominium over the crop, of holding it until the stipulated amount shall have been paid. He can prevent the con-acre holder from removing the crop from the ground before payment. Can he have the power of thus preventing the removal of the crop, if he has not possession of the ground? Does not the right to obstruct and prevent the removal of the crop involve the right to the possession of the soil on which the crop rests? It seems to me that it does."[117]

[20.27] These characteristics account for the popularity of such arrangements in the rural areas of Ireland. They enable a small-holding farmer without much capital to extend his farming activities without contravening private restrictions against subletting or, more common nowadays as a result of the Land Purchase Acts, statutory restrictions on sub-division attaching to the freehold of the land.[118] However convenient the system is, there seems little doubt that its economic consequences can be disastrous. The following views of an experienced Northern solicitor were reported some years ago.

"Because he may not hold the land after the end of the season, the conacre tenant will take everything he can out of the land and put nothing in. Any manure which he applies is of short term effect such as nitrogen to boost grass crop. He will not spend any money on repairs to fences and gates because he feels that he may lose the benefit at the end of the season. In the result, the state of the land let over a number of years deteriorates quite steadily and the yield falls off. One device to overcome the possibility of an unintended tenant right is the conacre agreement for one season with covenant to renew for a specified number of successive seasons. This is not widely used as its drafting is beyond the capacity of the average country Auctioneer who usually arranges these conacre lettings. I do not deny that conacre is of some value to the community as it enables the landless man without capital to get a start and I know of a few cases of a man starting with conacre takes who has been very successful. Far more numerous however are the cases where men, quite without resources, continue a kind of marginal farming on conacre land without ever bettering themselves and merely impoverishing the land they take."[119]

On the other hand, farming practices do change and some years ago the Northern Ireland Court of Appeal held that a commercial company, which had an 11-month conacre arrangement for growing seed potatoes on land, had exclusive occupation of the land, including buildings consisting of a dressing shed and store, sufficient to attract rating liability.[120] Gibson LJ, giving the main judgment of the Court, commented:

"The whole concept of conacre lettings has during the last 100 years undergone a radical change. No longer do the original considerations have any practical application, and

---

[117] (1861) 12 ICLR 418 at 435-6. See also *Foster v Cunningham* [1956] NI 29; *Carson v Jeffers* [1961] IR 44.

[118] Para **[18.03]**, *ante*.

[119] *Survey of the Land Law of Northern Ireland* (HMSO, 1971), para 287, wherein it was also reported that about 17 per cent of agricultural land in Northern Ireland was so farmed. See also the Land Law Working Group's *Final Report* (HMSO, 1990) Vol 1, Ch 4.9. Note the terms of the will considered in *Re Steele* [1976] NI 66.

with their disappearance have gone the early features which I have outlined. Nowadays it would be practically unknown for there to be a conacre letting of a small strip or area of ground having no obvious physical boundaries. The areas now correspond with the areas of fields or farms. The landowner no longer ploughs the land or provides the manure and he no longer reserves any right to exercise any control over or protection of the land, except in so far as the tenant may only grow one crop, is often obliged to fertilise the land and is required to vacate the land at the end of the term. The owner now merely has a claim in debt for the rent, and no longer has any lien or charge on the crop or right to prevent its removal. In perhaps most cases, as for example, where the farmer has retired or dies leaving a widow living in the house on the farm, the same land is let in conacre or agistment year after year, often to the same person, and in that case whether he vacates the land for a month is of little importance to the owner. In not a few cases as, for example, where the owner is in America, the lettings are made for long periods, occasionally by a single contract to the same tenant, and apart from any special covenants in the agreement no rights are reserved or exercised by or on behalf of the owner over the land during the period of the conacre or agistment agreements. The terms on which the company takes the lands for the growing of potatoes in this case illustrate the modern practice in so far as it is expressly found as a fact that the conacre landlord is, under the agreements, not to enter upon the land nor to permit anyone else to do so during the period of the take, and not to undersow the potato crop, nor make any other use of the land. Leaving aside for the moment the fact that the company has the right to be on the land for only 11 months, I am satisfied that the decisions of the Irish courts in the last century to the effect that a conacre tenant is not in occupation of the land for rating or other purposes have been overtaken both by the change in the nature of conacre lettings and also by the law. The facts found by the Lands Tribunal establish that the company has exclusive occupation of the various plots for the purpose of growing and harvesting the potatoes. It also has the right to exclude all other persons including the owners of the land, from the lands taken during the period of the take. Whereas, in earlier days, the landowner retained paramount occupation of the land, it is now clear that if there is any question of paramount occupation, which would only arise in the case of some rather exceptional contract, it now resides in the tenant.

Secondly, from the legal point of view the theory that a conacre agreement does not create a tenancy is so well established and embedded in our statute law that it cannot now be questioned. Yet the old notion that rateable occupation could only be found in the owner or lessee of the land has now disappeared from our law...."[121]

It should be noted that Gibson LJ did acknowledge the fundamental principle that a conacre agreement does not create a tenancy,[122] but the question remains how far the courts in Northern Ireland will take this new view of conacre agreements. Presumably the point still holds that each agreement must be examined according to its own terms, so that it is dangerous to generalise. However, the Northern Ireland Court of Appeal has clearly shown a willingness to tackle this matter with an open mind and a determination not to be ruled by the authorities of the last century. Whether this will result in a fresh approach being adopted in the Republic remains to be seen.

---

[120] *Maurice E Taylor (Merchants) Ltd v Commr of Valuation* [1981] NI 236 (see *A Casebook on Irish Land Law* (1984), p 680). And see *Northern Ireland Animal Embryo Transplant Ltd v Commr of Valuation* [1983] NI 105.

[121] *Ibid*, p 238.

[122] See para **[20.25]**, *ante*.

Part X

EXTINGUISHMENT OF INTERESTS

Chapter 23

ADVERSE POSSESSION

[23.01] One of the main ways in which an estate or interest in land may be extinguished is under the doctrine of "adverse possession", as it operates under modern statutes of limitations.[1] This doctrine, however, has become one of the most controversial features of modern land law.

I. BASIS OF DOCTRINE

[23.02] The modern doctrine of adverse possession finds expression in the statute of limitations[2] as it applies to land. This statute governs the extinguishment of "stale" claims generally, ie, rights of action are limited in point of time and are lost if not brought within that limit.[3] In its application to land the statute may have the effect of extinguishing the title of one person to the land and thereby leave some other person with "rights" to the land. One of the central points of controversy is the linking of these two aspects of its application to land.

[23.03] The underlying philosophy of the doctrine remains that of "quieting men's titles", for as Lord St Leonards (formerly Sir Edward Sugden), who was successively Lord Chancellor of Ireland and Great Britain, remarked:

> "All statutes of limitation have for their object the prevention of the rearing up of claims at great distances of time when evidences are lost; and in all well-regulated countries the quieting of possession is held an important point of policy."[4]

The doctrine thus operates as much to confirm long-held titles which can no longer be proved by documentary evidence as to sanction the activities of squatters deliberately setting out to dispossess the true owner of the land. In Ireland, the doctrine has played a vital role in regularising informal transfers of ownership, eg, where a farmer dies, but no

---

[1]   See Brady and Kerr, *The Limitation of Actions* (2nd ed, 1994), espec Chs 4-6. See also Darby and Bosanquet, *Statutes of Limitations in England and Ireland* (2nd ed, 1893, Supp 1899). Also Beytagh, *Statute of Limitations* (1846); Franks, *Limitation of Actions* (1959); Lightwood, *Possession of Land* (1894), *Time Limit of Actions* (1909); Pollock and Wright, *Possession in the Common Law* (1888); Preston and Newsom, *Limitation of Actions* (4th ed, 1989); *Prichard, Squatting* (1981). Goodman, 'Adverse Possession of Land Morality and Crime' (1970) 33 MLR 281; Prichard, 'Squatters - The Law and the Mythology' (1976) 40 Conv 255; Dockray, "Why Do We Need Adverse Possession?" [1985] Conv 272.

[2]   Ie, Statute of Limitations, 1957 (RI); Limitation (NI) Order 1989 (replacing the Statute of Limitations (NI), 1958). See Delany (1961) 63 JIBI 126.

[3]   *Cf* the equitable doctrine of *laches,* para **[3.066]**, *ante.* Also the common law doctrine of prescription, as extended by statute, para **[6.073]**, *ante.* Note that prescription is essentially a positive concept, *ie* the conferment of rights through a presumed grant, and is confined to minor interests in land, *ie,* easements and profits.

[4]   *Dundee Harbour Trustees v Dougall* (1852) 1 Macq 317 at 321.

representation is taken out of his estate and subsequent disputes arise between the beneficiaries under his will or between those entitled to distributive shares on his intestacy.[5]

A. Adverse Possession

[23.04] Prior to the Real Property Limitation Act 1833, "adverse possession" had a technical meaning.[6] Before 1833 there were several cases where a person could be in possession of land without any title to it and yet this possession was not regarded as "adverse". Thus possession by a younger brother was deemed to be possession by the heir to land;[7] possession by one co-owner was deemed to be possession by all the co-owners (whether joint tenants or tenants in common), unless an intention to claim the whole was expressed;[8] a tenant for years holding over after termination of his lease was deemed to hold possession for the lessor.[9] The 1833 Act, however, established the modern concept of fixed periods of limitation running from the time when a right of action accrues. The period fixed by the Act for actions in relation to land was generally 20 years.[10] This was reduced to 12 years by the Real Property Limitation Act 1874,[11] and this remains the general period under the latest Statutes of Limitations in both parts of Ireland.[12]

[23.05] Since 1833, "adverse possession" means simply possession of land which is inconsistent with the title of the true owner, ie, possession giving rise to a right of action in the owner which will be barred after lapse of the limitation period from the date of the right of action's accrual. As Lord St Leonards said in another case:

> "It is perfectly settled that adverse possession is no longer necessary in the sense in which it was formerly used, but that mere possession may be and is sufficient under many circumstances to give a title adversely."[13]

What these circumstances are we discuss later in this chapter, but the Republic's Statute of Limitations 1957 now adopts this meaning of adverse possession expressly:

> No right of action to recover land shall be deemed to accrue unless the land is in the possession (in this section referred to as adverse possession) of some person in whose favour the period of limitation can run.[14]

---

5   Paras **[23.40]**, *et seq, infra*.
6   See Lightwood, *op cit*, pp 159 *et seq. Howard v Sherwood* (1832) Alc & Nap 217; *Brownrigg v Cruikshank* (1849) 1 Ir Jur (os) 21; *Davies v D'Arcy* (1853) 3 ICLR 617.
7   *Cf* para **[23.37]**, *infra*.
8   *Cf* para **[23.36]**, *infra*.
9   *Cf* para **[23.31]**, *infra*.
10 Section 2.
11 Section 1.
12 1957 Act, s 13(2)(*a*); 1989 Order (NI), Article 21(1).
13 *Dean of Ely v Bliss* (1852) 2 De GM & G 459 at 476-7.
14 Section 18(1). See the discussion by Kenny J in *Browne v Fahy* Unrep (HC, RI) 24 October 1975 (Cir App) and the Republic's Supreme Court in *Murphy v Murphy* [1980] IR 183 (see *A Casebook on Irish Land Law* (1984), p 696) para **[23.21]**, *post*. See also *Hume v Tennyson* [1987] NI 139; Brady, 'Adverse Possession in Particular Circumstances' (1982) 4 DULJ 79.

The Limitation (NI) Order 1989 adopts a similar meaning:

> No right of action to recover land is to be treated as accruing unless the land is in the possession of some person in whose favour the period of limitation can run (in this paragraph referred to as 'adverse possession').[15]

B. Extinguishment

[23.06] The effect of adverse possession for the limitation period is expressed in the following form:

> ... at the expiration of the period fixed by this Act [Order] for any person to bring an action to recover land, the *title* of that person to the land shall be *extinguished*.[16]

This provision emphasises that the key concepts in relation to the operation of the statutes of limitations are those of "title" and "extinguishment".

1. Title

[23.07] Prior to 1833, possession for the limitation period barred the dispossessed owner's *right of action* only and left his *title* intact. The practical significance of this was that, if he subsequently came into lawful possession again, his title could be invoked against the dispossessor.[17] The modern system established since 1833, however, extinguishes the dispossessed's owner's title as well as his right of action, so that, if he subsequently re-enters without permission, he is a trespasser.[18] This highlights what is, perhaps, the central feature of ownership of land nowadays, namely the relativity of title.[19]

[23.08] Where a squatter bars the right of action and title of the dispossessed owner of land, he acquires a title good against anyone other than a person with a better title to the land. Unless such a person interferes with him, the squatter is free to defend his possession against trespass by another, who may not impugn the squatter's title by pleading a *jus tertii*, ie, that a superior title lies in some third party.[20] The question remains, however, as to how far such a superior title may affect the squatter. This is really another way of asking the basic question: what sort of title does the squatter obtain by adverse possession? Or, to put it yet another way, what do the Irish statutes of limitations mean when they say that the dispossessed owner's title to the land is "extinguished"?[21]

---

[15] Sched 1, para 8(1), replacing s 22(1) of the Statute of Limitations (NI) 1958.

[16] 1957 Act, s 24; 1989 Order (NI), Article 26. (Italics added)

[17] Lightwood, *Possession of Land* (1894), p 153.

[18] See *Incorporated Society for Protestant Schools v Richards* (1841) 1 Dr & War 258.

[19] See Rudden 'Terminology of Title' (1964) 80 LQR 63.

[20] See the discussion of the *jus tertii* rule by Keane J in *Gannon v Walsh* Unrep (HC, RI) 20 June 1996.

[21] See Omotola, 'Nature of Interest Acquired by Adverse Possession of Land under the Limitation Act, 1939' (1973) 37 Conv 85; Sweet, 'Title by Possession' (1906) 18 Jud Rev 415.

2. Parliamentary Conveyance

[23.09] Determination of the precise title obtained by a squatter under the statute of limitations has centred on the issue of whether or not the statute effects a "parliamentary conveyance" or "statutory transfer" of the dispossessed owner's title to the squatter. No less an authority than Parke B took the view that "the effect of the Act [Real Property Limitation Act 1833] is to make a parliamentary conveyance of the land to the person in possession after the period has elapsed."[22] Sir Edward Sugden (later, Lord St Leonards) held the same view and expressed it both while he was on the Bench in Ireland and England[23] and in his legal writings.[24] His view was accepted as the correct one by the Irish Queen's Bench Division in *Rankin v McMurtry*,[25] where Holmes J stated:

> "Whatever the mode of transfer, I am of opinion that the estate and interest the right to which is extinguished, so far as the original owner is concerned, became vested in the person whose possession has caused such extinction. The opposite conclusion would seriously affect leasehold tenancies in this country; and it is satisfactory to know that Lord St. Leonards seems to have had no doubt that the view I have expressed is the correct one."[26]

The court approved a passage from the leading treatise of the period which stated:

> "Though the title extinguished ... is not directly transferred by the statute to the wrongdoer who has been in possession, yet the title gained by such possession, being limited by rights yet remaining unextinguished, is clearly commensurate with the interest which the rightful owners have lost by operation of the statute, and must, therefore, it is apprehended, have the same legal character, and be freehold, leasehold or copyhold accordingly."[27]

It is important to note that *Rankin v McMurtry* concerned leasehold land, which, of course, was the predominant tenure in the rural parts of Ireland at the time and remains so today in urban areas. Furthermore, the existence of so many long leases in Ireland,

---

[22] *Doe d Jukes v Sumner* (1845) 14 M & W 39 at 42.

[23] *Incorporated Society for Protestant Schools v Richards* (1841) 1 Dr & War 258 at 289; *Scott v Nixon* (1843) 3 Dr & War 388 at 405-8; *Tuthill v Rogers* (1844) 1 Jo & Lat 36 at 72; *Burroughs v McCreight* (1844) 1 Jo & Lat 290 at 303; *Trustees of Dundee Harbour v Dougall* (1852) 1 Macq 317 at 321.

[24] Sugden, *Law of Vendors and Purchasers* (14th ed, 1862) p 476. See Meredith, 'A Paradox of Sugden' (1918) 34 LQR 253.

[25] (1889) 24 LR Ir 290. See also *Kennedy v Woods* (1868) IR 2 CL 436; *McCormack v Courtney* [1895] 2 IR 97; *Re Hayden* [1904] 1 IR 1. And see *Re Field* [1918] 1 IR 140.

[26] *Ibid*, p 301. *Cf* Gibson J at p 303 "If the statute has barred the right of the representative of the original lessee, in whom is the term now vested? I think it must be taken that the defendants, assuming the statutory bar has arisen, have in some way, whether by statutory estoppel, transfer, or otherwise, become owners of the lease."

[27] Darby and Bosanquet, *Statutes of Limitations in England and Ireland* (1st ed, 1867) p 390. Contrary views in Dart, *Vendors and Purchasers* (6th ed) Vol 1, p 463 and Hayes *Conveyancing* (5th ed) Vol 1, p 269 drew the following comment by Holmes J: "I dare say some speculation on the subject has been indulged in by textwriters whose contributions to legal learning consist in expressing doubts without venturing to offer a solution to them."

eg, 999 or 10,000 years, makes it crucial to determine the precise nature of the title obtained by the squatter and it is, perhaps, not surprising that the court held that the squatter took over the lease.

[23.10] The next development was the English decision in *Tichborne v Weir*,[28] where the English Court of Appeal rejected the concept of a parliamentary conveyance. Lord Esher MR took the view that "the effect of the statute is not that the right of one person is conveyed to another, but that the right is extinguished and destroyed,"[29] and Bowen LJ similarly refused to accept the "fiction of a transfer of title".[30] The views of Lord St Leonards[31] in the Irish cases were cited to the court, but were considered to be confined to cases of adverse possession relating to freehold land only.[32] The authority of *Tichborne v Weir* in Ireland was discussed by the Court of Appeal in *O'Connor v Foley*,[33] where the majority[34] seem to have accepted it as a correct statement of the law. Thus Fitzgibbon LJ said:

> "I do not question the authority of *Tichborne v Weir*. It is the decision of three eminent Judges of Appeal; it appears never to have been questioned in any text-book or subsequent case, and I respectfully say that it seems to me to be right."[35]

Holmes LJ dissented vigorously and felt unable to resist, despite *Tichborne v Weir*, "the steady current of Irish decisions".[36] He commented:

> "I should think every circuit-going Judge has taken the law as laid down in the cases I have mentioned. The title of the occupier who pays the rent for small agricultural holdings in this country is generally dependent on the Statute of Limitations, for personal representations in such cases are rarely raised, and even where the holding is transferred *inter vivos*, there is often no writing. A fair rent under the Irish Land Acts can only be fixed on the application of a tenant in occupation, and yet the cases in which the only title of the applicants to the tenancy is such as I have described may be counted by the hundreds."[37]

Nevertheless, later Irish judges still tended to adopt the view of the majority and to accept the authority of *Tichborne v Weir*, though usually *obiter*.[38]

---

[28] (1892) 67 LT 735, followed in *Taylor v Twinberrow* [1930] 2 KB 16.

[29] *Ibid*, p 737.

[30] *Ibid*, p 737.

[31] Recognised by Lord Esher as "a very great real property lawyer."

[32] *Ibid*, p 737 (*per* Bowen LJ).

[33] [1906] 1 IR 20. This discussion was *obiter*, since the court distinguished *Tichborne* on the ground that the squatter had become a tenant by estoppel, para [23.14], *infra*.

[34] Fitzgibbon and Walker LJJ.

[35] *Ibid*, p 26. Fitzgibbon LJ also explained Lord St Leonard's views as being applicable to freehold land only, *ibid*.

[36] Fn 25, *supra*.

[37] *Ibid*, p 39.

[38] *Ashe v Hogan* [1920] 1 IR 159, espec at 169 (*per* O'Connor MR); *Clibborn v Horan* [1921] 1 IR 93 at 101 (O'Connor MR); *RCB v Dublin Board of Assistance* [1948] IR 287 at 293-4 (Dixon J); *Re Ryan's Estate* [1960] IR 174 at 179 (Dixon J); *Cf Bank of Ireland v Domvile* [1956] IR 37 at 57 (Dixon J).

[23.11] Then the position under English law was reviewed by the House of Lords in *Fairweather v St Marylebone Property Co Ltd*,[39] which involved the acquisition of squatter's rights over part of a garden shed straddling the boundary line between adjoining properties, both held under 99-year leases. The dispossessed lessee purported to surrender his "lease" to the lessor, who claimed the right to eject the squatter immediately, ie, without having to await the expiration of the remainder of the 99-year term of the lease. The law lords unanimously confirmed the authority of *Tichborne v Weir* and the majority[40] held that, in the case of leasehold land, the title of the dispossessed lessee is extinguished as against the squatter only and not as against the lessor. Thus the majority held that the lease remained on foot as between the dispossessed lessee and lessor, so that the lessee could surrender it to the lessor. The consequences for the leasehold squatter were disastrous, for the majority then held that the effect of such a surrender was to remove the restriction created by the lease on the lessor's paramount right to possession of the land, so that he could immediately invoke that right.[41] The principle *nemo dat quod non habet* was held not to apply, ie, that the dispossessed lessee could surrender his lease only on the footing that it was subject to the squatter's right to possession for the remainder of the term of the lease.[42] In a subsequent case it was held that the lessor could forfeit the lease for non-payment of rent by the dispossessed lessee and the squatter had no right to claim relief against forfeiture.[43]

[23.12] The implications of the *Fairweather* decision were that a squatter on leasehold land was in an extremely precarious position. The dispossessed lessee and lessor could indulge in collusion to "squeeze" him out, through a surrender of the lease, ejectment by the lessor, followed, if the parties wished, by a regrant to the dispossessed lessee.[44] If the dispossessed lessee ceased to comply with the terms of his lease, the landlord might forfeit it and again eject the squatter. The risk to the squatter's title could have enormous significance in terms of policy in cases where a very long lease of land might be involved, as would often happen in Ireland. The title to such land could be in doubt for centuries rather than "quieted" as the doctrine of adverse possession was supposed to achieve.[45] Despite some Irish judges' apparent acceptance of the principle in *Tichborne v Weir*, which was the foundation of the House of Lords decision in *Fairweather*, one factor did, however, make it possible that the decision might not have such serious consequences in Ireland. This factor was the readiness with which the Irish judges have

---

[39] [1963] AC 510.

[40] Lord Morris *dissentiente*. See the criticism in Wade, 'Landlord, Tenant and Squatter' (1962) 78 LQR 541.

[41] [1963] AC 510 at 537 and 539 (*per* Lord Radcliffe) and at 543-5 (*per* Lord Denning).

[42] As Lord Morris thought, *ibid* p 550. *Walter v Yalden* [1902] 2 KB 304 supported him, as, subsequently, did Wade, *op cit.*

[43] *Tickner v Buzzacott* [1965] Ch 426.

[44] Lord Denning recognised this, [1963] AC 510 at 547. See also Lord Morris at p 554.

[45] See generally, Wallace, 'Adverse Possession of Leaseholds - The Case for Reform' (1975) 10 Jur (ns) 74; Wylie, 'Adverse Possession: An Ailing Concept?' (1965) 16 NILQ 467.

held that the squatter on leasehold land may be estopped from denying that he has become an assignee of the lease.

[23.13] In *O'Connor v Foley*[46] the Court of Appeal held that a squatter, who applied to have a fair rent fixed under the Irish Land Acts,[47] was estopped from denying that he had become an assignee of the lease, so as to be bound by its covenants. Similarly in *Ashe v Hogan*[48] it was held that a squatter, who took advantage of a proviso in the lease, whereby the rent was halved so long as the covenants were performed, and paid the reduced rent, which was accepted by the landlord, was bound by the covenants in the lease. As O'Connor MR said, "a person taking advantage of a clause in a lease and deriving benefit under it must accept the burdens."[49] The implication seems to have been that in such cases the landlord would similarly be estopped from denying the tenancy of the squatter by his acceptance of the rent and performance by the squatter of other obligations of the tenancy agreement.

[23.14] It seems to have been partly on this basis that the practice has been adopted in the Land Registries in both parts of Ireland of treating the squatter as if he had become a transferee of the registered land.[50] Section 52 of the Local Registration of Title (Ireland) Act 1891 preserved the operation of the doctrine of adverse possession, by providing that the squatter could apply to the court for an order declaring the title to the land he would have acquired if it had been unregistered land, and for an order for rectification of the register accordingly.[51] In practice, s 52 orders have directed rectification by registration of the squatter in the same folio as the dispossessed owner, ie, as if the squatter were a transferee of the same title. Yet if the *Tichborne* and *Fairweather* principle of there being no statutory transfer had been adopted, in strict theory a new folio should have been opened to deal with the new title acquired by the squatter. The problem would then have arisen, however, of determining what title the squatter should have been registered with and, in the case of leasehold land, it would have been difficult to answer this question, unless a tenancy by estoppel arose. According to the *Fairweather* case, he had neither the freehold nor the leasehold interest in the land. It is apparent, then, that the practice adopted by the Land Registries was extremely convenient, even though it might not have accorded with strict theory. For this reason it was recommended in Northern Ireland that the "parliamentary conveyance" theory should be expressly adopted by the legislation for both registered and unregistered land.[52]

---

[46] [1906] 1 IR 20. See also *Rankin v McMurtry* (1889) 24 LR Ir 290. *Cf Cullen v Cullen* [1962] IR 268 (para **[20.10]**, *ante*).

[47] Para **[1.49]**, *ante*.

[48] [1920] 1 IR 159.

[49] *Ibid*, p 164. *Cf Tichborne v Weir, op cit,* and *Tickner v Buzzacott* [1965] Ch 426, where it was held that mere payment of rent is *not* sufficient to raise an estoppel.

[50] See *Survey of the Land Law of Northern Ireland* (HMSO, 1971), para 413.

[51] On s 52, see *Re Skelton* [1976] NI 132. The new registration legislation adopts the same provision, except that an application to the court is no longer necessary, Registration of Title Act, 1964, s 49 (RI); Land Registration Act (NI) 1970, s 53. Para **[23.43]**, *post*.

[52] *1971 Survey (NI)* paras 4.11-13. See also the Land Law Working Group's *Final Report* (HMSO, 1990), Vol 1, paras 2.14.7-20.

[23.15] Since then, the whole matter has been reviewed by the Republic's Supreme Court in *Perry v Woodfarm Homes Ltd*,[53] which concerned a small plot of ground at the back of a house held under a 999-year lease granted in 1947. The plaintiff had been in exclusive possession of the plot since 1955 and clearly had extinguished the lessee's title by 12 years' adverse possession. In 1970 the defendants took an assignment of the 1947 lease and then, a month later, an assignment of the fee simple reversion. Their title to the freehold was registered in the Land Registry later the following month. The defendants argued that, on the basis of the *Fairweather* case, the plaintiff's title was good against the lessee's interest only and that had merged in their fee simple,[54] so as to give them an immediate right to possession, ie, the merger had the same effect as the surrender in the *Fairweather* case. The defendants indicated that they intended to take over the plot for building purposes and the plaintiff applied for an interlocutory injunction[55] to restrain them. On the parties agreeing to have the application treated as the hearing of the action, O'Keefe P granted a perpetual injunction.[56] On appeal to the Supreme Court, the majority upheld this decision.

[23.16] Walsh J took the view that the majority in *Fairweather* misconstrued the meaning of modern statutes of limitations in providing that the "title" to the land is "extinguished". He seemed to agree with much of the majority's analysis, but not with their conclusions. He agreed that the Statute did not destroy the lease itself, so that it remained an encumbrance preventing the freeholder from entering into immediate possession. He thought it "well established" that in relation to unregistered land "there is not a statutory conveyance or assignment of the estate to the squatter." Where he differed from the law lords was in his view that:

> "... a person who has lost all his title to a leasehold estate is not in a position to effectively deal with it at all and therefore he has nothing to surrender and nothing to assign. A person who takes from him a purported assignment or a surrender of the leasehold estate cannot be in any stronger position or have any better title than the person making the purported assignment or surrender."

In other words, Walsh J accepted the view of Lord Morris, who dissented in *Fairweather*, that the principle *nemo dat quod non habet* applied. He also accepted that the implication of saying the lease remained on foot as between the lessor and lessee was that the "squatter may be indirectly forced to carry out the covenants to preserve his possession from ejectment by forfeiture for non-observance of the covenants." Yet he did take the view, albeit *obiter*, that the position as regards a statutory transfer of title was different in the case of registered land. He commented on the effect of s 19 of the Registration of Title Act 1964:

---

[53] [1975] IR 104 (see *A Casebook on Irish Land Law* (1984), p 685) (Walsh and Griffin JJ, Henchy J *dissentiente*).

[54] Ch 24 *post*.

[55] Para **[3.133]**, *ante*.

[56] Para **[3.132]**, *ante*.

"This would appear to permit in the case of a squatter who has dispossessed a registered leaseholder where registered land is concerned to have himself registered as the owner of the leasehold."[57]

Griffin J agreed with Walsh J in accepting the view of Lord Morris as to the effect of a purported surrender or merger of the lease.

[23.17] He also reviewed the Irish and English cases on the question of a parliamentary conveyance and concluded:

"... though there is no statutory transfer or conveyance to the squatter, what the squatter ... has gained is the right to possession of the premises in dispute as against the fee simple owner ... for the unexpired portion of the term, subject to the risk and the possibility of a forfeiture. During the currency of the term limited by a lease, the lessor has no right to possession of the demised property unless the lessee has incurred a forfeiture for breach of one or more of the covenants in the lease ... The ousted lessee continues to be contractually liable to the lessor upon the covenants in the lease."

Since no forfeiture had occurred in this case, the squatter remained protected for the unexpired term of the 999-year lease.

[23.18] Henchy J, who dissented, also took the view that the Irish and English authorities had now established that no parliamentary conveyance took place. He, however, preferred the view that a merger took place between the fee simple and the lease so as to give the freeholders an immediate right to possession against the squatter.

"It seems to me to be inequitable and contrary to first principles that as a result of the merger of the leasehold in the fee simple the rights of the freeholder should be reduced and those of the squatter who had displaced the lessee should be enlarged."

[23.19] In the light of the *Fairweather* and *Perry* cases, it seems to be established now in both parts of Ireland[58] that the statutes of limitations have a negative effect only, at least as regards unregistered land. With respect to Walsh J, it is by no means clear that the position is different with respect to registered land and this point should be settled beyond doubt by appropriate legislation.[59] It should also be emphasised that the majority view in *Perry* gives the squatter on leasehold land limited protection only. He is still subject to the risk of forfeiture brought about by a default of the dispossessed lessee and to this extent there remains the failure of the doctrine of adverse possession to "quiet" the title. If the *Tickner* case is correct,[60] he may not even be able to apply for relief against the forfeiture by offering to take over the lease, though he may protect himself if he induces the landlord into co-operative acts sufficient to raise an estoppel. The ultimate conclusion must remain, therefore, that the recommendation in Northern

---

57 This seems to anticipate the view taken of the English Land Registry system in *Spectrum Investment Co v Holmes* [1981] 1 WLR 221. Neither Griffin J nor Henchy J dealt with this point.

58 Since the *Fairweather* decision was not an appeal from Northern Ireland, it is just possible that the courts there might still follow the earlier Irish decisions, but in view of the unanimous rejection by the Republic's Supreme Court in *Perry* the possibility is extremely remote.

59 See further para **[23.43]**, *infra.* Also Wylie, (1968) 19 NILQ 89 at 96-102.

60 Para **[23.11]**, *ante.*

Ireland for introduction of the parliamentary conveyance theory should still be considered by the legislators for both parts of Ireland.[61]

II. OPERATION OF DOCTRINE

Having considered the underlying theory of the doctrine of adverse possession, we must consider in some more detail its operation with respect to land.

A. Limitation Periods

[23.20] As mentioned above, the main limitation period for land is 12 years,[62] but other periods exist in certain special cases. The period is 30 years for recovery of land by a State authority in the Republic and the Crown in Northern Ireland,[63] and 60 years for recovery of foreshore.[64] In the case of arrears of rentcharges or conventional rents the period is 6 years.[65]

B. Running of Time

[23.21] The general rule is that time does not begin to run against the owner of land until a right of action accrues to him. Thus there must be both a dispossession of the true owner, or discontinuance of possession by him, and adverse possession by some other person. Mere abandonment or leaving land vacant is not enough, because, until someone else goes into adverse possession, the owner has no right of action against anyone. In *Browne v Fahy*,[66] Kenny J held that there was no adverse possession because the acts relied upon were not inconsistent with the enjoyment of the land in question by the owners. He stated:

> "The cattle were on the lands because of permission given by [the owners' predecessors] and the [owners] had no cattle. The planting of trees was to give shelter for the cattle which were on the lands. The erection of fences on the boundary with the public road was to keep the cattle in so that they would not stray while the erection of a

---

[61] *1971 Survey (NI)*, paras 411-3. See also the Land Law Working Group's Discussion Document No 4 (*Conveyancing and Miscellaneous* Matters) (HMSO, 1983), Ch 6 and *Final Report* (HMSO, 1990), Vol 1, paras 2.14.7-20.

[62] 1957 Act, s 13(2)(*a*); 1989 Order (NI), Article 21(1).

[63] 1957 Act, s 13 (1) (*a*); 1989 Order (NI), Article 21(3).

[64] Or 40 years (30 years in NI) from the date when the land has ceased to be foreshore, but remains State or Crown property, 1957 Act, s 13 (1)(*b*) and (*c*); 1989 Order (NI), Article 21 (5) and (6). Note also the Public Authorities Protection Act 1893, repealed in the Republic by the Public Authorities (Judicial Proceedings) Act 1954, s 2, and in Northern Ireland by the Law Reform (Misc Prov) Act (NI) 1954, ss 3, 9(2) and Sched. See *Carroll v Kildare CC* [1950] IR 258; *Donovan v Minister for Justice* (1951) 85 ILTR 134; *McDowell v Lynch* [1952] IR 264.

[65] 1957 Act, ss 27 and 28; 1958 Act (NI), ss 31 and 32. *Re Bryan's Estate* [1941] IR 446.

[66] (1975) Unrep (HC, RI). In *Murphy v Murphy* [1980] IR 183 (see *A Casebook on Irish Land Law* (1984), p 696) the Republic's Supreme Court emphasised that the question whether or not the person in possession of land was in *adverse* possession is ultimately a question of fact (see also para **[23.22]**, *infra*). In that case the claimant had farmed his mother's lands for many years and had mortgaged them to a bank. (See also *Re Skelton* [1976] NI 132). See also *McDonnell v McKinty* (1847) 10 Ir LR 514; *Fanning v Jenkinson* Unrep (HC, RI), 2 July 1997 (1994/4773).

fence between the lands and the avenue was intended to prevent the cattle from getting on to the avenue and from there on to the road. The draining and manuring of the land was consistent with a licence to use the lands for grazing and the collection of money from the campers was what would be expected when a person had the grazing of the lands and lived near them. Any person seeking permission to camp would naturally assume that the person whose cattle were on the lands was the owner. The property was of little value and the only way that [the owners] could use the lands was by walking on them and I accept the evidence that [one of the owners] walked over the lands on a number of occasions."

In England it was suggested some years ago that there could be no adverse possession despite the fact that the owner was making no present use of the land entered by the squatter, if the owner had some future plans to use the land,[67] and this approach was followed initially by the Republic's courts.[68] However, the English Court of Appeal reviewed its position later and reverted to the orthodox view that the primary consideration in each case is the establishment of factual possession by the squatter coupled with an intention to exclude all others.[69] This view has also now found favour with the Republic's courts[70] and would seem to be more consistent with the views of the Supreme Court expressed in *Murphy v Murphy*.[71]

Since the squatter has a title based on his possession which is good against everyone except the dispossessed owner, he can pass this title to others. Thus a squatter in the

---

[67] *Wallis's Cayton Bay Holiday Camp Ltd v Shell-Mex and BP Ltd* [1975] QB 94 (Lord Denning MR and Ormrod LJ, Stamp LJ dissenting), relying upon *Leigh v Jack* (1879) 5 Ex D 264. See also *Williams Brothers Direct Supply Ltd v Rafferty* [1958] 1 QB 159; *Tecbild Ltd v Chamberlain* (1969) 20 P & CR 633. Cf *Treloar v Nute* [1976] 1 WLR 1295. See also *McDonnell v McKinty* (1847) 10 Ir LR 514.

[68] See *Cork Corporation v Lynch* [1995] 2 ILRM 598 (decided by Egan J in July 1985 but reported 10 years late!).

[69] *Buckinghamshire County Council v Moran* [1990] Ch 623. Other aspects of the *Wallis* case (fn 67 *supra*) (eg the notion that owner of the land should be assumed to grant an implied licence to occupy on the squatter) were criticised by the English Law Reform Committee, 21st Report, paras 3.49-52 and this was dealt with specifically by the Limitation Amendment Act 1980, s 4 (later that year incorporated in the consolidating Limitation Act 1980, Sched 1, para 8(4)). A similar provision was included in the Limitation Amendment (NI) Order 1982, Article 7; see now Limitation (NI) Order 1989, Sched 1, para 8(5) and (6). It is, of course, still possible to establish on the facts of a particular case that the occupier of the land has possession with the licence, consent or permission of the title owner, in which case, of course, the possession will not be adverse and the limitation period will not run against the title owner: see *Bellew v Bellew* [1982] IR 447. Also *BP Properties Ltd v Buckler* (1988) P & CR 337; cf *Mount Carmel Investments Ltd v Thurlow Ltd* [1988] 3 All ER 129; Wallace, 'Limitation, Prescription and Unsolicited Permission' [1994] Conv 196.

[70] *Durack Manufacturing Ltd v Considine* [1987] IR 677; cf *Dundalk UDC v Conway* Unrep (HC, RI), 15 December 1987. See also *Belfast City Council v Donoghue* [1993] 5 BNIL 83.

[71] [1980] IR 183, fn 66 *ante*. See Brady and Kerr, *Limitations of Actions* (2nd ed, 1994), pp 99-106. The Law Reform Commission recommended enactment of a statutory provision to the effect that adverse possession is possession inconsistent with the title of the true owner, not inconsistent with the true owner's intention: *Report on Land Law and Conveyancing Law: (1) General Proposals* (LRC 30-1989), para 52-53.

process of barring the true owner by adverse possession, eg, 10 years' possession, can pass his interest in the land to someone else who can add the 10 years' possession to his own, ie, after another 2 years' possession he completes the acquisition of ownership by adverse possession.[72]

[23.22] It is also established that the adverse possession may take place without either party being aware of it.[73] Generally there is no relief for mistake and, indeed, the doctrine is often used to settle boundary disputes arising from some earlier mistake in the true line of the boundary between adjoining properties, which comes to light later only when a conveyance of one of them is being made.[74]

There may be special circumstances present, however, which will affect the running of the limitation period.

1. Postponement of Period

The date from which the limitation period begins to run may be postponed because of the existence of a disability, fraud or mistake.

(i) Disability

[23.23] In the case of a person under a disability,[75] eg, a minor[76] or person of unsound mind,[77] the limitation period may be extended to 6 years after that person ceases to be under the disability or dies, whichever happens first, even though the normal period has expired.[78] However, in the case of land there is a limit of 30 years from the date the action accrued.[79]

(ii) Fraud or Concealment

[23.24] The general rule is that, if the action is based on the defendant's or his agent's fraud or if any fact relevant to the plaintiff's right of action has been deliberately concealed from him by the defendant or his agent, time does not begin to run against the aggrieved party until he discovers the fraud or concealment or could with reasonable diligence have discovered it.[80] However, a plea of fraud or concealment will not

---

[72] *Asher v Whitlock* (1865) LR 1 QB 1; *Wallis v Howe* [1893] 2 Ch 545.

[73] *Murphy v Murphy* [1980] IR 183 (see *A Casebook on Irish Land Law* (1984), p 696). See Brady, 'Adverse Possession in Particular Circumstances' (1982) 4 DULJ (ns) 79.

[74] *Re Vernon's Estate* [1901] 1 IR 1. See also *Cartledge v Jopling & Sons Ltd* [1963] AC 758. See further, para **[23.25]**, *infra*.

[75] 1957 Act, s 48; 1989 Order (NI), Article 47.

[76] *Lambert v Browne* (1871) IR 5 CL 218; *Jennings v Coughlan* (1927) 61 ILTR 122; *Currie v Fairy Hill Ltd* [1968] IR 232.

[77] *Re PMK* [1944] IR 107; *Re R* [1941] Ir Jur Rep 67; *Re JS* [1941] IR 378; *Re Waters* [1945] IR 484; *Re Noblett* [1946] IR 155; *Re Nixon* [1949] Ir Jur Rep 37; *Re Dowd* [1960] Ir Jur Rep 64; *Re Gill* [1964] IR 143.

[78] 1957 Act, s 49 (1)(a); 1989 Order (NI), Article 48(1).

[79] 1957 Act, s 49 (1)(d); 1989 Order (NI), Article 48(4).

[80] 1957 Act, s 71(1); 1989 Order (NI), Article 71(1). See the discussion of fraudulent concealment by Carroll J in *Morgan v Park Developments Ltd* [1983] ILRM 156; *McDonald v McBain* [1991] 1 IR 284. Brady and Kerr, *The Limitation of Actions* (2nd ed, 1994), pp 188-98.

postpone the running of time where the property has been purchased for valuable consideration, by a person who was not a party to the fraud or concealment and did not at the time of the purchase know or have reason to believe that any fraud or concealment had been committed.[81]

(iii) Mistake

[23.25] As mentioned above, the general rule is that mistake does not stop time running[82] and squatter's rights are often acquired by such means, eg, where neighbouring landowners make a mistake as to where the boundary lies between their adjoining lands. However, where the action in question is for relief from the consequences of mistake, time does not run until the plaintiff discovers the mistake, or could have done so with reasonable diligence.[83] In the case of land, relief for mistake usually involves an application for *equitable* relief, ie, rescission[84] or rectification,[85] and as such is not subject to the statute of limitations anyway. Like all equitable relief, on the other hand, it is subject to the doctrine of *laches*.[86]

2. Fresh Accrual

In certain cases time may start running afresh.

(i) Acknowledgment

[23.26] Time may start afresh and run from the date of a written and signed acknowledgment by or on behalf of the defendant of the plaintiff's title.[87] No particular form of acknowledgment, however, is laid down and it may be inferred from the actions of the party concerned.[88]

(ii) Part Payment

[23.27] Time may also begin to run afresh where payment of part of the principal or interest due in respect of a debt is made to or for the account of the person whose title is being barred.[89]

It is important to note, however, that, once the full limitation period has run in respect of land, no acknowledgment or part payment can revive any action to recover the land. This was the change first introduced by the Real Property Limitation Act 1833,[90] namely

---

[81] 1957 Act, s 71 (2); 1989 Order (NI), Article 71(3) and (4).

[82] *Re Jones's Estate* [1914] 1 IR 188.

[83] 1957 Act, s 72 (1); 1989 Order (NI), Article 71(1) and (4).

[84] Para **[3.157]**, *ante*.

[85] Para **[3.162]**, *ante*.

[86] Para **[3.066]**, *ante*.

[87] 1957 Act, ss 50-60; 1989 Order (NI), Articles 52-61. *Johnston v Smith* [1896] 2 IR 82; *Re Matthew's Estate* (1904) 38 ILTR 246; *Howard v Hennessy* [1947] IR 336; *Murphy v Allied Irish Banks Ltd* [1994] 2 ILRM 220.

[88] *Hobson v Burns* (1850) 13 Ir LR 286; *Re Deeney* [1933] NI 80; *Re Mitchell's Estate* [1943] IR 74; *Hart v Carswell* [1973] NI 15.

[89] 1957 Act, ss 61-70; 1989 Order (NI), Articles 62-70. *McAuliffe v Fitzsimons* (1889) 26 LR Ir 29; *Beamish v Whiting* [1909] 1 IR 360; *Re Irwin's Estate* [1907] 1 IR 357; *Addiscott v Fagan* [1946] IR 194.

that not only is the remedy to recover the land barred but the title to it is also barred.[91] The opposite position remains with respect to other actions, eg, for debts. Thus an acknowledgment or part payment by a mortgagor in favour of his mortgagee, after time has run, revives the mortgagor's liability on his personal covenant for the debt, but does not revive the mortgagee's security on the mortgagor's land.[92]

C. Particular Cases

We must now examine the operation of the doctrine of adverse possession in particular cases involving land, both unregistered and registered.

1. Unregistered Land

In the case of unregistered land the following are the situations most likely to arise.

(i) Freehold in Possession

[23.28] This is the straightforward case where the only problem is the basic question of whether or not the squatter on such land obtains a transfer of the freeholder or leaseholder's title. This matter we discussed at length earlier in the chapter.

(ii) Leases

[23.29] The position of a squatter on leasehold land was also discussed earlier. Time does not run against the freehold reversioner until the lease ends, eg, by expiry or forfeiture by the reversioner.[93]

[23.30] As between a tenant and his landlord, there can be no adverse possession by the tenant during the currency of the tenancy. He is estopped from denying his landlord's title.[94] Any "encroachment" by the tenant on another person's land generally enures for the landlord's benefit, unless the conduct of the landlord or tenant indicates a contrary intention.[95] Non-payment of rent for six years merely bars the landlord's right to the rent[96] and does not destroy his title to the land.[97] Similarly, failure to exercise a right of

---

[90] Para **[23.04]**, *ante.*

[91] 1957 Act, s 24; 1989 Order (NI), Article 26. See *Re Field* [1918] 1 IR 140. See para **[23.06]**, *ante.*

[92] *Re Conlon's Estate* (1892) 29 LR Ir 199; *Beamish v Whiting* [1909] 1 IR 360; *Re Lloyd* [1911] 1 IR 153; *Re Lohan* [1936] IR 621.

[93] 1957 Act, s 15 (1); 1989 Order (NI), Article 22(1).

[94] *Cf* licensees or other occupiers, *eg,* caretakers or "service tenants", *Ellis v Crawford* (1842) Long & Town 664; *Moore v Doherty* (1842) 5 Ir LR 449; *Musgrave v McAvey* (1907) 41 ILTR 230.

[95] *Meares v Collis* [1927] IR 397; *Creavin v Donnelly* Unrep (HC, RI), 25 June 1993 (1992 No 6523 P).See also *Kingsmill v Millard* (1855) 11 Exch 313; *Att-Gen v Tomline* (1880) 15 Ch D 150; *King v Smith* [1950] 1 All ER 553. Pye, 'Adverse Possession and Encroachments by Tenants' (1987) 81 Gaz ILSI 5; Wylie, *Irish Landlord and Tenant Law*, para 28.11; Brady and Kerr, *The Limitation of Actions* (2nd ed, 1994), pp 124-7. *Cf* the law of "accretion", whereby, as a result of gradual and imperceptible action of *natural* forces (eg, a fall in the level of a river or lake), land accretes to an adjacent landowner (eg, the owner of land on the bank of the river or lake): see *Att-Gen v McCarthy* [1911] 2 IR 260; *Hume v Tennyson* [1987] NI 139. See also Howarth, 'The Doctrine of Accretion: Qualifications, Ancient and Modern' [1986] Conv 247; Wilkinson, 'Accretion, Avulsion and Diluvion' (1982) NLJ 1164.

[96] 1957 Act, s 28; 1989 Order (NI), Article 29.

[97] Note that this rule applies only to "conventional" rents which do *not* include a fee farm rent payable under a grant creating the relationship of landlord and tenant: see 1957 Act, s 2(1); (contd.../)

re-entry under a forfeiture clause bars the right after 12 years,[98] but the landlord's title remains and he can still claim possession on expiration of the lease. However, if the tenant holding under a lease, reserving of rent of at least £1, pays the rent to a person wrongfully claiming to be the immediate reversioner, this is equivalent to adverse possession against the true reversioner and his title is barred after 12 years.[99]

[23.31] In the case of a tenancy at will, in the Republic time runs against the landlord in favour of the tenant after one year, or earlier determination of the tenancy,[100] unless rent is paid or a written acknowledgment is made.[101] Time runs against the landlord from the beginning of a "tenancy" at sufferance, since this is really adverse possession without the landlord's consent.[102] Yearly or other periodic tenancies are in a similar position to tenancies at will, provided there is no lease in writing,[103] ie, the tenancy is deemed to determine after the first year or other period of the tenancy.[104] However, if rent is subsequently received, time runs from the date of the last receipt.[105]

---

[97] (\...contd) 1989 Order (NI), Article 2(1). The vital point here is that fee farm rents are treated like rentcharges (see *ibid*), which are regarded as an incumbrance on land, the title to which can be extinguished by 12 years' adverse possession, ie non-payment of the rent: 1957 Act ss 2(7)(a) and 18(4)(a); 1989 Order (NI) Article 2(8)(a) and Sched 1, para 8(4)(a): see *Re Maunsell's Estate* [1911] 1 IR 271. The effect of 12 years' non-payment of a fee farm rent would, therefore, appear to be that not only does the person previously entitled to the rent lose his remedies for enforcement of the rent (see *Wright v Redmond* (1936) 70 ILTR 227), but also the right to enforce other covenants in the fee farm grant: see Wylie, 'The Effect of Non-payment of a Fee Farm Rent' The Western Law Gazette (Dli), Winter 1993, p 50.

[98] 1957 Act, s 16; 1989 Order (NI), Sched 1, para 7.

[99] 1957 Act, s 17(3); *cf* 1989 Order (NI), Sched 1, para 6(1) (minimum of £10, substituted originally by Article 6(3) of the Limitation Amendment (NI) Order 1982).

[100] 1957 Act, s 17(1). See the discussion by the Republic's Supreme Court in *Bellew v Bellew* [1982] IR 447. See also *Woodhouse v Hooney* [1915] 1 IR 296; *Trappe v Halpin* (1928) 62 ILTR 15; *McAuliffe v Irish Sailors and Soldiers Land Trust* [1959] IR 78. No mortgagor or beneficiary is to be deemed a tenant at will to his mortgagee or trustee, 1957 Act, s 17 (1) (c). *Cf* guests, *Peakin v Peakin* [1895] 2 IR 359; *Jennings v Coughlan* (1927) 61 ILTR 122.

[101] Para **[23.26]**, *ante*. A similar rule existed in s 21 ot the Statue of Limitations (NI) 1958, but this was abolished by the Limitation Amendment (NI) Order 1982, Article 6 (2)(a). Since then time runs against the landlord only after the tenancy at will has been determined.

[102] Para **[4.012]**, *ante*.

[103] The writing must amount to a "lease", ie, a *grant* of a leasehold interest and not mere evidence of an oral grant: see *Long v Tower Hamlets LBC* [1996] 2 All ER 683. The distinction between oral periodic tenancies and those created by a lease in writing has been much criticised and the Republic's Law Reform Commission has recommended its abolition: see *Report on Land Law and Conveyancing Law: (1) General Proposals* (LRC 30-1989), paras 54-55.

[104] 1957 Act, s 17(2)(a); 1989 Order (NI), Sched 1, para 5(1). See *Sauerzweig v Feeney* [1986] IR 224; *cf Foreman v Mowlds* unrep (HC, RI), 28 January 1985 (noted (1985) 3 ILT (ns) 47). Brady, 'Periodic Tenancies and the Running of Time' (1986) 80 Gaz ILSI 253; Brady and Kerr, *The Limitation of Actions* (2nd ed, 1994), pp 119-24. In *Jessamine Investment Co v Schwartz* [1978] QB 264, the English Court of Appeal held that a weekly tenancy was a "tenancy from year to year or other period" and time continued to run against the reversioner even though that contractual tenancy was transformed into a statutory tenancy under the Rent Acts.

[105] 1957 Act, s 17 (2)(b); 1989 Order (NI), Sched 1, para 5(2).

(iii) Future Interests

[23.32] The general rule is that in the case of a future interest, whether in reversion or remainder, time runs from the date on which the future interest falls into possession by determination of the preceding estate.[106] However, if the previous owner[107] has been dispossessed, the reversioner or remainderman must sue within 12 years from the adverse possession or 6 years from his own interest vesting in possession,[108] whichever is the longer.[109] This alternative 6 year period is not available to a reversioner or remainderman entitled upon determination of an entail in possession, whose estate or interest might have been barred by the tenant in tail.[110]

(iv) Mortgages

[23.33] A mortgagor's right to redeem is barred if the mortgagee has been in possession for 12 years, without acknowledgment of the mortgagor's title or receiving part payment on account of principal or interest.[111] Where a mortgagee takes possession (which is rare), it is a temporary measure to ensure payment of interest or preservation of the value of his security and he is liable to account strictly to the mortgagor.[112] Thus in this case there is an exception to the rule that time does not run unless there is "adverse" possession[113] and, if there is a mortgage by demise, an exception to the rule that a lessee cannot bar his lessor's title.[114]

[23.34] So far as the mortgagee's rights to enforce his security are concerned, his right of action for sale of the land or to sue for possession is barred after 12 years from the date where repayment became due and his title is extinguished.[115] His right to sue for recovery of principal is also barred after 12 years and thereafter his right to recover

---

[106] 1957 Act, s 15(1); 1989 Order (NI), Sched 1, para 4. *Barcroft v Murphy* [1896] 1 IR 590; *Blake v Bracken* (1901)1 NIJR 246.

[107] Unless he holds a "term of years absolute" (RI) or "leasehold estate or interest" (NI).

[108] 30 and 12 years respectively where the State or Crown is the reversioner or remainderman, 1957 Act, s 15(2)(b), 1989 Order (NI), Article 22(2).

[109] 1957 Act, s 15(2)(a); 1989 Order (NI), Article 22(1). *Re Keone's Estate* (1905) 5 NIJR 145.

[110] 1957 Act, s 15(3); 1989 Order (NI), Article 22(3).

[111] 1957 Act ss 33, 34(1)(a), 54 and 64; 1989 Order (NI), Arts 34(1), 35, 55 and 64. *Re Huddleston's Estate* [1920] 1 IR 29. Where under a welsh mortgage (para **[12.22]**, *ante*) the rents and profits received by the mortgagee in possession are to be applied in reduction of principal and interest, the mortgagor is barred 12 years after he knows the principal and interest have been satisfied, 1957 Act, s 34(2); 1989 Order (NI), Article 34(3). *Shields v Shields* (1904) 38 ILTR 188; *Johnston v Moore* (1904) 4 NIJR 218; *Fenton v Walsh* (1909) 43 ILTR 54; *Re Gonin* [1914] 1 IR 23.

[112] Para **[13.046]**, *ante* See *Forster v Forster* [1918] 1 IR 95.

[113] Para **[23.05]**, *supra*. See also *1971 Survey (NI)*, para 416.

[114] Para **[23.30]**, *supra*.

[115] 1957 Act, ss 32 and 33; 1989 Order (NI), Articles 32 and 33. Once again the period is 30 years in the case of the State or Crown, *ibid*, but 12 years is the period for rights of residence (para **[20.17]**, *ante*), 1957 Act ss 40 and 41; 1989 Order (NI), Articles 40 and 41.

principal or interest is extinguished.[116] The period is 6 years in respect of arrears of interest.[117] If an action is brought to realise the amount due on a mortgage by a sale of the property, other mortgagees may prove their claims in the action, as it is regarded as being for the benefit of all incumbrancers. Since it is so regarded, the order for sale normally stops the statute of limitations running against all persons who could prove in the action and, in this sense, the order might enure for the benefit of all incumbrancers.[118] However, it seems that the action enures for the benefit only of those mortgagees who prove their claims in the action. The statute continues to run against those who do not do so.

[23.35] It has also been held that, where a third party is in adverse possession against the mortgagor when the mortgage is created, title so acquired against the mortgagor is also valid against the mortgagee, notwithstanding an action by him in respect of principal or interest within the limitation period.[119]

(v) Co-Ownership

[23.36] The pre-1833 rule that possession by one co-owner, ie, joint tenant, tenant in common or co-parcener, was deemed to be possession of them all, so that there could be no adverse possession unless there was some additional "ouster",[120] no longer applies.[121]

(vi) Younger Brother

[23.37] The pre-1833 rule that possession by a younger brother or other relation was deemed to be possession by the heir to any land has also been abolished,[122] though it should be noted that the law of inheritance no longer applies (except to a fee tail) in either part of Ireland.

---

[116] 1957 Act, ss 36 and 39; 1989 Order (NI), Articles 36 and 39. The period is 30 years for certain mortgages eg, those payable into the Church Temporalities Fund (para **[6.128]**, *ante*), 1957 Act s 36(1)(b); 1989 Order (NI), Article 36(2). Note that the Fund was dissolved by s 7 of the Republic's Land Act, 1984 and any sums which would have been paid into it are now paid as directed by the Minister for Finance for the benefit of the Exchequer: s 7(4).

[117] 1957 Act s 37; 1989 Order (NI), Article 37. *Re Howlin's Estate* (1906) 40 ILTR 207; *Re Finnegan's Estate* [1906] 1 IR 370; *Harpur v Buchanan* [1919] 1 IR 1; *Re Huggard's Estate* [1930] IR 532.

[118] *Bennett v Bernard* (1849) 12 Ir Eq R 229; *Harpur v Buchanan* [1919] 1 IR 1; *Royal Bank of Ireland v Sproule* [1940] Ir Jur Rep 33.

[119] *Eyre v Walsh* (1859) 10 ICLR 346; *Munster and Leinster Bank Ltd v Croker* [1940] IR 185. *Cf Halpin v Cremin* [1954] IR 19 (adverse possession before "crystallisation" of floating debenture charge).

[120] *O'Sullivan v McSweeny* (1840) 2 Ir LR 89, (1841) Long & Town 111; *Scott v Knox* (1841) 4 Ir Eq R 397.

[121] See now 1957 Act, s 21; 1989 Order (NI), Article 24. *Re Dane's Estate* (1871) IR 5 Eq 498; *Hawkesworth v Ryan* (1902) 36 ILTR 238; *Broome v Lundy* (1906) 40 ILTR 88; Battersby 'Adverse Possession and Concurrent Owners of Land' (1971) 35 Conv 6. See also *Re McCann* (1966) 17 NILQ 292; *Fagan v McParland* (1977) 28 NILQ 201.

[122] See now 1957 Act, s 22; in NI the rule was abolished by the 1958 Act (NI), s 26.

(vii) Trusts

[23.38] The general rule is that the 12-year period of limitation applies to equitable estates in land,[123] including interests in the proceeds of the sale of land under a trust for sale, in the same manner as it applies to legal estates in land.[124] However, a stranger in adverse possession of trust property does not bar the trustees' legal title until all the beneficiaries' equitable interests are barred.[125] As a general rule trustees cannot bar their own beneficiaries' rights to the trust property, though there is a 6-year period of limitation laid down for actions to recover trust property, or for any breach of trust, where no other period is prescribed.[126] But this does not apply to claims against trustees founded on fraud or fraudulent breach of trust or to recover trust property or its proceeds still retained by the trustees or previously received by them and converted to their own use.[127] In these cases the trustee can never bar the beneficiaries' rights.

[23.39] So far as adverse possession by a beneficiary is concerned, it is provided that time does not run in favour of a beneficiary in possession of settled land, or land held on trust for sale, as against the trustees or other beneficiaries.[128] However, adverse possession can occur where the beneficiary in possession is solely and absolutely entitled to the property, eg, where a purchaser under an uncompleted contract for the sale of land[129] takes possession.[130] Presumably the usual 12 year period of limitation applies in such cases.[131]

(viii) Deceased Persons' Estates

[23.40] This is a subject upon which there has been much litigation in Ireland, partly due to the emigration of younger people from rural areas. It is very common on the death of a farmer[132] for his will to remain unproved or for no letters of administration of his estate to be taken out, and for his widow and one of his sons to continue living on the farm regardless of the rights of absent beneficiaries or next-of-kin entitled to distributive shares on intestacy. In these situations the rights of the various parties often can be determined only by the doctrine of adverse possession. Until recently in both parts of Ireland, the limitation period in respect of estates of deceased persons was 12 years,

---

[123] 1957 Act, s 25 (1); 1989 Order (NI), Article 27(1).

[124] See definition of "land" in 1957 Act, s 2 (1); 1989 Order (NI), Article 2(2).

[125] 1957 Act, s 25 (2); 1989 Order (NI), Article 27(2).

[126] 1957 Act, s 43; 1989 Order (NI), Article 42. As regards personal representatives who may also be trustees see para **[16.26]**, *ante*.

[127] 1957 Act, s 44; 1989 Order (NI), Article 43. *Clarke v Crowley* (1930) 64 ILTR 1. See also *Nelson v Rye* [1996] 2 All ER 186.

[128] 1957 Act, s 25(4); 1989 Order, Sched 1, para 9. *Commrs of Charitable Donations and Bequests v Wybrants* (1845) 7 Ir Eq R 580; *Re Drake's Estate* [1909] 1 IR 136; *McAuliffe v Irish Sailors and Soldiers Land Trust* [1959] IR 78; *Fagan v McParland* (1977) 28 NILQ 201. Goodman, 'Adverse Possession by a *Cestui Que Trust* - A Renewed Plea' (1965) 29 Conv 356.

[129] For whom the vendor is to some extent a constructive trustee, para **[9.061]**, *ante*.

[130] See *Bridges v Mees* [1957] Ch 475.

[131] See *Re Cussons Ltd* (1904) 73 LJ Ch 296.

[132] So that in most cases the land is registered land, para **[21.02]**, *ante*.

with 6 years for recovery of arrears of interest on a legacy,[133] excluding actions against personal representatives for fraud.[134] This remains the case in Northern Ireland, but in the Republic these periods have been reduced to 6 years and 3 years respectively and the exclusion for fraud actions repealed.[135]

[23.41] Until recently, there were difficulties about the position of personal representatives, if they, as is often the case, are left in possession of the land. Generally personal representatives are trustees for the beneficiaries entitled under the deceased's will or his intestate successors, as the case may be.[136] For some time the Irish courts held that a personal representative entering into possession could not, as express trustee, bar the claims of beneficiaries or intestate successors.[137] Then the Northern Ireland Court of Appeal in *McNeill v McNeill*[138] and the Republic's Supreme Court in *Vaughan v Cottingham*[139] held that, despite their position as trustees under the law of devolution, personal representatives could bar the claims of beneficiaries or intestate successors by adverse possession. This view has now been confirmed by legislation in both parts of Ireland, which provides that a personal representative in his capacity as personal representative is not a trustee for the purposes of the statute of limitations.[140] In the Republic, legislation has also overruled the line of Irish authority applying the maxim "once a bailiff always a bailiff" to persons entering into possession of a deceased person's estate.[141] Section 124 of the Succession Act 1965 now provides that, notwithstanding any rule of law, "trustee" in the Statute of Limitations 1957 does not include a person whose fiduciary relationship arises merely because he is in possession of a deceased person's property in the capacity of bailiff for another person. This resolves the difficulty of proving a change in the character of the possession to being adverse to the claimant, eg, where the widow of an intestate runs the farm and her children, who are entitled to distributive shares on the intestacy, never live there.[142]

---

[133] 1957 Act, s 45; 1989 Order (NI), Article 44.

[134] 1957 Act, s 46: 1989 Order (NI), Article 45.

[135] Succession Act 1965, s 126 (substituting a new s 45 in the 1957 Act) and ss 8 and 9, 2nd Sched, Pt IV. See *JH v WJH* Unrep (HC, RI), 20 December 1979 (1977/5831 P); *Drohan v Drohan* [1981] ILRM 473.

[136] Succession Act 1965, s 10 (3); Administration of Estates Act (NI), s 2 (3). And under the Trustee Act 1893, s 50 and Trustee Act (NI), 1958, s 67, "trust" generally includes the duties of personal representatives for the purposes of those Acts. See the discussion by the Republic's Supreme Court in *Gleeson v Feehan* [1997] 1 ILRM 522 and para **[15.14]**, *ante*.

[137] *Nugent v Nugent* (1884) 15 LR Ir 321; *Re Laughlin's Application* (1941) 75 ILTR 24; *Re Loughlin* [1942] IR 15. *Cf Toates v Toates* [1926] 2 KB 30. Also *Re McCausland's Trusts* [1908] 1 IR 327; *Owens v McGarry* [1948] IR 226. And *Molony v Molony* [1894] 2 IR 1.

[138] [1957] NI 10, followed in *Re Hughes* [1974] NI 83. See also *Fagan v McParland* (1977) 28 NILQ 201.

[139] [1961] IR 184. See also *Ruddy v Gannon* [1965] IR 283 at 292 (*per* O'Dálaigh (CJ).

[140] 1957 Act, s 2(2)(d) (as substituted by s 123 of Succession Act 1965); 1989 Order (NI), Article 45(1).

[141] *McMahon v Hastings* [1913] 1 ER 395; *Rice v Begley* [1920]1 IR 243; *Leonard v Walsh* [1941] IR 25. See also *Moloney v Moloney* (1924) 58 ILTR 81.

[142] See *Re Maguire and McClelland's Contract* [1907] 1 IR 393.

Bailiffship is usually presumed in cases involving land to which a minor[143] or lunatic[144] is entitled. A similar distinction between adverse and non-adverse possession has been drawn as between husband and wife, eg, on their separation or the husband's desertion leaving the wife in possession.[145]

[23.42] A next-of-kin entitled to a share in an intestate's estate may bar the rights of other next-of-kin by adverse possession.[146] Once again this is common in the rural areas of Ireland, where one of a deceased farmer's sons is left to run the farm and the others emigrate or leave home. However, if one of the next-of-kin is in possession at the date of death, it would appear that his possession is adverse to the holder of the *legal* title, ie, the President of the High Court in the Republic or the Probate Judge in Northern Ireland,[147] and *not* adverse to the other next-of-kin, because at that stage they have no equitable or other interest vested in them. No interest vests in them until, at the earliest, a grant of representation is made in favour of administrators vesting the legal title in them and they complete administration of the estate, so that the *net* estate is available for distribution to the next-of-kin as intestate successors. This was the view of the Republic Supreme Court in the recent case of *Gleeson v Feehan*.[148] The result is that, if the one next-of-kin bars the title of the legal owner before that point is reached, there is no estate or interest left to be distributed to *any* of the next-of-kin. It is not then a case of one next-of-kin barring the rights of other next-of-kin, because these rights have never arisen.[149] The position is different where one next-of-kin enters after administration is completed. Apart from this point, the Irish courts have generally taken the view, though they have not always been consistent, that next-of-kin in adverse possession acquire title as tenants in common in respect of their own shares, but as joint tenants of the shares of the barred next-of-kin.[150] This rule has now been reversed in the Republic by s 125(1) of the Succession Act 1965 which provides:

> Where each of two or more persons is entitled to any shares in land comprised in the estate of a deceased person, whether such shares are equal or unequal, and any or all of

---

[143] *Graham v Chambers* (1902) 2 NIJR 194; *Re Codd and Pettitt* (1910) 44 ILTR 193; *McMahon v Hastings* [1913] 1 IR 395; *Mallon v McAlea* [1923]1 IR 30; *Ruddy v Gannon* [1905] IR 283. *Cf Re McGee* [1964] Ir Jur Rep 26.

[144] *Smyth v Byrne* [1914] 1 IR 53; *Leonard v Walsh* [1941] IR 25.

[145] See *McArdle v Gaughran* [1903] 1 IR 106; *Keelan v Garvey* [1925] 1 IR 1; *Re Daily* [1944] NI 1; *Re Downey* (1946) 80 ILTR 44; *Re McCann* (1966) 17 NILQ 292. See also *Murland v Despard* [1956] IR 170; *O'Shea v O'Shea* (1966) 100 ILTR 16.

[146] See Pearce, 'Adverse Possession by the Next-of-Kin of an Intestate' (1987) 5 ILT 281; Brady and Kerr, *The Limitation of Actions* (2nd ed, 1994), p 157.

[147] Paras **[16.02-3]**, *ante*.

[148] [1997] 1 ILRM 522.

[149] *Ibid*, p 540.

[150] *Coyle v McFadden* [1901] 1 IR 298; *Martin v Kearney* (1902) 36 ILTR 117; *Morteshed v Morteshed* (1902) 36 ILTR 142; *Smith v Savage* [1906] 1 IR 469; *Tobin v Brett* (1906) 40 ILTR 249; *Re Christie* [1917] 1 IR 17; *cf Ward v Ward* (1871) 6 Ch App 789 and *Maher v Maher* [1987] ILRM 582. Note that some of the reasoning in these earlier cases was held to be fallacious by the Republic's Supreme Court in *Gleeson v Feehan supra*.

them enter into possession of the land, then, notwithstanding any rule of law to the contrary, those who enter shall (as between themselves and as between themselves and those (if any) who do not enter) be deemed, for the purposes of the Statute of Limitations 1957, to have entered and to acquire title by possession as joint tenants (and not as tenants in common) as regards their own respective shares and also as regards the respective shares of those (if any) who do not enter.[151]

This new rule applies whether or not the person entered into possession as personal representative of the deceased,[152] or, having entered, was subsequently granted representation of the deceased's estate.[153] Once the limitation period has run, subsequent taking out of representation of the deceased's estate generally does not affect the title acquired by the adverse possession.[154]

2. Registered Land

[23.43] In view of the numerous applications of the doctrine of adverse possession to farm land in Ireland, it is hardly surprising that the Local Registration of Title (Ireland) Act 1891 preserved the doctrine in relation to registered land, which agricultural land has become.[155] Section 52 provided that, once the title to the land was registered,[156] the right to be registered as owner in derogation of the registered owner's title could not be acquired by "mere possession", but the possessor was given the right to apply for a court order declaring his title and for rectification of the register accordingly. The court could make such an order only "if satisfied that such title would have been acquired but for the provisions of this [1891] Act." The problem about this condition was that it appeared to import the rules relating to unregistered land and, in particular, the rule, recently confirmed by the House of Lords and the Republic's Supreme Court, that there is no parliamentary conveyance of the previous owner's title to the squatter.[157] Yet the Irish judges have adopted the practice, which has had to be followed by the Land Registries in Dublin and Belfast, of directing that the squatter's title be registered in the same folio as the dispossessed owner's title, ie, as if in effect there had been a conveyance or transfer of title. The predicament of the judges and Registrars was clear, if one considered leasehold land. If the dispossessed lessee's title was not "extinguished" as regards the lessor, how could his registered title be cancelled in the register? If the squatter did not become the new owner of the leasehold title, with what title could he be registered as owner? Fortunately this conundrum was usually solved in respect of

---

[151] In *Gleeson v Feehan* it was not necessary to determine whether s 125 was drafted on the "mistaken assumption" that the next-of-kin were entitled to an interest as from the date of death, *op cit*, p 541.

[152] *Cf Re Ryan's Estate* [1960] IR 174; *Ruddy v Gannon* [1965] IR 283.

[153] Section 125(2).

[154] *Re McClure and Garrett's Contract* [1899] 1 IR 225; *Re Deeny* [1933] NI 80; *Brennan v Brennan* [1948] Ir Jur Rep 3; *Re Fallon* (1949) 83 ILTR 77. *Cf Duffy v Duffy* [1906] 1 IR 205.

[155] Land sold under the Land Purchase Acts was compulsorily registrable, 1891 Act, s 23.

[156] See *Re Healy* [1947] Ir Jur Rep 24; *Re Greaney* [1956] IR 226; *Fagan v McParland* (1977) 28 NILQ 201; *Re Skelton* [1976] NI 132. *Cf O'Regan v White* [1919] 2 IR 339.

[157] Paras **[23.11-9]**, *supra*.

leasehold land by regarding the squatter as estopped from denying that he had become an assignee of the lease, and, presumably, his landlord from denying the tenancy.[158]

[23.44] It is questionable how far the new registration legislation in both parts of Ireland changes the position, apart from enabling the respective Registrars to deal with applications for rectification of the registers, without the need for reference to the court except in cases of doubt or opposition by one party. Section 49(1) of the Republic's Registration of Title Act 1964, indeed, introduces the replacement for s 52 of the 1891 Act by providing that, subject to the rest of the section, the Statute of Limitations 1957 "shall apply to registered land as it applies to unregistered land." This would seem to import the unregistered law laid down by the House of Lords and the Republic's Supreme Court. Subsection (2) then provides that the applicant may be registered "*as owner of the land* with an absolute, good leasehold, possessory or qualified title, as the case may require, but without prejudice to any right not *extinguished* by such possession." Subsection (3) concludes by providing that, on such registration "the title of the person whose right of action to recover the land has expired shall be *extinguished*." The difficulty is to reconcile the words italicised, bearing in mind the general principle enunciated in subs (1).

[23.45] On the one hand, it is arguable that subs (2) means that the squatter must be registered as the new "owner" of the land, ie, it effects a parliamentary conveyance which the Statute of Limitations does not do. This seems to have been the view of Walsh J in the *Perry* case,[159] but, unfortunately, he appears to have been the only Supreme Court judge to have adverted to the point. This is certainly in line with the Dublin Registry's practice under the 1891 Act and seems to have been the view adopted in drafting the rules made under the 1964 Act.[160] The doubt remains, however, about the use in subss (2) and (3) of the key word in the statute of limitations, ie, "extinguished", which, taken with subs (1), still seems to import the rules of unregistered land. And the last clause of subs (2) seems to be a precise description of the lessor's right of forfeiture for breach of covenant by the dispossessed lessee, which the Supreme Court held in *Perry* was a risk which would continue to affect the squatter's interest for the remainder of the term of the lease. One cannot help concluding that this matter would have been

---

[158] Para **[23.13]**, *supra.* In these cases, the courts and Registries also seem to have resolved the doubts whether s 52 of the 1891 Act applied to leasehold land at all (see also s 53), see Wylie, (1965) 16 NILQ 467 at 484-5, (1968) 19 NILQ, 89 at 97-8; *cf* McAllister, *Registration of Title in Ireland* (1973), p 95; Fitzgerald, *Land Registry Practice* (2nd ed, 1995), p 84 and Ch 11.

[159] Para **[23.16]**, *supra.* But see now on the English Land Registry system, *Spectrum Investment Co v Holmes* [1981] 1 WLR 221.

[160] See 1972, rr 17 and 46 and Sched, Form 5, which requires a declaration from the applicant that he is "entitled for [his] own benefit to the fee simple interest in the property (*or, otherwise as the case may be*) and [he is] not aware of any contract or agreement for sale, or of any mortgage, charge, lease, agreement for lease, restrictive covenant, or incumbrance ... affecting the property." In the *Perry* case, the leasehold squatter was held to be subject to the lease remaining on foot as between the dispossessed lessee and lessor.

better settled if the word "cancelled" had been substituted for "extinguished" in subs (3).[161]

[23.46] It is arguable that s 53 of the Land Registration Act (NI) 1970, leaves the same lingering doubt. Subsection (1) enunciates the same general principle that the Statute of Limitations (NI) 1958 (now the Limitation (NI) Order 1989) applies to registered land as it applies to unregistered land. Subsection (2), however, does not use the word "extinguished" and, instead, speaks of a "defeasance of an estate in any registered land" and of a person claiming to have acquired a "right by possession to be registered as owner of an estate in that land." Such a person may apply for registration of "the title to that estate." This seems to contemplate a transfer of title, but, then, subs (4) introduces the doubt by providing that the registration is not "to prejudice any estate of any other person in the land to which the application relates, being an estate which is not *extinguished* by operation of the said Statute."[162]

---

[161] *Cf* s 32 (rectification of errors, issue of new land certificate and cancellation of old certificate).

[162] See Wallace, *Land Registry Practice in Northern Ireland* (2nd ed, 1987), pp 71-2; 'Adverse Possession of Registered Land' (1981) 32 NILQ 254; *cf* Kenny, 'Limitation and Registered Leases' [1982] Conv 201. See also *McLean and Another v McErlean* [1983] NI 258.